Formal Languages and Automata Theory

PRINCIPLES OF COMPUTER SCIENCE SERIES

Series Editors

Alfred V. Aho, Bell Telephone Laboratories, Murray Hill, New Jersey
Jeffrey D. Ullman, Stanford University, Stanford, California

Computer Organization
Michael Andrews
Trends in Theoretical Computer Science
Egon Börger, Editor
Formal Languages and Automata Theory
Vladimir Drobot
Advanced C: Food for the Educated Palate
Narain Gehani
C: An Advanced Introduction
Narain Gehani
C for Personal Computers: IBM, PC, AT&T PC 63000, and Compatibles
Narain Gehani
An Introduction to the Theory of Computation
Eitan Gurari
Theory of Relational Databases
David Maier
An Introduction to Solid Modeling
Martti Mäntylä
Principles of Computer Design
Leonard R. Marino
The Theory of Database Concurrency Control
Christos Papadimitriou
Algorithms for Graphics and Image Processing
Theo Pavlidis
A Logical Language for Data and Knowledge Bases
Shamim Naqvi and Shalom Tsur
The Elements of Artificial Intelligence
Steve Tanimoto
Computational Aspects of VLSI
Jeffrey D. Ullman
Principles of Database and Knowledge-Base Systems, Volumes I and II
Jeffrey D. Ullman

OTHER BOOKS OF INTEREST

Jewels of Formal Language Theory
Arto Salomaa
Principles of Database Systems
Jeffrey D. Ullman
Fuzzy Sets, Natural Language Computations, and Risk Analysis
Kurt J. Schmucker
LISP: An Interactive Approach
Stuart C. Shapiro

Formal Languages and Automata Theory

Vladimir Drobot

Santa Clara University

COMPUTER SCIENCE PRESS

Library of Congress Cataloging-in-Publication Data

Drobot, Vladimir.
Formal languages and automata theory / Vladimir Drobot.
p. cm.—(Principles of computer science series)
Bibliography: p.
Includes index.
ISBN 0-7167-8186-7
1. Formal languages. 2. Sequential machine theory. I. Title.
II. Series.
QA267.3.D76 1989 89-549
511.3—dc19 CIP

Printed in the United States of America

Computer Science Press
1803 Research Boulevard
Rockville, MD 20850

An imprint of W. H. Freeman and Company
41 Madison Avenue, New York, NY 10010
20 Beaumont Street, Oxford OX1 2BQ, England

1 2 3 4 5 6 7 8 9 0 RRD 7 6 5 4 3 2 1 0 8 9

CONTENTS

PREFACE

Formal Languages and Automata Theory is the outgrowth of lecture notes for a course with the same title, which I have taught several times at Santa Clara University. It is intended as a text for an undergraduate course dealing with the concepts of formal languages, finite automata, and theoretical computing, and it conforms to courses CS15 and CS16 of the ACM Curriculum '78. The book also contains much of the preliminary material discussed in a compiler design course and could be used as an auxiliary text in such a course.

When writing this book, I had two main objectives in mind. First, the students should be able to read it with relative ease, and second, the amount of material included should be such that it is possible to cover it from beginning to end in one semester. I have pared most of the material that might be considered optional in an introductory course. I have included all formal mathematical definitions, but each one of these is preceded by a considerable amount of informal discussion explaining the underlying ideas. Some of the more complex proofs are totally omitted, some are only sketched, but a large number of them are given in full to give students an appreciation of the techniques. For further explanation, complete references to the literature are always given for the missing proofs. The definite emphasis is, however, on what a theorem means rather than on how to prove it.

There are numerous examples throughout the book, some of them worked out in considerable detail, to demonstrate the concepts under discussion. Whenever possible, figures also illustrate the ongoing discussion. Many of the end-of-chapter exercises are quite straightforward; they are intended to help students to test their grasp of the main ideas. There are, however, many others that require ingenuity to solve.

Readers who wish to go into greater detail with the theory and acquaint themselves with the current research trends are encouraged to consult *Introduction to Automata Theory, Languages, and Computation* by J. E. Hopcroft and J. E. Ullman and other titles cited in the References.

Major portions of this book were written while I was on sabbatical leave at Wrocław Politechnic Institute in Wrocław, Poland. I would like to express my gratitude to my hosts for the kindness and generosity shown me during my stay. I would also like to thank Professor Dave Logothetti for expertly and promptly supplying the art work, and Professor Dennis C. Smolarski, S.J. for his help with proofreading and for several valuable suggestions.

Vladimir Drobot

CHAPTER 1

FORMAL LANGUAGES

1.1. BASIC CONCEPTS

We are all familiar with some higher-level language, such as Pascal, FORTRAN, BASIC, C, and others. We write our programs in these languages and when we read a program or a description of an algorithm written in one of them, we can usually tell what the program or the algorithm is supposed to do (at least, when such a program is reasonably short and well written). We can also spot mistakes in the programs or sentences written in these manmade languages. Thus, for instance, the sentence in FORTRAN,

$$IF\ (IND.EQ.1)\ N = N + 1 \tag{1.1}$$

is a correct one, while

$$IF\ (IND.EQ.1)\ N = \tag{1.2}$$

is not. It is truly amazing that not only can we, supposedly intelligent beings, spot mistakes like this and decipher the meaning of statements and programs, but also machines (which consist essentially of bunches of hardware) can do the same thing. How is it done? After all, when we enter the program into the machine we do it symbol by symbol. When a sentence such as (1.1) is presented to the computer, what is fed first is the letter I, then the letter F, then the symbol (, and so on. The machine dutifully accepts these symbols one by one, and after all of them are entered, it "knows" what to do. It is also able to determine if the string of symbols it has just received is "correct" or not. To do this, the machine must know what "correct" means, and then it must be able to determine that the string (1.1) is "correctly written," while the string (1.2) is not. In this chapter we discuss primarily how to define a language in a completely rigorous way. This definition should enable us to determine, in a completely automatic way, whether a given string of symbols is in the language or not. It is not clear that such a completely formal and deterministic definition is possible for all languages—in fact, for natural languages such as English, French, and Russian, it is probably not possible at all. It *is* clearly possible, however, for the computer languages—after all, the computers do work.

We begin with an alphabet—every language obviously ought to have one. Thus, the alphabet for FORTRAN, say, consists of 26 letters: A, B, . . . , X, Y, Z; 10 digits: 0, 1, 2, . . . , 9, and assorted other symbols, such as =, +, /, *, (, (space). The exact alphabet, also known as the character set, of any language can be found in the opening pages of any manual for that language.

Definition 1.1. An ***alphabet*** is a nonempty, finite set of symbols.

We will usually denote the alphabets by the symbol Σ. The definition of a language over some given alphabet is now very simple.

Definition 1.2. A ***language*** L over an alphabet Σ is a collection of finite strings of elements of Σ.

The elements of an alphabet Σ are also called ***characters.*** The strings from a language L are also called ***sentences*** of L.

Example 1.1. Let the alphabet Σ consist of only two symbols 0 and 1, i.e., $\Sigma = \{0, 1\}$. Two examples of languages over Σ might be

a) $L_1 = \{0, 01, 110\}$. This language contains only three sentences: 0, 01 and 110.
b) L_2 = All strings of 0's and 1's with equal number of 0's and 1's.

Thus, 010011 and 1010 are in the language L_2, while 110 and 010 are not. It is clear that the language L_2 (unlike L_1) contains an infinite number of sentences.

We will deal quite often with strings of symbols throughout the book. For convenience, we summarize some notational conventions about them. If $\sigma = x_1x_2 \ldots x_n$ and $\tau = y_1y_2 \ldots y_m$ are two strings, the concatenation of σ and τ, denoted by $\sigma\tau$, is defined as $\sigma\tau = x_1x_2 \ldots$

$x_n y_1 y_2 \ldots y_m$. Thus, $\sigma\tau$ is obtained from σ and τ by joining the strings σ and τ (in that order). For instance, if $\sigma = 01011$ and $\tau = 001$, then $\sigma\tau = 01011001$. Notice that $\tau\sigma = 00101011$, so in general $\sigma\tau \neq \tau\sigma$. If x is a character, then x^n is defined to be the string $xx \ldots x$ (n times). Thus, $x^2 = xx$, $y^3 = yyy$, etc. The length of a string $\sigma = x_1 x_2 \ldots x_m$ is the number of characters in σ. Thus, the length of $\sigma = abaa$ is 4. It is quite often very convenient to introduce the concept of an empty string. Such a string has no characters at all; its length is 0. It will always be denoted by λ, and, conversely, the symbol λ will be reserved for such a string. If σ is any string and λ is the empty string, then the concatenation of σ and λ always produces σ: $\sigma\lambda = \lambda\sigma = \sigma$. For that reason, if x is any symbol, we define x^0 to be the empty string λ: $x^0 = \lambda$. The length of the empty string λ is 0, and it is the only string having that length.

Definition 1.3. Let Σ be a nonempty set. The language of all possible finite strings of elements of Σ (including the empty string) will be denoted by Σ^*. The language of all possible nonempty strings of elements of Σ will be denoted by Σ^+.

We note that, in general, a language L over an alphabet Σ does not contain all possible strings of elements of Σ, only some of them. This corresponds to a well-known fact that not every sequence of symbols forms a valid program. What we would like to do now is to describe a rigorous rule for deciding if a given string belongs to a language or not. An example of such a rule may be the description of the language L_2 from Example 1.1. The rule is indeed very simple and rigorous; moreover, given a string σ of 0's and 1's it is very easy to check if σ is a sentence in L_2 or not. It is, however, difficult to imagine such a simple rule for a more realistic language, such as Pascal. Such a rule should be sophisticated and precise enough so that given any proposed Pascal program (which we view as one long string), it should determine if it is a valid program: Are all BEGIN's closed with END's? Are all algebraic expressions well formed? and so forth.

A very useful and general method of describing languages is based on so-called ***grammars***. Roughly speaking, a grammar is a set of rules that, when followed, will produce a valid sentence in a language. The detailed and precise description of the concept of a grammar is as follows.

Definition 1.4. A ***grammar*** G consists of four objects:

1. A finite, nonempty set Σ called an ***alphabet***. The language generated by the grammar G will consist of strings formed from

the symbols of Σ. The elements of Σ will be called ***terminals*** and will be usually denoted by the lowercase letters a, b, c, etc.;

2. A finite, nonempty set N of symbols, all of them different from the terminals in Σ (i.e., $N \cap \Sigma = \emptyset$). The elements of N will be called ***nonterminals***, or variables; they are usually denoted by the uppercase letters A, B, C, etc.
3. One distinguished element S of N. This nonterminal S is called the ***start symbol.***
4. A set P of ***productions*** (also called production rules or substitution rules). This set P consists of expressions of the form

$$A \rightarrow X_1X_2 \ldots X_n,$$

where A is a nonterminal and $X_1X_2 \ldots X_n$ is a finite string of terminals or nonterminals (i.e., $X_i \in \Sigma \cup N$).

The grammars so defined are also called the ***context-free grammars***; we will discuss this a little bit later.

The string $X_1X_2 \ldots X_n$ in part 4 of the above definition is allowed to contain no symbols at all, i.e., it may be an empty string λ. The corresponding production is then of the form $A \rightarrow \lambda$, and is called an ***empty production.*** A grammar G with Σ, N, S, and P as in Definition 1.4 will be denoted by $G = \{\Sigma, N, S, P\}$.

Example 1.2. The following is a description of a grammar $G = \{\Sigma, N, S, P\}$:

1. The set Σ of terminals (the alphabet) is $\{a, b, c\}$.
2. The set N of nonterminals is $\{S, A, B, C\}$.
3. The start symbol is S.
4. The set P of productions consists of the following productions:

$$S \rightarrow AaB \qquad S \rightarrow B \qquad A \rightarrow aB \qquad A \rightarrow a$$
$$B \rightarrow bC \qquad C \rightarrow ac \qquad C \rightarrow \lambda$$

In the last production, λ, as usual, is the empty string and $C \rightarrow \lambda$ is an empty production. This grammar has three terminals (a, b, c), four nonterminals (S, A, B, C) and seven productions.

We now proceed to describe how a grammar generates a language. We need the following terminology:

Definition 1.5. Let $G = \{\Sigma, N, S, P\}$ be a grammar. A ***sentential***

form of G is any string $X_1X_2 \ldots X_n$ of symbols, each X_i being either a terminal or a nonterminal (i.e., $X_i \in \Sigma \cup N$).

A sentential form may contain no symbols at all, i.e., it may be the empty string λ. In Example 1.2, the strings AaB, $AAaCB$, aba, and λ are examples of sentential forms.

Definition 1.6. Let $G = \{\Sigma, N, S, P\}$ be a grammar. Suppose σ is a sentential form expressed as $\sigma = \gamma_1 A \gamma_2$, where γ_1 and γ_2 are strings of terminals or nonterminals (i.e., they are sentential forms themselves), and A is a nonterminal. Suppose also that $A \rightarrow X_1X_2 \ldots X_n$ is a production in P. Let τ be the sentential form obtained from σ by replacing A with $X_1X_2 \ldots X_n$, i.e., $\tau = \gamma_1 X_1 X_2 \ldots X_n \gamma_2$. We say that the sentential form τ is ***immediately derivable*** from σ using the production $A \rightarrow X_1X_2 \ldots X_n$. We denote this by

$$\sigma \Rightarrow \tau$$

Consider the grammar $G = \{\Sigma, N, S, P\}$ from Example 1.2. The sentential form $\sigma = aBabC$ immediately derives the sentential form $\tau = abCabC$ using the production $B \rightarrow bC$:

$$\sigma = aBabC \Rightarrow abCabC$$

In other words, to say that $\sigma \Rightarrow \tau$ means that one can replace one of the nonterminals of σ with the corresponding right-hand side of the production and arrive at the string τ. Here, in the sentential form $\sigma = aBabC$, we replaced B with bC (since $B \rightarrow bC$ is a production) and obtained $\tau = abCabC$. As another example, let $\sigma = aaCba$. Applying the production $C \rightarrow \lambda$ to σ we obtain

$$\sigma = aaCba \Rightarrow aaba$$

Here we substituted the right-hand side of the production $C \rightarrow \lambda$, (i.e., the empty string) for C. Since λ is the empty string, it has no symbols, so $aa\lambda ba = aaba$, that is, the symbol C "disappears."

Definition 1.7. Let σ_1 and σ_2 be two sentential forms of a grammar G. Suppose there is a sequence of sentential forms $\tau_1, \tau_2, \ldots, \tau_n$ such that

$$\sigma_1 \Rightarrow \tau_1 \Rightarrow \tau_2 \Rightarrow \cdots \Rightarrow \tau_n \Rightarrow \sigma_2$$

We say then that σ_1 ***derives*** σ_2, or σ_2 is derivable from σ_1, and denote it by

$$\sigma_1 \Rightarrow^* \sigma_2$$

For instance, in the grammar of Example 1.2, we have $S \Rightarrow^* aabC$ because

$$\begin{array}{ccccccc} S & \Rightarrow & AaB & \Rightarrow & aaB & \Rightarrow & aabC \\ & \uparrow & & \uparrow & & \uparrow & \\ & S \rightarrow AaB & & A \rightarrow a & & B \rightarrow bC & \end{array}$$

Under each symbol $\Rightarrow$ we have indicated the relevant production of G used in the immediate derivation.

Given a grammar $G = \{\Sigma, N, S, P\}$, the language $L(G)$ generated by G is the collection of all possible strings of terminals that are derivable from the starting symbol S. Formally, we have the following:

Definition 1.8. Let $G = \{\Sigma, N, S, P\}$ be a grammar. The language $L(G)$ generated by G is defined to be the set of strings

$$L(G) = \{\sigma | \ \sigma \in \Sigma^*, S \Rightarrow^* \sigma\}$$

The elements (strings) of $L(G)$ are called ***sentences*** of $L(G)$.

Thus, in Example 1.2, the strings b, $aabac$, and bac all belong to $L(G)$:

$$S \Rightarrow B \Rightarrow bC \Rightarrow b$$

$$S \Rightarrow AaB \Rightarrow aaB \Rightarrow aabC \Rightarrow aabac$$

$$S \Rightarrow B \Rightarrow bC \Rightarrow bac$$

A little experimentation, on the other hand, shows that the string cb is not in the language $L(G)$. Indeed, beginning with the start symbol S, the first sentential form derivable from S is going to be either AaB or B. By inspection, it is seen that neither of these strings will derive a sentence that begins with the symbol c.

Example 1.3. The grammar given in this example will generate the language consisting of all correctly formed algebraic expressions that can be obtained using the symbols a, $+$, $*$, (, and). Thus, the expression $(a + a) * a$ will be in the language, while $(a + a) * (a +$ will not. This grammar will be denoted by G_0 and will be discussed frequently throughout the book. The alphabet of G_0 is $\Sigma = \{a, +, *, (,)\}$, the set N of nonterminals is $N = \{E, T, F\}$, and the start symbol is E. The productions of G_0 are

1. $E \rightarrow E + T$
2. $E \rightarrow T$
3. $T \rightarrow T * F$
4. $T \rightarrow F$
5. $F \rightarrow (E)$
6. $F \rightarrow a$

Thus, for instance, the expression $(a + a) * a$ is in the language $L(G_0)$, its derivation being

$$E \overset{2}{\Rightarrow} T \overset{3}{\Rightarrow} T * F \overset{4}{\Rightarrow} F * F \overset{5}{\Rightarrow} (E) * F \overset{1}{\Rightarrow} (E + T) * F$$

$$\overset{2}{\Rightarrow} (T + T) * F \overset{4}{\Rightarrow} (F + T) * F \overset{6}{\Rightarrow} (a + T) * F$$

$$\overset{4}{\Rightarrow} (a + F) * F \overset{6}{\Rightarrow} (a + a) * F \overset{6}{\Rightarrow} (a + a) * a$$

The numbers above the symbol $\Rightarrow$ indicate the production number used in each derivation. To see that the string $(a + a) *(a +$ is not in $L(G_0)$, we observe that the only way the symbols) and (will appear in a sentential form is through the application of the production $F \rightarrow (E)$. Hence, any string derivable from E will have the same number of)'s as ('s, and the string in question does not have this property. The letters E, T, and F, which form the set of nonterminals, are mnemonics for expression, term, and factor.

There are several conventions commonly used in describing grammars. Unless specified to the contrary, the terminals of the alphabet Σ will be denoted by the lowercase letters a, b, c, etc., or the digits 0, 1, 2, . . . , 9, or some special symbols such as $+$, $*$, (,). The nonterminals are usually denoted by the capital letters A, B, C, . . . , and the start symbol is commonly denoted by S. (For traditional reasons, this was not done in Example 1.3.) The empty string will always be denoted by λ. The first production listed will have the start symbol on the left-hand side. The elements of the set $\Sigma \cup N$ will be called ***grammatical symbols***; thus, a grammatical symbol is either a terminal or a nonterminal. If

$$\begin{aligned} A &\rightarrow \alpha_1 \\ A &\rightarrow \alpha_2 \\ &\ \ \vdots \\ A &\rightarrow \alpha_k \end{aligned}$$

are all the productions with the same left-hand side A, to save space, they will be usually listed as

$$A \rightarrow \alpha_1 \mid \alpha_2 \mid \cdots \mid \alpha_{k-1} \mid \alpha_k$$

Thus, the grammar from Example 1.2 will be written as

$$\begin{aligned} S &\rightarrow AaB \mid B \\ A &\rightarrow a \mid aB \\ B &\rightarrow bC \\ C &\rightarrow ac \mid \lambda \end{aligned}$$

and the grammar G_0 from Example 1.3 as

$$\begin{aligned} E &\rightarrow E + T \mid T \\ T &\rightarrow T * F \mid F \\ F &\rightarrow (E) \mid a \end{aligned}$$

Which symbols have which meaning should be clear from the context. Thus, for instance, unless it is specified otherwise, given a description of a grammar as

$$\begin{aligned} S &\rightarrow AB \\ A &\rightarrow BSB \mid BB \mid 1 \\ B &\rightarrow 0A1 \mid 0 \mid \lambda \end{aligned}$$

we conclude that the set Σ of terminals is $\{0, 1\}$, the set N of nonterminals is $\{S, A, B\}$, and the productions are

$$\begin{aligned} S &\rightarrow AB \\ A &\rightarrow BSB \\ A &\rightarrow BB \\ A &\rightarrow 1 \\ B &\rightarrow 0A1 \\ B &\rightarrow 0 \\ B &\rightarrow \lambda \end{aligned}$$

We will frequently use this abbreviated form to describe grammars.

The derivation of a sentence in a language generated by a grammar can be depicted by a derivation tree. Consider, for example, a grammar G:

$$S \rightarrow aBa \qquad B \rightarrow Sb \mid bCC \qquad C \rightarrow abb$$

and a derivation of the sentence *aababbabbaba*:

$$S \Rightarrow aBa \Rightarrow aSba \Rightarrow aaBaba \Rightarrow aabCCaba$$
$$\Rightarrow aababbCaba \Rightarrow aababbabbaba$$

This derivation may be schematically represented by a graph, called a ***derivation tree***, or a ***parse tree***, as in Figure 1.1.

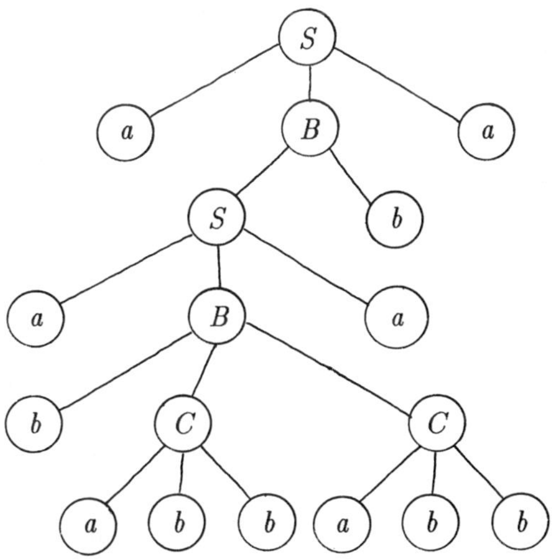

Figure 1.1. A parse (derivation) tree of a string.

The circled objects in the graph are called nodes. The node at the top, S, is called the ***root*** of the tree. If a node X is connected to a node Y below, X is called the ***parent*** of Y, and Y is called a ***child*** of X. The nodes with no children are called the ***leaves***, the nodes with both child(ren) and parent are called the ***internal nodes***. The formation of the graph, called the derivation tree, is almost self-evident. If A is a nonterminal which is being replaced by the right-hand side of a production $A \rightarrow X_1X_2 \ldots$

X_n, then the node A has children $X_1, X_2, \ldots, X_n$ (from left to right). The root of a tree is the node S, where S is the start symbol of the grammar, and the leaves are nodes of the form x, where $x \in \Sigma$ are terminals. Given a derivation tree of a string, we obtain this string by concatenating its leaves from left to right.

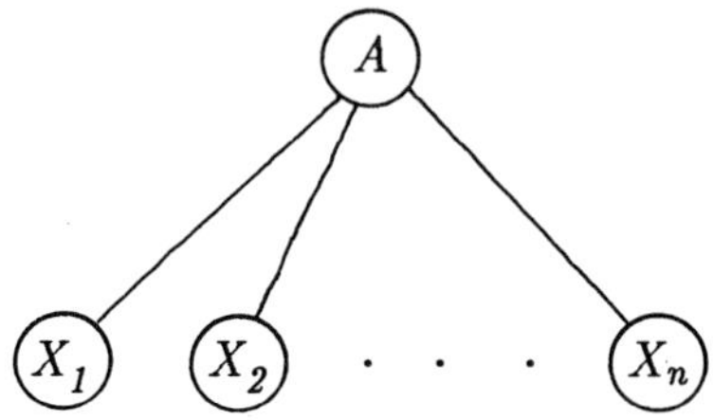

Figure 1.2. Formation of a parse tree.

Hence, the sentence $(a + a) * a$ in the language $L(G_0)$ of Example 1.3 has the derivation tree depicted in Figure 1.3.

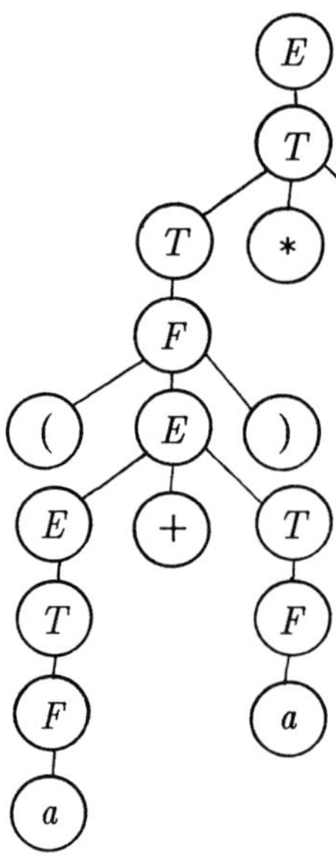

Figure 1.3. The derivation tree of $(a + a) * a$.

Example 1.4. As another example, we present a grammar for the language consisting of all valid FORTRAN real constants. The FOR-

TRAN manuals describe such constants in various ways. A fairly typical example is "A real constant is represented by a string of digits; it contains a decimal point or an exponent representing a power of 10, or both. Real constants may be in the following forms:

$$n.n, \quad n., \ .n, \quad n.n\mathrm{E}\pm s, \quad n.\mathrm{E}\pm s, \quad .n\mathrm{E}\pm s, \quad n\mathrm{E}\pm s$$

Examples are 3.E1, 3.1415768, 31.41592E−01, 314.0749162, .31415E01, −3.141592E+279, .31415E+01" [10]. An example of a grammar generating such a language would be as follows:

$$\begin{array}{lll}
S & \rightarrow & AB \\
A & \rightarrow & XD \\
B & \rightarrow & \mathrm{E}XI \mid \lambda \\
D & \rightarrow & .\,I \mid I\,. \mid I\,.\,I \mid I \\
X & \rightarrow & + \mid - \mid \lambda \\
I & \rightarrow & M \mid M\ I \\
M & \rightarrow & 0 \mid 1 \mid 2 \mid 3 \mid 4 \mid 5 \mid 6 \mid 7 \mid 8 \mid 9
\end{array}$$

The terminals form the set $\Sigma = \{0, 1, 2, 3, 4, 5, 6, 7, 8, 9, \mathrm{E}, +, -, .\}$, the set of nonterminals is $N = \{S, A, B, D, I, M, X\}$ and the start symbol is S. The derivation tree of −3.14E01 is given in Figure 1.4. It should be reasonably clear that all the FORTRAN constants (and only those) can be derived using this grammar.

This is, of course, not the only grammar that can be used to describe this language; it is perfectly possible to have two distinct grammars G_1 and G_2 such that $L(G_1) = L(G_2)$. We will discuss this concept later. Actually, the entire Pascal language, as well as any other computer language, can be described by giving its grammar. These grammars are typically rather long and may include several hundred productions. This method of describing the computer languages is also called ***Backus Normal Form*** or ***BNF***. The notation used in such a description is slightly different from the one we just introduced. The arrow → is represented by the symbol ::= and the nonterminals are written as self-explanatory phrases enclosed in < · · · >. Thus, for example, a BNF description of integer constants in FORTRAN (or just about any language for that matter) might be:

<*IntegerConstant*> ::= <*Sign*><*Number*>
<*Sign*>::= + | − | λ
<*Number*> :: = <*Digit*> | <*Digit*><*Number*>
<*Digit*> ::= 0 | 1 | 2 | 3 | 4 | 5 | 6 | 7 | 8 | 9

It should be obvious that this form of describing grammars (and languages), except for notational conventions, is identical with the one just described.

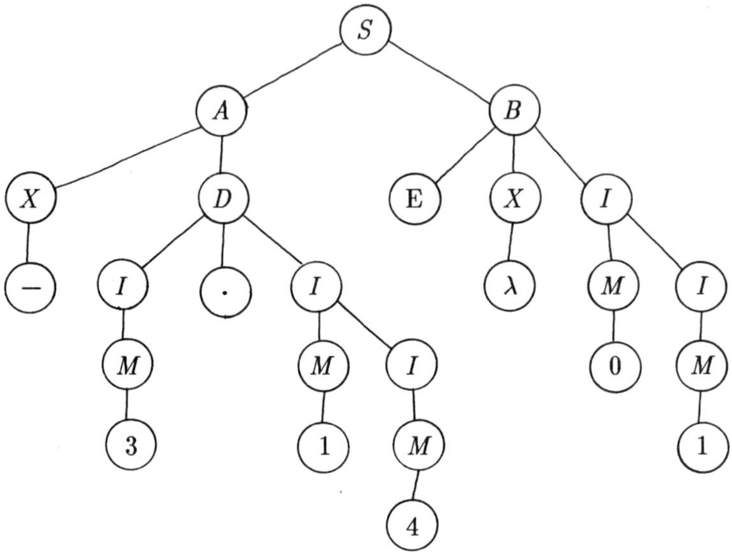

Figure 1.4. Parse tree of $-3.14\text{E}01$.

1.2. TYPES OF GRAMMARS AND THEIR CLASSIFICATION

The idea of rigorous description of a language by a grammar is due to N. Chomsky (see [4], [5]). In the early part of his work he was primarily interested in natural languages, such as English and German. To this end he analyzed grammars considerably more general than the kind described here. For the sake of completeness we now present these more general definitions.

I. ***Type-0*** grammars, also called ***phrase-structure*** grammars or ***unrestricted*** grammars. As before, an unrestricted grammar G consists of four objects: a nonempty set Σ of terminals, a nonempty set N of nonterminals, with $N \cap \Sigma = \emptyset$, a start symbol $S \in N$, and a finite collection P of productions. A production in an unrestricted grammar has the form

$$u \to v$$

where u and v are arbitrary strings of terminals or nonterminals; we only require that $u \neq \lambda$. Such a production allows for a completely arbitrary replacement of one string (u) by another (v). A sentential form σ is then said to immediately derive a sentential form τ if $\sigma = \alpha u \beta$, $\tau = \alpha v \beta$ and $u \to v$ is a production of the grammar. We denote this by $\sigma \Rightarrow \tau$. The language $L(G)$ is then defined to be the set of strings of terminals that are derivable from the start symbol S.

Example 1.5. Let the alphabet of a grammar G be $\Sigma = \{a, c, d\}$, let the set of nonterminals be $N = \{S, X, Y\}$, let S be the start symbol, and let the set P of productions be given by

1. $S \to aXYc$
2. $aX \to cad$
3. $Xc \to aXa$
4. $XYc \to Xcc$
5. $Yc \to \lambda$

An example of a derivation in this grammar would be

$$S \Rightarrow \underline{aX}Yc \Rightarrow cad\underline{Yc} \Rightarrow cad$$

or

$$S \Rightarrow a\underline{XYc} \Rightarrow a\underline{Xc}c \Rightarrow a\underline{aX}ac \Rightarrow acadac$$

In each of the sentential forms above we have underlined the left-hand side of the relevant production. Grammars such as these are extremely general, just about every language (set of strings) can be described by such a type-0 grammar. A language generated by a type-0 grammar is called a type-0 language.

II. *Type-1* grammars, also called ***context-sensitive*** grammars. The terminals, nonterminals and the start symbol are all as usual. Each production now has a form

$$\alpha A \beta \to \alpha \sigma \beta$$

where A is a nonterminal, and $\sigma \neq \lambda$ is any nonempty string of terminals or nonterminals. The point is that we may replace the nonterminal A by σ, but only if A is surrounded by, or in the context of,

α and β. It is clear that the context-sensitive grammars are also type-0 grammars, but not conversely. We will come back to these issues in Chapter 9.

III. ***Type-2*** grammars, also called ***context-free*** grammars. If all the productions of a grammar are of the form $A \rightarrow \sigma$, where A is a single nonterminal and σ is any string of terminals or nonterminals, the grammar is called context-free, abbreviated to CFG (context-free grammars). Type-2 grammars are thus restrictions of type-1 grammars: we require that $\alpha = \beta = \lambda$. Hence, given a sentential form $\gamma_1 A \gamma_2$ and a production $A \rightarrow \sigma$, we may replace A by σ to derive a form $\gamma_1 \sigma \gamma_2$, irrespective of the "context" of γ_1 and γ_2. This explains the name "context-free." This is, however exactly the definition of a grammar given in Definition 1.4. Strictly speaking, type-2 grammars are not restrictions of type-1 grammars, since we allow productions of the form $A \rightarrow \lambda$ in the former, but not in the latter. This is, however, somewhat superficial. We will show in Chapter 7 that, given a context-free grammar with empty productions, there exists an equivalent, context-free grammar (i.e., generating the same language) with no empty productions, except possibly one: $S \rightarrow \lambda$ (here S is the start symbol). In particular, if G is a context-free grammar such that $\lambda \notin L(G)$—the language generated by G—then $L(G) = L(G')$ for some context-free grammar G' with no empty productions whatsoever. Hence, if L is a type-2 language not containing λ, it is also type-1. The converse is not true: there are type-1 languages that have no context-free grammar. We will discuss some of these issues in Chapter 9. Most of the grammars discussed in this book will be context-free—they are just much easier to analyze. Practically all of the actual computer languages, such as Pascal, C, etc., are context-free.

IV. ***Type-3*** grammars, also called ***regular*** grammars. There is an interesting subclass of context-free grammars, called regular, or linear, grammars.

Definition 1.9. We say that a grammar G is ***right linear***, or ***right regular***, if every one of its productions has one of the following forms:

$$S \rightarrow \lambda \qquad\qquad A \rightarrow aB \qquad\qquad A \rightarrow a$$

In the above, S is the start symbol, λ is the empty string, A and B are arbitrary nonterminals, and a is any terminal. A grammar is called ***left linear***, or ***left regular***, if all of its productions are in one of the following forms:

$S \to \lambda$ $\qquad$ $A \to Ba$ $\qquad$ $A \to a$

A grammar is called ***regular* (*linear*)** if it is either right regular (linear) or left regular (linear).

It is clear that regular grammars are context-free. In Chapter 2 we will study the regular grammars in considerable detail. This classification of grammars (type-j, $j = 0, 1, 2, 3,$) is known as ***Chomsky's hierarchy.***

1.3. REPRESENTATION OF LANGUAGES BY THEIR GRAMMARS

We have seen in Sections 1.2 and 1.3 how to describe a language in terms of a grammar. From the point of view of computer science the following two "inverse" problems are much more important (and difficult):

I. Given a string σ of terminals, does it belong to the language?
II. Given that a string σ is in the language, how was it derived?

The importance of problem I is obvious—given a program written in some language we wish to determine if it is correctly written. We do not address the question of whether the program will do what it is supposed to do, only whether it is a valid program. All we wish to determine at this point is whether the program is "grammatically correct." Are all the statements in the proper form? Are all the DO loops closed? Do all BEGIN's terminate with proper END's? and so on. Examining these kinds of questions is known as lexical analysis. Problem II is even more important, for it allows us to interpret the "meaning" of the program and decide how the program is going to be executed. Studying the second problem is called parsing or syntax analysis. We illustrate both of these points on the following example.

Example 1.6. Consider the grammar G_0 of all valid arithmetic expressions that can be formed from positive unsigned integers and symbols +, ∗, (, and). This grammar has the productions

1. $E \to E + T$ $\qquad$ 3. $T \to T * F$ $\qquad$ 5. $F \to (E)$
2. $E \to T$ $\qquad$ 4. $T \to F$ $\qquad$ 6. $F \to a$

Here the symbol a represents any positive, unsigned integer. Given a sentence in the language $L(G_0)$, say $(5 + 3) * 4$, we have to decide:

I. Is this a valid sentence?

II. What does this sentence mean?

What is involved in question II is the interpretation, or evaluation, of the string (5 + 3) * 4. When this string is presented to the machine, it should "know" that it supposed to take the numbers 5 and 3, load them into appropriate memory or register locations, perform the addition, take the result of this addition and load it in a proper place, then load the number 4 where needed and perform the final multiplication. All this should be done completely automatically; the machine should be programmed in such a way that when the string (5 + 3) * 4 is presented to it, all of the above are performed in correct order. We will show now that if the machine can reproduce the derivation tree of the sentence, it can figure out how to do all of the above, i.e., it can decipher the "meaning" or the value of the sentence.

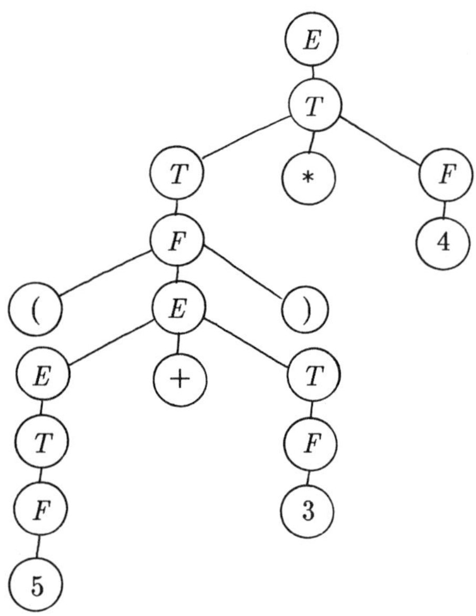

Figure 1.5. Derivation tree of (5 + 3) * 4.

Indeed, suppose we have the derivation tree of (5 + 3) * 4, as in Figure 1.5. Verifying that the string is in the language is easy enough: Concatenate the leaves of the tree from left to right and check if the resulting string matches, symbol by symbol, the original input. We do not discuss how such a tree would be stored in the memory, how the nodes would be accessed, etc. These are problems of implementation, they can be accomplished, and to some extent they depend on the actual hardware of the machine. What we claim is that given this derivation tree we can actually recapture the meaning of the string.

To this end we will rewrite the tree in a slightly different way. Each node will be represented by a cell $\boxed{X \mid n}$: The symbol X will be the grammatical symbol of the node, (i.e., a terminal or a nonterminal) and n will denote the production number used in obtaining the children of the node.

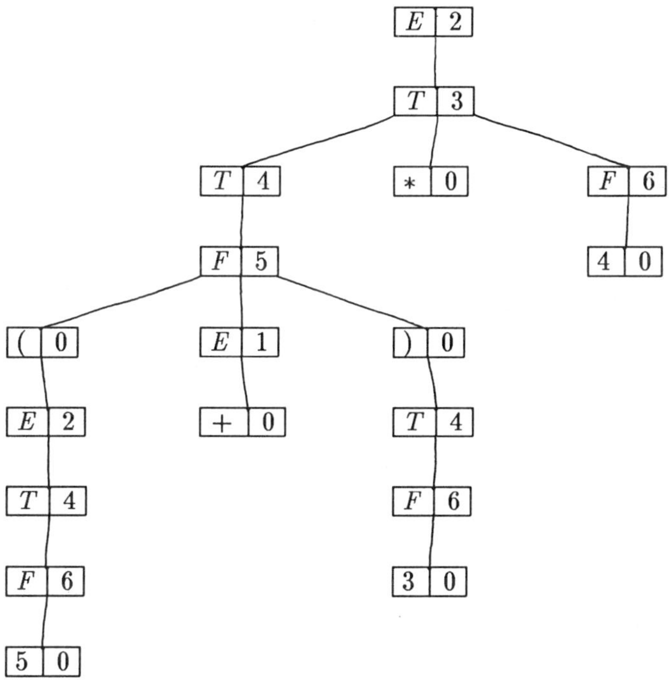

Figure 1.6. Derivation of (5 + 3) $*$ 4.

If X is a terminal, i.e., when the node is a leaf, we set $n = 0$. The derivation tree of (5 + 3) $*$ 4 then becomes as shown in Figure 1.6. Define now a function $V(\boxed{X \mid n}) = V(X, n)$ on the nodes as follows:

$$V(X,\ n) = \begin{cases} X \quad \text{if } n = 0 \\ V(LeftChild(X,\ n)) + V(RightChild(X,\ n)) \quad \text{if } n = 1 \\ V(Child(X,\ n)) \quad \text{if } n = 2,\ 4, \text{ or } 6 \\ V(LeftChild(X,\ n)) * V(RightChild(X,\ n)) \quad \text{if } n = 3 \\ V(MiddleChild(X,\ n)) \quad \text{if } n = 5 \end{cases}$$

The function $V(X, n)$ is then defined for those X and n for which $\boxed{X \mid n}$ can be a node in a derivation tree of an arithmetic expression. Strictly speaking, we should also define the functions *LeftChild*, *RightChild*, *MiddleChild*, and *Child*, but these should be self-explanatory. Given the derivation tree of an expression, to find the meaning, or the value, of this expression is easy enough: We evaluate $V(Root)$. In the example under discussion, the evaluation proceeds as follows:

$$\begin{aligned} V(Root) &= V(E,\ 2) \\ &= V(T,\ 3) \\ &= V(T,\ 4) * V(F,\ 6) \\ &= V(F,\ 5) * V(4,\ 0) \\ &= V(E,\ 1) * 4 \\ &= (V(E,\ 2) + V(T,\ 4)) * 4 \\ &= (V(T,\ 4) + V(F,\ 6)) * 4 \\ &= (V(F,\ 6) + V(3,\ 0)) * 4 \\ &= (V(5,\ 0) + 3) * 4 \\ &= (V(5,\ 0) + 3) * 4 \\ &= (5 + 3) * 4 = 32 \end{aligned}$$

It should be clear that the function V will correctly calculate the value of every properly formed arithmetic expression, provided it knows the derivation tree of the expression. The function V has the property of being recursive, that is, when it is called it may call itself to evaluate some of its arguments. It may not be clear to the reader how evaluation of such a function can be implemented on a computer, i.e., done in a completely automatic way. Suffice it to say that, indeed, it can be accomplished, although the specific implementation will depend on the actual language in which the implementation is done as well as on the hardware to some extent. We will not discuss these matters any further. Rather we will be studying the process of reconstructing the derivation tree from a given string. The only reason the function V is introduced is to convince the reader that such a process of reconstruction of the derivation tree is indeed useful and, in fact, necessary.

The following problem arises immediately when we talk of parsing (i.e., of the reconstruction of the derivation tree): Given a grammar G and a string σ in the language $L(G)$, can it happen that σ has two distinct derivation trees? It turns out that, indeed, such phenomena can happen.

Example 1.7. Let G be the grammar

$$S \to A \qquad\qquad A \to A0A \mid 1$$

Figure 1.7 shows two distinct derivation trees of the string $\sigma = 10101$.

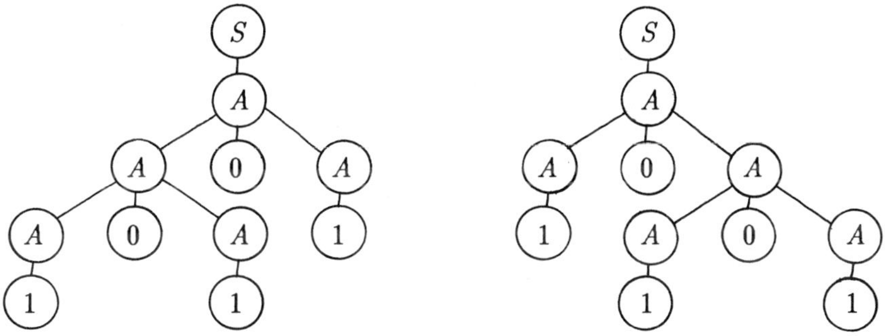

Figure 1.7. Distinct derivation trees of $\sigma = 10101$.

This leads to the following concept:

Definition 1.10. A grammar G is said to be ***ambiguous*** if there is a sentence σ in $L(G)$ with two distinct derivation trees. If a grammar is not ambiguous, it is called ***unambiguous.***

Example 1.8. The following is a more concrete example relating to the "***if*** C_1 ***then*** C_2 ***else*** C_3" construction in Pascal and many other languages. A fragment of a grammar for Pascal dealing with these constructions can be given by the following:

<statement> → ***if*** *<condition>* ***then*** *<statement>* |
if *<condition>* ***then*** *<statement>* ***else*** *<statement>* |
<other kind of statement> (1.3)

If this construction were indeed described by the above grammar, the derivation tree of some sentences would not be unique. Indeed, consider the following sentence:

$$\textit{if}\ \ C = 0\ \ \textit{then}\ \ \textit{if}\ \ D = 1\ \ \textit{then}\ \ A := 3\ \ \textit{else}\ \ A := 4 \tag{1.4}$$

It has two distinct derivation trees, as in Figure 1.8. The "meaning" or the "value" of the sentence σ under consideration, is different for both of the trees. Suppose that during the execution of the program, the variable C has value 1, D is also 1, and A is 5, and the statement σ above is encountered. If it is assumed that the derivation tree is given by Figure 1.8(a), the value $A = 5$ remains. If, on the other hand, the tree of Figure 1.8(b) is taken to be the right one, the value of A becomes 4. Thus, when compiling programs derived from an ambiguous grammar, an arbitrary decision must be taken as to which derivation tree is to be used, i.e., which meaning is to be assigned to the sentence. In this particular example, the meaning implied by the tree from Figure 1.8(a) is assumed. The arbitrarily chosen, but fixed rule is: "Each *else* is associated with the closest previous ***then***."

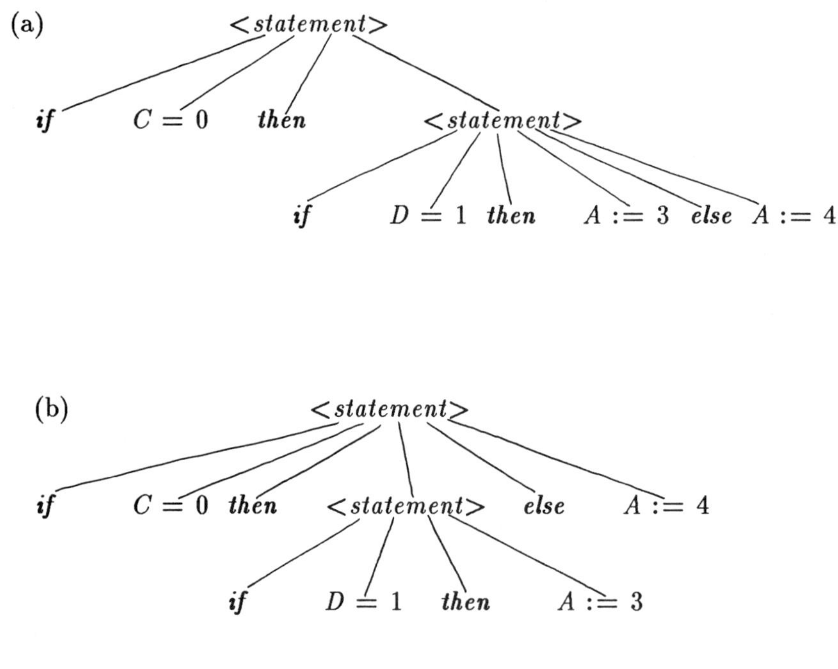

Figure 1.8. Ambiguity of ***if . . . then . . . else.***

It is clear from the above example that unambiguous grammars are preferable to ambiguous ones. Given a grammar G, in general there is no algorithm to determine whether G is ambiguous or not. For some specific grammars this can, however, be done—in Chapter 8 we will show that the grammar G_0 of arithmetic expressions is unambiguous.

It may well happen that for a given grammar G generating a language $L(G)$, there may exist a different grammar G' that generates the same language, i.e., $L(G') = L(G)$. Here is an example of this phenomenon.

Example 1.9. Let G be the grammar

$$\begin{aligned} S &\to 0A0 \\ A &\to S \mid \lambda \end{aligned}$$

and let G' be the grammar

$$\begin{aligned} S &\to 0B \\ B &\to 0S \mid 0 \end{aligned}$$

It is clear that both grammars generate the same language L—the set of all strings having an even number of 0's. The grammars themselves are actually quite distinct: G' is a regular grammar with no empty productions, while G has none of these properties.

It may happen that given an ambiguous grammar G, there is another, unambiguous grammar G' such that $L(G) = L(G')$. We could, for instance, rewrite the grammar of ***if* . . . *then* . . . *else*** in Example 1.8 as follows:

$$\begin{array}{lcl} \langle \textit{statement} \rangle & \to & S_1 \mid S_2 \mid \langle \textit{other kind of sentence} \rangle \\ S_1 & \to & \textbf{\textit{if}}\ \langle \textit{condition} \rangle\ \textbf{\textit{then}}\ S_1 \mid \\ & & \textbf{\textit{if}}\ \langle \textit{condition} \rangle\ \textbf{\textit{then}}\ S_2\ \textbf{\textit{else}}\ S_1 \mid \\ & & \langle \textit{other kind of sentence} \rangle \\ S_2 & \to & \textbf{\textit{if}}\ \langle \textit{condition} \rangle\ \textbf{\textit{then}}\ S_2\ \textbf{\textit{else}}\ S_2 \mid \\ & & \langle \textit{other kind of sentence} \rangle \end{array} \tag{1.5}$$

This grammar generates the same sentences as the grammar from Example 1.8, but the ambiguity is removed. Thus, when the sentence

$$\textbf{\textit{if}}\ \ C = 0\ \textbf{\textit{then}}\ \ \textbf{\textit{if}}\ \ D = 1\ \textbf{\textit{then}}\ A := 3\ \textbf{\textit{else}}\ A := 4$$

is parsed, its meaning is interpreted as

$$\textbf{\textit{if}}\ C = 0\ \textbf{\textit{then}}\ (\textbf{\textit{if}}\ D = 1\ \textbf{\textit{then}}\ A := 3\ \textbf{\textit{else}}\ A := 4)$$

as opposed to

$$\textbf{\textit{if}}\ C = 0\ \textbf{\textit{then}}\ (\textbf{\textit{if}}\ D = 1\ \textbf{\textit{then}}\ A := 3)\ \textbf{\textit{else}}\ A := 4.$$

Definition 1.11. A language is said to be ***inherently ambiguous*** if every grammar generating L is ambiguous.

It is not obvious that inherently ambiguous languages exist, but in fact they do. One example of such a language is

$$L = \left\{ a^k b^l c^m d^n \mid k,\ l,\ m, \text{ and } n \geq 1, \text{ either } (k = l \text{ and } m = n) \text{ or } (k = n \text{ and } l = m) \right\}$$

Examples of strings in L are *aabbcccddd* ($k = l = 2$, $m = n = 3$) and *aabbbcccdd* ($k = n = 2$, $l = m = 3$). The proof that this is indeed an inherently ambiguous language is beyond the scope of this book. The interested reader may find it on p. 99 of [13].

1.4. INTRODUCTION TO PARSING

We now consider the problem of reconstructing the derivation tree for a given sentence in a language, i.e., the problem of parsing. This question will be discussed throughout the book; the present section deals only with preliminaries. One may suspect that in order to specify the derivation tree it is enough to exhibit the sequence of productions used in the derivation. Without some additional restrictions there are some difficulties with this idea. First of all, two formally distinct sequences of productions may lead to the same tree. For example, consider the grammar G_0 of arithmetic expressions

1. $E \to E + T$	3. $T \to T * F$	5. $F \to (E)$
2. $E \to T$	4. $T \to F$	6. $F \to a$

and the string $a + a$ in this language. The sequences 1, 2, 4, 6, 4, 6, and 1, 4, 6, 2, 4, 6 are formally different and they correspond to two formally different derivations of $a + a$.

$$E \overset{1}{\Rightarrow} E + T \overset{2}{\Rightarrow} T + T \overset{4}{\Rightarrow} T + F \overset{6}{\Rightarrow} T + a \overset{4}{\Rightarrow} F + a \overset{6}{\Rightarrow} a + a$$

and

$$E \overset{1}{\Rightarrow} E + T \overset{4}{\Rightarrow} E + F \overset{6}{\Rightarrow} E + a \overset{2}{\Rightarrow} T + a \overset{4}{\Rightarrow} F + a \overset{6}{\Rightarrow} a + a$$

Both of these derivations, however, generate the same tree, as in Figure 1.9.

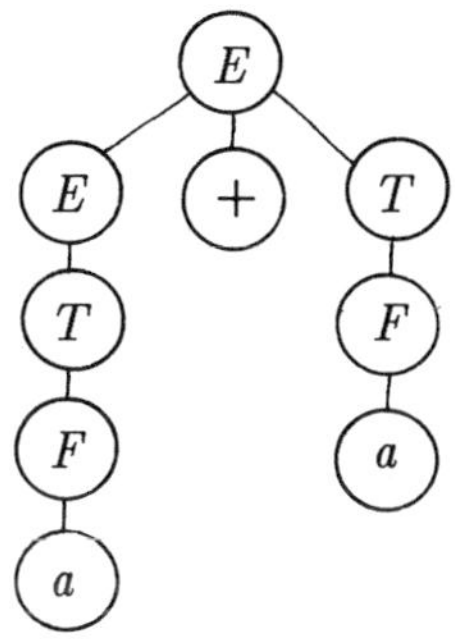

Figure 1.9. Parse tree for $a + a$.

The converse may also happen: Unless we specify at each step which nonterminal is being replaced, the same sequence of productions may lead to two distinct derivation trees. To see this, consider the grammar

1. $S \rightarrow A$
2. $A \rightarrow A0A$
3. $A \rightarrow 1$

The sequence of productions 1, 2, 2, 3, 3, 3 gives rise to two distinct derivations:

$$\underline{S} \overset{1}{\Rightarrow} \underline{A} \overset{2}{\Rightarrow} \underline{A}0A \overset{2}{\Rightarrow} \underline{A}0A0A \overset{3}{\Rightarrow} 10\underline{A}0A \overset{3}{\Rightarrow} 1010\underline{A} \overset{3}{\Rightarrow} 10101$$

and

$$\underline{S} \overset{1}{\Rightarrow} \underline{A} \overset{2}{\Rightarrow} A0\underline{A} \overset{2}{\Rightarrow} A0A0\underline{A} \overset{3}{\Rightarrow} A0\underline{A}01 \overset{3}{\Rightarrow} \underline{A}0101 \overset{3}{\Rightarrow} 10101$$

(In each sentential form the nonterminal that is being replaced is underlined.) The derivation trees of both of these derivations, as depicted in Figure 1.10, are distinct.

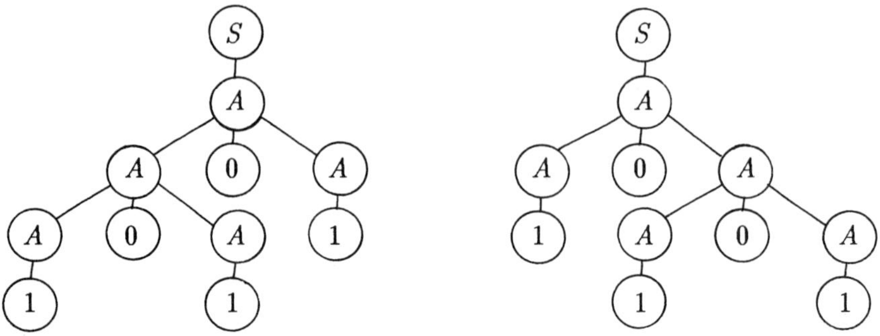

Figure 1.10. Ambiguous grammar.

Thus, in order to specify the derivation tree by means of the sequence of productions used, it is also necessary to specifically describe, at each stage, the nonterminal that is being replaced. This is quite cumbersome and, it turns out, unnecessary since we can specify in advance which nonterminal is singled out for replacement.

Definition 1.12. Let G be a grammar, let σ be a sentence in the language $L(G)$ and let

$$S \Rightarrow \sigma_1 \Rightarrow \sigma_2 \Rightarrow \cdots \Rightarrow \sigma_n = \sigma \qquad (1.6)$$

be the derivation of σ. We say that (1.6) is the ***leftmost derivation*** of σ, if at each stage $\sigma_i \Rightarrow \sigma_{i+1}$ the nonterminal of σ_i which is being replaced is the leftmost one. We say that (1.6) is the ***rightmost derivation*** if at each stage we replace the rightmost nonterminal.

For example, the leftmost derivation of $(a + a) * a$ in G_0 (the grammar of arithmetic expressions form Example 1.3) is

$$E \overset{1}{\Rightarrow} T \overset{3}{\Rightarrow} T * F \overset{4}{\Rightarrow} F * F \overset{5}{\Rightarrow} (E) * F \overset{1}{\Rightarrow} (E + T) * F \overset{2}{\Rightarrow}$$

$$(T + T) * F \overset{4}{\Rightarrow} (F + T) * F \overset{6}{\Rightarrow} (a + T) * F \overset{4}{\Rightarrow} (a + F) * F$$

$$\overset{6}{\Rightarrow} (a + a) * F \overset{6}{\Rightarrow} (a + a) * a$$

The rightmost derivation of the same sentence is given by

$$E \overset{2}{\Rightarrow} T \overset{3}{\Rightarrow} T * F \overset{6}{\Rightarrow} T * a \overset{4}{\Rightarrow} F * a \overset{5}{\Rightarrow} (E) * a \overset{1}{\Rightarrow}$$

$$(E + T) * a \overset{4}{\Rightarrow} (E + F) * a \overset{4}{\Rightarrow} (E + a) * a \overset{6}{\Rightarrow} (T + a) * a$$

$$\overset{4}{\Rightarrow} (F + a) * a \overset{1}{\Rightarrow} (a + a) * a$$

Thus, if we know in advance what kind of derivation is used (leftmost or rightmost), the sequence of productions used in deriving a sentence will completely describe the derivation tree.

Definition 1.13. A ***left parse*** of a string σ is the sequence of productions used in the leftmost derivation of σ. A ***right parse*** of σ is the reverse of the sequence of productions used in the rightmost derivation of σ.

The reason for the "reverse" in the definition of the right parse will be discussed briefly later on in this section, and in more detail in Chapter 8. Thus, the left parse of $(a + a) * a$ is: 2, 3, 4, 5, 1, 2, 4, 6, 4, 6, 6. The right parse of the same string is: 6, 4, 2, 6, 4, 1, 5, 4, 6, 3, 2. Clearly we can also speak of the left parse and the right parse of any sentential form derivable from the start symbol S. Thus, for instance, the left parse of $a * (E)$ in the grammar G_0 is 2, 3, 4, 6, 5, because

$$E \overset{2}{\Rightarrow} T \overset{3}{\Rightarrow} T * F \overset{4}{\Rightarrow} F * F \overset{6}{\Rightarrow} a * F \overset{5}{\Rightarrow} a * (E)$$

All this, of course, provides no clue of how to find a parse of a given string (be it the right or the left parse). Given a string $\sigma = a_1 a_2 \ldots a_n$ of terminals, the only thing we know about its derivation tree is that it has the symbol S on top, and its leaves on the bottom form the string $a_1 a_2 \ldots a_n$:

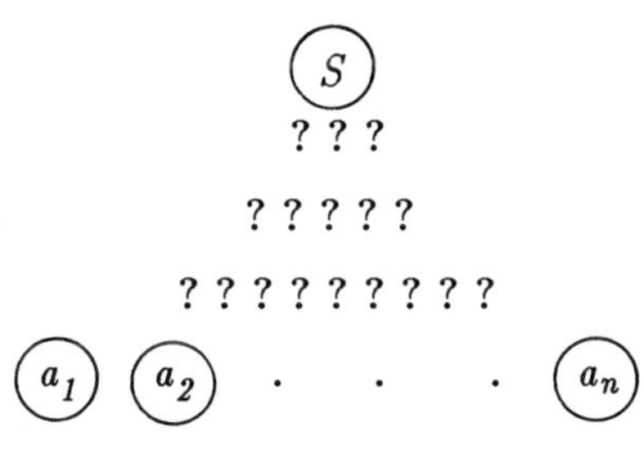

Figure 1.11. Derivation tree of $a_1 a_2 \ldots a_n$.

There are two ways we may try to fill in the inside of this tree: One way is to reconstruct it from the top down, the other way is to do it from the bottom up.

In the top-down parsing scheme, we start with the nonterminal S and try to figure out what is the first production $S \rightarrow \sigma_1$ that will guarantee that the derivation of $a_1a_2 \ldots a_n$ has the form

$$S \Rightarrow \sigma_1 \cdots \Rightarrow a_1a_2 \ldots a_n.$$

Once this is determined, we have to examine the string σ_1 and figure out which one of its nonterminals, say A, has to be replaced by the right-hand side of the production $A \rightarrow \alpha$, which will produce the sentential form σ_2 in the derivation

$$S \Rightarrow \sigma_1 \Rightarrow \sigma_2 \cdots \Rightarrow a_1a_2 \ldots a_n$$

This procedure is repeated over and over until the entire derivation is reconstructed. It turns out that if restrict ourself to the leftmost derivation, i.e., at each stage we wish to guess the leftmost nonterminal within a sentential form σ to be replaced, there is a very good way to make such educated guess. It will be presented in Chapter 6.

In the bottom-up parsing scheme, the process is reversed: Starting with the string $a_1a_2 \ldots a_n$, we try to find a sentential form σ_k such that the derivation of $a_1a_2 \ldots a_n$ has the form

$$S \Rightarrow \cdots \Rightarrow \sigma_k \Rightarrow a_1a_2 \ldots a_n.$$

To do this, we must locate a substring α of $a_1a_2 \ldots a_n$ that is a right-hand side of some production $A \rightarrow \alpha$, and replace this α by A. (Such a substring α is called the handle.) When this is accomplished, we repeat the procedure with the string σ_k in place of $a_1a_2 \ldots a_n$. We continue this until we reach S. It is not obvious how to accomplish this, but if we restrict ourself to the reconstruction of the rightmost derivation, it can be done. We will explain the process in Chapter 8. This explains, incidentally, why the right parse was defined to be the reverse of the sequence of the productions used in the rightmost derivation of a string: In the bottom-up parsing we first determine the last production used in the derivation, then the next to last, and so forth.

PROBLEMS

1. Let G_0 be the language of algebraic expressions from Example 1.3. Give the derivation tree, the left parse, and the right parse of the

following strings:

a) $a + a + a$, b) $(a + a) * a + a * (a + a)$, c) $a * a * a + a * a$

In each of problems 2–12 give a context-free grammar describing the given language and give a derivation tree of the indicated string σ_0.

2. All strings $\sigma \in \{0,1\}^*$ having a substring 001; $\sigma_0 = 01001110$.
3. All strings $\sigma \in \{0,1\}^*$ of odd length; $\sigma_0 = 0011011$.
4. $L = \{ a^{m+n} b^m d^n \mid m \geq 0,\ n \geq 0\}$; $\sigma_0 = aaaabccc$.
5. $L = \{ a^m b^n \mid 1 \leq n \leq m \leq 2n\}$; $\sigma_0 = aaabb$.
6. $L = \{ a^m b^n \mid 2 \leq 2n \leq m \leq 3n\}$; $\sigma_0 = aaaabb$.
7. The set of all strings over $\Sigma = \{0,\ 1\}$ of odd length; $\sigma_0 = 0010111$.
8. The set of all strings over $\Sigma = \{a,\ b\}$ in which the number of a's is the same as the number of b's; $\sigma_0 = abbaaabb$.
9. The set of all strings over $\Sigma = \{a,\ b\}$ in which there is one more a than b; $\sigma_0 = aabbbaa$.
10. The set of strings over $\Sigma = \{0,\ 1\}$ in which 1 occurs at least 3 times; $\sigma_0 = 001101$.
11. The set of strings over $\Sigma = \{a,\ b\}$ in which the first symbol is different from the last symbol; $\sigma_0 = aababab$.
12. The set of all valid dates for the years 1900 through 1999 given in the form

    NOVEMBER 30, 1959

    Notice that the year 1900 was not a leap year so that there was no February 29 in 1900; $\sigma_0 =$ OCTOBER 30, 1941.

In problems 13–15, describe the language generated by the given grammar.

13. $S \rightarrow aaSb \mid A, \quad A \rightarrow cAdd \mid cd$
14. $S \rightarrow ASBB \mid AB, \quad A \rightarrow aA \mid b, \quad B \rightarrow Bc \mid d$
15. $S \rightarrow aSb \mid aSbb \mid aSbbb \mid ab$

Each of the grammars in problems 16–21 is ambiguous. For each one of these grammars, find a sentence with two distinct derivation trees.

16. $S \rightarrow SaSa \mid b$
17. $S \rightarrow aSb \mid Sb \mid Sa \mid a$
18. $S \rightarrow aaS \mid aaaS \mid a$
19. $S \rightarrow aS \mid aSb \mid A, \quad A \rightarrow Aa \mid a$
20. $S \rightarrow AA, \quad A \rightarrow AAA \mid a \mid bA \mid Ab$
21. $S \rightarrow AaA, \quad A \rightarrow aA \mid bA \mid \lambda$

22. Show that every left linear language has also a right linear grammar, and conversely.
23. A fragment of the grammar dealing with the ***if . . . then . . . else*** constructs given in (1.3) on page 19 was ambiguous, since the sentence (1.4) had two distinct derivation trees, as exhibited in Figure 1.8. This fragment was then rewritten in (1.5) so as to force the sentence (1.4) to have the derivation tree given by Figure 1.8(a). Rewrite the grammar in (1.3) so the sentence (1.4) has the unique parse tree given by Figure 1.8 (b).

CHAPTER 2

FINITE STATE MACHINES

In this chapter we introduce the concept of finite state machines, also called finite automata. These mathematical devices have their origin in modeling the behavior of sequential electrical circuits; their use and applications, however, are much wider. They can be thought as the simplest model of an "algorithm," or of a parser of a language, or even of a computer. More sophisticated devices such as push-down automata, or even Turing machines, can be viewed as finite state machines with various "bells and whistles" attached to them. The theory of finite automata is simple enough to provide a motivation and an insight in studying these more powerful models.

2.1. DEFINITIONS

We now consider the mathematical concept of a finite state machine (abbreviated FSM), or finite automaton (FA). Initially, we restrict our attention to deterministic finite state machines (DFSM). These machines consist of a finite number of states together with an input device, which reads, one by one (from left to right), symbols from some input string of characters. If the machine is in some state Q and the input symbol is x, the machine changes the state (or moves) to a state $\delta(Q, x)$. It then reads the next input symbol to the right and the process repeats. The machine is initialized to an initial state Q_0, and the first symbol of the string it reads is the leftmost symbol of that string. The rule $\delta(Q, x)$ describing the next state is called the transition function. It depends only on the present state Q and the present input x, and is completely independent of past moves and inputs. The machine stops after it reads all the symbols of the input string. Some variations of the concept allow the possibility of the function $\delta(Q, x)$ being undefined for certain Q's and x's. In this case the machine will also halt when it reaches a configuration in which $\delta(Q, x)$ is undefined. Before giving the formal definitions, let us consider some examples.

Example 2.1. Suppose the machine M has four states: Q_0, Q_1, Q_2, and Q_3, and the allowable input strings are formed from the symbols a, b, and c. Let Q_0 be the initial state and let the transition function δ be given by the table in Figure 2.1.

		Current input		
		a	b	c
State	Q_0	Q_1	Q_2	Q_0
	Q_1	Q_0	Q_0	Q_3
	Q_2	Q_3	Q_1	Q_2
	Q_3	Q_3	Q_1	Q_0

Figure 2.1. Table of a transition function.

Such a machine can also be represented, in a self-explanatory way, by what is called a ***state diagram***, or ***transition diagram***, as depicted in Figure 2.2. The arrow $\rightarrow$ pointing to Q_0 indicates that Q_0 is the initial state. Notice that in some situations the machine remains in the same state, for instance $\delta(Q_3, a) = Q_3$. Thus, if the machine is in the state Q_3 and the input symbol is a, the machine remains in the state Q_3 and the next symbol is read. If the original input of the machine is $aacbbca$, then the machine would go through the following sequence of moves:

$$Q_0 \xrightarrow{a} Q_1 \xrightarrow{a} Q_0 \xrightarrow{c} Q_0 \xrightarrow{b} Q_2 \xrightarrow{b} Q_1 \xrightarrow{c} Q_3 \xrightarrow{a} Q_3$$

Here $Q_i \xrightarrow{x} Q_j$ means that the machine changes state from Q_i to Q_j upon reading the input x, i.e., $\delta(Q_i, x) = Q_j$. After the entire input string has been read the machine is in the state Q_3.

Finite state machines may be used to "recognize" or "accept" certain kind of strings and reject others, depending on the state the machine is in after the string has been read. Given a finite state machine M, we designate some of its states as "accepting" or "final." When a string $\sigma =$

$x_1x_2 \ldots x_n$ of characters is presented to M, it executes the sequence of moves as described above (beginning with the initial state Q_0 and the symbol x_1). After the symbol x_n has been read we observe the state in which the machine M stops.

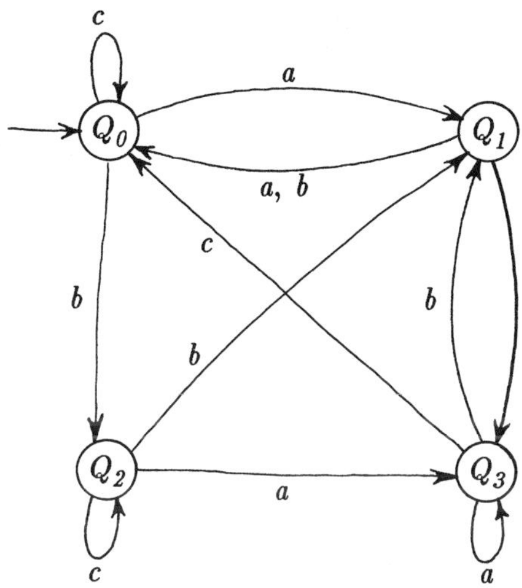

Figure 2.2. Transition diagram.

If this state is one of the accepting states, we say that M accepts σ, otherwise we say that M does not accept σ. In the transition diagram of M we enclose the accepting states in a double circle.

Figure 2.3. Accepting state Q.

The initial state is allowed to be one of the accepting states. Any machine in which this takes place will accept the empty string λ. (It may, of course, also accept other strings.)

Example 2.2. We construct a machine M that will accept strings of 0's and 1's with even number of 1's (and no others). The transition diagram of this machine is given in Figure 2.4. Thus, for instance, when the input $\sigma_1 = 01001011$ is presented to M the sequence of moves is

$$Q_0 \xrightarrow{0} Q_0 \xrightarrow{1} Q_1 \xrightarrow{0} Q_1 \xrightarrow{0} Q_1$$
$$\xrightarrow{1} Q_0 \xrightarrow{0} Q_0 \xrightarrow{1} Q_1 \xrightarrow{1} Q_0$$

The machine halts in the accepting state Q_0, thus σ_1 is accepted by M. On the other hand, if the input is $\sigma_2 = 01101$ the sequence of moves is

$$Q_0 \xrightarrow{0} Q_0 \xrightarrow{1} Q_1 \xrightarrow{1} Q_0 \xrightarrow{0} Q_0 \xrightarrow{1} Q_1$$

The last state is Q_1, which is not accepting, and thus the string σ_2 is not accepted by M.

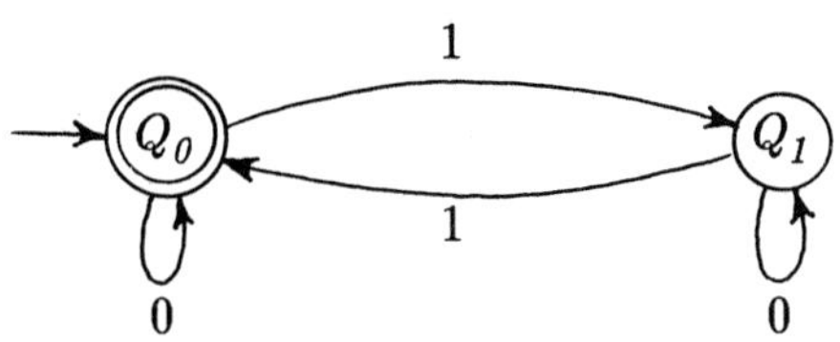

Figure 2.4. Transition diagram of a FA.

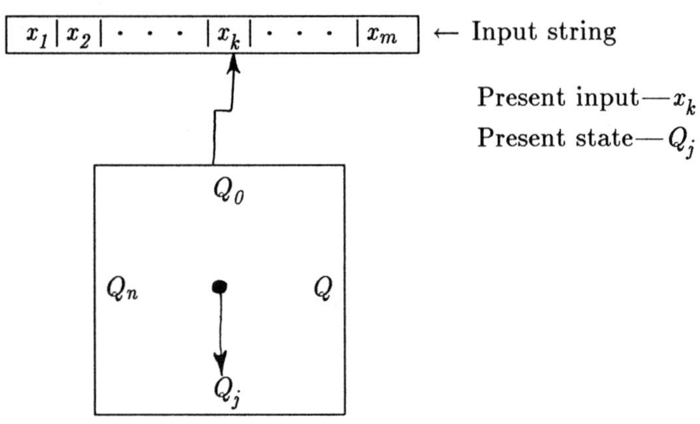

Figure 2.5. Schematic representation of a FSM.

Finite state machines may be schematically represented as in Figure 2.5. The input head moves only to the right, the arrow pointing to the symbol Q_j indicates the current state. The formal definition of a finite state machine is as follows:

Definition 2.1. A ***finite state machine*** M consists of the following five objects:

1. A finite, nonempty set $\mathcal{Q} = \{Q_0, Q_1, \ldots, Q_n\}$. The elements Q of $\mathcal{Q}$ are called ***states***;
2. A finite, nonempty set $\Sigma = \{a_1, a_2, \ldots, a_k\}$ of symbols allowable in the input strings. The set Σ is called the ***input alphabet*** of M;
3. A designated state $Q_0 \in \mathcal{Q}$, called the ***initial state***;
4. A ***transition function*** $\delta(Q, a)$ defined for all states $Q \in \mathcal{Q}$ and all $a \in \Sigma$. For each $Q \in \mathcal{Q}$ and each $a \in \Sigma$ the value of $\delta(Q, a)$ is another state of $\mathcal{Q}$. Thus $\delta: \mathcal{Q} \times \Sigma \mapsto \mathcal{Q}$.
5. A nonempty collection $\mathcal{F}$ of states from $\mathcal{Q}$. The elements of $\mathcal{F}$ are called ***final***, or ***accepting*** states.

A finite state machine M will then be a quintuple $M = \{\mathcal{Q}, \Sigma, Q_0, \delta, \mathcal{F}\}$.

Thus, for the machine in Example 2.2 we have $\mathcal{Q} = \{Q_0, Q_1\}$, $\Sigma = \{0, 1\}$, $Q_0 = Q_0$, and δ is given by $\delta(Q_0, 0) = \delta(Q_1, 1) = Q_0$, $\delta(Q_0, 1) = \delta(Q_1, 0) = Q_1$. There are minor variations of this definition in the literature. Sometimes it is not required that the transition function $\delta(Q, x)$ be defined for all Q's and all x's; also, the set $\mathcal{F}$ of the accepting states may be allowed to be empty.

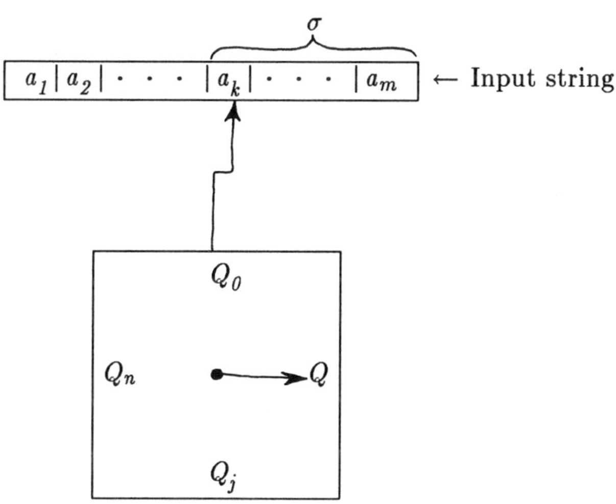

Figure 2.6. Finite state machine in configuration $[\![Q, a_k a_{k+1} \ldots a_m]\!]$.

To facilitate describing the movements of a machine, we introduce concept of ***configuration.*** A configuration of a machine M is a pair $[\![Q, \sigma]\!]$, where Q is a state and $\sigma = a_k a_{k+1} \ldots a_m$ is the portion of the input string under and to the right of the input head, as depicted in Figure 2.6. If a machine M is in configuration $[\![Q, a_k a_{k+1} \ldots a_m]\!]$ and $\delta(Q, a_k) = \hat{Q}$, the next configuration of M is $[\![\hat{Q}, a_{k+1} a_{k+2} \ldots a_m]\!]$. We denote this by

$$[\![Q, a_k a_{k+1} \ldots a_m]\!] \rightarrow [\![\hat{Q}, a_{k+1} a_{k+2} \ldots a_m]\!]$$

and call it a move. When the input string is empty, e.g., when the entire string has been read, the configuration of M is $[\![Q, \lambda]\!]$, where λ, as usual, stands for the empty string. Hence the movements of the machine from Example 2.2 on input 01101 are described by the following sequence of configurations:

$$[\![Q_0, 01101]\!] \rightarrow [\![Q_0, 1101]\!] \rightarrow [\![Q_1, 101]\!] \rightarrow [\![Q_0, 01]\!] \rightarrow [\![Q_0, 1]\!] \rightarrow [\![Q_1, \lambda]\!]$$

If for some sequence of configurations we have the sequence of moves

$$[\![Q_1, \sigma_1]\!] \rightarrow [\![Q_2, \sigma_2]\!] \rightarrow \cdots \rightarrow [\![Q_p, \sigma_p]\!]$$

we denote this by $[\![Q_1, \sigma_1]\!] \rightarrow^* [\![Q_p, \sigma_p]\!]$ and call it a ***transition.***

Example 2.3. The machine M will have as its alphabet the set $\Sigma = \{0, 1, 2\}$. We may think of the inputs of M the nonnegative integers expressed in ternary notation (base 3). Thus, the string $\epsilon_1 \epsilon_2 \ldots \epsilon_n$ represents the number

$$x = \epsilon_n + \epsilon_{n-1} \cdot 3 + \epsilon_{n-2} \cdot 3^2 + \cdots + \epsilon_1 \cdot 3^{n-1}$$

The machine under construction will accept such a string $\epsilon_1 \epsilon_2 \ldots \epsilon_n$ if and only if the corresponding number x is even. Thus, it will accept 121 $(=1 + 2 * 3 + 1 * 9 = 16$, base 10), but it will not accept 210 $(= 0 + 1 * 3 + 2 * 9 = 21$, base 10). The key to understanding the behavior of M is the following rule for evenness of numbers expressed in the ternary notation: If

$$x = \epsilon_n + \epsilon_{n-1} \cdot 3 + \epsilon_{n-2} \cdot 3^2 + \cdots + \epsilon_1 \cdot 3^{n-1} \tag{2.1}$$

then x is even if and only if $\epsilon_1 + \epsilon_2 + \cdots + \epsilon_n$ is even. To see this, suppose x is given by (2.1). Each power of 3, when divided by 2, gives the remainder 1. Thus, when we divide x by 2, each term $\epsilon_k \cdot 3^{n-k}$ will contribute ϵ_k to the remainder. The formal proof may be given using congruences. The machine M is then given by the diagram in Figure 2.7.

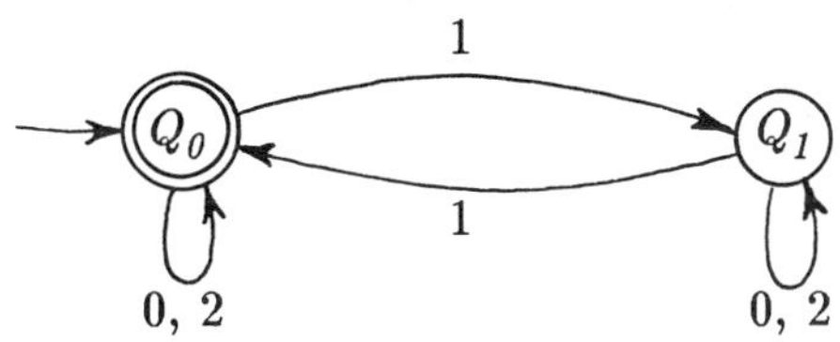

Figure 2.7. Divisibility by 2.

The transition function δ is such that $\delta(Q_i, \epsilon) = Q_j$, where j is the remainder obtained from dividing $i + \epsilon$ by 2 ($j \equiv i + \epsilon (\text{mod } 2)$). On the input $\sigma = 121$ the machine goes through the sequence of configurations

$$[\![Q_0, 121]\!] \rightarrow [\![Q_1, 21]\!] \rightarrow [\![Q_1, 1]\!] \rightarrow [\![Q_0, \lambda]\!]$$

and on the input $\sigma = 1122$ the movements are

$$[\![Q_0, 1122]\!] \rightarrow [\![Q_1, 122]\!] \rightarrow [\![Q_0, 22]\!] \rightarrow [\![Q_0, 2]\!] \rightarrow [\![Q_0, \lambda]\!]$$

2.2. DESCRIPTION OF A LANGUAGE USING MACHINES

The concept of a finite state machine gives another method of describing languages. Let M be a finite state machine with an alphabet Σ. We define the language $L(M)$ generated by M as the collection of all strings of elements of Σ that are accepted by M. In other words, a string $\sigma = x_1 x_2 \ldots x_n$ from Σ^* will be in $L(M)$ if and only if the machine M, when started on input σ, will halt in an accepting state. Formally, we have the following.

Definition 2.2. Let $M = \{\mathcal{Q}, \Sigma, Q_0, \delta, \mathcal{F}\}$ be a finite state machine. The language $L(M)$ ***generated*** (or ***recognized***, or ***accepted***) by M is defined as

$$L(M) = \{\sigma \in \Sigma^* \mid [\![Q_0, \sigma]\!] \rightarrow^* [\![Q, \lambda]\!] \text{ for some } Q \in \mathcal{F}\}$$

This description of a language is a very convenient one. Finite state machines can be easily simulated on a computer, in fact they can be easily implemented in hardware. Thus, given a language L, if one can construct a finite state machine accepting L, one has in effect constructed an automatic parser of L. This brings a natural (and practical) question: Given a grammar G, can we construct a finite state machine M such that $L(G) = L(M)$? Unfortunately (or fortunately, depending on one's point of view), this is possible only for special kind of grammars—the regular grammars. Recall that G is regular if it is either right linear (all productions of the form $A \rightarrow aB$, $A \rightarrow a$, or $S \rightarrow \lambda$) or left linear (all productions of the form $A \rightarrow Ba$, $A \rightarrow a$, or $S \rightarrow \lambda$). We have the following result.

Theorem 2.1. Let L be a language. There exists a finite state machine M such that $L = L(M)$ if and only if there exists a regular grammar G such that $L = L(G)$.

In this section we will prove the "only if" part, i.e., given a finite state machine M, we will construct a regular grammar G such that $L(M) = L(G)$. Let the states of M be $Q_0, Q_1, \ldots, Q_n$, let the alphabet of M be $\Sigma = \{a_1, a_2, \ldots, a_k\}$, let $\delta(Q, a)$ be the transition function, let Q_0 be the initial state, and let $\mathcal{F}$ be the collection of final states. The grammar G is constructed as follows:

1. The alphabet (i.e., the set of terminals) is $\Sigma = \{a_1, a_2, \ldots, a_k\}$.
2. The set of nonterminals is the set of symbols in $\mathcal{Q}$ (i.e., $N = \mathcal{Q}$).
3. The start symbol of G is Q_0 — the initial state of M.
4. The productions of G are formed according to the following rules:

I. For every transition $\delta(Q_i, a) = Q_j$, where Q_j is not a final state, include production $Q_i \rightarrow aQ_j$.
II. For every transition $\delta(Q_i, a) = Q_j$ where Q_j is a final state, include productions $Q_i \rightarrow aQ_j$ and $Q_i \rightarrow a$.
III. If Q_0 is a final state, include production $Q_0 \rightarrow \lambda$.

It is evident that the resulting grammar is regular (it is right linear).

Example 2.4. Let M be defined by the diagram in Figure 2.8. The corresponding grammar G is then constructed as follows.

$$\left.\begin{array}{l} 1.\ Q_0 \rightarrow bQ_0 \\ 2.\ Q_0 \rightarrow b \end{array}\right\} \quad \text{Rule II: } Q_0 \xrightarrow{b} Q_0$$

$$3.\ Q_0 \rightarrow aQ_0 \qquad \text{Rule I: } Q_0 \xrightarrow{a} Q_1$$

$$
\begin{array}{llll}
4. & Q_0 \to \lambda & & \text{Rule III: } Q_0 \in \mathcal{F} \\
5. & Q_1 \to aQ_0 & \multirow{2}{*}{\}} & \text{Rule II: } Q_1 \xrightarrow{a} Q_0 \\
6. & Q_1 \to a & & \\
7. & Q_1 \to bQ_2 & & \text{Rule II: } Q_1 \xrightarrow{b} Q_2 \\
8. & Q_1 \to b & & \\
9. & Q_2 \to aQ_1 & & \text{Rule I: } Q_2 \xrightarrow{a} Q_1 \\
10. & Q_2 \to bQ_0 & & \text{Rule II: } Q_2 \xrightarrow{b} Q_0 \\
11. & Q_2 \to b & &
\end{array}
$$

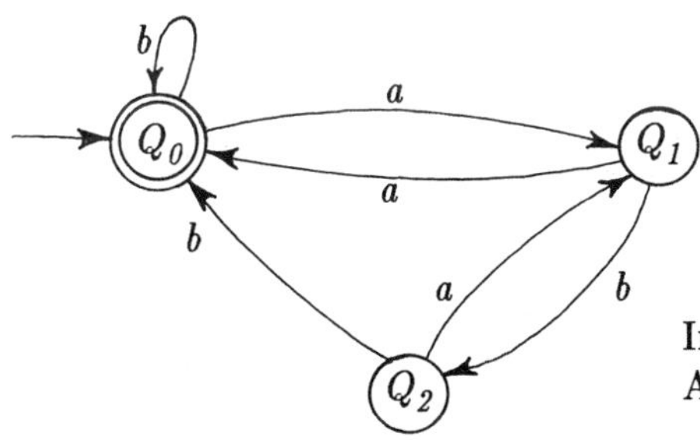

Initial state—Q_0
Accepting states—Q_0 and Q_2

Figure 2.8. Construction of a grammar for a FSM.

The proof that $L(M) = L(G)$ is intuitively straightforward. Suppose a string $\sigma = x_1x_2 \ldots x_p$ is accepted by a machine. Then the sequence of configurations of M is given by

$$
\begin{aligned}
[\![Q_0, x_1x_2 \ldots x_p]\!] &\to [\![\hat{Q}_1, x_2x_3 \ldots x_p]\!] \to [\![\hat{Q}_2, x_3x_4 \ldots x_p]\!] \\
&\to^* [\![\hat{Q}_i, x_{i+1}x_{i+2} \ldots x_p]\!] \to [\![\hat{Q}_{i+1}, x_{i+2} \ldots x_p]\!] \\
&\to^* [\![\hat{Q}_{p-1}, x_p]\!] \to [\![\hat{Q}_p, \lambda]\!] \qquad (2.2)
\end{aligned}
$$

where each $X_j \in \Sigma$, $\hat{Q}_j \in \mathcal{Q}$, and $\hat{Q}_p \in \mathcal{F}$. Each transition follows from the corresponding value of the transition function in (2.3).

$$\delta(Q_0, x_1) = \hat{Q}_1,\ \delta(\hat{Q}_1, x_2) = \hat{Q}_2, \ldots,$$
$$\delta(\hat{Q}_i, x_{i+1}) = \hat{Q}_{i+1}, \ldots, \delta(\hat{Q}_{p-1}, x_p) = \hat{Q}_p \tag{2.3}$$

Hence, the grammar G includes the following productions (among others):

$$Q_0 \to x_1\hat{Q}_1,\ \hat{Q}_1 \to x_2\hat{Q}_2, \ldots, \hat{Q}_i \to x_{i+1}\hat{Q}_{i+1}, \ldots,$$
$$\hat{Q}_{p-1} \to x_p\hat{Q}_p, \qquad \hat{Q}_{p-1} \to x_p \tag{2.4}$$

The last production is included because $\hat{Q}_p$ is a final state. Thus, the string $\sigma = x_1x_2 \ldots x_p$ can be derived in the grammar G as

$$Q_0 \Rightarrow x_1\hat{Q}_1 \Rightarrow x_1x_2\hat{Q}_2 \Rightarrow \ldots \Rightarrow x_1x_2 \ldots x_i\hat{Q}_i$$
$$\Rightarrow x_1x_2 \ldots x_ix_{i+1}\hat{Q}_{i+1} \Rightarrow x_1x_2 \ldots x_{p-1}\hat{Q}_{p-1} \Rightarrow x_1x_2 \ldots x_{p-1}x_p \tag{2.5}$$

In all but the last derivation we used a production of the form $\hat{Q}_i \to x_{i+1}\hat{Q}_{i+1}$; the last derivation used the production $\hat{Q}_{p-1} \to x_p$. The converse is proved in a similar fashion: Suppose the derivation of a sentence $x_1x_2 \ldots x_p$ in the grammar G is given by (2.5). This implies that all the productions in (2.4) are productions in G, which in turn implies that the transition function δ satisfies relations (2.3), which finally implies that the machine M goes through the sequence of configurations (2.3), i.e., $x_1x_2 \ldots x_p \in L(M)$. Hence, the "only if" part of Theorem 2.1 is proved.

As an illustration, we consider the machine M and the grammar G from Example 2.4. The string $\sigma = abaab$ is in the language $L(M)$ since

$$[\![Q_0, abaab]\!] \to [\![Q_1, baab]\!] \to [\![Q_2, aab]\!] \to [\![Q_1, ab]\!] \to [\![Q_0, b]\!] \to [\![Q_0, \lambda]\!]$$

and Q_0 is an accepting state. The derivation of σ in the grammar G is then

$$Q_0 \overset{3}{\Rightarrow} aQ_1 \overset{7}{\Rightarrow} abQ_2 \overset{9}{\Rightarrow} abaQ_1 \overset{5}{\Rightarrow} abaaQ_0 \overset{2}{\Rightarrow} abaab$$

Production numbers are indicated above the arrows.

A comment, perhaps, should be made about the acceptance of the empty string λ by a finite state machine M. When such a string is presented to M, the machine starts in the configuration (Q_0, λ), where

Q_0 is the initial state, and halts without making a move. Thus, $\lambda \in L(M)$ if and only if the initial state Q_0 is also one of the accepting states.

2.3. NONDETERMINISTIC FINITE STATE MACHINES

It may seem straightforward to prove the "if" part of Theorem 2.1 as follows. Given a grammar G, we construct a finite state machine M which accepts $L(G)$ by having the nonterminals play the role of the states and include a transition $A \xrightarrow{a} B$ (i.e., $\delta(A, a) = B$) for every production of the form $A \rightarrow aB$. This idea, however, does not quite work, as the following example shows. Let G be the grammar

$$S \rightarrow aA \qquad A \rightarrow aB \qquad B \rightarrow b$$
$$S \rightarrow bB \qquad A \rightarrow aS$$

When we try to construct the machine according to the indicated scheme, two kind of difficulties arise. First of all, what should be $\delta(B, a)$? There is no production of the form $B \rightarrow aX$ for any nonterminal X. This is actually only a minor annoyance that can be repaired, as we shell see later. The more serious difficulty arises from two productions $A \rightarrow aB$ and $A \rightarrow aS$. In an attempt to construct the machine M along the lines indicated above, we face the dilemma of how to define $\delta(A, a)$, i.e., what to do when M is in the state A and it reads the symbol a. The production $A \rightarrow aB$ implies that the next state $\delta(A, a)$ should be B, while the production $A \rightarrow aS$ suggests that perhaps it should be S. Thus, the fragment of the diagram description of M would look like Figure 2.9.

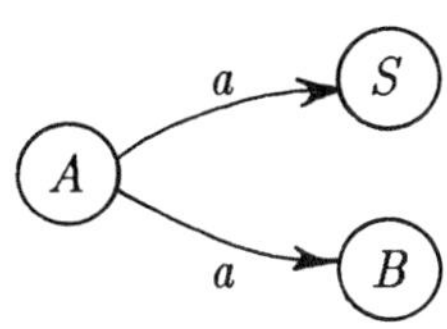

Figure 2.9. Ambiguous transition diagram.

When the concept of a finite state machine was defined in Definition 2.1, it was carefully stipulated that $\delta(Q, x)$ was defined for each state Q and every input symbol x, and that given Q and x, the next state, i.e., the value of the transition function $\delta(Q, x)$, was uniquely defined. The machine was not allowed to make any choices along the way. The way out of this predicament is to extend the definition of a finite state machine, and allow it to include peculiarities just described. Such devices will be called nondeterministic finite automata (NDFA) or nondeterministic finite state machines (NDFSM). It turns out that given one of these new machines, say M, there exists an ordinary deterministic finite automaton (as defined in Definition 2.1) accepting the same language as M. We now proceed to describe these concepts precisely.

Definition 2.3. A ***nondeterministic finite state machine*** (NDFSM for short) consists of the following five objects:

1. A finite, nonempty set $\mathfrak{Q} = \{Q_0, Q_1, \ldots, Q_n\}$ of states.
2. A finite, nonempty set $\Sigma = \{a_1, a_2, \ldots, a_k\}$ of allowable input symbols (the alphabet).
3. A designated state $Q_0 \in \mathfrak{Q}$, called the initial state.
4. A transition function $\delta(Q, x)$, which need not be defined for all Q's from $\mathfrak{Q}$ and all x's from Σ. For those Q's and x's for which it is defined, $\delta(Q, x)$ is a set of one or more states of $\mathfrak{Q}$. Strictly speaking, if $\mathfrak{P}(\mathfrak{Q})$ denotes the set of all subsets of $\mathfrak{Q}$, then the transition function $\delta\colon \mathfrak{Q} \times \Sigma \mapsto \mathfrak{P}(\mathfrak{Q})$. With this notation, $\delta(Q, x)$ is "not defined" means $\delta(Q, x) = \emptyset$ (the empty set). The interpretation of the function δ is the same as in the deterministic case: It is the next state. The difference now is that we allow several possibilities (or none).
5. A nonempty collection $\mathfrak{F}$ of states. The elements of $\mathfrak{F}$ will be called accepting, or final states.

Such machines M will be denoted by $\{\mathfrak{Q}, \Sigma, Q_0, \delta, \mathfrak{F}\}$ (in the same way as the deterministic machines). They are also called ***nondeterministic finite automata*** (NDFA). Thus, everything is the same as in the deterministic case, except for the definition of the transition function δ. The movements of such a NDFSM are given as follows.

1. Given an input string $\sigma = x_1x_2 \ldots x_p$ of symbols from Σ, the initial configuration of M is $[\![Q_0, x_1x_2 \ldots x_p]\!]$, i.e., M is in the initial state Q_0 and the input symbol is x_1.
2. Suppose at some instant of time, the configuration of M is $[\![Q, x_ix_{i+1} \ldots x_p]\!]$. If $\hat{Q}$ is one of the possible values of $\delta(Q, x_i)$ (or, more precisely, $\hat{Q} \in \delta(Q, x_i)$) then M is allowed to move into configuration $[\![\hat{Q}, x_{i+1} \ldots x_p]\!]$. Thus, if M is in the state Q and the input symbol is x, M is allowed to change into any one of the states in $\delta(Q, x_i)$, but not into any others. If $\delta(Q, x_i) = \emptyset$, then Q is not allowed to move at all. The move, if possible, from one configuration to another is denoted by

$$[\![Q, x_ix_{i+1} \ldots x_p]\!] \rightarrow [\![\hat{Q}, x_{i+1} \ldots x_p]\!]$$

and is called a legal move.

3. The machine stops either when it has read all its input (i.e., in configuration $[\![Q, \lambda]\!]$), or when $\delta(Q, x_i) = \emptyset$ (i.e., when $\delta(Q, x_i)$ does not contain any possibilities for the next state).

Example 2.5. Let M be a NDFSM as follows. The set $\mathcal{Q}$ of the states has four elements: $\mathcal{Q} = \{Q_0, Q_1, Q_2, Q_3\}$, the alphabet $\Sigma = \{0, 1, 2\}$, the initial state is Q_0, and the set of final states is $\mathcal{F} = \{Q_2, Q_3\}$.

State		Current input: 0	1	2
S	Q_0	$\{Q_0, Q_1\}$	$\{Q_0\}$	$\emptyset$
t	Q_1	$\emptyset$	$\{Q_2\}$	$\{Q_0, Q_3\}$
a	Q_2	$\{Q_2\}$	$\{Q_0, Q_3\}$	$\emptyset$
t e	Q_3	$\{Q_2\}$	$\{Q_1, Q_3\}$	$\{Q_3\}$

Figure 2.10. A nondeterministic transition function δ.

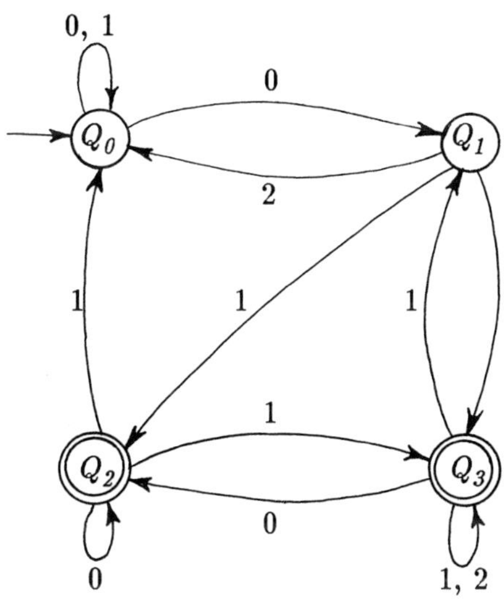

Figure 2.11. A nondeterministic FSM.

The transition function is given by the table in Figure 2.10, or the diagram in Figure 2.11. Thus, if the machine is in the state Q_1 and the input symbol is 2, M is allowed to move to state Q_0 or Q_3. It follows that, on a given input σ, the machine M is allowed to go through many different sequences of moves. For example, if $\sigma = 01021$ some of the possible movements are as follows:

$$[\![Q_0, 01021]\!] \to [\![Q_0, 1021]\!] \to [\![Q_0, 021]\!] \to [\![Q_1, 21]\!] \to [\![Q_3, 1]\!] \to [\![Q_1, \lambda]\!] \text{ — stop}$$

$$[\![Q_0, 01021]\!] \to [\![Q_0, 1021]\!] \to [\![Q_0, 021]\!] \to [\![Q_0, 21]\!] \text{ — stop}$$

$$[\![Q_0, 01021]\!] \to [\![Q_1, 1021]\!] \to [\![Q_2, 021]\!] \to [\![Q_2, 21]\!] \text{ — stop}$$

$$[\![Q_0, 01021]\!] \to [\![Q_0, 1021]\!] \to [\![Q_0, 021]\!] \to [\![Q_1, 21]\!] \to [\![Q_3, 1]\!] \to [\![Q_3, \lambda]\!] \text{ — stop}$$

In the first sequence, the input is read entirely but the machine halts in a nonaccepting state; in the second and third sequences, M stops before the string is read completely; and in the fourth sequence, the whole string is read and the last state is an accepting one.

If $[\![Q, \sigma]\!]$ and $[\![\hat{Q}, \hat{\sigma}]\!]$ are two configurations such that it is possible for M to get from $[\![Q, \sigma]\!]$ to $[\![\hat{Q}, \hat{\sigma}]\!]$ through a sequence of allowable moves, we say that $[\![\hat{Q}, \hat{\sigma}]\!]$ is ***derivable*** from $[\![Q, \sigma]\!]$, and denote this by

$$[\![Q, \sigma]\!] \to^* [\![\hat{Q}, \hat{\sigma}]\!]$$

In Example 2.5, for instance, we have $[\![Q_0, 01021]\!] \to^* [\![Q_1, 21]\!]$ and $[\![Q_0, 01021]\!] \to^* [\![Q_3, \lambda]\!]$. We are now ready to define a language generated (also called accepted, or recognized) by a nondeterministic finite state machine.

Definition 2.4. Let $M = \{\mathcal{Q}, \Sigma, Q_0, \delta, \mathcal{F}\}$ be a NDFSM. We say that a string $\sigma = x_1 x_2 \ldots x_p$ of elements of Σ is ***accepted by M*** if

$$[\![Q_0, x_1 x_2 \ldots x_p]\!] \to^* [\![Q, \lambda]\!]$$

and $Q \in \mathcal{F}$. The set of all strings accepted by M is denoted by $L(M)$ and is called the language generated by M.

Note that in order for a string σ to be accepted by M, we only require that there be ***some*** legal sequence of moves getting from $[\![Q_0, \sigma]\!]$

to $[\![Q, \lambda]\!]$, where Q is an accepting state, and not that ***all*** legal sequences will get us there. Thus, in Example 2.5, $[\![Q_0, 01021]\!] \rightarrow^* [\![Q_3, \lambda]\!]$, so $\sigma = 01021$ is in $L(M)$ because Q_3 is an accepting state. Notice, however, that beginning with the configuration $[\![Q_0, 01021]\!]$, the machine M may get stuck in some blind alleys: $[\![Q_0, 01021]\!] \rightarrow^* [\![Q_0, 21]\!]$, $[\![Q_0, 01021]\!] \rightarrow^* [\![Q_2, 21]\!]$, etc.

It is quite clear that the deterministic finite state machines from Definition 2.1 are special cases of the nondeterministic machines. They are characterized by the property that for each state Q and each input x, the set $\delta(Q, x)$ consists of exactly one state. It is reasonable therefore to expect that the class of languages accepted by nondeterministic machines should be larger than the class accepted by the deterministic machines, i.e., there should be a NDFSM, say M, such that for no deterministic machine K we do have $L(M) = L(K)$. It is somewhat surprising that this is not the case. We have the following theorem.

Theorem 2.2. Let M be a nondeterministic finite state machine. Then there exists a deterministic machine K such that $L(M) = L(K)$, i.e., the machines M and K accept the same strings.

Proof. Let M be a nondeterministic finite state machine, as specified by Definition 2.3. Let $\mathcal{Q} = \{Q_0, Q_1, \ldots, Q_n\}$ be the set of the states of M, with Q_0 being the initial state, let $\Sigma = \{a_1, a_2, \ldots, a_k\}$ be its alphabet, let δ be the transition function, and let $\mathcal{F}$ be the set of accepting states. The machine K is specified as follows:

1. The input alphabet of K is Σ—the same as for M.
2. The states of K will be all possible subsets of $\mathcal{Q}$. Thus, for example, if M were to have three states—say Q_0, Q_1, and Q_2—the states of K would be $S_0 = \{Q_0\}$, $S_1 = \{Q_1\}$, $S_2 = \{Q_2\}$, $S_3 = \{Q_0, Q_1\}$, $S_4 = \{Q_0, Q_2\}$, $S_5 = \{Q_1, Q_2\}$, $S_6 = \{Q_0, Q_1, Q_2\}$, and last (but not the least) $S_7 = \emptyset$—the empty set. (We ***do*** include the empty set as a subset of any set.) Hence, if M has n states, the machine K has 2^n states: $S_0, S_1, S_2, \ldots, S_{2^n-1}$. The collection of the states of K will be denoted by $\mathcal{S}$.
3. The initial state of K is the state $S_0 = \{Q_0\}$, where Q_0 is the initial state of M.
4. A state $S \in \mathcal{S}$ will be a final state of K if and only if it contains a final state $Q \in \mathcal{F}$ of M. Thus, for example, if M is the machine from Example 2.5, the final states of K will be sets containing Q_2 or Q_3 (or both). These are $\{Q_2\}$, $\{Q_3\}$, $\{Q_0, Q_2\}$, $\{Q_0, Q_3\}$, $\{Q_1, Q_2\}$, $\{Q_1, Q_3\}$, $\{Q_2, Q_3\}$, $\{Q_0, Q_1, Q_2\}$, $\{Q_0, Q_1, Q_3\}$, $\{Q_0, Q_2,$

$Q_3\}$, $\{Q_1, Q_2, Q_3\}$, and $\{Q_0, Q_1, Q_2, Q_3\}$—there are 12 of them altogether.

5. The transition function Δ of K is defined as follows. Let $S = \{Q_{i_1}, Q_{i_2}, \ldots, Q_{i_p}\}$ be a state of K and let $x \in \Sigma$. The value of $\Delta(S, x)$ is another state of K, i.e., a set of Q's, which we define by the following rule:

   If $Q \in \delta(Q_j, x)$ for some Q_j in S, then $Q \in \Delta(S, x)$

   Formally, we have, of course,

$$\Delta(S, x) \quad = \quad \bigcup_{Q \in S} \delta(Q, x) \tag{2.6}$$

In other words, if for some Q_j in S it is possible for the machine M to move from the state Q_j to Q on the input x, then $Q \in \Delta(S, x)$. A slight ambiguity arises when $S = \emptyset$ (the empty set, which is a state of K). Formally this presents no problem since the formula (2.6) gives in this case $\Delta(\emptyset, x) = \emptyset$ for all x's (an empty union of sets is empty).

The machine K is thus completely defined and it is clear that it is deterministic: For each state S of K and each input symbol x, the transition function $\Delta(S, x)$ uniquely defines another state of K. Before proceeding with the proof that both of these machines accept the same language, let us consider an example of how K is actually constructed.

Example 2.6. Let M be the machine from Example 2.5. The corresponding deterministic machine K has 16 ($= 2^4$) states:

$S_0 = \{Q_0\}$, $S_1 = \{Q_1\}$, $S_2 = \{Q_2\}$, $S_3 = \{Q_3\}$,
$S_4 = \{Q_0, Q_1\}$, $S_5 = \{Q_0, Q_2\}$, $S_6 = \{Q_0, Q_3\}$,
$S_7 = \{Q_1, Q_2\}$, $S_8 = \{Q_1, Q_3\}$, $S_9 = \{Q_2, Q_3\}$,
$S_{10} = \{Q_0, Q_1, Q_2\}$, $S_{11} = \{Q_0, Q_1, Q_3\}$, $S_{12} = \{Q_0, Q_2, Q_3\}$,
$S_{13} = \{Q_1, Q_2, Q_3\}$, $S_{14} = \{Q_0, Q_1, Q_2, Q_3\}$, and $S_{15} = \emptyset$.

The initial state is $S_0 = \{Q_0\}$, and the accepting states are S_2, S_3, S_5, S_6, S_7, S_8, S_9, S_{10}, S_{11}, S_{12}, S_{13}, and S_{14}, i.e., those S's that contain Q_2 and/or Q_3—the final states of M. Let us calculate some of the values of the transition function Δ. Consider, for example, $\Delta(S_5, 1)$. Since $S_5 = \{Q_0, Q_2\}$ and $\delta(Q_0, 1) = \{Q_0\}$, $\delta(Q_2, 1) = \{Q_0, Q_3\}$, then $\Delta(S_5, 1) = \delta(Q_0, 1) \cup \delta(Q_2, 1) = \{Q_0\} \cup \{Q_0, Q_3\} = \{Q_0, Q_3\} = S_6$, i.e., $\Delta(S_5, 1) = S_6$. Similarly, since $S_7 = \{Q_1, Q_2\}$, we have $\Delta(S_7, 0) = \delta(Q_1, 0) \cup \delta(Q_2, 0) = \emptyset \cup \{Q_2\} = \{Q_2\} = S_2$. Also, $\Delta(S_0, 2) =$

$\delta(Q_0, 2) = \emptyset = S_{15}$. By previous remarks, $\Delta(S_{15}, x) = S_{15}$ for all $x =$ 0, 1, 2. The full description of the transition function Δ is given by the table in Figure 2.12. The machine K does, of course, have its own transition diagram, but the entire picture of it is quite messy. A cursory glance at the table of Δ shows that the machine K has many more states than are actually needed. For example, the state S_7 cannot be reached from the initial state S_0. As a matter of fact it cannot be reached from any state at all. Thus, we could remove the state S_7 altogether and the new machine would accept the same strings. We will discuss the question of how to make a given FSM as "small as possible" shortly. What we are trying to show now is that given a nondeterministic FSM, there is some deterministic FSM that accepts exactly the same strings; we are not trying to find the most efficient such machine.

State		Input x		
	$S_0 = \{Q_0\}$	S_4	S_0	S_{15}
	$S_1 = \{Q_1\}$	S_{15}	S_2	S_6
	$S_2 = \{Q_2\}$	S_2	S_6	S_{15}
	$S_3 = \{Q_3\}$	S_2	S_3	S_3
	$S_4 = \{Q_0, Q_1\}$	S_4	S_5	S_6
	$S_5 = \{Q_0, Q_2\}$	S_{10}	S_5	S_{15}
	$S_6 = \{Q_0, Q_3\}$	S_{10}	S_{11}	S_3
	$S_7 = \{Q_1, Q_2\}$	S_2	S_{12}	S_6
	$S_8 = \{Q_1, Q_3\}$	S_2	S_{13}	S_6
	$S_9 = \{Q_2, Q_3\}$	S_2	S_{11}	S_3
	$S_{10} = \{Q_0, Q_1, Q_2\}$	S_{10}	S_{12}	S_6
	$S_{11} = \{Q_0, Q_1, Q_3\}$	S_{10}	S_{14}	S_6
	$S_{12} = \{Q_0, Q_2, Q_3\}$	S_{10}	S_{11}	S_3
	$S_{13} = \{Q_1, Q_2, Q_3\}$	S_2	S_{14}	S_6
	$S_{14} = \{Q_0, Q_1, Q_2, Q_3\}$	S_{10}	S_{14}	S_6
	$S_{15} = \emptyset$	S_{15}	S_{15}	S_{15}

Figure 2.12. Table of the transition function Δ.

We now return to the proof that $L(K) = L(M)$. Indeed, suppose that a string $\sigma = x_1x_2 \ldots x_p$ is accepted by M. This means that for some sequence of states $Q_0, \hat{Q}_1, \hat{Q}_2, \ldots, \hat{Q}_p$ the sequence of moves

$$Q_0 = \hat{Q}_0 \xrightarrow{x_1} \hat{Q}_1 \xrightarrow{x_2} \hat{Q}_2 \rightarrow \cdots \rightarrow \hat{Q}_i \xrightarrow{x_{i+1}} \hat{Q}_{i+1} \rightarrow \cdots \rightarrow \hat{Q}_{p-1} \xrightarrow{x_p} \hat{Q}_p \tag{2.7}$$

is legal, and $\hat{Q}_p$ is an accepting state of M. It follows then, that for each $i = 0, 1, 2, \ldots, p - 1$, the transition function δ satisfies

$$\hat{Q}_{i+1} \in \delta(\hat{Q}_i, x_{i+1}), \quad i = 0, 1, \ldots, p - 1 \tag{2.8}$$

When the string σ is presented to the machine K, the machine executes the following sequence of moves:

$$S_0 = \hat{S}_0 \xrightarrow{x_1} \hat{S}_1 \xrightarrow{x_2} \hat{S}_2 \rightarrow \cdots \rightarrow \hat{S}_i \xrightarrow{x_{i+1}} \hat{S}_{i+1} \rightarrow \cdots \rightarrow \hat{S}_{p-1} \xrightarrow{x_p} \hat{S}_p \tag{2.9}$$

Now, from (2.8) with $i = 0$, $\hat{Q}_1$ is in $\delta(\hat{Q}_0, x_1)$, because $\hat{Q}_0 \xrightarrow{x_1} \hat{Q}_1$ is a legal transition for M, so $\hat{Q}_1$ is in $\hat{S}_1 = \Delta(\hat{S}_0, x_1)$. Similarly, with $i = 1$, $\hat{Q}_2$ is in $\delta(\hat{Q}_1, x_2)$, so $\hat{Q}_2 \in \hat{S}_2 = \Delta(\hat{S}_1, x_2)$. Proceeding in this manner, we see that $\hat{Q}_j$ is in $\hat{S}_j$ for all j's, so in particular, $\hat{Q}_p \in \hat{S}_p$. Since $\hat{Q}_p$ is a final state of M (σ was accepted by M), we see that $\hat{S}_p$ is a final state of K, i.e., σ is accepted by K.

Conversely, suppose that a string $\sigma = x_1x_2 \ldots x_p$ is accepted by K, and let (2.9) be the sequence of moves by K on input σ. For every $\hat{Q}_1 \in \hat{S}_1$ the move $\hat{Q}_0 \xrightarrow{x_1} \hat{Q}_1$ is a legal one for the machine M ($\hat{S}_1$ consists of those Q's for which $\hat{Q}_1 \xrightarrow{x_1} Q$ is a legal move in M). Similarly, for every $\hat{Q}_2 \in \hat{S}_2$ there is a $\hat{Q}_1$ in $\hat{S}_1$ such that the sequence of moves

$$\hat{Q}_0 \xrightarrow{x_1} \hat{Q}_1 \xrightarrow{x_2} \hat{Q}_2$$

is legal in M. Indeed, we choose $\hat{Q}_1$ to be the state for which the transition $\hat{Q}_1 \xrightarrow{x_1} \hat{Q}_2$ is legal (such $\hat{Q}_1$ exists because $\Delta(\hat{S}_1, x_2) = \hat{S}_2$). In exactly the same way, we show that if $\hat{Q}_3 \in \hat{S}_3$, then we can find $\hat{Q}_1 \in \hat{S}_1$ and $\hat{Q}_2 \in \hat{S}_2$ such that

$$\hat{Q}_0 \xrightarrow{x_1} \hat{Q}_1 \xrightarrow{x_2} \hat{Q}_2 \xrightarrow{x_3} \hat{Q}_3$$

is a legal sequence of moves. Continuing in this way, we see that for every $\hat{Q}_p$ in $\hat{S}_p$ we can find $\hat{Q}_1 \in \hat{S}_1$, $\hat{Q}_2 \in \hat{S}_2, \ldots, \hat{Q}_{p-1} \in \hat{S}_{p-1}$ such that (2.7) is a legal sequence of moves in M. If we now choose $\hat{Q}_p$ in $\hat{S}_p$ which is an accepting state of M, we ascertain that σ is accepted by M, i.e., it is in the language $L(M)$. Q.E.D.

Definition 2.5. Let M_1 and M_2 be two FSM's. The machines M_1 and M_2 are said to be ***equivalent*** if they generate (accept) the same language, i.e., if $L(M_1) = L(M_2)$.

It is readily seen from the proof of Theorem 2.2 that given a nondeterministic machine M_1, the corresponding deterministic machine M_2 may be quite large. Indeed, if M_1 has n states, then the construction calls for M_2 to have 2^n states. When $n = 10$, say, then M_2 will have $2^{10} = 1024$ states. In Section 2.5 we will show how to make M_2 smaller, in fact how to find the smallest possible machine equivalent to M_2. In certain situations, however, the construction of M_2 can be greatly simplified. Recall that a machine $M = \{\mathcal{Q}, \Sigma, Q_0, \delta, \mathcal{F}\}$ may fail to be deterministic for two reasons:

1. $\delta(Q, x) = \emptyset$ for some $Q \in \mathcal{Q}$ and $x \in \Sigma$ (i.e., if M is in the state Q and the input symbol is x, the next state is undefined).
2. $\delta(Q, x)$ contains more then one state (for some Q and x).

The nature of case 1 is quite different from case 2; the machine M is not "really" nondeterministic, the problem is that it can get "stuck" in a blind alley. Some authors, for this reason, do not consider such machines nondeterministic. In cases when 1 occurs but 2 does not (that is when $\delta(Q, x)$ is always either empty or contains exactly one state) the construction of an equivalent deterministic machine can be greatly simplified.

Theorem 2.3. Let $M = \{\mathcal{Q}, \Sigma, Q_0, \delta, \mathcal{F}\}$ be a nondeterministic finite state machine such that for each $Q \in \mathcal{Q}$ and each $x \in \Sigma$ the set $\delta(Q, x)$ is either empty or contains exactly one state. Let K be a machine obtained from M by adding one state D, and whose transition function Δ is defined as follows:

$$\Delta(Q, x) = \begin{cases} \delta(Q, x) \text{ if } \delta(Q, x) \neq \emptyset \\ \{D\} \text{ if } \delta(Q, x) = \emptyset \end{cases} \qquad \Delta(D, x) = \{D\} \text{ for all } x \in \Sigma$$

The initial and the final states of K are the same as those of M—in particular D is ***not*** an accepting state. Then K is a deterministic machine and is equivalent to M.

The state D introduced above is referred to as a "trap" or "dead" state. The intuitive idea behind Theorem 2.3 is quite clear: If the machine M gets stuck in some state, the string σ which is being read cannot be accepted. We thus send the machine to this "dead" state.

Proof. The fact that K is deterministic is quite obvious: For each state $Q \in \mathcal{Q} \cup \{D\}$ and each $x \in \Sigma$ the set $\Delta(Q, x)$ contains exactly one state. If a string $\sigma = x_1 x_2 \ldots x_p$ is accepted by M, then the sequence of moves K on the input σ is the same as the sequence of moves of M on this input—the only time the moves could be different is when M gets stuck in a configuration

$$[\![Q, x_i x_{i+1} \ldots x_p]\!] \qquad \delta(Q, x_i) = \emptyset \tag{2.10}$$

Since M accepts σ, this does not happen. Conversely, if M does not accept σ, then either M moves from the configuration $[\![Q_0, \sigma]\!]$ to $[\![Q, \lambda]\!]$ with Q not being an accepting state, in which case K does the same thing, or M gets stuck in configuration (2.10). In that case, K continues by changing to the state D and remains there until the rest of the string has been read. Since D is not an accepting state, K does not accept σ. Q.E.D.

Example 2.7. Consider the machine M whose transition diagram is given in Figure 2.13. It is clear that M satisfies the conditions of Theorem 2.3. The corresponding machine K equivalent to M is given by the diagram in Figure 2.14.

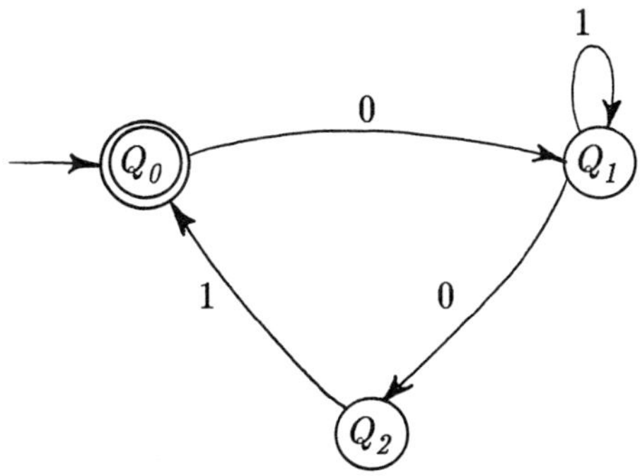

Figure 2.13. Incomplete transition function.

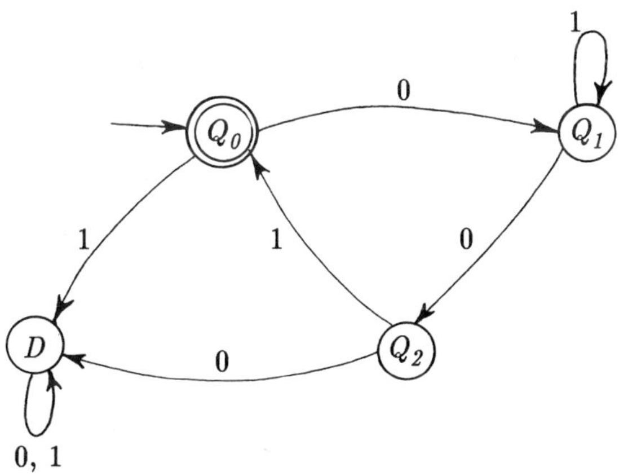

Figure 2.14. Completion of transition function.

2.4. REGULAR GRAMMARS AND FINITE STATE MACHINES

In this section we complete the proof of Theorem 2.1 by showing that, given a regular grammar G, there exists a deterministic finite state machine M such that $L(M) = L(G)$. We will do it only for the right linear grammars (all productions are of the form $S \to \lambda$, $A \to aB$, or $A \to a$); the case of left linear grammars is very similar and is left as an exercise. In view of Theorem 2.2 it is actually enough to show that given a right linear grammar, there exists a nondeterministic machine M such that $L(M) = L(G)$.

Theorem 2.4. Let G be a right linear grammar. Then there exists a nondeterministic finite state machine M such that $L(G) = L(M)$.

Proof. Let the alphabet of G be $\Sigma = \{a_1, a_2, \ldots, a_k\}$, let the set N of nonterminals be $\{S, A, B, \ldots\}$ with S being the start symbol, and let P be the set of productions. The input alphabet of M will also be Σ, the states of M will be the nonterminals $S, A, B, \ldots$, plus an additional state X, which is different from the other nonterminals. The initial state of M is S. The accepting states of M are X and, if $S \to \lambda$ is a production in G, the state S. The transition function δ of M is defined by the following rules:

1. For every production of the form $A \to aB$ in G include B in $\delta(A, a)$, i.e., include the transition $A \xrightarrow{a} B$ in the transition diagram.
2. For every production of the form $A \to a$ include the state X in $\delta(A, a)$, i.e., include the transition $A \xrightarrow{a} X$ in the transition diagram.

In general, of course, the resulting machine will be a nondeterministic one. We must show that the strings accepted by M are exactly those that are derivable in G. Let $\sigma = x_1x_2 \ldots x_n$ be a string that is acceptable by M. By definition, there exists a legal sequence of moves

$$S = Z_1 \xrightarrow{x_1} Z_2 \xrightarrow{x_2} Z_3 \xrightarrow{x_3} \cdots \to Z_n \xrightarrow{x_n} Z_{n+1} \tag{2.11}$$

where Z_{n+1} is an accepting state, and $Z_{n+1} = X$ or (possibly) $Z_{n+1} = S$. For each $i < n$ the transition $Z_i \xrightarrow{x_i} Z_{i+1}$ is a legal one, which implies that $Z_{i+1} \in \delta(Z_i, x_i)$, so that $Z_i \to x_iZ_{i+1}$ is a production in G. Consider now the last transition $Z_n \xrightarrow{x_n} Z_{n+1}$. If $Z_{n+1} = X$, this means that G has a production of the form $Z_n \to x_n$; if $Z_{n+1} = S$, then G must have productions $Z_n \to x_nS$ and $S \to \lambda$. Thus the sequence of derivations of σ in G is given either by (2.12) or (2.13):

$$S = Z_1 \Rightarrow x_1Z_2 \Rightarrow x_1x_2Z_3 \Rightarrow \ldots \Rightarrow x_1x_2 \ldots x_{n-1}Z_n \Rightarrow \Rightarrow x_1x_2 \ldots x_{n-1}x_n \tag{2.12}$$

$$S = Z_1 \Rightarrow x_1Z_2 \Rightarrow x_1x_2Z_3 \Rightarrow \ldots \Rightarrow x_1x_2 \ldots x_{n-1}Z_n \Rightarrow \Rightarrow x_1x_2 \ldots x_{n-1}x_nS \Rightarrow x_1x_2 \ldots x_n \tag{2.13}$$

In either case, σ is derivable in G. The converse is also true. Suppose σ is in $L(G)$; its derivation must be of the form (2.12) or (2.13). In either case this makes (2.11) a legal sequence of moves of M. A certain amount of care must be taken when $\sigma = \lambda$ is the empty string. If $S \rightarrow \lambda$ is a production of G then clearly $\lambda \in L(G)$. In this case S is also an accepting state, so when λ is presented to M, the initial configuration of M is $[\![S, \lambda]\!]$ and the machine immediately halts without making any moves. Since S is an accepting state, M accepts λ, i.e., $\lambda \in L(M)$. Q.E.D.

Example 2.8. Consider the grammar

$$\begin{aligned} S &\rightarrow aA \mid aB \mid \lambda \\ A &\rightarrow aA \mid b \\ B &\rightarrow bS \mid b \end{aligned}$$

The diagram of the nondeterministic machine M such that $L(G) = L(M)$ is given in Figure 2.15. The state S is an accepting one since $S \rightarrow \lambda$ is a production. The transition $A \xrightarrow{b} X$ is the result of the production $A \rightarrow b$; $B \xrightarrow{b} S$ follows from the production $B \rightarrow bS$; $A \xrightarrow{b} A$ from $A \rightarrow aA$, etc.

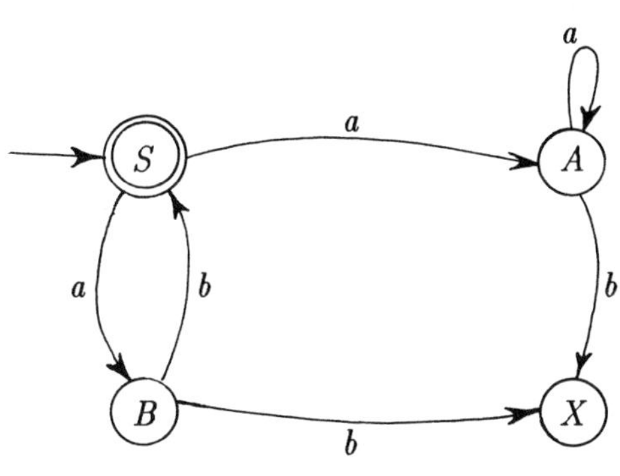

Figure 2.15. Nondeterministic FSM that recognizes a language.

We can use the method in the proof of Theorem 2.2 to construct a deterministic machine K such that $L(K) = L(G)$. The resulting machine K has 16 states and the transition function given by the table in Figure 2.16. Many of its states cannot be reached from the initial state Q_0. For instance, Q_4 cannot be reached from any state whatsoever, and hence can be deleted altogether. Thus, the resulting machine is certainly not the smallest possible. The main content of Theorem 2.2 is that such a machine K can be constructed at all. We will discuss the question of finding the smallest such machine in the next section. The initial state of K is Q_0, and the accepting states are Q_0, Q_3, Q_4, Q_5, Q_6, Q_8, Q_9, Q_{10}, Q_{11}, Q_{12}, Q_{13}, and Q_{14} (i.e., those Q's that contain either S or X).

		Input x	
		a	b
State	$Q_0 = \{S\}$	Q_7	Q_{15}
	$Q_1 = \{A\}$	Q_1	Q_3
	$Q_2 = \{B\}$	Q_{15}	Q_6
	$Q_3 = \{X\}$	Q_{15}	Q_{15}
	$Q_4 = \{S, A\}$	Q_7	Q_3
	$Q_5 = \{S, B\}$	Q_7	Q_6
	$Q_6 = \{S, X\}$	Q_7	Q_{15}
	$Q_7 = \{A, B\}$	Q_1	Q_2
	$Q_8 = \{A, X\}$	Q_1	Q_3
	$Q_9 = \{B, X\}$	Q_7	Q_6
	$Q_{10} = \{S, A, B\}$	Q_7	Q_6
	$Q_{11} = \{S, A, X\}$	Q_7	Q_3
	$Q_{12} = \{S, B, X\}$	Q_7	Q_6
	$Q_{13} = \{A, B, X\}$	Q_1	Q_6
	$Q_{14} = \{S, A, B, X\}$	Q_7	Q_6
	$Q_{15} = \emptyset$	Q_{15}	Q_{15}

Figure 2.16. Transition function of the machine K.

Consider now, for instance, the derivation

$$S \Rightarrow aB \Rightarrow abS \Rightarrow abaA \Rightarrow abaaA \Rightarrow abaab$$

The moves of the nondeterministic machine M corresponding to this derivation, will be

$$[\![S,\ abaab]\!] \rightarrow [\![B,\ baab]\!] \rightarrow [\![S,\ aab]\!] \rightarrow [\![A,\ ab]\!] \rightarrow [\![A,\ b]\!] \rightarrow [\![X,\ \lambda]\!]$$

The deterministic machine K, on the other hand, will execute the sequence of moves

$$[\![Q_0,\ abaab]\!] \rightarrow [\![Q_7,\ baab]\!] \rightarrow [\![Q_6,\ aab]\!] \rightarrow [\![Q_7,\ ab]\!] \rightarrow [\![Q_1,\ b]\!] \rightarrow [\![Q_3,\ \lambda]\!]$$

2.5. MINIMIZATION

The examples of previous sections show that even simple grammars may lead to rather large machines. It would be very useful to have a method of reducing the sizes of these machines, if possible. Consider for example the FSM M_1 in Figure 2.17. The states Q_3 and Q_4 can clearly be combined into a single state, say T, without changing the language generated by M_1. This results in an equivalent machine M_2, shown in Figure 2.18.

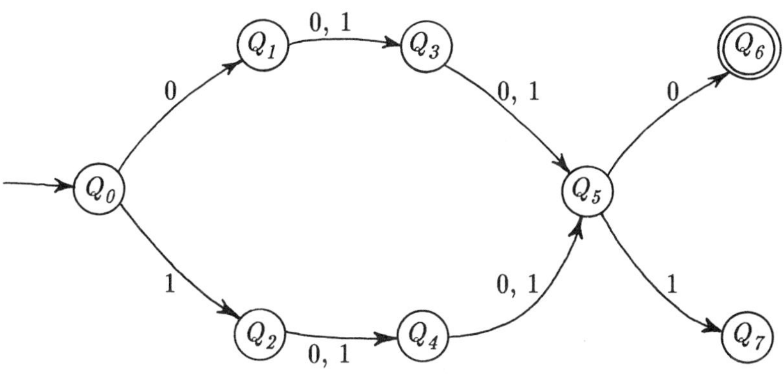

Figure 2.17. A finite state machine with too many states.

Any input σ accepted by M_1 is also accepted by M_2 and conversely. The machine M_2 can be reduced further by combining the states Q_1 and Q_2 into a single state, R say. This results in a FSM M_3 as in Figure 2.19. The description of the language generated by M_3 (and hence by M_1) is now evident: $L(M_3)$ consists of all strings of 0's and 1's of length four, ending with 0.

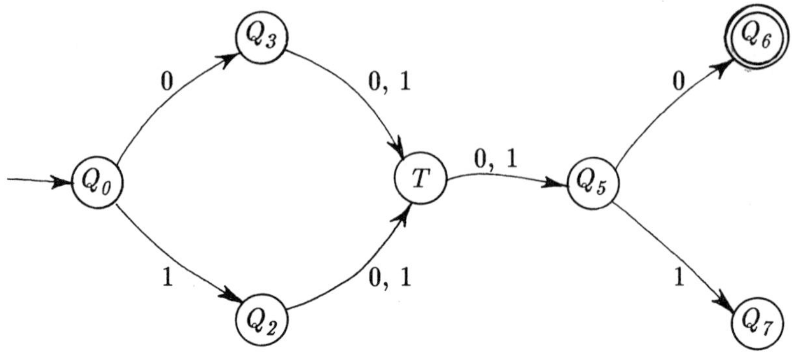

Figure 2.18. Removal of a state.

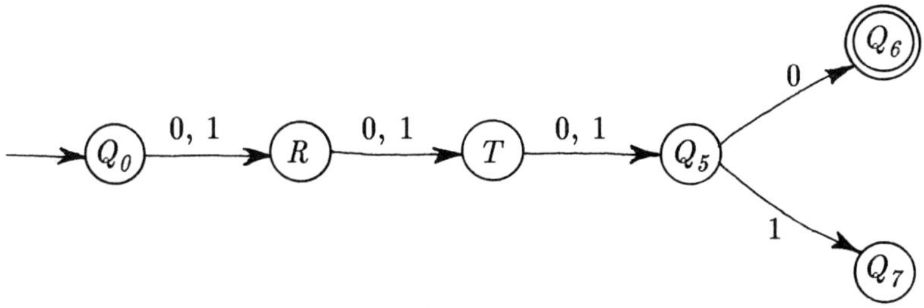

Figure 2.19. Minimal finite state machine.

There is an algorithm that, given a deterministic finite state machine M_1, will produce the smallest possible finite state machine M_2 such that $L(M_1) = L(M_2)$. We devote this section to the description of this algorithm. We begin by showing how to eliminate from a machine so-called inaccessible states.

Definition 2.6. Let M be a finite state machine. We say that a state Q of M is ***inaccessible*** if there is no input string σ such that $[\![Q_0, \sigma]\!] \to^* [\![Q, \lambda]\!]$. Here Q_0 is the initial state of M.

In other words, a state Q of M is inaccessible if, beginning with the initial state Q_0, the machine will never reach the state Q, no matter what the input may be. For example, the state Q_1 of the machine in Figure 2.20 is inaccessible.

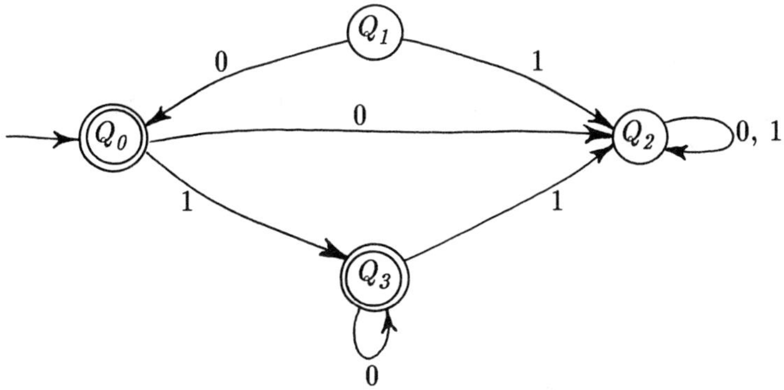

Figure 2.20. A finite state machine with inaccessible state.

The following result is quite clear.

Theorem 2.5. Let M_1 be a finite state machine and let M_2 be obtained from M_1 by removing all of the inaccessible states. Then $L(M_1) = L(M_2)$.

Given a machine M, all of its inaccessible states can be found using the following algorithm.

Algorithm 2.1. Inaccessible states of a finite state machine.
Input: A finite state machine $M = \{\mathcal{Q}, \Sigma, Q_0, \delta, \mathcal{F}\}$.
Output: Collection $\mathcal{I}$ of inaccessible states.

First, the collection $\mathcal{A}$ of accessible states is constructed as follows. We form a sequence $\{\mathcal{A}_n\}$ of sets of states of M according to these rules:

1. $\mathcal{A}_0 = \{Q_0\}$, i.e., $\mathcal{A}_0$ consists of the single state Q_0—the initial state of M.
2. Suppose $\mathcal{A}_k$ is already constructed for some $k \geq 0$. Form the set $\mathcal{A}_{k+1}$ by adding to $\mathcal{A}_k$ all the states of M, which are accessible from $\mathcal{A}_k$ in a single move, i.e.,

$$\mathcal{A}_{k+1} = \mathcal{A}_k \cup \{Q\text{: For some } \hat{Q} \text{ in } \mathcal{A}_k \text{ and some } x \text{ in } \Sigma,\ \delta(\hat{Q}, x) = Q\}$$

3. If $\mathcal{A}_k = \mathcal{A}_{k+1}$, i.e., if no new states are added to $\mathcal{A}_k$, we stop and set $\mathcal{A} = \mathcal{A}_k$. Otherwise, go back to step 2.

Since there are only finite number, say n, of states in M, this process will eventually terminate in at most $n - 1$ iterations. The set $\mathcal{I}$ of inaccessible sets in now obtained from $\mathcal{Q}$ by removing from it all the elements of $\mathcal{A}$, i.e., $\mathcal{I} = \mathcal{Q}\backslash\mathcal{A}$ (we remove from the set $\mathcal{A}$ the elements of the set $\mathcal{Q}$).

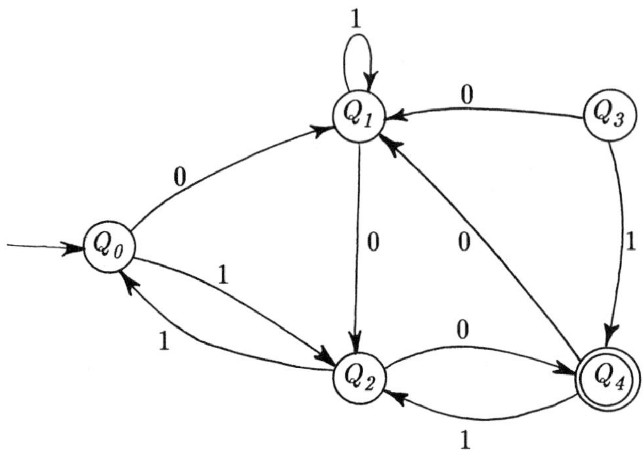

Figure 2.21. Removal of inaccessible states.

Example 2.9. Let M be the machine given by the transition diagram in Figure 2.21. The construction proceeds as follows.

$\mathcal{A}_0 = \{Q_0\}$—by definition
$\mathcal{A}_1 = \{Q_0\} \cup \{Q_1, Q_2\} = \{Q_0, Q_1, Q_2\}$, since $\delta(Q_0, 0) = Q_1$ and $\delta(Q_0, 1) = Q_2$
$\mathcal{A}_2 = \mathcal{A}_1 \cup \{Q_4\} = \{Q_0, Q_1, Q_3, Q_4\}$ since $\delta(Q_2, 0) = Q_4$
$\mathcal{A}_3 = \mathcal{A}_2$—no new states can be reached from $\mathcal{A}_2$

Thus $\mathcal{A} = \mathcal{A}_2 = \{Q_0, Q_1, Q_2, Q_3\}$, and $\mathcal{I} = \{Q_3\}$ is the collection of inaccessible states. The state Q_3 may be removed from the machine M.

Notice that this algorithm applies also to nondeterministic machines. For instance, the machine from Example 2.8 has only six accessible states. We leave it as an exercise to verify this statement. From now on we assume that every finite state machine has no inaccessible states and concentrate on eliminating "structurally redundant" states. The procedure for doing it is based on the concept of congruence.

Definition 2.7. Let $M = \{\mathcal{Q}, \Sigma, Q_0, \delta, \mathcal{F}\}$ be a deterministic finite state machine and let $k \geq 0$ be an integer. We say that two states Q and $\hat{Q}$ are k-***congruent*** if the following is true:

> Let σ be any input string of length at most k, and suppose $[\![Q, \sigma]\!] \to^* [\![P, \lambda]\!]$, $[\![\hat{Q}, \sigma]\!] \to^* [\![\hat{P}, \lambda]\!]$ describe the movements of M on the input σ, beginning with the states Q and $\hat{Q}$, respectively. Then either both P and $\hat{P}$ are accepting, or both P and $\hat{P}$ are not accepting.

If Q and $\hat{Q}$ are k-congruent, we denote this by $Q \equiv_k \hat{Q}$. If Q and $\hat{Q}$ are k-congruent for all $k = 0, 1, \ldots$, we say that Q and Q are ***congruent*** and denote it by $Q \equiv \hat{Q}$.

The heuristic meaning of k-congruence is as follows. Suppose τ is a string to be tested for membership in $L(M)$. We start the machine M in configuration $[\![Q_0, \tau]\!]$; M moves along until it reaches configuration $[\![Q, \sigma]\!]$, where σ is a string of length at most k. If Q and $\hat{Q}$ are k-congruent we may change the state from Q to $\hat{Q}$ and let it run from there (on the input σ), without changing the ultimate result: If, starting from configuration $[\![Q, \sigma]\!]$, the machine will end up in an accepting state, the same would be true if the machine started in configuration $[\![\hat{Q}, \sigma]\!]$. Suppose now Q and $\hat{Q}$ are k-congruent for all $k = 0, 1, \ldots$. We then may combine Q and $\hat{Q}$ into a single state—it will have no effect on the set of strings accepted by M. Thus, to minimize a finite state machine M, we must determine which states are congruent to each other. It is clear from the definition that

1. If $Q_1 \equiv_k Q_2$ then $Q_2 \equiv_k Q_1$. (Symmetric)
2. For any state Q we have $Q \equiv_k Q$. (Reflexive)
3. If $Q_1 \equiv_k Q_2$ and $Q_2 \equiv_k Q_3$ then $Q_1 \equiv_k Q_3$. (Transitive)

Thus, the relation $\equiv_k$ is symmetric, reflexive, and transitive, i.e., it is an equivalence relation. It is also clear that the statements 1, 2, and 3, above, remain true if $\equiv_k$ is replaced by $\equiv$, so the congruence $\equiv$ is also an equivalence relation among the states of M. The task of minimization of the machine M consists essentially of dividing all the states of M into equivalence classes; any two states within one class will be equivalent to each other, and any two states from different classes will not be equivalent. The minimized machine will then have these equivalence classes as its states. It also turns out that this process yields the smallest possible machine equivalent to the original one, i.e., the one with the fewest states.

Before presenting an algorithm for doing this, we need two lemmas.

Lemma 2.1. If two states of a machine are $(k+1)$-congruent, they are also k-congruent.

The proof is immediate from the definition.

Lemma 2.2. Let $M = \{\mathcal{Q}, \Sigma, Q_0, \delta, \mathcal{F}\}$ be a finite state machine. Let $k \geq 0$ be a fixed integer and let $\mathcal{G}_1, \mathcal{G}_2, \ldots, \mathcal{G}_n$ be the partition of the states of M into equivalence classes: Two states from each class are k-congruent to each other, and two states from different classes are not k-congruent. Let $\mathcal{G}$ be one of these classes and let $Q_1, Q_2, \ldots, Q_m$ be the states of $\mathcal{G}$. For each symbol $x \in \Sigma$ and each $Q \in \mathcal{G}$ let $h_k(Q, x)$ be the class $\mathcal{G}_i$ containing $\delta(Q, x)$. Then the states Q and $\hat{Q}$ from $\mathcal{G}$ are $(k+1)$-congruent if and only if

$$h_k(Q, x) = h_k(\hat{Q}, x) \text{ for each } x \in \Sigma \tag{2.14}$$

Proof. Suppose Q and $\hat{Q}$ are two states belonging to the same class $\mathcal{G}$ and suppose that (2.14) is true. We want to show that Q and $\hat{Q}$ are $(k+1)$-congruent, that is, if σ is a string of length at most $k + 1$, $[\![Q, \sigma]\!] \rightarrow^* [\![P, \lambda]\!]$, and $[\![\hat{Q}, \sigma]\!] \rightarrow^* [\![\hat{P}, \lambda]\!]$, then either both P and $\hat{P}$ are accepting states, or both of them are not accepting states. If the string σ is of length at most k, we are done, since by hypothesis Q and $\hat{Q}$ are in the same $\equiv_k$-equivalence class $\mathcal{G}$, hence, $Q \equiv_k \hat{Q}$. Suppose then that σ has length $k + 1$, i.e., $\sigma = x\tau$, where $x \in \Sigma$ and τ is of length exactly k. But then

$$[\![Q, \sigma]\!] = [\![Q, x\tau]\!] \rightarrow [\![Q_1, \tau]\!] \rightarrow^* [\![P, \lambda]\!]$$

and

$$[\![\hat{Q}, \sigma]\!] = [\![\hat{Q}, x\tau]\!] \rightarrow [\![\hat{Q}_1, \tau]\!] \rightarrow^* [\![\hat{P}, \lambda]\!]$$

and both Q_1 and $\hat{Q}_1$ belong to the same class $\mathcal{G}'$ (because (2.14) holds, so $h_k(Q, x) = \mathcal{G}' = h_k(\hat{Q}, x)$). Thus $Q_1 \equiv_k \hat{Q}_1$ and since τ has length k, we see that P and $\hat{P}$ are either both accepting or both nonaccepting.

Conversely, suppose that Q and $\hat{Q}$ are two $(k+1)$-congruent states; we wish to prove that (2.14) is true. Indeed, if $h_k(Q, x) \neq h_k(\hat{Q}, x)$ for some $x \in \Sigma$, then $\delta(Q, x) = Q_1 \in h_k(Q, x)$ and $\delta(\hat{Q}, x) = \hat{Q}_1 \in h_k(\hat{Q}, x)$, so Q_1 and $\hat{Q}_1$ are not k-congruent. This implies that for some string σ

of length at most k, the configurations $[\![Q_1, \sigma]\!]$ and $[\![\hat{Q}_1, \sigma]\!]$ will "end up" differently: one in an accepting state and the other in a nonaccepting one. But the same is then true of configurations $[\![Q, x\sigma]\!]$ and $[\![\hat{Q}, x\sigma]\!]$. However, the length of $x\sigma$ is $k + 1$ so this contradicts the hypothesis that Q and $\hat{Q}$ are $(k + 1)$-congruent. Q.E.D.

When $k = 0$ the division of the states into 0-congruence classes is particularly simple. A moment of reflection shows that two states are 0-congruent if and only if they are either both accepting or both non-accepting. Thus, for $k = 0$, there are two equivalence classes: $\mathcal{G}_1^{(0)}$—all the nonaccepting states, and $\mathcal{G}_2^{(0)}$—all the accepting states. The algorithm for dividing up the states into $\equiv$-equivalence classes will basically operate as follows. First we divide the states of M into two groups $\mathcal{G}_1^{(0)}$ and $\mathcal{G}_2^{(0)}$—the equivalence classes for the relation $\equiv_0$ (we have just shown what they are). Next, using Lemma 2.2, we divide each one of these into further subgroups; the resulting partition will form the equivalence classes for $\equiv_1$. The operation is repeated over and over again, until no new subdivisions occur. The formal, precise description of this algorithm is as follows.

Algorithm 2.2. Minimal finite state machine.
Input: A finite state machine $M = \{\mathcal{Q}, \Sigma, Q_0, \delta, \mathcal{F}\}$.
Output: A finite state machine K, with the fewest possible states, such that $L(K) = L(M)$.

I. Construction of states of K. The states of K will be the equivalence classes of the states of M under the equivalence relation $\equiv$. That is, the states of K are the sets $\mathcal{G}_1, \mathcal{G}_2, \ldots, \mathcal{G}_r$ of states of M such that Q_1, Q_2 are members of the same $\mathcal{G}$ if and only if $Q_1 \equiv Q_2$. The construction of these classes is as follows.

1. Let $\mathcal{G}_1^{(0)}$ be the set of all nonaccepting states and $\mathcal{G}_2^{(0)}$ be the set of all accepting states of M.
2. Suppose the sets of M have been split into equivalence classes

$$\mathcal{G}_1^{(k)}, \mathcal{G}_2^{(k)}, \ldots, \mathcal{G}_{m_k}^{(k)} \tag{2.15}$$

under the relation $\equiv_k$. For each state Q and each $x \in \Sigma$ let $h_k(Q, x)$ be the class $\mathcal{G}_i^{(k)}$ that contains $\delta(Q, x)$. Subdivide each of the sets $\mathcal{G}_i^{(k)}$ of (2.15) further as follows. Two states Q and $\hat{Q}$ of $\mathcal{G}_i^{(k)}$ will belong to the same class if and only if $h_k(Q, x) = h_k(\hat{Q}, x)$ for every x in Σ. Let the resulting partition of the states of M be

$$\mathcal{G}_1^{(k+1)}, \ \mathcal{G}_2^{(k+1)}, \ldots, \ \mathcal{G}_{m_{k+1}}^{(k+1)} \tag{2.16}$$

3. If the sets in (2.16) are identical with those in (2.15), stop. The desired partition into equivalence classes has been obtained. If there are more classes in (2.16) than in (2.15), go back to step 2.

II. The input alphabet of K is the same as the input alphabet of M, i.e., the set Σ.

III. The initial state of K is the equivalence class containing the initial state Q_0 of M.

IV. The transition function Δ of K is defined as follows: Let

$$\mathcal{G}_1, \ \mathcal{G}_2, \ldots, \ \mathcal{G}_r \tag{2.17}$$

be the states of K. These are actually equivalence classes for that k for which the equivalence classes in (2.16) are identical with those of (2.15). From the construction in part I it follows that if Q and $\hat{Q}$ are in the same $\mathcal{G}_i$, then $h_k(Q, x) = h_k(\hat{Q}, x)$ for all $x \in \Sigma$. Thus the function

$$\Delta(\mathcal{G}, x) = h_k(Q, x) \text{ for any } Q \in \mathcal{G}$$

is well defined, i.e., independent of Q. (We emphasize that $\Delta(\mathcal{G}, x)$ is an equivalence class, i.e., one of the $\mathcal{G}$'s, since $h_k(Q, x)$ is the equivalence class containing $\delta(Q, x)$.) We take this function Δ to be the transition function of K.

V. A state $\mathcal{G}$ is an accepting state if and only if it consists of accepting states of M.

We illustrate Algorithm 2.2 in the following example.

Example 2.10. Let M be the finite state machine given by the diagram in Figure 2.22. The class $\mathcal{G}_1^{(0)}$ (all nonaccepting states) is $\{Q_0, Q_1, Q_2, Q_3, Q_4, Q_6, Q_7, Q_9\}$. The class $\mathcal{G}_2^{(0)}$ (all accepting states) is $\{Q_5, Q_8\}$. The next subdivision is obtained by considering the function

$$h_0(Q, x) = \text{the class } \mathcal{G}_i^{(0)} \text{ containing } \delta(Q, x).$$

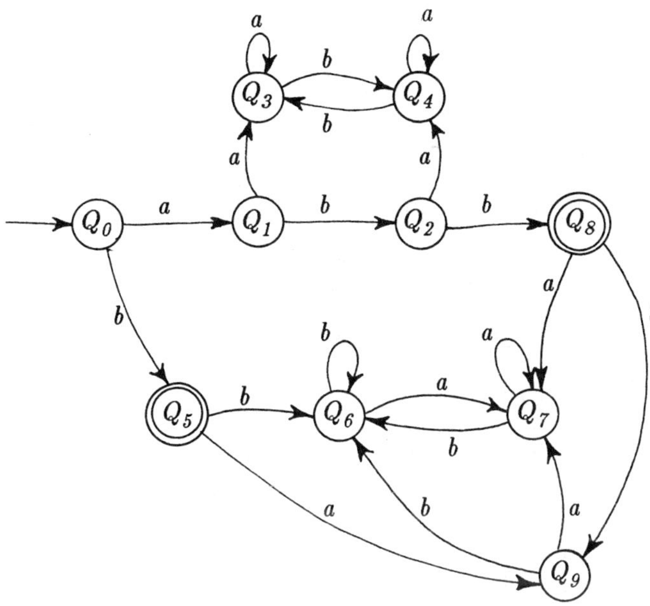

Figure 2.22. Minimization of a finite state machine.

Thus for $k = 1$ the class $\mathcal{G}_1^{(0)}$ splits into two subclasses

$$\mathcal{G}_1^{(1)} = \{Q_0, Q_2\} \text{ and } \mathcal{G}_2^{(1)} = \{Q_1, Q_3, Q_4, Q_6, Q_7, Q_9\}$$

The class $\mathcal{G}_2^{(0)}$ does not split (Q_5 and Q_8 produce identical rows) and it becomes $\mathcal{G}_3^{(1)}$. Further splitting is summarized by the table in Figure 2.24. We have omitted $\mathcal{G}$'s and Q's, retaining only the relevant subscripts. (Thus, $\mathcal{G}_3^{(3)}$ is entered as 3 and Q_5 as 5.) The portion of the table in Figure 2.24 above Pass #1 is identical to the table of Figure 2.23. No new subclasses are introduced during pass #4 ($k = 3$), so the equivalence classes of M, and thus the states of K, are

$$\mathcal{G}_1 = \{Q_0\} \quad \mathcal{G}_2 = \{Q_2\} \quad \mathcal{G}_3 = \{Q_1\}$$
$$\mathcal{G}_4 = \{Q_3, Q_4, Q_6, Q_7, Q_9\} \quad \mathcal{G}_5 = \{Q_5, Q_8\}$$

The initial state of K is $\mathcal{G}_1$ and the final state is $\mathcal{G}_5$. The transition function Δ is essentially given by the function h_3 in the table in Figure 2.24. For example, $\Delta(\mathcal{G}_4, a) = \mathcal{G}_4$ since $h_3(Q_3, a) = h_3(Q_4, a) = h_3(Q_6, a) = h_3(Q_7, a) = h_3(Q_9, a) = \mathcal{G}_4$. In exactly the same way $\Delta(\mathcal{G}_5, b) = \mathcal{G}_4$ since $h_3(Q_5, b) = h_3(Q_8, b) = \mathcal{G}_4$. Finally, the transition diagram of K is given in Figure 2.25.

$\mathcal{G}^{(0)}$	Q	h_0	
		$h_0(Q, a)$	$h_0(Q, b)$
$\mathcal{G}_1^{(0)}$	Q_0	$\mathcal{G}_1^{(0)}$	$\mathcal{G}_2^{(0)}$
	Q_1	$\mathcal{G}_1^{(0)}$	$\mathcal{G}_1^{(0)}$
	Q_2	$\mathcal{G}_1^{(0)}$	$\mathcal{G}_1^{(0)}$
	Q_3	$\mathcal{G}_1^{(0)}$	$\mathcal{G}_1^{(0)}$
	Q_4	$\mathcal{G}_1^{(0)}$	$\mathcal{G}_1^{(0)}$
	Q_6	$\mathcal{G}_1^{(0)}$	$\mathcal{G}_1^{(0)}$
	Q_7	$\mathcal{G}_1^{(0)}$	$\mathcal{G}_1^{(0)}$
	Q_9	$\mathcal{G}_1^{(0)}$	$\mathcal{G}_1^{(0)}$
$\mathcal{G}_2^{(0)}$	Q_5	$\mathcal{G}_1^{(0)}$	$\mathcal{G}_1^{(0)}$
	Q_8	$\mathcal{G}_1^{(0)}$	$\mathcal{G}_1^{(0)}$

These rows are distinct, so Q_0 and Q_1 will belong to different classes $\mathcal{G}^{(1)}$

These rows are identical, so Q_2 and Q_3 will belong to the same class $\mathcal{G}^{(1)}$

Figure 2.23. First step in Algorithm 2.2.

$\mathcal{G}^{(0)}$	h_0			$\mathcal{G}^{(1)}$	h_1			$\mathcal{G}^{(2)}$	h_2			$\mathcal{G}^{(3)}$	h_3		
	Q	a	b		Q	a	b		Q	a	b		Q	a	b
1	0	1	2	1	0	2	3	1	0	2	4	1	0	3	5
	1	1	1		2	2	3		2	3	4	2	2	4	5
	2	1	2	2	1	2	1	2	1	3	1	3	1	4	2
	3	1	1		3	2	2	3	3	3	3	4	3	4	4
	4	1	1		4	2	2		4	3	3		4	4	4
	6	1	1		6	2	2		6	3	3		6	4	4
	7	1	1		7	2	2		7	3	3		7	4	4
	9	1	1		9	2	2		9	3	3		9	4	4
2	5	1	1	3	5	2	2	4	5	3	3	5	5	4	4
	8	1	1		8	2	2		8	3	3		8	4	4
Pass #1 $k = 0$				Pass #2 $k = 1$				Pass #3 $k = 2$				Pass #4 $k = 3$			

Figure 2.24. Complete Algorithm 2.2.

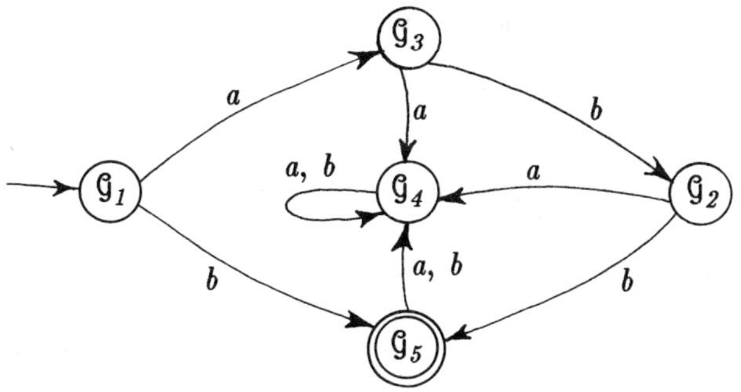

Figure 2.25. Minimized machine.

We conclude this section by showing that Algorithm 2.2 works correctly.

Theorem 2.6. Let M and K be the deterministic finite state machines from Algorithm 2.2. Then $L(K) = L(M)$. Moreover, if K_1 is any other DFSM such that $L(K_1) = L(M)$ then the number of states of K_1 is at least as large as the number of states of K.

Proof. Let Q and $\hat{Q}$ be two states of M and let $\mathcal{G}$ and $\hat{\mathcal{G}}$ be the states of K such that $Q \in \mathcal{G}$ and $\hat{Q} \in \hat{\mathcal{G}}$. From the construction of K it follows that for any $x \in \Sigma$

$$\text{If } \delta(Q, x) = \hat{Q} \text{ then } \Delta(\mathcal{G}, x) = \hat{\mathcal{G}}. \tag{2.18}$$

Let now $\sigma = x_1 x_2 \ldots x_p$ be a string accepted by M. The sequence of moves of M on input σ is

$$Q_0 \xrightarrow{x_1} Q_{i_1} \xrightarrow{x_2} Q_{i_2} \xrightarrow{x_3} \cdots \xrightarrow{x_p} Q_{i_p} \tag{2.19}$$

where Q_{i_p} is an accepting state of M. Let $\mathcal{G}_{i_1}, \mathcal{G}_{i_2}, \ldots, \mathcal{G}_{i_p}$ be the states of K such that $Q_{i_j} \in \mathcal{G}_{i_j}$. It follows from (2.18) that the sequence of moves of K is

$$\mathcal{G}_0 \xrightarrow{x_1} \mathcal{G}_{i_1} \xrightarrow{x_2} \mathcal{G}_{i_2} \xrightarrow{x_3} \cdots \xrightarrow{x_p} \mathcal{G}_{i_p} \tag{2.20}$$

Since $Q_{i_p} \in \mathcal{G}_{i_p}$, the state $\mathcal{G}_{i_p}$ is an accepting state of K, so $\sigma \in L(K)$.

Conversely, if σ is not in $L(M)$ then the state Q_{i_p} in (2.19) is not a final state of M, and again, since $Q_{i_p} \in \mathcal{G}_{i_p}$, the state $\mathcal{G}_{i_p}$ is not a final state of K, so $\sigma \notin L(K)$. Thus, $L(K) = L(M)$.

To show that the machine K has the fewest possible states, we argue as follows. Let K_1 be any deterministic finite state machine with fewer states than K. We will show that $L(K_1) \neq L(M) = L(K)$. Since all the states of M are accessible, all the states of K are also accessible. Thus, for every $\mathcal{G}$ of K there is a string $\sigma = \sigma(\mathcal{G})$ such that $[\![\mathcal{G}_0, \sigma]\!] \to^* [\![\mathcal{G}, \lambda]\!]$. Let P_0 be the initial state of K_1, and consider the movements of K_1 on the inputs $\sigma(\mathcal{G})$ for all possible states $\mathcal{G}$ of K. For each such $\mathcal{G}$ the machine K_1 will end up in some configuration $[\![P(\mathcal{G}), \lambda]\!]$ for some state $P(\mathcal{G})$ of K_1. Since K_1 has fewer states than K, there are going to be two distinct states of K, say $\mathcal{G}'$ and $\mathcal{G}''$, such that $P(\mathcal{G}') = P(\mathcal{G}'')$. In other words, there are two distinct strings $\sigma' = \sigma(\mathcal{G}')$ and $\sigma'' = \sigma(\mathcal{G}'')$ such that

1. On the input of both σ' and σ'' the machine K_1 moves from P_0 to the same state P.
2. On the input of σ' and σ'' the machine K moves from $\mathcal{G}_0$ to two distinct states $\mathcal{G}'$ and $\mathcal{G}''$.

Let Q' be a state of M which is contained in $\mathcal{G}'$ and let Q'' be a state of M which is contained in $\mathcal{G}''$. Since $\mathcal{G}' \neq \mathcal{G}''$, the states Q' and Q'' are not congruent. Thus for some input τ, the machine M will move from Q' to $\overline{Q}$ and from Q'' to $\overline{\overline{Q}}$ where one of the states $\overline{Q}$ and $\overline{\overline{Q}}$ is accepting and the other one is not. This implies that one of the strings $\sigma'\tau$ and $\sigma''\tau$ is in $L(M)$ while the other one is not. Consider however, what happens when these strings are fed into the machine K_1. On the input $\sigma'\tau$ the machine K_1 moves from the configuration $[\![P_0, \sigma'\tau]\!]$ to $[\![P, \tau]\!]$. Similarly, on the input $\sigma''\tau$ the machine K_1 moves from $[\![P_0, \sigma''\tau]\!]$ to the same configuration $[\![P, \tau]\!]$ and then proceeds further, until the string τ is exhausted. Thus, K_1 must either accept both strings $\sigma'\tau$ and $\sigma''\tau$ or reject both of these strings. Thus $L(K_1) \neq L(M)$, since by construction the machine $L(M)$ accepts exactly one of the strings. Q.E.D.

2.6. TWO-WAY FINITE STATE MACHINES

There is an interesting modification of the concept of the finite state machine as follows. Recall that when the finite automata were defined, it was stipulated that when the machine reads a symbol x and is in a state Q, it then changes the state to $\delta(Q, x)$ and moves the input head one symbol to the ***right***. Suppose now we allow the input head to move not only to the right, but also to the left, and also perhaps, not to move at all. Thus, when the machine is in a state Q and the symbol input is x, the machine is allowed to do one of the following:

1. Change the state to Q' and move the input head to the right.
2. Change the state to Q' and move the input head to the left.
3. Change the state to Q' and not move the input head at all.

The decision of what to do is, however, still based only on the present state and the present input symbol, and is independent of the past states and past inputs. The value of the transition function for such machines should now be a pair:

$$\delta(Q, x) = (Q', R) \text{ or } (Q', L) \text{ or } (Q', S)$$

If $\delta(Q, x) = (Q', R)$, the machine changes the state to Q' and moves the input pointer one symbol to the right; when $\delta(Q, x) = (Q', L)$, the machine changes to the state Q' and moves the input pointer one symbol to the left; similarly, when $\delta(Q, x) = (Q', S)$, the input head does not move at all, the present symbol x is read again. Formally, we have the following:

Definition 2.8. A *two-way deterministic finite state machine* M consists of the following five objects:

1. A finite, nonempty set $\mathfrak{Q} = \{Q_0, Q_1, \ldots, Q_n\}$. The elements of $\mathfrak{Q}$ are called states.
2. A finite, nonempty set $\Sigma = \{a_1, a_2, \ldots, a_k\}$ of symbols allowable in the input strings. The set Σ is called the alphabet of M.
3. A designated state $Q_0 \in \mathfrak{Q}$, called the initial state.
4. A transition function $\delta(Q, x)$ defined for all states $Q \in \mathfrak{Q}$ and all $x \in \Sigma$. For each $Q \in \mathfrak{Q}$ and each $x \in \Sigma$ the value of $\delta(Q, x)$ is a pair (Q', Z), where Q' is another state of $\mathfrak{Q}$ and Z is one of the symbols R, L, or S.
5. A nonempty collection $\mathfrak{F}$ of states from $\mathfrak{Q}$. The elements of $\mathfrak{F}$ are called final, or accepting, states.

A finite state machine described as above will be a quintuple $M = \{\mathfrak{Q}, \Sigma, Q_0, \delta, \mathfrak{F}\}$ and will be denoted by *2DFSM.*

Example 2.11. Let M be a 2DFSM machine with four states Q_0 (the initial state), Q_1, Q_2, and Q_3; with the input alphabet $\Sigma = \{a, b, c\}$; with one final state Q_3; and whose transition function is given by the table in Figure 2.26.

		Current input		
		a	b	c
State	Q_0	(Q_0, R)	(Q_1, R)	(Q_2, R)
	Q_1	(Q_0, R)	(Q_3, L)	(Q_1, L)
	Q_2	(Q_0, R)	(Q_1, R)	(Q_2, S)
	Q_3	(Q_0, L)	(Q_3, L)	(Q_0, S)

Figure 2.26. A two-way deterministic finite state machine.

To facilitate the description of the movements of a 2DFSM we need a method of describing the configuration of a machine at any given time. Since the input head is allowed to move backward and forward, we need to know the content of the string to the left of the input pointer, as well as to the right. Thus, a configuration of a 2DFSM will be a triple $[\![\sigma, Q, \tau]\!]$, where σ is the input string to the left of the input head, Q is the present state, and τ is the input string to the right of the input head—we assume that the input head is scanning the first symbol of the string τ. The entire input string is, of course, given by $\sigma\tau$. Both σ and τ can be the empty string λ: If $\sigma = \lambda$, this means that the input string is on the leftmost symbol of the input string, and $\tau = \lambda$ means that the entire input string has been read. Such a configuration of the machine is depicted in Figure 2.27.

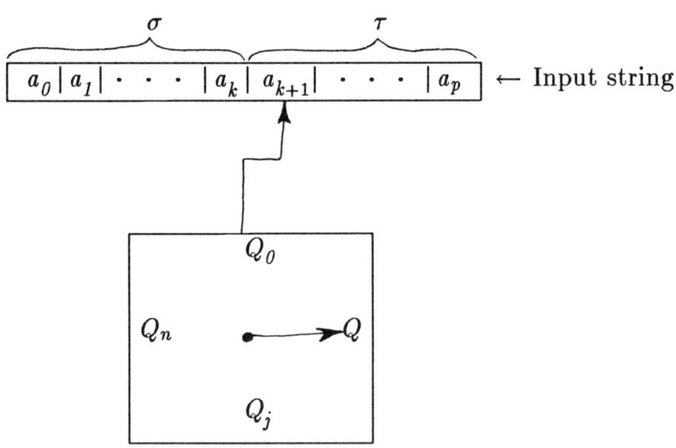

Figure 2.27. A 2DFSM in configuration $[\![a_0 a_1 \ldots a_k, Q, a_{k+1} \ldots a_p]\!]$.

The possible movements of the machine M are then as follows

$$[\![a_1 \ldots a_k, Q, a_{k+1}, \ldots a_p]\!] \rightarrow \begin{cases} [\![a_1 \ldots a_k a_{k+1}, P, a_{k+2} \ldots a_p]\!] \\ \qquad \text{if } \delta(Q, a_{k+2}) = (P, R) \\ [\![a_1 \ldots a_{k-1}, P, a_k \ldots a_p]\!] \\ \qquad \text{if } \delta(Q, a_{k+1}) = (P, L) \\ [\![a_1 \ldots a_k, P, a_{k+1} \ldots a_k]\!] \\ \qquad \text{if } \delta(Q, a_{k+1}) = (P, S) \end{cases}$$

The machine, as usual, is started in the configuration $[\![\lambda, Q_0, a_1a_2 \ldots a_k]\!]$. As it moves along the following situations can develop:

1. The machine reads the entire input string σ and reaches the configuration $[\![\sigma, Q, \lambda]\!]$ for some state Q. We say in this case that M halts. For instance, the machine M from Example 2.11 will execute the following sequence of movements on the input $\sigma = aabcac$:

$$[\![\lambda, Q_0, aabcac]\!] \rightarrow [\![a, Q_0, abcac]\!] \rightarrow [\![aa, Q_0, bcac]\!] \rightarrow [\![aab, Q_1, cac]\!]$$
$$\rightarrow [\![aabc, Q_2, ac]\!] \rightarrow [\![aabca, Q_0, c]\!] \rightarrow [\![aabcac, Q_2, \lambda]\!] \text{ — halts.}$$

2. The machine reaches configuration $[\![\lambda, Q, a \ldots]\!]$ and $\delta(Q, a) = (Q', L)$, i.e., the input head reads the leftmost symbol of the input string and the instructions call for moving the input head to the left. We say in this case that the machine hangs. For instance, on the input $\sigma = abbbca$, the machine from Example 2.11 will move as follows:

$$[\![\lambda, Q_0, abbbca]\!] \rightarrow [\![a, Q_0, bbca]\!] \rightarrow [\![ab, Q_1, bca]\!]$$
$$\rightarrow [\![a, Q_3, bbca]\!] \rightarrow [\![\lambda, Q_3, abbca]\!] \text{ — hangs}$$

3. The machine enters into an infinite loop. We say that in this case, the machine loops. For instance, on the input $\sigma = abccab$, the movements of the machine M from Example 2.11 are:

$$[\![\lambda, Q_0, abccab]\!] \rightarrow [\![a, Q_0, bccab]\!] \rightarrow [\![ab, Q_1, ccab]\!]$$
$$\rightarrow [\![abc, Q_2, cab]\!] \rightarrow [\![ab, Q_1, ccab]\!] \text{ — loops}$$

We define now the language accepted, or generated by a 2DFSM M to be the collection of strings σ such that the machine M, when started in configuration $[\![\lambda, Q_0, \sigma]\!]$, will ***halt*** in configuration $[\![\sigma, Q, \lambda]\!]$ for some final state $Q \in \mathcal{F}$. Formally,

$$L(M) = \{\sigma \in \Sigma^* \mid [\![\lambda, Q_0, \sigma]\!] \to^* [\![\sigma, Q, \lambda]\!], Q \in \mathcal{F}\}$$

Hence, if M is the machine from Example 2.11, $aabcac \in L(M)$, but $abccab$ and $abbbca$ do not belong in $L(M)$. Ordinary finite state machines can obviously be viewed as special cases of the two-way machines: $\delta(Q, a) \neq (Q', L)$ or (Q', S) in this case. Thus it is reasonable to expect that the class of languages generated by the 2DFSM's would be larger than the class generated by the ordinary FSM's. It is somewhat surprising that this is not the case. In fact, we have the following theorem:

Theorem 2.7. Let $M = \{\mathcal{Q}, \Sigma, Q_0, \delta, \mathcal{F}\}$ be a 2DFSM. Then there exists a deterministic FSM K such that $L(M) = L(K)$.

Proof. We will prove this theorem under an additional hypothesis that the machine M always moves its reading head to the right or to the left, i.e., $\delta(Q, x) \neq (Q', S)$. This is done mainly to simplify the exposition; the proof in the general case is based on the same idea.

Let the states of M be $Q_0, Q_1, Q_2, \ldots, Q_n$, and let D be a symbol not used in the description of M. For any string $\sigma \in \Sigma$, define two functions $\phi_\sigma(Q)$ and $\psi_\sigma(Q, x)$ as follows. If Q is a state, define $\phi_\sigma(Q)$ to be the state P, such that the machine M, when started in configuration $[\![\lambda, Q, \sigma]\!]$, will halt in configuration $[\![\sigma, P, \lambda]\!]$. This means that M will read all the symbols of σ and halt in the state P. If no such P exists, set $\phi_\sigma(Q) = D$. This will happen, for instance, when the machine M, once started on the input σ, will go into an infinite loop, or if it hangs. For example, in the machine from Example 2.11 we have $\phi_{cac}(Q_1) = Q_2$ because

$$[\![\lambda, Q_1, cac]\!] \to [\![c, Q_2, ac]\!] \to [\![ca, Q_0, c]\!] \to [\![cac, Q_2, \lambda]\!] \text{ — halts}$$

On the other hand, $\phi_{bca}(Q_1) = D$ because

$$[\![\lambda, Q_1, bca]\!] \to [\![\lambda, Q_3, bca]\!] \text{ — hangs}$$

Formally we have $\phi_\sigma\colon \mathcal{Q} \mapsto \mathcal{Q} \cup \{D\}$ given by

$$\phi_\sigma(Q) = \begin{cases} P & \text{if } [\![\lambda, Q, \sigma]\!] \to^* [\![\sigma, P, \lambda]\!] \\ D & \text{if no such } P \text{ exists} \end{cases}$$

The function ψ_σ has two arguments—a state Q and a symbol $x \in \Sigma$—

and is defined as follows: We set $\psi_\sigma(Q, x)$ to be the state P such that the machine M, when started in configuration $[\![\sigma, Q, x]\!]$ will move to configuration $[\![\sigma, P, x]\!]$, but such that there is no state R so that

$$[\![\sigma, Q, x]\!] \to^* [\![\sigma, R, x]\!] \to^* [\![\sigma, P, x]\!]$$

In other words, $\psi_\sigma(Q, x)$ is defined to be the first state P such that, when M is started in configuration $[\![\sigma, Q, x]\!]$, the input head of M moves to the left and stays entirely within σ, until it reaches configuration $[\![\sigma, P, x]\!]$. If no such state P exists, we set $\psi_\sigma(Q, x) = D$. Referring to the Example 2.11 again, we have $\psi_{bca}(Q_3, a) = Q_0$ because

$$[\![bca, Q_3, a]\!] \to [\![bc, Q_0, aa]\!] \to [\![bca, Q_0, a]\!]$$

Formally, we have $\psi_\sigma: \mathbb{Q} \times \Sigma \mapsto \mathbb{Q} \cup \{D\}$ given by

$$\psi_\sigma(Q, x) = \begin{cases} P \text{ if } [\![\sigma, Q, x]\!] \to^+ [\![\sigma, P, x]\!], \text{ but there is no } R \neq P \\ \quad \text{such that } [\![\sigma, Q, x]\!] \to^* [\![\sigma, R, x]\!] \to^* [\![\sigma, P, x]\!] \\ \\ D \text{ if no such } P \text{ exists} \end{cases}$$

In the above definition, the notation $[\![\sigma, Q, x]\!] \to^+ [\![\sigma, P, x]\!]$ means that the machine actually makes a positive number of moves between the configurations. The important thing to remember about the function ψ is this: if $\psi_\sigma(Q, x) = P$, this means that when M is started in configuration $[\![\sigma, Q, x]\!]$, the input head moves left and stays entirely within σ until the configuration $[\![\sigma, P, x]\!]$ is reached.

We now observe that there is only a finite number of such functions ψ and ϕ. This is because the sets $\mathbb{Q}$ and Σ are finite. Thus, there will be many pairs of strings σ_1 and σ_2 in Σ^* such that $\psi_{\sigma_1}(Q, x) = \psi_{\sigma_2}(Q, x)$ and $\phi_{\sigma_1}(Q) = \phi_{\sigma_2}(Q)$ for every $Q \in \mathbb{Q}$ and every $x \in \Sigma$. We call two such strings equivalent and denote this by $\sigma_1 \simeq \sigma_2$. It is clear that the relation $\simeq$ is an equivalence relation, and because there are only a finite number of functions ψ and ϕ, there are only a finite number of equivalence classes of this relation.

The equivalence relation $\simeq$ has an additional property as follows: Suppose $\sigma_1 \simeq \sigma_2$. Then for any τ,

$$\sigma_1\tau \in L(M) \text{ if and only if } \sigma_2\tau \in L(M) \tag{2.21}$$

Indeed, let τ be given and suppose $\sigma_1\tau \in L(M)$; we wish to prove that $\sigma_2\tau$ is also in $L(M)$. We may assume that $\tau \neq \lambda$, since otherwise the conclusion is obvious. Let then $\tau = x\tau_1$ and consider the movements of the machine M on the input $\sigma_1 x\tau_1$, in particular let P_1 be the state of M when its input head first reaches the symbol x—the first symbol of τ: $[\![\lambda, Q_0, \sigma_1 x\tau_1]\!] \to^* [\![\sigma_1, P_1, x\tau_1]\!]$ and during the transition between these configurations the input head stays entirely within σ_1. But this means that $P_1 = \phi_{\sigma_1}(Q_0)$, and because the strings σ_1 and σ_2 are equivalent, P_1 is also the state of the machine M when its input head first reaches x (starting from the configuration $[\![\lambda, Q_0, \sigma_2\tau]\!]$). Thus, on the inputs $\sigma_1 x\tau_1$ and $\sigma_2 x_1\tau$ the initial movements of M are

$$\begin{aligned} [\![\lambda, Q_0, \sigma_1 x\tau_1]\!] &\to^* [\![\sigma_1, P_1, x\tau_1]\!] \\ [\![\lambda, Q_0, \sigma_2 x\tau_1]\!] &\to^* [\![\sigma_2, P_1, x\tau_1]\!] \end{aligned} \tag{2.22}$$

and during the intermediate configurations, the reading head is entirely contained within σ_1 and σ_2, respectively. Let now $P_1, P_2, \ldots, P_k$ be the states of the machine M during the consecutive times its reading head points at x—the first symbol of τ. (We still trace the movements of M on the input $\sigma_1\tau$.) In other words, let $P_1, P_2, \ldots, P_k$ be the states such that

$$[\![\sigma_1, P_1, x\tau_1]\!] \to^* [\![\sigma_1, P_2, x\tau_1]\!] \to^* \cdots \to^* [\![\sigma_1, P_k, x\tau_1]\!] \to^* \cdots \tag{2.23}$$

where the movements in (2.23) are such that

1. Before the configuration $[\![\sigma_1, P_1, x\tau_1]\!]$ is reached, the machine M has its input head entirely within σ_1.
2. Between the configurations $[\![\sigma_1, P_j, x\tau_1]\!]$ and $[\![\sigma_1, P_{j+1}, x\tau_1]\!]$ the reading head is either entirely within σ_1 or entirely within $x\tau_1$.
3. After the configuration $[\![\sigma_1, P_k, x\tau_1]\!]$ the reading head is entirely within $x\tau_1$.

It follows from the definition of the function ψ and the fact that $\sigma_1 \simeq \sigma_2$ that the movements of M on the input σ_2, after configuration $[\![\sigma_2, M, x\tau_1]\!]$ are

$$[\![\sigma_2, P_1, x\tau_2]\!] \to^* [\![\sigma_2, P_2, x\tau_2]\!] \to^* \cdots \to^* [\![\sigma_2, P_k, x\tau_2]\!] \to^* \cdots \tag{2.24}$$

Indeed, consider the movements of M beginning with the first confi guration in (2.24). If the head moves to the right, the movements will be the same as those of M when started in the first configuration of (2.23). Thus, after the input pointer comes back to x, M will be in the configuration $[\![\sigma_2, P_2, x\tau_1]\!]$. If, on the other hand, the input pointer makes the move to the left, then because $P_2 = \psi_{\sigma_1}(P_1, x)$, and since σ_2 is equivalent to σ_1, the next time the input head encounters x, M will enter the state P_2. Repeating the argument with the states P_2 and P_3 in place of P_1, P_2, etc., we see that (2.24) holds. But after M reaches the last configuration in (2.24), it proceeds in the same way as if it were to begin with the last configuration of (2.23); in other words, it accepts $\sigma_2\tau$. Since the role of σ_1 and σ_2 in this discussion was completely symmetric, we conclude that (2.21) holds.

We are now, finally, ready to construct the machine K. Its input alphabet is Σ, the same as the alphabet of M, of course. Its states are the equivalence classes of the relation $\simeq$. If σ is any string in Σ^*, let $\bar{\sigma}$ denote the equivalence class containing σ. The starting state of K is then taken to be the class $\bar{\lambda}$—the equivalence class containing the empty string. The accepting states of K will be those equivalence classes that consist only of strings from $L(M)$. (It is an easy exercise to show that if $\sigma_1 \simeq \sigma_2$, then either both σ_1, σ_2 are in $L(M)$, or both are not in $L(M)$). The transition function Δ of K is then defined as follows:

$$\Delta(\bar{\sigma}, x) = \overline{\sigma x} \tag{2.25}$$

This means that if $\bar{\sigma}$ is an equivalence class (i.e., a state of K), and x is the present input symbol, then the next state of K is the equivalence class containing $\overline{\sigma x}$. It is clear that K is a deterministic finite state machine, whose input head moves only to the right. It is also a very easy exercise, using the property (2.21), to show that $L(M) = L(K)$. Q.E.D.

PROBLEMS

In each of the problems 1–9 construct a deterministic finite state machine accepting the given language.

1. The set of all strings of 0's and 1's of length at most 5.
2. The set of strings from $\{a, b\}^*$ having even number of b's.
3. The set of strings of a's and b's having both aa and bb as a substring.
4. The language of all signed or unsigned integer constants. Thus, $+345$, -345 and 345 are all in the language.
5. The language of all strings over $\{0, 1\}^*$ that do not contain the substring 0011.
6. The language $L \subseteq \{a, b\}^*$ of strings with even number of a's and

odd number of b's.

7. The set of strings of 0's and 1's that begin with 000 but in which the string 000 does not occur anywhere else. Thus 000 is in the language, but 0000 is not.
8. The language of all strings of 0's and 1's in which the substring 001 occurs at least three times.
9. The set of strings from $\{a, b\}^*$ in which neither aa nor bb occur as a substring.

In each of the problems 10–14 construct a finite state machine that accepts the language generated by the indicated grammar. The finite state machine need not be deterministic.

10. $S \rightarrow aS \mid bS \mid b \mid \lambda$
11. $S \rightarrow 0A \mid 1B, \quad A \rightarrow 0C \mid 1A \mid 0, \quad B \rightarrow 1B \mid 1A \mid 1, \quad C \rightarrow 0 \mid 0A$
12. $S \rightarrow aA \mid aB, \quad A \rightarrow aA \mid bS, \quad B \rightarrow b \mid bA$
13. $S \rightarrow aS \mid bB \mid \lambda, \quad B \rightarrow aA \mid b, \quad A \rightarrow aS \mid aB$
14. $S \rightarrow aS \mid bS \mid cA, \quad A \rightarrow cB, \quad B \rightarrow cC, \quad C \rightarrow aC \mid bC \mid \lambda$
15. Construct a deterministic finite state machine accepting each one of the languages generated in Problems 10–14.
16. For each machine from Figure 2.28 construct an equivalent deterministic machine.

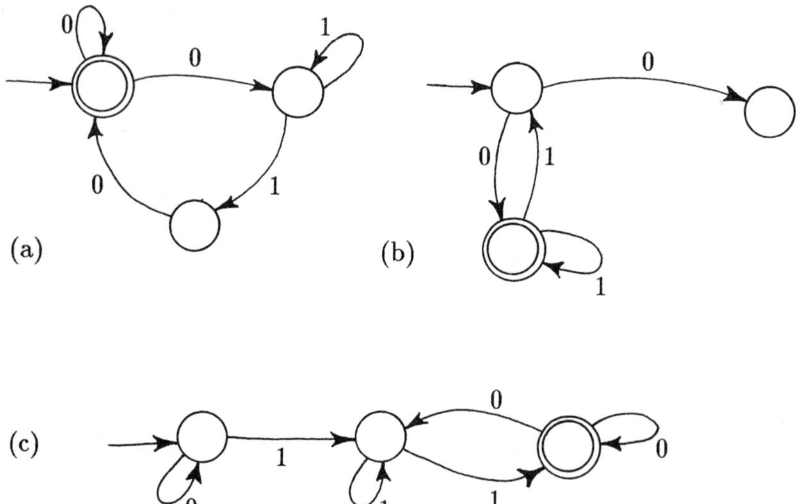

Figure 2.28. Nondeterministic finite state machines.

17. Minimize the finite state machine whose transition function is given in Figure 2.16 on p. 52. (Eliminate the inaccessible states first).
18. Minimize the finite state machines from Figure 2.29.
19. Complete the proof of Theorem 2.7 by showing the following (in the notation introduced there):
    a. If $\sigma_1 \simeq \sigma_2$ then either both σ_1 and σ_2 are in $L(M)$, or both are not in $L(M)$.
    b. The machine K introduced in the proof is equivalent to M.

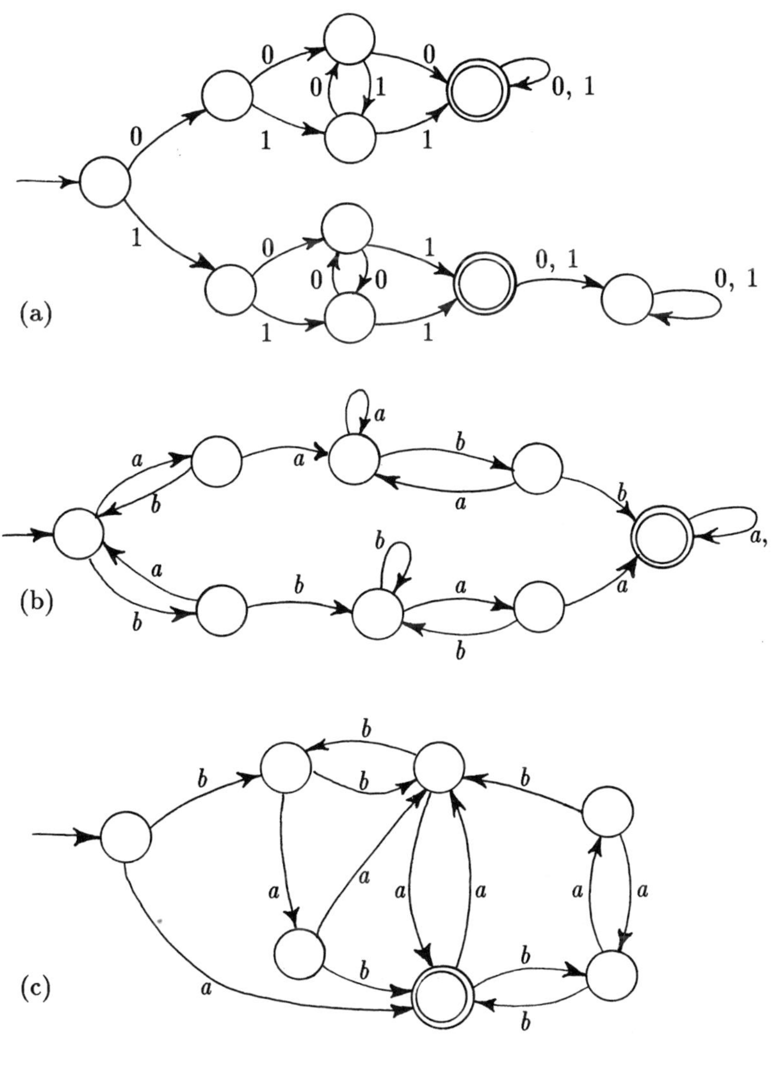

Figure 2.29. Some finite automata.

CHAPTER 3

REGULAR LANGUAGES

3.1. PUMPING LEMMA

We have seen in Chapter 2 that if G is a regular grammar (i.e., all the productions are of the form $S \rightarrow \lambda$, $A \rightarrow aB$, or $A \rightarrow a$), then there exists a deterministic finite state machine M such that $L(G) = L(M)$. Since such machines can easily be simulated on a computer—in fact, they can be implemented in the hardware—the solution to the parsing problem seems to be at hand: Given a language L, write a grammar G for L in such a way that G is regular, and then construct an appropriate finite automaton. However things are not quite that simple. Consider, for instance, the language

$$L(G) = \{0^n 1^n \mid n = 0, 1, 2, \ldots\}$$

that is the collection of all strings consisting of n 0's followed by n 1's. An example of a grammar for this language might be

$$S \rightarrow 0S1 \mid \lambda$$

which is evidently not regular. It turns out that there is no regular grammar G such that $L(G) = L$. We show this by demonstrating that there is no finite state machine M such that $L(M) = L$. Indeed, suppose such a machine M exists and let $Q_0, Q_1, \ldots, Q_{k-1}$ be its states (k of them). Let $\sigma = 0^m 1^m$ be a string in the language L, whose length is larger than k, that is, $2m > k$ (one can certainly find such strings in L.) When M is started on σ, it goes through the following sequence of moves:

$$Q_0 = \hat{Q}_0 \xrightarrow{0} \hat{Q}_1 \xrightarrow{0} \hat{Q}_2 \xrightarrow{0} \cdots \xrightarrow{0} \hat{Q}_m$$
$$\xrightarrow{1} \hat{Q}_{m+1} \xrightarrow{1} \cdots \xrightarrow{1} \hat{Q}_{2m} \qquad (3.1)$$

where $\hat{Q}_{2m}$ is an accepting state. Since M has only $k < 2m$ states, some of the $\hat{Q}$'s in (3.1) must repeat, that is $\hat{Q}_i = \hat{Q}_{i+p}$ for some i and $p > 0$. Let

$$\hat{Q}_i \xrightarrow{\epsilon_1} \hat{Q}_{i+1} \xrightarrow{\epsilon_2} \cdots \xrightarrow{\epsilon_p} \hat{Q}_{i+p} = \hat{Q}_i \qquad \epsilon_j = 0 \text{ or } 1 \qquad (3.2)$$

be the portion of the sequence (3.1) between these states. Let τ be the sequence $\epsilon_1\epsilon_2 \ldots \epsilon_p$. The length of τ is $p > 0$. Thus $\sigma = \sigma_1\tau\sigma_2$ and $\tau \neq \lambda$. Consider now the sequence $\rho = \sigma_1\tau\tau\sigma_2$—that is, the τ-portion of σ is repeated twice—and consider what happens when ρ is fed into M. Originally M is in the configuration $[\![Q_0, \sigma_1\tau\tau\sigma_2]\!]$. When all the symbols of σ_1 are read, the machine will be in configuration $[\![\hat{Q}_i, \tau\tau\sigma_2]\!]$. After the symbols of the "first τ" are processed, the configuration of M will be $[\![\hat{Q}_{i+p}, \tau\sigma_2]\!] = [\![\hat{Q}_i, \tau\sigma_2]\!]$ since $\hat{Q}_{i+p} = \hat{Q}_i$. From then on, the machine M will proceed as in the sequence (3.1), ending up in an accepting configuration $[\![\hat{Q}_{2m}, \lambda]\!]$. Schematically we have, on input $\rho = \sigma_1\tau\tau\sigma_2$,

$$\hat{Q}_0 \xrightarrow{\sigma_1}{}^* \hat{Q}_i \xrightarrow{\tau}{}^* \hat{Q}_{i+p} = \hat{Q}_i \xrightarrow{\tau\sigma_2}{}^* \hat{Q}_{2m}$$

Thus ρ is accepted by M, so $\rho = \sigma_2\tau\tau\sigma_2$ must belong to the language L, i.e., it must be of the form 0^n1^n for some n. That, however, is impossible. If τ consists only of 0's, then $\rho = \sigma_1\tau\tau\sigma_2$ has more 0's than 1's (since $\sigma = \sigma_1\tau\sigma_2$ has equal number of 0's and 1's, and $\tau \neq \lambda$); if τ consists only of 1's, then ρ will have more 1's than 0's. If τ has both 0's and 1's, then in the string $\rho = \sigma_1\tau\tau\sigma_2$ some of the 1's will precede some of the 0's, which also does not happen for strings in the language L. In all cases we see that ρ cannot be in L, thus $L \neq L(M)$.

The phenomenon described here is, in fact, common to all regular languages.

Theorem 3.1. (Pumping Lemma) Let G be a regular grammar. There exists an integer k with the following property: If σ is a string from $L(G)$ of length longer than k, then σ can be written as $\sigma = \sigma_1\tau\sigma_2$, where $\tau \neq \lambda$, and such that all the strings $\sigma_1\sigma_2$, $\sigma_1\tau\sigma_2$, $\sigma_1\tau\tau\sigma_2$, $\sigma_1\tau\tau\tau\sigma_2$, . . . ,

$\sigma_1\tau^n\sigma_2, \ldots$, belong also to the language $L(G)$.

Proof. We essentially mimic the arguments from the preceding discussion. Since G is a regular grammar, there exists a finite state machine M such that $L(G) = L(M)$ (Theorem 2.1). We take the integer k to be the number of the states in M; let these states be $Q_0, Q_1, \ldots, Q_{k-1}$. Let now $\sigma = x_1x_2 \ldots x_l$ be a string in $L(G)$ of length $l > k$. This string is accepted by the machine M, thus, on input σ, the machine M moves through the following sequence of configurations

$$Q_0 = \hat{Q}_0 \xrightarrow{x_1} \hat{Q}_1 \xrightarrow{x_2} \cdots \xrightarrow{x_l} \hat{Q}_l \tag{3.3}$$

where $\hat{Q}_l$ is a final state of M. Since $l > k$, there are two states occurring in (3.3) that are identical, i.e., $\hat{Q}_i = \hat{Q}_{i+p}$ for some i and $p > 0$. Let the transition between these states be

$$\hat{Q}_i \xrightarrow{x_{i+1}} \hat{Q}_{i+1} \xrightarrow{x_{i+2}} \cdots \xrightarrow{x_{i+p}} \hat{Q}_{i+p} = \hat{Q}_i, \quad x_j \in \Sigma \tag{3.4}$$

We take $\tau = x_{i+1}x_{i+2} \ldots x_{i+p}$. Since $p > 0$, $\tau \neq \lambda$ and we can write $\sigma = \sigma_1\tau\sigma_2$. For any $n \geq 0$, the motion of M on the input $\sigma_1\tau^n\sigma_2$ will be

$$\hat{Q}_0 \xrightarrow{\sigma_1}{}^{*} \underbrace{\hat{Q}_i \xrightarrow{\tau} \hat{Q}_i \xrightarrow{\tau} \cdots \xrightarrow{\tau} \hat{Q}_i}_{n \text{ times}} \xrightarrow{\sigma_2}{}^{*} \hat{Q}_l$$

and thus $\sigma_1\tau^n\sigma_2$ is accepted by M, so it is in the language $L(G)$. Q.E.D.

The Pumping Lemma is used mainly in demonstrating that certain languages do not have regular grammars. Given a language L, one shows that it does not have a regular grammar by assuming that it does, and then applying the Pumping Lemma to get a contradiction, as in the example at the beginning of the chapter. We illustrate this on once more.

Example 3.1. Let $L = \{a^n \mid n \text{ is a square of an integer}\}$. Thus L consists of strings of a's of length 1, 4, 9, 16, 25, ..., etc. We will show that L does not have a regular grammar. Indeed, suppose that there is a regular grammar G such that $L = L(G)$, and let k be the integer as described in the Pumping Lemma. Let $\sigma = aa \ldots a = a^{m^2}$ be a string of length longer than k, that is $m^2 > k$. The string σ can then be written as $\sigma = \sigma_1\tau\sigma_2$, with $\tau \neq \lambda$, and such that for each n the string $\sigma_1\tau^n\sigma_2$

is again in L. Let the length of σ_1 be r_1, the length of τ be t, and the length of σ_2 be r_2, so that $r_1 + t + r_2 = m^2$ and $t > 0$. The foregoing discussion shows that for each integer n, the number $r_1 + nt + r_2$ is again a perfect square, thus for each n we have $r_2 + nt + r_2 = j_n^2$, where j_n is an integer. Hence,

$$t = (r_1 + (n+1)t + r_2) - (r_1 + t + r_2) =$$
$$= j_{n+1}^2 - j_n^2 \geq (j_n^2 + 1)^2 - j_n^2 = 2j_n + 1 \qquad (3.5)$$

The left side of (3.5) is a fixed number t, while the right side gets larger and larger as $n \rightarrow \infty$. This contradiction shows that L does not have a regular grammar.

3.2. REGULAR EXPRESSIONS

Another way of describing languages is by using what are called regular expressions. This method attempts to mimic the "verbal" description of a language. For example we may describe a language L by saying that L consists of strings beginning with two 1's, followed by three 0's, and followed by an arbitrary number of either 2's or 3's. Thus 110002322 is in the language, while 11000201 is not. It turns out that it is possible to develop a precise mathematical formalism for such descriptions. We begin with preliminary concepts and terminology.

Definition 3.1. Let L, L_1, and L_2 be languages.

1. The language L_1L_2 is defined to be the collection of all strings obtained by concatenating a string from L_1 with a string from L_2. Formally,

$$L_1L_2 = \{\sigma_1\sigma_2 \mid \sigma_1 \in L_1, \sigma_2 \in L_2\}$$

2. The language $L_1 + L_2$ is the collection of all strings that either belong to L_1 or to L_2. Thus, $L_1 + L_2$ is just the set theoretic union of L_1 and L_2:

$$L_1 + L_2 = \{\sigma \mid \sigma \in L_1 \text{ or } \sigma \in L_2\} = L_1 \cup L_2$$

3. The language L^* is the collection of strings obtained from concatenating an arbitrary but finite number of strings from L. Thus:

$$L^* = \{\sigma_1\sigma_2 \ldots \sigma_n \mid \sigma_1 \in L, \sigma_2 \in L, \ldots, \sigma_n \in L\}$$

In this definition of L^* we allow $n = 0$, in which case $\sigma_1\sigma_2 \ldots \sigma_n$ is to be interpreted as λ—the empty string. Thus for any language L, $\lambda \in L^*$.

4. The language L^+ is defined as the collection of strings obtained by concatenating an arbitrary positive number of strings from L. Hence

$$L^+ = \{\sigma_1\sigma_2 \ldots \sigma_n \mid \sigma_1 \in L, \ldots, \sigma_n \in L, n \geq 1\}$$

The language L^+ is quite similar to L^*, the only difference being that we do not allow $n = 0$ in the above definition. If $\lambda \notin L$, then $\lambda \notin L^+$, but of course $\lambda \in L^*$.

We illustrate this by some examples. Let $L_1 = \{01, 1001\}$ and $L_2 = \{11, 00, 1\}$. Then

$$L_1L_2 = \{\underline{01}\,\underline{11}, \underline{01}\,\underline{00}, \underline{01}\,\underline{1}, \underline{1001}\,\underline{11}, \underline{1001}\,\underline{00}, \underline{1001}\,\underline{1}\}$$
$$L_1 + L_2 = \{01, 1001, 11, 00, 1\}$$

In the definition of L_1L_2 we underlined the parts of the string belonging to L_1 and to L_2. It should be noted that in general $L_1L_2 \neq L_2L_1$. Thus, for example, 101 is in L_2L_1, but not in L_1L_2. An example of a string in L_2^* might be the string 1100111:

$$\underset{\sigma_1}{\underline{1\,1}}\;\underset{\sigma_2}{\underline{0\,0}}\;\underset{\sigma_3}{\underline{1}}\;\underset{\sigma_4}{\underline{1\,1}}$$

where each $\sigma_i \in L_2$. Such a representation (partition) is not unique. The same string could be represented as

$$\underset{\sigma_1}{\underline{1}}\;\underset{\sigma_2}{\underline{1}}\;\underset{\sigma_3}{\underline{0\,0}}\;\underset{\sigma_4}{\underline{1}}\;\underset{\sigma_5}{\underline{1}}\;\underset{\sigma_6}{\underline{1}}\;.$$

We now come to the concept of a regular expression over an alphabet Σ. Regular expressions will be written in bold type and will denote certain languages as follows.

Definition 3.2. Let Σ be an alphabet, i.e., a nonempty finite set of symbols.

1. $\boldsymbol{\emptyset}$ is a regular expression over Σ and $\boldsymbol{\emptyset}$ denotes the empty language, that is the language with no strings whatsoever.

2. λ is a regular expression over Σ and it denotes the language $\{\lambda\}$, i.e., the language containing the empty string λ.
3. For each $a \in \Sigma$, $\mathbf{a}$ is a regular expression and it denotes the language $\{a\}$—the language consisting of the single string a.
4. If $\mathbf{r}$ and $\mathbf{s}$ are regular expressions over Σ denoting languages L_1 and L_2, respectively, then $\mathbf{rs}$, $\mathbf{r} + \mathbf{s}$, and $\mathbf{r}^*$ are regular expressions, where $\mathbf{rs}$ denotes the language L_1L_2, $\mathbf{r} + \mathbf{s}$ denotes $L_1 + L_2$, and $\mathbf{r}^*$ denotes L_1^* .
5. Any regular expression can be obtained by a finite number of applications of rules 1–4.

The reason for denoting the regular expressions in bold type is to distinguish them from the symbols of the language they represent. A comment should be made about points 1 and 2 of the above definition. the regular expression λ is different from the regular expression $\emptyset$. The symbol λ denotes the language consisting of one empty string, while $\emptyset$ denotes the language which contains no strings at all—not even the empty string. Perhaps the distinction looks artificial, but it is logically correct and very useful.

Example 3.2. Let $\Sigma = \{a, b, c\}$. Examples of regular expressions over Σ are $\mathbf{a}$, $\mathbf{a} + \mathbf{b}$, $\mathbf{ab} + c$, and $\mathbf{a}^* + \mathbf{bc}$. The languages they represent are as follows:

$\mathbf{a}$ represents the language $\{a\}$ consisting of the single string a
$\mathbf{a} + \mathbf{b}$ represents the language $\{a\} \cup \{b\} = \{a, b\}$ consisting of two strings: a and b
$\mathbf{ab}$ represents the language $\{a\}\{b\} = \{ab\}$, thus $\mathbf{ab} + c$ represents the language $\{ab, c\}$
$\mathbf{a}^*$ represents the language $\{\lambda, a, aa, aaa, \ldots, a^n, \ldots\}$
$\mathbf{a}^* + \mathbf{bc}$ represents the language $\{bc, \lambda, a, aa, aaa, \ldots, a^n, \ldots\}$

Regular expressions may be considerably more complicated than that. Consider, for instance, a regular expression $\mathbf{x} = \mathbf{ab(a + bc)^*(bc + ca)}$. A verbal description of a string σ in the language $\mathbf{x}$ is as follows: σ must begin with ab, followed by some finite number (or none) of strings each one of which is either a or bc, and ending with either bc or ca. Thus, for instance, $ababcaaca$ is in $\mathbf{x}$, but $baabcab$ is not.

There are several notational conventions commonly used when dealing with regular expressions. We summarize them here.

Definition 3.3. Let $\mathbf{r}$ be a regular expression. We set

$$r^n = rr \ldots r \ (n \text{ times}), \quad \text{and } r^+ = rr^*$$

Thus, r^n denotes the language of strings obtained by concatenating n strings—all of them from the language r. The language r^+ is obtained by taking all possible concatenations of finite number of strings, each one of which is from the language r, with the proviso that this finite number is strictly positive. It is easy to see that $r^* = r^+ + \lambda$; thus, in particular, if $\lambda \in r$ then $r^+ = r^*$. In dealing with regular expressions we adopt precedence conventions analogous to those from algebra: * has precedence over concatenation, which in turn has precedence over $+$. Thus $a(b^*)$ may be written as ab^* and $(ab) + c$ may be written as $ab + c$. The algebra of regular expressions has many, but not all, of the properties of ordinary algebraic expressions. We summarize some of them here.

Theorem 3.2. Let $r_1, r_2, \ldots$ be regular expressions. The following hold:

1. $r_1 + (r_2 + r_3) = (r_1 + r_2) + r_3$ Associativity of $+$
2. $r_1 + r_2 = r_2 + r_1$ Commutativity of $+$
3. $r_1(r_2r_3) = (r_1r_2)r_3$ Associativity of concatenation
4. α) $r_1(r_2 + r_3) = r_1r_2 + r_1r_3$
   β) $(r_1 + r_2)r_3 = r_1r_3 + r_1r_3$ Distributive laws
5. $r_1 + \emptyset = \emptyset + r_1 = r_1$
6. $\lambda r_1 = r_1\lambda = r_1$
7. $\emptyset r_1 = r_1\emptyset = \emptyset$

Proof. The properties $1-5$ are entirely clear from the definition. The meaning of 6 is this: If we take the empty string λ from λ and concatenate it with a string σ from r_1, we obtain the same string σ. The reason 7 is true is that $\emptyset r_1$ denotes the set of strings σ of the form $\sigma = \sigma_1\sigma_2$, where $\sigma_1 \in \emptyset$ and $\sigma_2 \in r_1$. Since it is impossible to find a string σ_1 in the empty set $\emptyset$, there are no strings σ of the indicated form. Thus, $\emptyset r_1 = \emptyset$. Q.E.D.

It should be noted, perhaps, that in general $r_1r_2 \neq r_2r_1$. Indeed, $10 \neq 01$, since the language 10 contains only one string 10 and the language 01 contains only one string 01. Evidently these languages are not the same.

Example 3.3. Regular expressions allow us to describe certain languages in an easy and natural way. Consider, for instance, the language of FORTRAN real constants discussed in Example 1.4. The alphabet of this language is

$$\Sigma = \{0, 1, 2, 3, 4, 5, 6, 7, 8, 9, +, -, ., E\}$$

Let $d = 0 + 1 + 2 + 3 + 4 + 5 + 6 + 7 + 8 + 9$ be a regular expression over Σ; d represents the language consisting of single digits: $d = \{0, 1, 2, 3, 4, 5, 6, 7, 8, 9\}$. The language of FORTRAN real constants can now be described in a natural way as

$$(+ + - + \lambda)\,(d^+.\,d^+ + d^+. + .\,d^+)\,(\lambda + E\,(\lambda + + + -)d^+))$$

Another example would be the language of FORTRAN identifiers. These are defined, for instance, as "any combination of 1–7 characters beginning with a letter" (see [10].). The regular expression denoting precisely this language is

$$u\,(\lambda + v + v^2 + v^3 + v^4 + v^5 + v^6)$$

where $u = A + B + C + \cdots + X + Y + Z$, and $v = u + 0 + 1 + \cdots + 8 + 9 = u + d$.

3.3. REGULAR LANGUAGES AND REGULAR EXPRESSIONS

Having introduced a new way of describing languages, we quite naturally inquire how this new method compares with the old one. It turns out that aside from notational convenience we have not gained much.

Theorem 3.3. A language L can be described by a regular expression if and only if it is a regular language (i.e., it has a regular grammar).

Proof. We begin with some heuristics. Suppose we have a language L that is regular, and we wish to find a regular expression describing it (assuming that one exists). Since L is regular, there is a finite state machine M which accepts L. Suppose, for example, that this machine is given in Figure 3.1. In this figure the accepting state is Q_2, but we intentionally do not specify the initial state. For each $i = 0, 1, 2$, let M_i be the above machine whose initial state is Q_i, and let $L(M_i)$ be the language accepted by M_i. Supposing that Theorem 3.3 is true, let Q_i be the regular expression describing the language $L(M_i)$. We now show that these regular expressions must satisfy certain algebraic relations. Consider, for instance, Q_0. We claim that

$$Q_0 = bQ_0 + aQ_1 \tag{3.6}$$

Indeed, suppose σ is a string accepted by M_0, i.e., $\sigma \in Q_0$. Such a string must begin with either a or b. If σ begins with a, then $\sigma = a\tau_1$, so after reading the symbol a, the machine will move to the state Q_1 and begin to read τ_1. If M_0 accepts $\sigma = a\tau_1$, then M_1 (i.e., the machine whose initial state is Q_1) must accept τ_1, thus $\tau_1 \in Q_1$ and $a\tau_1 \in \boldsymbol{a}Q_1$.

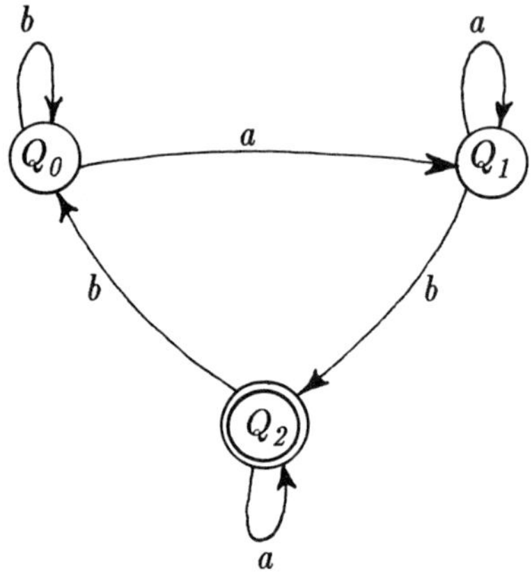

Figure 3.1. Construction of a regular expression from a FSM.

Similarly, if σ begins with b, then $\sigma = b\tau_2$ and τ_2 must be accepted by M_0 (since M_0, after reading symbol b, remains in the state Q_0). Thus $\sigma \in \boldsymbol{b}Q_0$ in this case. This shows that for any string $\sigma \in Q_0$, σ is in $\boldsymbol{b}Q_0 + \boldsymbol{a}Q_1$. It is just as easy to see that if a string σ belongs to the right side of (3.6), it must also belong to the left side. Indeed, any such string must be either of the form $b\tau_1$, with $\tau_1 \in Q_0$ (i.e., τ is accepted by M_0), or of the form $a\tau_2$, with $\tau_2 \in Q_1$ (i.e., τ is accepted by M_1). In either case σ is accepted by M_0. Thus (3.6) must hold. Arguing in exactly the same way, starting with the state Q_1, we get the equation

$$Q_1 = \boldsymbol{a}Q_1 + \boldsymbol{b}Q_2 \tag{3.7}$$

Consider now the state Q_2 and the regular expression Q_2 describing the language $L(M_2)$. Q_2 must contain the regular expression $\boldsymbol{a}Q_2 + \boldsymbol{b}Q_0$. However, since Q_2 is an accepting state, Q_2 must also contain the string λ. Thus the equation for Q_2 is

$$Q_2 = \boldsymbol{a}Q_2 + \boldsymbol{b}Q_0 + \lambda \tag{3.8}$$

This shows that if the languages $L(M_i)$ are described by regular expressions Q_i, $i = 0, 1, 2$, then these expressions are the solutions of the system of equations

$$\begin{aligned} X_0 &= bX_0 + aX_1 \\ X_1 &= aX_1 + bX_2 \\ X_2 &= aX_2 + bX_0 + \lambda \end{aligned} \tag{3.9}$$

Hence, to show that each one of the languages $L(M_i)$ can be described by a regular expression, it is enough to show the following two things:

I. The system of equations (3.9) does have a solution
II. If Q_0, Q_1, and Q_2 are regular expressions which satisfy (3.9), then each Q_i is equal to $L(M_i)$ (3.10)

We take up II first. Assume that the system of equations (3.9) does have a solution $X_0 = Q_0$, $X_1 = Q_1$, and $X_2 = Q_2$. We claim that these regular expressions Q_i describe the languages $L(M_i)$, i.e., $Q_i = L(M_i)$. What we have to show is that given a string σ, this string belongs to $L(M_i)$ if and only if it belongs to Q_i, $i = 1, 2, 3$. (We have not established that the system (3.9) has a solution or, if one exists, how to find it. This will be done shortly.) The argument is by induction on the length k of σ. Assume σ has length 0; this means that $\sigma = \lambda$. It is clear that σ is accepted only by $L(M_2)$ and it belongs only to Q_2 (any string in Q_1 say, will have to begin either with a or b, because of the first equation in (3.9), likewise for strings in Q_0). Thus the assertion is true for $k = 0$. Suppose it is true for k, and let σ be a string of length $k + 1$, say $\sigma = x\tau$, where τ is of length k. If σ is in Q_2, say, then, on account of the third equation in (3.), x must be either a, in which case τ is in Q_2, or b, in which case τ must be in Q_0. By inductive hypothesis, τ is accepted either by M_2 or by M_0, whichever is the case. But this means that σ is accepted by M_2, since after M_2 reads x, it moves to either M_2 or M_0, and then it reads τ. The same argument holds for strings in Q_0 and Q_1: Any string σ of length $k + 1$ that is in Q_i must be in $L(M_i)$. Conversely, suppose the string σ is accepted by, say M_1, then x must be either a or b. If $x = b$, then τ is accepted by M_2, so by inductive hypothesis τ is in Q_2, and σ is in Q_1 by the second equation of (3.9). The same argument holds when $x = a$, and when σ is accepted by other M_i's. This proves II of (3.10).

All that remains is to prove that the system of equations (3.9) has a solution and show how to find it. The arguments here are based on the following lemma.

Lemma 3.1. Consider an equation

$$x = ux + v \tag{3.11}$$

where u and v are given regular expressions and x is a regular expression to be found. The following is then true:

1. The regular expression $x = u^*v$ is a solution of (3.11).
2. If the empty string λ does not belong to the language described by u, then $x = u^*v$ is the only solution of (3.11).

Proof. To prove 1, we must show that

$$u^*v = uu^*v + v \tag{3.12}$$

which means that both sides of (3.12) denote the same collection of strings. Let σ be a string in u^*v. This means that σ may be written as $\sigma = \sigma_1\sigma_2$, where $\sigma_1 \in u^*$ and $\sigma_2 \in v$. If $\sigma_1 \neq \lambda$ then $\sigma_1 \in uu^* \subset uu^* + v$. ($\sigma_1$ is a concatenation of a positive, finite number of strings from u). If $\sigma_1 = \lambda$ then $\sigma = \sigma_2 \in v \subset uu^* + v$. Thus, the left-hand side of (3.11) is a subset of the right-hand side. Conversely, suppose $\sigma \in uu^*v + v$. If $\sigma \in uu^*v$, then it also belongs to u^*v; if σ is in v, then it is in u^*v, too. This shows that (3.12) holds.

To show 2 it is enough to prove that if $\lambda \notin u$, then the solution of (3.11) is unique. (The preceding argument shows that $x = u^*v$ is always a solution). Suppose then that we have two solutions $x_1 \neq x_2$, both satisfying (3.11):

$$\begin{aligned} x_1 &= ux_1 + v \\ x_2 &= ux_2 + v \end{aligned} \tag{3.13}$$

The meaning of the hypothesis $x_1 \neq x_2$ is that x_1 and x_2 describe different languages, i.e., there is a string that is contained in one of them but not in the other. Without loss of generality, we may assume that there is a string contained in x_1 but not in x_2; let σ be the shortest such string (σ need not be unique, but it does not matter). Thus $\sigma \in x_1$ and $\sigma \notin x_2$, and if $\hat{\sigma}$ is any other string in x_1 of length shorter than the length of σ, then $\hat{\sigma}$ belongs to x_2. Since $\sigma \in x_1$, we see from the first equation of (3.13) that $\sigma \in ux_1$ or $\sigma \in v$. But σ cannot belong to v, since, by the second equation of (3.13), it would then belong to x_2. Thus, $\sigma = \tau_1\sigma_1$, where $\tau_1 \in u$ and $\sigma_1 \in x_1$. Since $\lambda \notin u$, the string $\tau_1 \neq \lambda$, so the string σ_1 is strictly shorter then σ and, by the previous remark, must also belong to x_2. But this implies that $\tau_1\sigma_1$, and thus σ, belongs to ux_2, and thus, by the second equation of (3.13), to x_2 . This however, contradicts the choice of σ.Q.E.D.

We are now ready to solve the system of equations (3.9), which we reproduce here.

$$\begin{aligned} X_0 &= bX_0 + aX_1 \\ X_1 &= aX_1 + bX_2 \\ X_2 &= aX_2 + bX_0 + \lambda \end{aligned} \tag{3.14}$$

We solve the third equation of (3.14) for X_2 (using Lemma 3.1 with $u = a$ and $v = bX_0 + \lambda$).

$$X_2 = a^*(bX_0 + \lambda) = a^*bX_0 + a^*$$

and the solution is unique. Substituting this expression into the first two equations of (3.14) we get two equations in two unknowns.

$$\begin{aligned} X_0 &= bX_0 + aX_1 \\ X_1 &= aX_1 + ba^*bX_0 + ba^* \end{aligned} \tag{3.15}$$

Solving the second equation for X_1 (with $u = a$ and $v = ba^*bX_0 + ba^*$) we get

$$X_1 = a^*(ba^*bX_0 + ba^*) = a^*ba^*bX_0 + a^*ba^*$$

Substituting this into the first equation of (3.15) we get, after some algebra,

$$X_0 = (b + aa^*ba^*b)X_0 + aa^*ba^*$$

which finally gives $X_0 = Q_0 = (b + aa^*ba^*b)^*aa^*ba^*$—a regular expression describing the language $L(M_0)$ from Figure 3.1. In a similar way we can solve for X_1 and X_2; thus, we can find a regular expression describing each one of the languages $L(M_i)$, $i = 1, 2, 3$, of Figure 3.1.

The method extends to the general case without any difficulty. Given a finite state machine $M = \{\mathcal{Q}, \Sigma, Q_0, \delta, \mathcal{F}\}$, to find a regular expression describing the language $L(M)$ we proceed as follows. For each state $Q_0, Q_1, \ldots, Q_n$ write down an equation in regular expressions:

$$X_i = \sum_k r_{i\,k}\ ,\ i = 0, 1, 2, \ldots n \tag{3.16}$$

where for each i, the r_{ik} are defined as:

1. If Q_i is an accepting state, include λ among the r_{ik}'s.
2. If $\delta(Q_i, a) = Q_j$ is a valid transition, include aX_j among the r_{ik}'s.

Formally, the equations (3.16) may be written as

$$X_i = \sum_{\delta(Q_i,\ a)=Q_j} aX_j \ + \ \mu_i \tag{3.17}$$

where $\mu_i = \lambda$ if Q_i is an accepting state, and $\mu_i = \emptyset$ if Q_i is not an accepting state. One can than show that the system of equations (3.17) has a solution $X_0 = Q_0, X_1 = Q_1, \ldots, X_n = Q_n$, (using Lemma 3.1) and that each Q_i is a regular expression describing the language of the machine M_i obtained from M by changing the initial state to Q_i. The machine M itself is then given by Q_0. To solve for Q_0 from the system (3.17) we proceed "backwards": Using Lemma 3.1 we solve for X_n from the last equation and substitute the result into the previous $n - 1$ equations. After repeating this $n - 1$ times, we arrive at a single equation of the form

$$X_0 = \alpha X_0 \ + \beta$$

which we solve, again using Lemma 3.1. The arguments are almost verbatim repetitions of the proof presented in the special case, and we omit them. We illustrate the process on one more example.

Example 3.4. Consider finite state machine in Figure 3.2. Corresponding equations (3.17) are

$$\begin{aligned} X_0 &= aX_1 + bX_2 \\ X_1 &= bX_1 + aX_3 \\ X_2 &= bX_1 \\ X_3 &= aX_2 + \lambda \end{aligned}$$

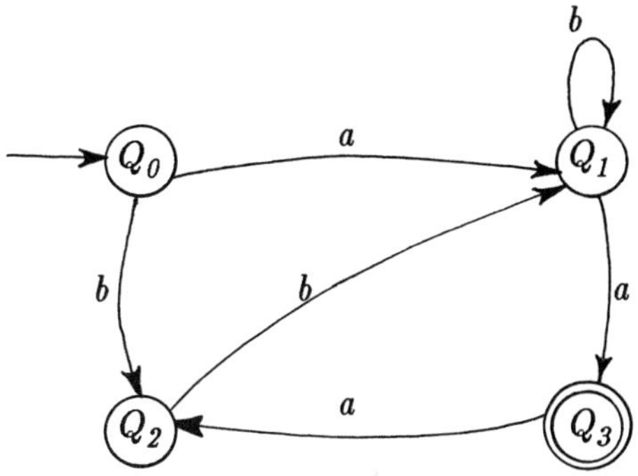

Figure 3.2. A finite state machine.

Substituting the values for X_3 from the last equation into the previous three, we obtain the system

$$X_0 = aX_1 + bX_2$$
$$X_1 = bX_1 + aaX + a$$
$$X_2 = bX_1$$

The expression X_2 is again "solved for" and we substitute it into the top two equations to get a system

$$X_0 = aX_1 + bbX_1$$
$$\begin{aligned} X_1 &= bX_1 + aabX_1 + a \\ &= (b + a^2b)X_1 + a \end{aligned}$$

Solving for X_1 from the last equation (using Lemma 3.1), we get $X_1 = (b + a^2b)^*a$, and finally, substituting this into the first equation and solving for X_0, we get a description of the machine $L(M_0)$ by a regular expression: $(a + b^2)(b + a^2b)^*a$.

A few words should perhaps be said about Lemma 3.1. (The assertion that the equation $x = ux + v$ has a solution $x = u^*v$ and this solution is unique if $\lambda \notin u$.) If $\lambda \in u$, the solution need not be unique. Consider an equation

$$x = (a + \lambda)x + ab$$

One solution, according to Lemma 3.1, is $x_1 = (a + \lambda)^*ab$, but $x_2 =$

$(\boldsymbol{a} + \lambda)^* \boldsymbol{ab} + \boldsymbol{b}$ is also a solution and $x_1 \neq x_2$, as can easily be checked. A special case arises when $\boldsymbol{v} = \emptyset$. If $\lambda \notin \boldsymbol{u}$, then the only solution of $x = x\boldsymbol{u} + \emptyset$ is $x = \emptyset$. Indeed, according to Lemma 3.1, the only solution is $x = \boldsymbol{u}^*\emptyset = \emptyset$, by Theorem 3.2. We have thus established the first half of Theorem 3.3: Any regular language can be described by a regular expression.

We now proceed to show how to construct a finite state machine from a regular expression. First, we do this for extremely simple regular expressions: $\emptyset$, λ, and $\boldsymbol{a}$.

Theorem 3.4. Let the finite state machines M_1, M_2, and M_3 be given by the diagrams in the Figure 3.3. Then $L(M_1) = \emptyset$, $L(M_2) = \lambda$, and $L(M_3) = \boldsymbol{a}$.

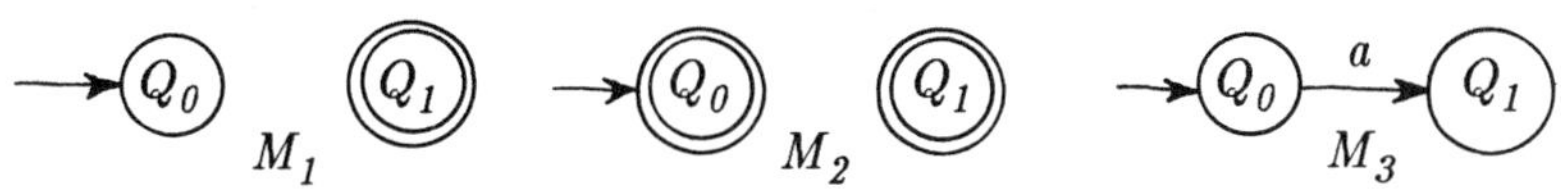

Figure 3.3. Simple finite automata.

The proof is entirely obvious. We have made the machines M_1 and M_2 intentionally more complicated than they need to be, the reason for which will be explained below. Notice that the machines M_1 and M_2 have no transitions whatsoever; $\delta(Q, x) = \emptyset$ for all states Q and all input symbols x.

Now let L, L_1, and L_2 be some regular languages accepted by finite state machines M, M_1, and M_2, respectively. Also suppose we have a method of constructing machines N, N_1, and N_2 (using M, M_1, and M_2) such that $L^* = L(N)$, $L_1 + L_2 = L(N_1)$ and $L_1L_2 = L(N_2)$. (See Definition 3.1.) If we do have such a method, then given any regular expression $\boldsymbol{r}$, we will be able to construct a finite state machine K such that $L(K) = \boldsymbol{r}$. Indeed, $\boldsymbol{r}$ is obtained by taking regular expressions $\emptyset$, λ, and $\boldsymbol{a}$, and successively applying operations of concatenation, +, and *—see Definition 3.2. But the machines for $\emptyset$, λ, and $\boldsymbol{a}$ are known—they are given in Theorem 3.4.

Intuitively, the method for constructing N, N_1, and N_2 is clear. If the machines M_1 for L_1 and M_2 for L_2 are known, to construct the machine for L_1L_2 we "string" M_1 and M_2 together, as in Figure 3.4. To construct the machine for $L_1 + L_2$, we join M_1 and M_2 in a "parallel" fashion, as in Figure 3.5. Finally, to construct the machine N for $L(M)^*$, we "tie M around," as in Figure 3.6.

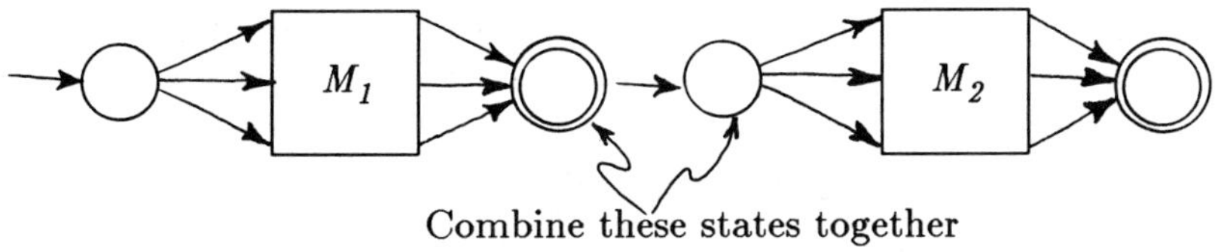

Figure 3.4. Machine for the language $L_1 L_2$.

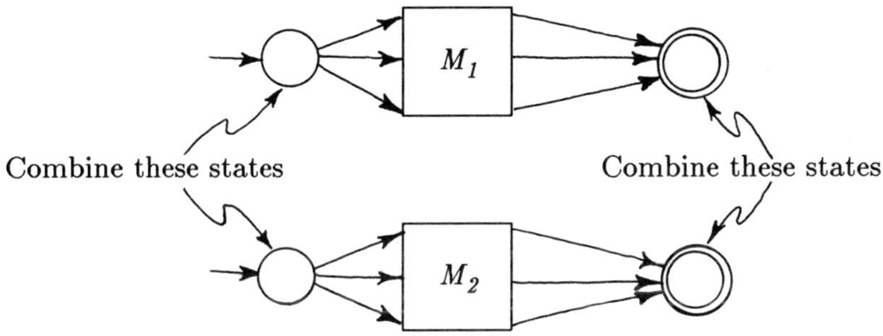

Figure 3.5. Machine for the language $L_1 + L_2$.

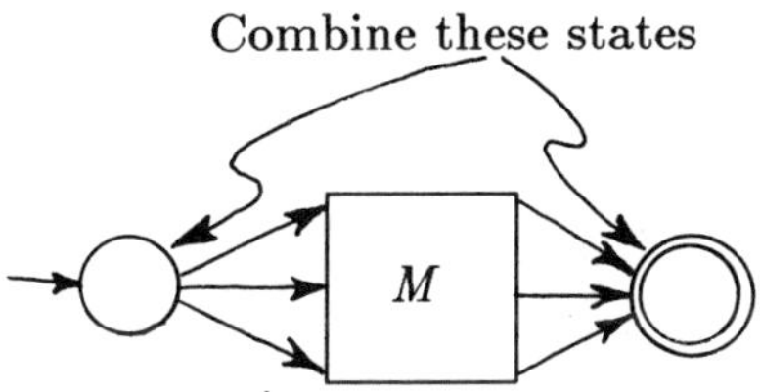

Figure 3.6. Machine for the language L^*.

It is also clear that we have to be much more precise in describing these constructions. The machines M, M_1, and M_2 may have more than one accepting state, and there is a difficulty in choosing exactly which states are to be combined. We now develop precise mathematical descriptions of these processes.

Definition 3.4. Let M be a finite state machine. We say that M is ***straight*** if it satisfies the following conditions:

1. There are no transitions leading into the initial state Q_0 of M. In other words, for any state Q and any input symbol x, $Q_0 \notin \delta(Q, x)$.

2. The machine M has either one or two accepting states. One of these states, say Q_F, is different from the initial state Q_0 and has the property that there are no transitions leading out of it, i.e., $\delta(Q_F, x) = \emptyset$ for all x's. The other accepting state, if there is one, must be the initial state Q_0.

Schematically, a straight machine has one of the forms indicated in Figure 3.7. We will use these straight machines to make the constructions indicated above.

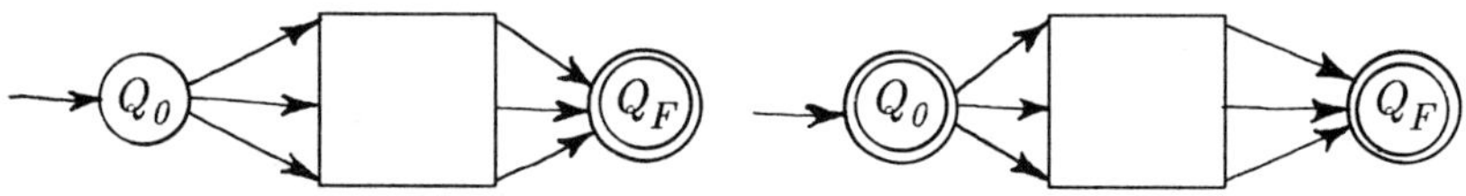

One accepting state Q_F Two accepting states Q_0 and Q_F

Figure 3.7. Straight machines.

First, we have the following:

Lemma 3.2. Given any finite state machine M, there is a straight machine K such that $L(M) = L(K)$.

Proof. Let the states of $M = \{\mathcal{Q}, \Sigma, Q_0, \delta, \mathcal{F}\}$ be $Q_0, Q_1, \ldots, Q_n$. To construct the machine K, add two new states I and F and make the following modifications.

1. The initial state of K is I.
2. F is an accepting state of K. In addition, if Q_0 is an accepting state of M, then I is also an accepting state of K.
3. For every transition of the form $Q_0 \xrightarrow{x} Q$ in M, add the transition $I \xrightarrow{x} Q$ in K.
4. For every transition of the form $Q \xrightarrow{x} \hat{Q}$ in M, where $\hat{Q}$ is an accepting state, add the transition $Q \xrightarrow{x} F$ in K.
5. For every transition of the form $Q_0 \xrightarrow{x} Q$ in M, where Q_0 is an initial state and Q is a final state, add the transition $I \xrightarrow{x} F$ in K.
6. The transition relations between the Q's remain unchanged, the state Q_0 is not the initial state anymore (I is), and the accepting states of M become nonaccepting.

It should be emphasized that a transition in M may generate several transitions in K. For instance, if M has 3 states: Q_0 (initial), Q_1, and

Q_2(accepting), then the transition $Q_0 \xrightarrow{x} Q_2$ will generate transitions $I \xrightarrow{x} Q_2$ (rule 3), $Q_0 \xrightarrow{x} F$ (rule 4), and $I \xrightarrow{x} F$ (rule 5).

We now show that M and K accept the same strings. Suppose $\sigma = \lambda$ is accepted by M, then Q_0 must be an accepting state of M, so I is an accepting state of K, hence $\lambda \in L(K)$. Conversely, $\lambda \in L(K)$ if and only if I is an accepting state of K, but this happens if and only if Q_0 is an accepting state of M, so $\lambda \in L(M)$. Now let $\sigma = x_1x_2 \ldots x_m$ be a nonempty string in $L(M)$. On the input σ the machine M goes through the following sequence of configurations:

$$[\![Q_0, x_1x_2 \ldots x_{m-1}x_m]\!] \rightarrow [\![\hat{Q}_1, x_2 \ldots x_{m-1}x_m]\!]$$
$$\rightarrow^* [\![\hat{Q}_{m-1}, x_m]\!] \rightarrow [\![\hat{Q}_m, \lambda]\!]$$

where $\hat{Q}_m$ is an accepting state of M. Thus $Q_0 \xrightarrow{x_1} \hat{Q}_1$ and $\hat{Q}_{m-1} \xrightarrow{x_m} \hat{Q}_m$ are legal transitions of M, so $I \xrightarrow{x_1} \hat{Q}_1$ and $\hat{Q}_{m-1} \xrightarrow{x_m} F$ are transitions in K. Thus, on input σ, the machine K goes through the following sequence of moves:

$$[\![I, x_1x_2 \ldots x_{m-1}x_m]\!] \rightarrow [\![\hat{Q}_1, x_2 \ldots x_{m-1}x_m]\!] \rightarrow^* [\![\hat{Q}_{m-1}, x_m]\!] \rightarrow [\![F, \lambda]\!]$$

so $\sigma \in L(K)$. Using an entirely similar argument, we see that if $\sigma \in L(K)$ then σ will also be in $L(M)$. Q.E.D.

Example 3.5. Suppose the machine M is given by a diagram in Figure 3.8. The corresponding straight machine K is then described by Figure 3.9.

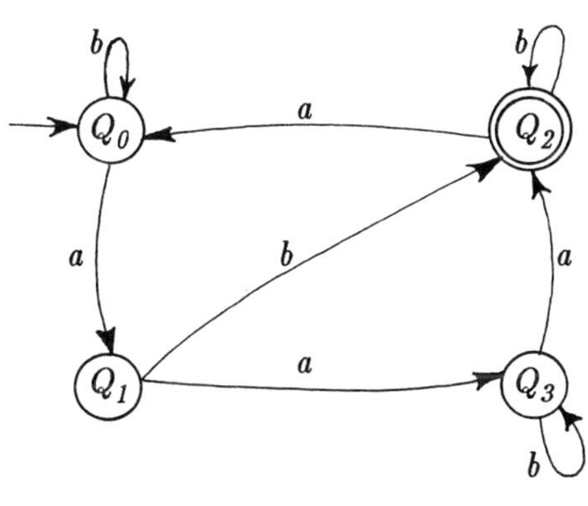

Figure 3.8. A twisted machine.

For instance, the transition $Q_1 \xrightarrow{b} F$ is included because $Q_1 \xrightarrow{b} Q_2$ (rule 4); $I \xrightarrow{a} Q_1$ is included because $Q_0 \xrightarrow{a} Q_1$ (rule 2). If Q_0 were an accepting state of M, then I would have been an accepting state of K, and we would have three additional transitions: $Q_0 \xrightarrow{b} F$ (rule 4 applied to $Q_0 \xrightarrow{b} Q_0$), $Q_2 \xrightarrow{a} F$ (rule 4 applied to $Q_2 \xrightarrow{a} Q_0$), and $I \xrightarrow{b} F$ (rule 5 applied to $Q_0 \xrightarrow{b} Q_0$).

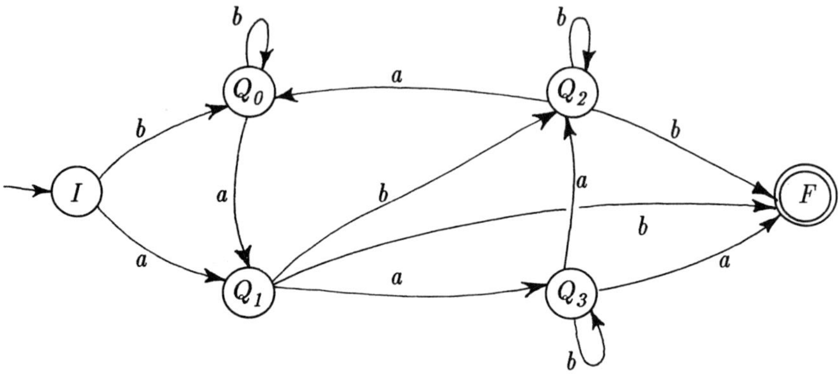

Figure 3.9. Straight machine.

We are now ready to describe precisely the constructions discussed prior to Definition 3.4.

Theorem 3.5. Let M_1, M_2, and M be finite state machines. Then each of the languages $L(M_1) + L(M_2)$, $L(M_1)L(M_2)$, and $L(M)^*$ is accepted by a finite state machine.

Proof. Without loss of generality, we may assume that M_1, M_2, and M are straight machines, if not, they can be converted to straight machines using Lemma 3.2. Let the initial states of M_1, M_2, and M be I_1, I_2, and I, respectively, and let the final states of M_1, M_2, and M be F_1, F_2, and F. To construct a machine accepting the language $L(M_1) + L(M_2)$ we "fuse" the initial states of M_1 and M_2, and do the same to the final states F_1 and F_2. Schematically, the new machine has its diagram represented in Figure 3.10. The initial state is indicated by an arrow $\rightarrow$ and the final states by the double circle. If either I_1 or I_2 (or both) is an accepting state, then the state $I_1 = I_2$ is also an accepting state of the machine. It is quite evident that the language accepted by this FSM is exactly $L(M_1) + L(M_2)$. To construct a machine accepting the state $(L(M))^*$ is also straightforward: We "tie the machine M around," that is we combine I and F into a new state, which will be both initial and accepting. This is schematically represented in Figure 3.11. Again, it is quite evident that this construction gives the correct result.

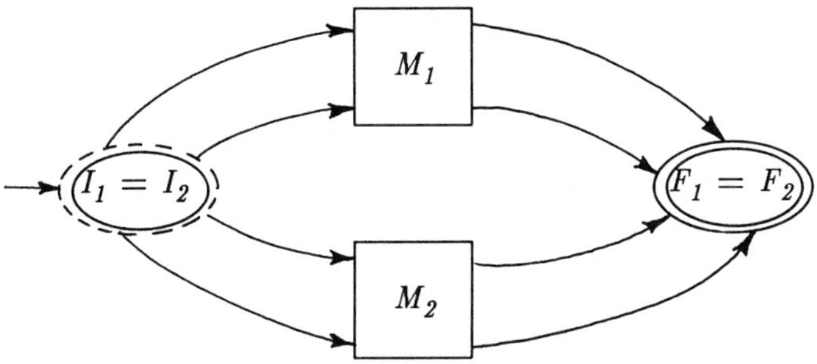

Figure 3.10. Machine for the language $L(M_1) + L(M_2)$.

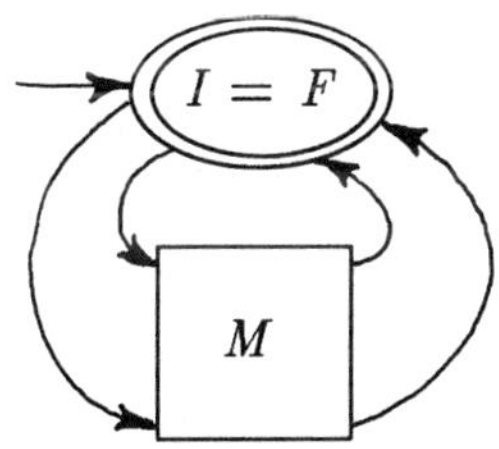

Figure 3.11. Machine for the language $(L(M))^*$.

There are minor complications in constructing the composite machine $L(M_1)L(M_2)$. Intuitively, we should attach M_2 to the end of M_1, i.e., the states I_2 and F_1 should be combined into one, and the resulting diagram should be as in Figure 3.12. This is essentially what will be done, except care has to be taken when one of the languages contains an empty string. Consider, for example, the situation when $\lambda \in L(M_1)$ (i.e., I_1 is an accepting string), and some nonempty string σ is in $L(M_2)$. The string σ is then, of course, in $L(M_1)L(M_2)$, but there is no way for σ to be "sent through M_1 to reach M_2."

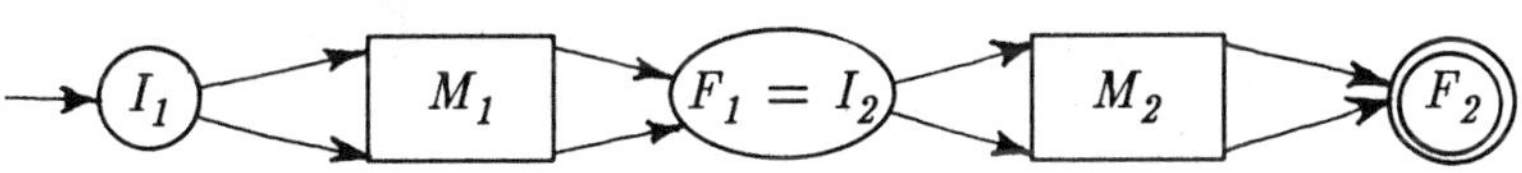

Figure 3.12. Hypothetical machine for $L(M_1)L(M_2)$.

To circumvent this, we have to consider several cases depicted in Figure 3.13. A moment of reflection shows that these machines will accept the language $L(M_1)L(M_2)$ in all four cases. Q.E.D.

Case I: $\lambda \notin L(M_1)$ and $\lambda \notin L(M_2)$—I_1 is nonaccepting and I_2 is nonaccepting.

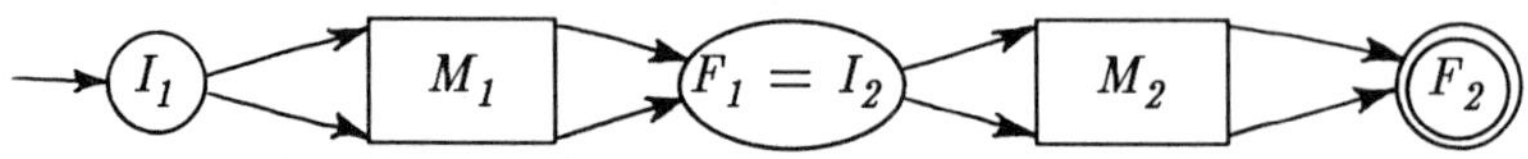

Case II: $\lambda \notin L(M_1)$ and $\lambda \in L(M_2)$—I_1 is nonaccepting and I_2 is accepting.

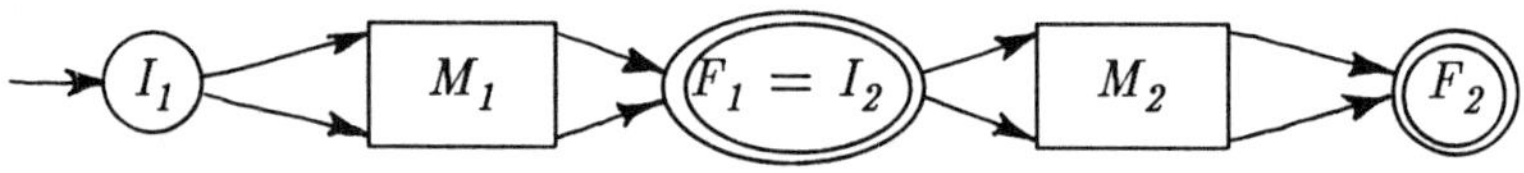

Case III: $\lambda \in L(M_1)$ and $\lambda \notin L(M_2)$—I_1 is accepting and I_2 is nonaccepting.

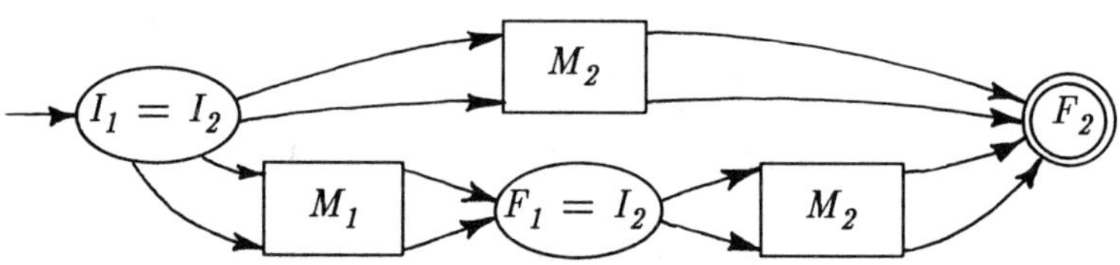

The machine M_2 must be reproduced twice.

Case IV: $\lambda \in L(M_1)$ and $\lambda \in L(M_2)$—I_1 is accepting and I_2 is accepting.

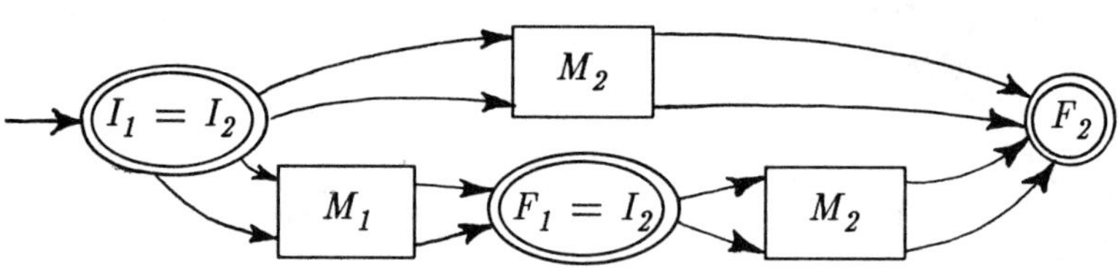

The machine M_2 must be reproduced twice.

Figure 3.13. Machines for the language $L(M_1)L(M_2)$.

Example 3.6. Let M_1 and M_2 be two finite state machines described by diagrams in Figure 3.14.

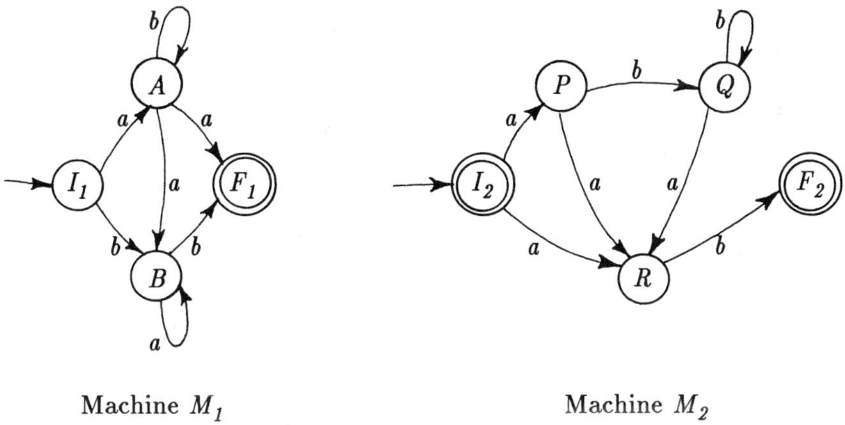

Figure 3.14. Two finite state machines.

The machines for $L(M_1) + L(M_2)$, $(L(M_2))^*$, $L(M_1)L(M_2)$, and $L(M_2)L(M_1)$ are then given by the diagrams in Figure 3.15. In the diagram for $L(M_2)L(M_1)$ the machine M_1 had to be reproduced twice, as required by Figure 3.13, Case III. To distinguish between the two copies, we denote the states of one copy of M_1 by I_1, A, B, F_1, and the states of the other copy by $\overline{I}_1$, $\overline{A}$, $\overline{B}$, and $\overline{F}_1$.

We have thus proved Theorem 3.3: A language is regular if and only if it can be described by a regular expression. Before giving an example of a construction of a finite state machines from a regular expressions, we prove one additional property of regular languages. If L is a language over an alphabet Σ, denote by $\overline{L}$ the language of all strings from Σ^* which do not belong to L—this language is called the complement of L. If L_1 and L_2 are two languages, denote by $L_1 \cap L_2$ all the strings which are in both languages L_1 and L_2. (This is not to be confused with the language L_1L_2 of all strings from L_1 concatenated with all strings from L_2.) We have the following.

Theorem 3.6. Suppose L, L_1, and L_2 are regular languages. Then all of the following languages are also regular: L^*, L_1L_2, $L_1 + L_2$, $\overline{L}$, $L_1 \cap L_2$.

Proof. The only languages not covered by Theorem 3.6 are the

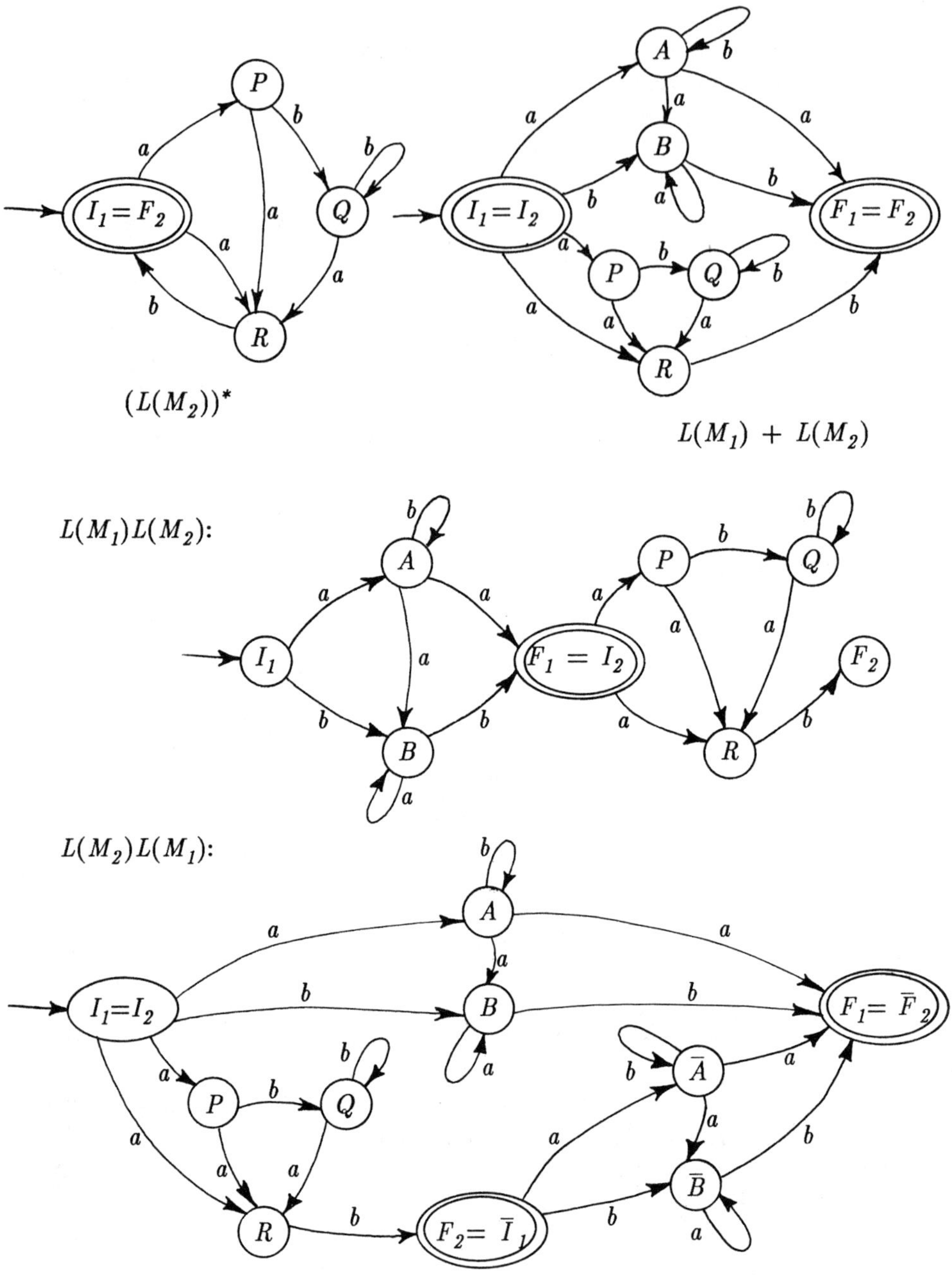

Figure 3.15. Combinations of machines.

languages $\bar{L}$ and $L_1 \cap L_2$. If L is a regular language, let M be a finite state machine accepting L. Now construct a finite state machine $\bar{M}$ by interchanging the accepting and the nonaccepting states of M—the nonaccepting states will become accepting and vice versa. It is clear that $\overline{L} = L(\overline{M})$, thus $\overline{L}$ is also a regular language. Finally, it is easy to see that $L_1 \cap L_2 = \overline{\overline{L_1} + \overline{L_2}}$, so $L_1 \cap L_2$ is also a regular language. Q.E.D.

Example 3.7. We construct a finite state machine recognizing the language **01(10)* + 1(1* + 0)**. We proceed step by step. Machines for **01** and **10** are

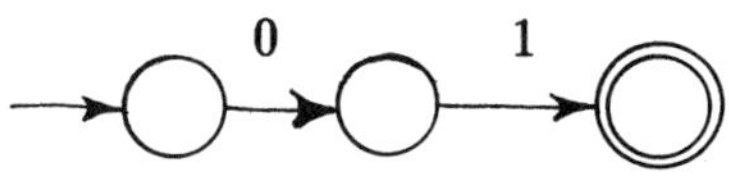

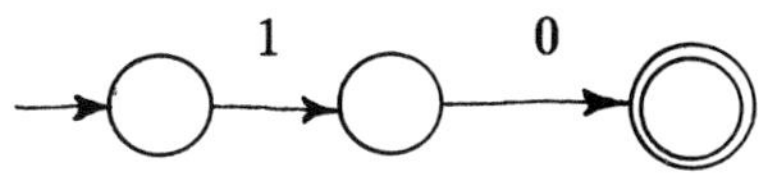

The machine for **(10)*** is, by Theorem 3.6,

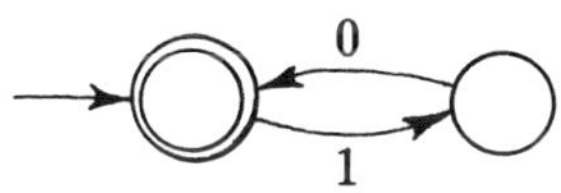

The straight machine for **(10)*** is, by Lemma 3.2,

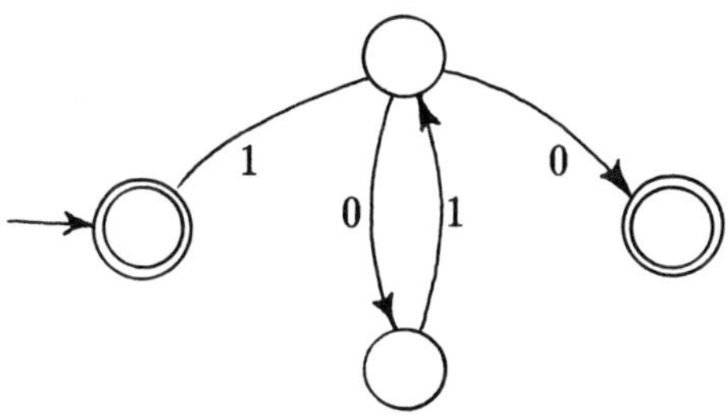

Thus, the machine for **01(10)*** is (Theorem 3.6)

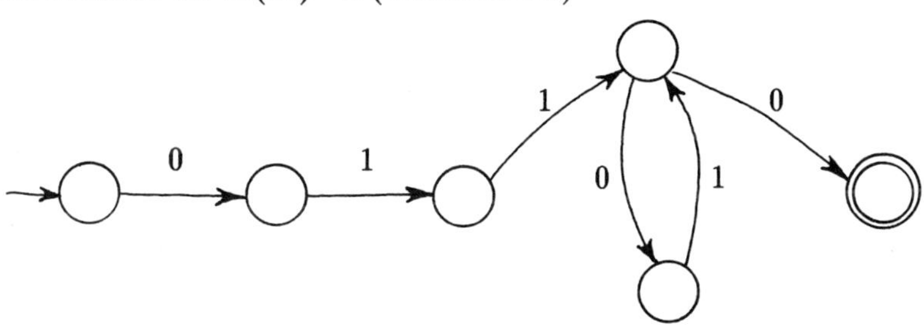

The straight machine for **01(10)*** is, by Lemma 3.2,

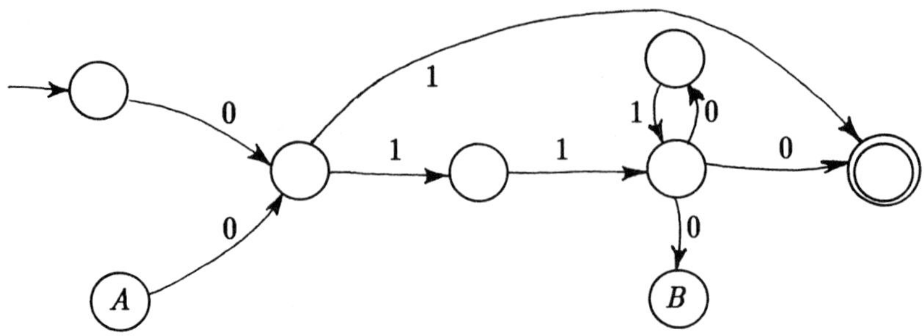

(Notice that states A and B may be removed)

The machines for **1** and **1*** are (Theorem 3.6)

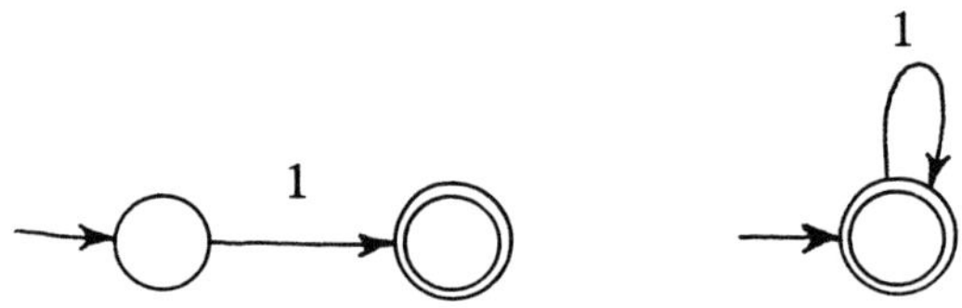

The straight machine for **1*** is (Lemma 3.2)

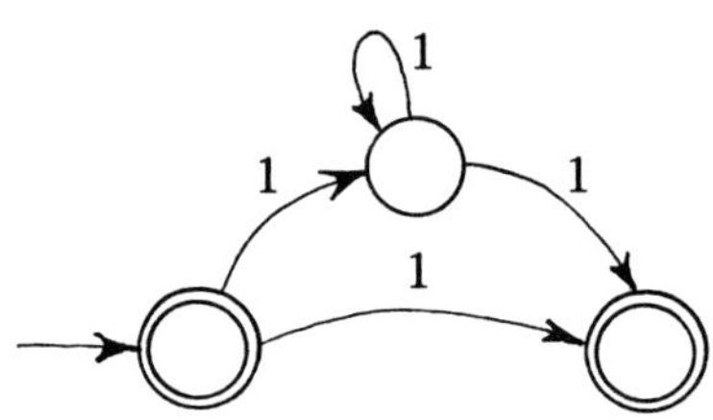

The machine for **1*** + **0** is then

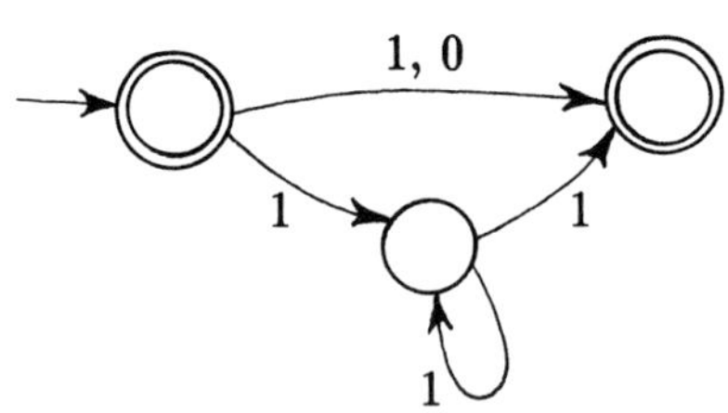

And thus, the machine for $\mathbf{1(1^* + 0)}$ is (Theorem 3.6)

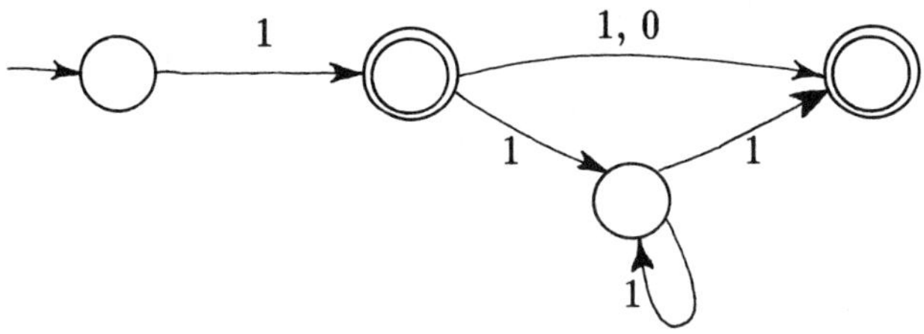

The straight machine for $\mathbf{1(1^* + 0)}$ is then

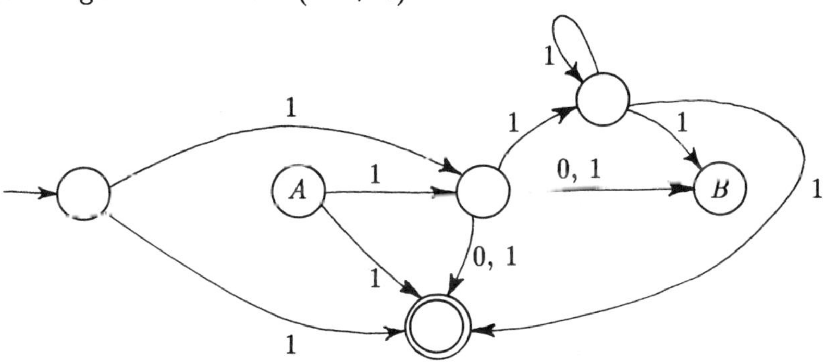

(Notice that the states A and B may be removed)

Finally, the machine for $\mathbf{01(10)^* + 1(1^* + 0)}$ is, by Theorem 3.6

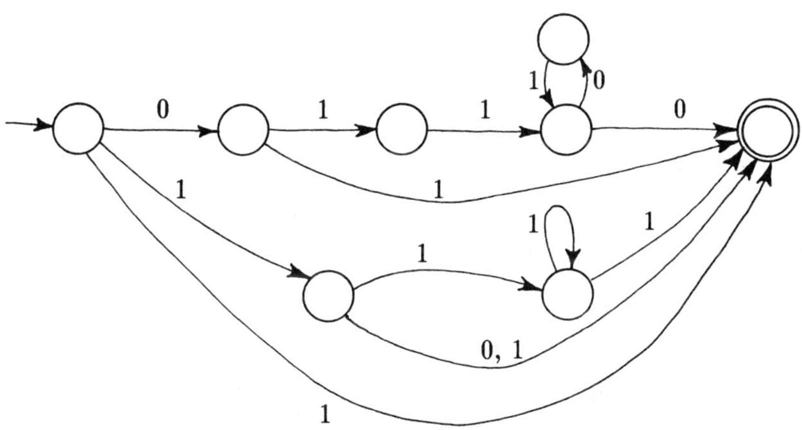

3.4. MACHINES WITH OUTPUT

It is often convenient to consider finite state machines that, in addition to moving through the internal states, also have an output device. As an example, suppose we receive a stream of 0's and 1's and wish to ring a bell each time three or more 1's are received in succession. For instance, in the sequence

$$0\,1\,1\,0\,1\,1\,\underset{\uparrow}{1}\,\underset{\uparrow}{1}\,0\,1\,1\,\underset{\uparrow}{1}\,0\,0\,1\,0$$

an arrow ↑ indicates when the bell is to be rung. One way of formally describing such a process is as follows: Consider a finite state machine M having 4 states, which we suggestively denote by [00], [01], [10], and [11]. If a string of 0's and 1's is $\epsilon_1\epsilon_2 \ldots \epsilon_{k-1}\epsilon_k \ldots$, we stipulate that upon receiving symbol ϵ_k the machine is in the state $[\epsilon_{k-1}\epsilon_k]$ (each ϵ_j is either 0 or 1). After receiving two ϵ's, the initial state is specified and further movements of the machine are determined by the diagram in Figure 3.16.

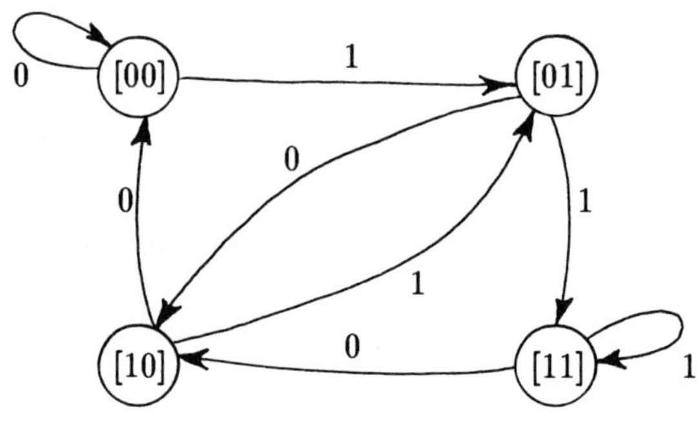

Figure 3.16. Machine with output.

Thus, for instance, suppose the first two symbols received were 00 so that the machine begins its operation with the initial state being [00]. Suppose also that the subsequent symbols are 101110. The machine then will go through the following sequence of transitions:

$$[00] \xrightarrow{1} [01] \xrightarrow{0} [10] \xrightarrow{1} [01] \xrightarrow{1} [11] \xrightarrow{1} [11] \xrightarrow{0} [10]$$

In view of the requirement of the problem, some action has to be taken (the bell is to be rung) when the machine moves from the state [11], on the input 1, back to the state [11], that is during the transition

$[11] \xrightarrow{1} [11]$, and some other action is to be taken (i.e., the bell is not to be rung) during all other transitions. This may be described mathematically by a function $F(Q, x)$, where Q is a state and x is an input symbol. In the example under discussion the function F is given by

$$F(Q, x) = \begin{cases} A \text{ if } Q = [11] \text{ and } x = 1 \\ B \text{ in all other cases} \end{cases} \tag{3.18}$$

Thus, $F(Q, x)$ describes the output of the machine during the transition from Q to $\delta(Q, x)$ (δ is the transition function of our machine). Machines of this type are called Mealy machines, see [16]. Formally, we have the following:

Definition 3.5. A ***Mealy machine*** Me is a pair $Me = (M, F)$, where M is an ordinary finite state machine and $F = F(Q, x)$ is a function defined for all states Q and all input symbols x, and taking values in some nonempty set S ($F\colon \mathcal{Q} \times \Sigma \mapsto S$, where $\mathcal{Q}$ is the collection of the states of M and Σ is the input alphabet of M). The set S is called the output alphabet of Me.

The interpretation of F is that during the transition $Q \xrightarrow{x} \hat{Q}$ the machine generates the output $F(Q, x)$. As in the case of finite state machines, Mealy machines may be deterministic or nondeterministic, depending upon whether the underlying finite automaton is deterministic or not. A convenient way of describing a Mealy machine is by the use of diagrams similar to those used to describe finite automata. Suppose a machine is in state Q and the input symbol is x, so that the next state is $\hat{Q} = \delta(Q, x)$ and the output is $X = F(Q, x)$. This is indicated in the diagram by

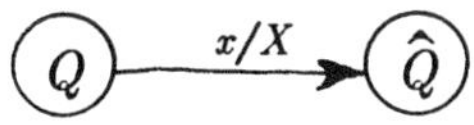

Hence, the finite state machine from Figure 3.16, in conjunction with the output function from (3.18), gives a Mealy machine whose diagram is shown in Figure 3.17.

Example 3.8. Suppose we receive a stream of symbols, each one of which is 0, 1, or 2, and we wish to construct a machine that will emit symbol a whenever the sum of three consecutive symbols is 0, 1, or 4; will emit symbol b when the sum of three consecutive symbols is 2 or 3; and will emit symbol c when the sum of three consecutive symbols is 5 or

6. The Mealy machine *Me* simulating this situation may be described as follows. The input alphabet is the set $\Sigma = \{0, 1, 2\}$. The states are the pairs $[xy]$, where x and y are in Σ—the machine is in the state $[xy]$ if the last two input symbols are x and y (in that order).There are 9 such states, and after the first two symbols are received, the initial state is determined.

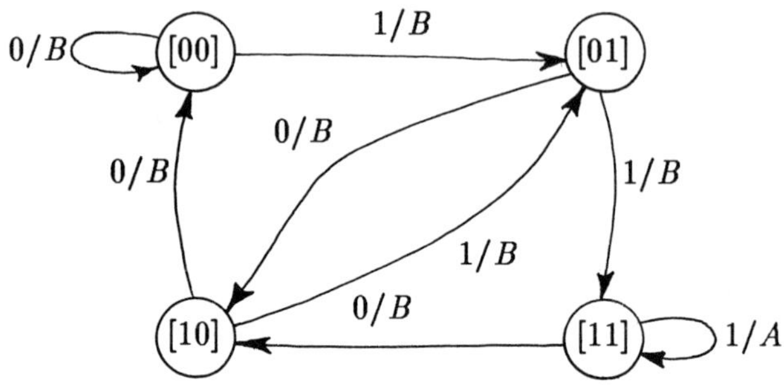

Figure 3.17. A Mealy machine.

The entire diagram of such a machine is too complex to draw here; a fragment of it is given in Figure 3.18.

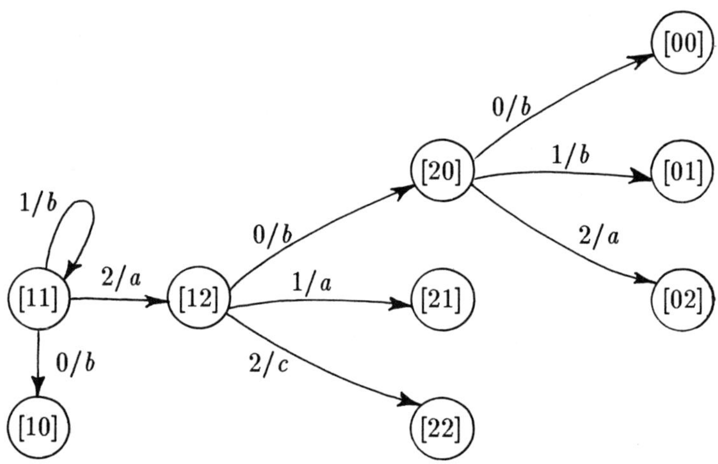

Figure 3.18. A fragment of Mealy machine.

For example,the transition $[12] \xrightarrow{1/a} [21]$ means that if the machine is in the state [12] and the input 1 is received, the machine changes to state [21], and outputs symbol a during the transition. This corresponds to the specification of the machine, since being in the state [12] means the last two received symbols were 1 and 2 in that order. The input 1 makes the sum of the last three inputs equal to 4, so the output a is called for and the next state is [21]. The entire machine Me may be presented in tabular form, as in Figure 3.19. In the table in Figure 3.19, $\delta(Q, x)$ denotes the next state and $F(Q, x)$ denotes the output of the machine during the transition from Q to $\delta(Q, x)$.

Present state Q	Input symbol					
	0		1		2	
	$\delta(Q, 0)$	$F(Q, 0)$	$\delta(Q, 1)$	$F(Q, 1)$	$\delta(Q, 2)$	$F(Q, 2)$
[00]	[00]	a	[01]	a	[02]	b
[01]	[10]	a	[11]	b	[12]	b
[02]	[20]	b	[21]	b	[22]	a
[10]	[00]	a	[01]	b	[02]	b
[11]	[10]	b	[11]	b	[12]	c
[12]	[20]	b	[21]	a	[22]	c
[20]	[00]	b	[01]	b	[02]	b
[21]	[10]	b	[11]	a	[12]	c
[22]	[20]	a	[21]	c	[22]	c

Figure 3.19. Transition table of a Mealy machine.

Suppose, for instance, that the first two symbols received are 2, 0, so that the initial state is [20], and the next four inputs are 1, 2, 2, 0. The machine will make the following sequence of moves:

$$[20] \xrightarrow{1/b} [01] \xrightarrow{2/b} [12] \xrightarrow{2/c} [22] \xrightarrow{0/a} [20]$$

Thus, the input sequence 1, 2, 2, 0 produces the output sequence b, b, c, a.

There is another way of associating an output with a finite state machine, and that is to stipulate that this output takes place during the time the machine remains in some state (and not during the transition between the states, as is the case for Mealy machines). For instance, consider again the problem of a stream of 0's and 1's in which we wish to signal an occurrence of three successive 1's. Another way to simulate this situation is to consider a finite state machine with 8 states:

$$[000] \quad [001] \quad [010] \quad [011] \quad [100] \quad [101] \quad [110] \quad [111].$$

The interpretation of the state $[\epsilon_1\epsilon_2\epsilon_3]$ is that the three most recent symbols received are ϵ_1, ϵ_2, and ϵ_3 (in that order). The transition function δ is easily defined:

$$\delta([\epsilon_1\epsilon_2\epsilon_3], \epsilon_4) = [\epsilon_2\epsilon_3\epsilon_4]$$

As soon as three symbols are received, the initial state is established and the machine proceeds to move through the states. We now construct an output function G, defined for each state by

$$G([\epsilon_1\epsilon_2\epsilon_3]) = \begin{cases} A & \text{if } [\epsilon_1\epsilon_2\epsilon_3] = [111] \\ B & \text{in all other cases} \end{cases}$$

This function G depends only on the state of the machine, unlike the output function F of Mealy machines, which depends both on the state and the input. Machines of this kind are called Moore machines, see [17]. Formally, their definition is as follows.

Definition 3.6. A ***Moore machine*** Mo consists of two objects:

1. A finite state machine
2. A function $G(Q)$ defined for all states Q of Mo and taking values in some nonempty set S, called the output alphabet of Mo

As in the case of finite automata and Mealy machines, the Moore machines can be conveniently represented by a diagram. In such a diagram, each state will be represented by a pair (Q, X), where Q is a state and $X = G(Q)$ is the output associated with the state Q. For instance, the Moore machine just described (detecting an occurrence of three 1's in a stream of 0's and 1's) has a diagram depicted in Figure 3.20. This should be compared with a diagram of the Mealy machine for the same problem. The essential difference is the output function.

When the empty string λ is presented to a Mealy machine, it produces no output since no transition takes place. The Moore machine, on the other hand, will produce the output $G(Q_0)$ associated with the initial state. Thus, on a given input, the output of a Moore machine will always be one symbol longer than the output of a Mealy machine. For example, suppose the initial state of the Mealy machine from Figure 3.17 is [00] and the initial state of the Moore machine from Figure 3.20 is [000].

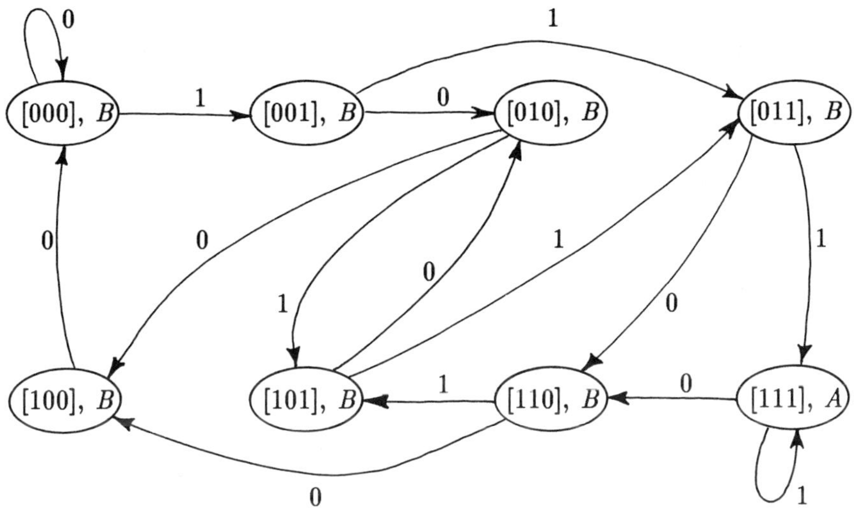

Figure 3.20. A Moore machine.

If the input $\sigma = 11101$ is given, the Mealy machine will produce an output $BBABB$, while the output of the Moore machine will be $BBBABB$ —it has one extra B in front. For this reason, strictly speaking, it is impossible to construct a Mealy machine that is equivalent to a given Moore machine, and conversely. If, however, we disregard the initial symbol of the output of a Moore machine, the two devices turn out to be equivalent. We now introduce the following definitions.

Definition 3.7. Let M be either a Mealy or a Moore machine. For each input string σ let $H_M(\sigma)$ denote the output string generated by M on the input σ. We say that two machines M and $\bar{M}$ (both either Mealy or Moore) are ***equivalent*** if for every input σ we have $H_M(\sigma) = H_{\bar{M}}(\sigma)$.

Let M be a Mealy machine and let K be a Moore machine. We say that M and K are ***equivalent*** if for every input string σ we have $H_K(\sigma) = XH_M(\sigma)$, where X is some symbol from the output alphabet. In other words, both M and K will produce the same outputs on the same inputs, provided we disregard the initial symbol of the output of K.

It turns out that with this definition, given a machine of one kind one can construct an equivalent machine of the other kind.

Theorem 3.8. If M is a Mealy machine, there exists a Moore machine K that is equivalent to M. Conversely, given a Moore machine K, there is a Mealy machine M equivalent to K.

Proof. Let M be a Mealy machine with states Q_0 (initial state), Q_1, . . . , Q_n, output alphabet $\{X_1, \ldots, X_m\}$, input alphabet $\{x_1, \ldots, x_j\}$ and output function $F(Q, x)$. The states of the corresponding Moore machine K will be all possible pairs $\{Q, X\}$, where Q is a state of M and X is an output symbol of M. The initial state of K is taken to be $\{Q_0, X_1\}$. The output function G of K is defined by

$$G(\{Q, X\}) = X$$

The transitions of K are defined by the following rule:

$$\text{If } Q \xrightarrow{x/X} \hat{Q} \text{ is a transition of } M\text{, then } \{Q, B\} \xrightarrow{x} \{\hat{Q}, X\} \text{ is a transition of } K \text{ for all output symbols } B \tag{3.19}$$

In other words, if the transition diagram of M contains the fragment

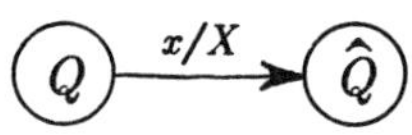

then the transition diagram of K will contain a fragment

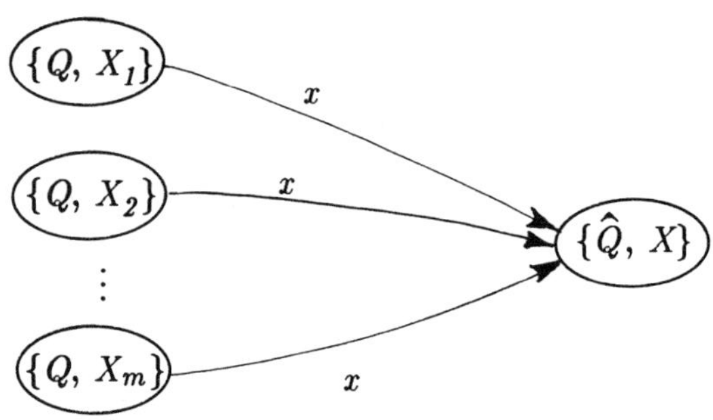

It is clear that if M, on input $\hat{x}_1\hat{x}_2 \ldots \hat{x}_r$, goes through the sequence of states $\hat{Q}_0(= Q_0)$, $\hat{Q}_1, \ldots, \hat{Q}_r$ and emits output $\hat{X}_1\hat{X}_2 \ldots \hat{X}_r$, then the machine K will go through the sequence of states $\{Q_0, X_1\}$, $\{\hat{Q}_1, \hat{X}_1\}$, $\{\hat{Q}_2, \hat{X}_2\}$, . . . ,$\{\hat{Q}_r, \hat{X}_r\}$ and emit the same output $X_1\hat{X}_1\hat{X}_2 \ldots \hat{X}_r$ (aside from the initial symbol X_1). Indeed, the first transition of M is

$$\hat{Q}_0 \xrightarrow{\hat{x}_1/\hat{X}_1} \hat{Q}_1$$

that is, M changes the state to $\hat{Q}_1$ and emits symbol $\hat{X}_1$. Now, K starts in the state $\{Q_0, X_1\}$ so it emits symbol X_1 and upon input $\hat{x}_1$ it moves to $\{\hat{Q}_1, \hat{X}_1\}$, where it emits symbol $\hat{X}_1$, see (3.19). The second transitions of K and M are thus, by (3.19),

$$Q_1 \xrightarrow{x_2/\hat{X}_2} \hat{Q}_2 \quad \text{and} \quad \{\hat{Q}_1, \hat{X}_1\} \xrightarrow{x_2} \{\hat{Q}_2, \hat{X}_2\}$$

so that $\hat{X}_2$ is the second symbol emitted by M, and $\hat{X}_2$ is the third symbol emitted by K. Continuing this argument, we see that M and K are equivalent.

To construct a Mealy machine from a given Moore machine K we proceed as follows. Denote the states of K by Q_0 (the initial state), Q_1, $Q_2, \ldots, Q_n$, the output symbols by $X_1, \ldots, X_m$, and the input symbols by $x_1, x_2, \ldots, x_j$. Let $G(Q)$ be the output function of K (it depends only on the state Q). The states, and the input and the output alphabets of M, will be the same as those of K. We can think of each state of K as a pair $\{Q, G(Q)\}$, where Q is a state and $G(Q)$ is the output symbol emitted by K while in the state Q. The transition and the output function of M are given by the following rule:

$$\text{If } \{Q, X\} \xrightarrow{x} \{\hat{Q}, \hat{X}\} \text{ is a transition of } K$$

$$\text{then } Q \xrightarrow{x/\hat{X}} \hat{Q} \text{ is a transition of } M. \tag{3.20}$$

In terms of the transition diagram, each fragment of the transition diagram of K in Figure 3.21(a) generates a fragment of the transition diagram of M as in Figure 3.21(b).

$$\{Q, X\} \xrightarrow{x} \{\hat{Q}, \hat{X}\} \qquad\qquad Q \xrightarrow{x/\hat{X}} \hat{Q}$$

(a) (b)

Figure 3.21. Mealy and Moore transitions.

It is quite clear that if, on input $\hat{x}_1\hat{x}_2 \ldots \hat{x}_r$, the machine K goes through the sequence of states $\{Q_0, X_0\}, \{\hat{Q}_1, \hat{X}_1\}, \ldots, \{\hat{Q}_r, \hat{X}_r\}$

emitting the symbols X_0, $\hat{X}_1$, . . ., $\hat{X}_r$, then M will go through the sequence of states Q_0, $\hat{Q}_1$, . . . , $\hat{Q}_r$ emitting the symbols $\hat{X}_1$, $\hat{X}_2$, . . . , $\hat{X}_r$. Q.E.D.

Example 3.9. Consider the Mealy machine given by the diagram in Figure 3.22.

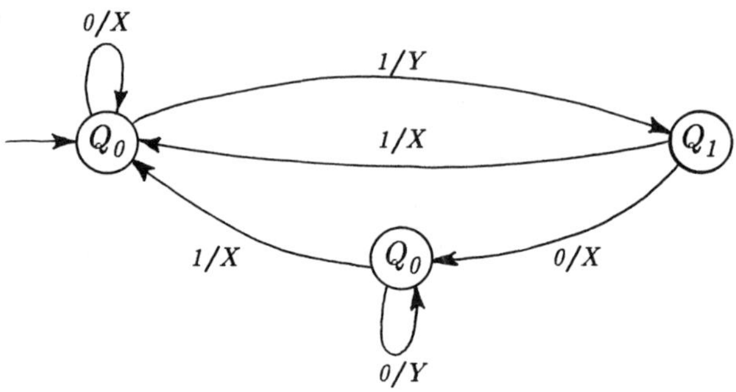

Figure 3.22. A Mealy machine.

The corresponding equivalent Moore machine has six states $\{Q_0, X\}$ (= the initial state), $\{Q_0, Y\}$, $\{Q_1, X\}$, $\{Q_1, Y\}$, $\{Q_2, X\}$, and $\{Q_2, Y\}$. Its transition diagram is given by Figure 3.23.

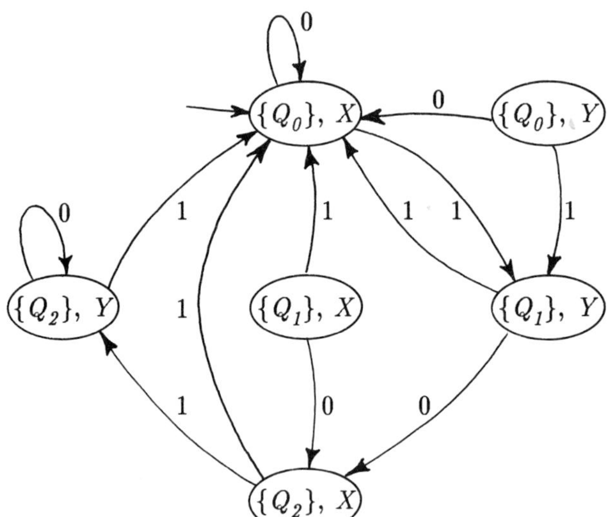

Figure 3.23. A Moore machine.

For example, the transition $\{Q_1, Y\} \xrightarrow{1} \{Q_0, X\}$ of the Moore machine is included because $Q_1 \xrightarrow{1/X} Q_0$ is a transition of the Mealy machine. This last transition is also responsible for $\{Q_1, X\} \xrightarrow{1} \{Q_0, Y\}$. Similarly, $\{Q_2, Y\} \xrightarrow{0} \{Q_2, Y\}$ is included because $Q_2 \xrightarrow{0/Y} Q_2$ generates $\{Q_2, X\} \xrightarrow{0} \{Q_2, Y\}$ and $\{Q_2, Y\} \xrightarrow{0} \{Q_2, Y\}$. The machine from Figure 3.23 can be simplified somewhat, for example the states $\{Q_1, X\}$ and $\{Q_0, Y\}$ may be removed because they are inaccessible.

Example 3.10. Consider a Moore machine as in Figure 3.24(a). The corresponding Mealy machine is drawn in Figure 3.24(b). For example, the transition $\{Q_1, Y\} \xrightarrow{1} \{Q_2, Y\}$ induces transition $Q_1 \xrightarrow{1/Y} Q_2$, $\{Q_2, Y\} \xrightarrow{1} \{Q_3, Y\}$ induces $Q_2 \xrightarrow{1/Y} Q_3$, etc. On the input 100 the Moore machine will produce the output $XYXY$, while the Mealy machine emits the output YXY. These outputs are considered identical, since in comparing them we disregard the initial character of the output of the Moore machine.

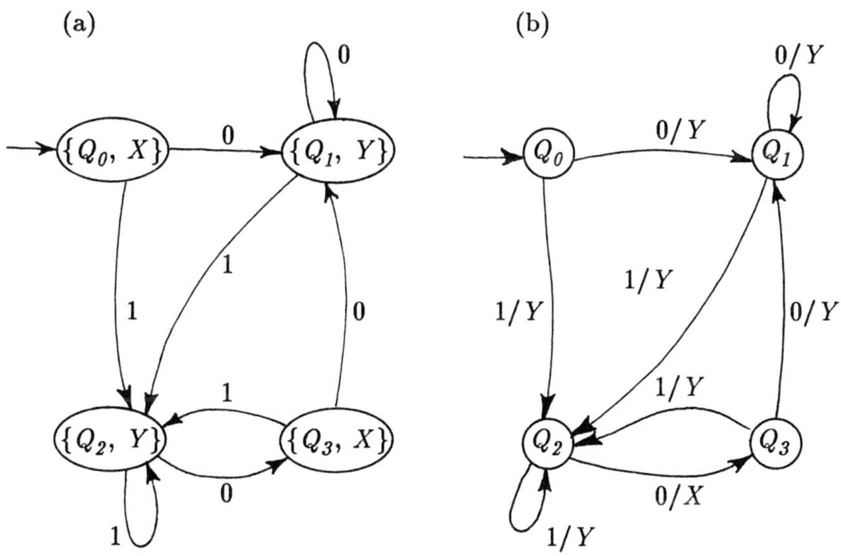

Figure 3.24. Mealy and Moore machines.

PROBLEMS

In each of problems 1–7, show that the given language is not regular.

1. $L = \{a^{2n}b^n c^n \mid n = 1, 2, 3, \ldots\}$
2. $L = \{a^n b^n c^n \mid n = 0, 1, 2, \ldots\}$
3. $L = \{a^n b c^n \mid n = 0, 1, 2, \ldots\}$
4. $L = \{a^{3n} b^n \mid n = 1, 2, 3, \ldots\}$
5. $L = \{a^{n+m} b^n c^n \mid n, m = 1, 2, 3, \ldots\}$
6. $L = \{a^n b^m c^{n-m} \mid n, m = 0, 1, 2, \ldots\}$
7. $L = \{(a^n b)^p (c^m d)^p \mid n, m, p = 0, 1, 2, \ldots\}$

In each of problems 7–14, write down the regular expression describing the given language.

8. $L = \{\sigma \in \{0, 1\}^* \mid \sigma$ has a substring $111\}$
9. $L = \{\sigma \in \{a, b\}^* \mid \sigma$ has substrings aa and $bb\}$
10. $L = \{\sigma \in \{a, b\}^* \mid$ The length of σ is divisible by $3\}$
11. L is the language of all strings from $\{a, b, c\}$ that contain even number of a's.
12. $L = \{\sigma \in \{0, 1\}^* \mid \sigma$ begins with 0 and has an even number of 1's$\}$
13. $L = \{\sigma \in \{a, b, c\}^* \mid$ There are no a's to the right of any b in $\sigma\}$
14. $L = \{\sigma \in \{a, b, c\}^* \mid \sigma$ has no two consecutive a's$\}$
15. Prove or disprove the following assertions about regular expressions:

    a. $(rs + r)^* r = r(sr + r)^*$
    b. $(a + b)^* = a^*(ba^*)^*$
    c. $(a + b)^* = a^* + b^*$
    d. $a + (a + bc)^* = (a + bc)^*$
    e. $(x + y)^* = (x^* + y)^*$
    f. $(a^* b)^* = \lambda + (a + b)^* b$

16. Construct a finite state machine that accepts each of the following languages:

    a. $1^*(0 + 11) + 1(0^* + 10) + \lambda$
    b. $(ab + ba)^* + 1$
    c. $a^*(b + c)(a^* + b^*)$
    d. $(a + b^* c)^*$
    e. $((bc)^* + a)^*(ac + b^* c)$
    f. $(a + (ab + a)^*)^* + b$

17. Find a regular expression describing the language accepted by each of the machines in Figure 3.25.
18. Construct a straight machine equivalent to each one of the FSM in Figure 3.25(a) and (b).

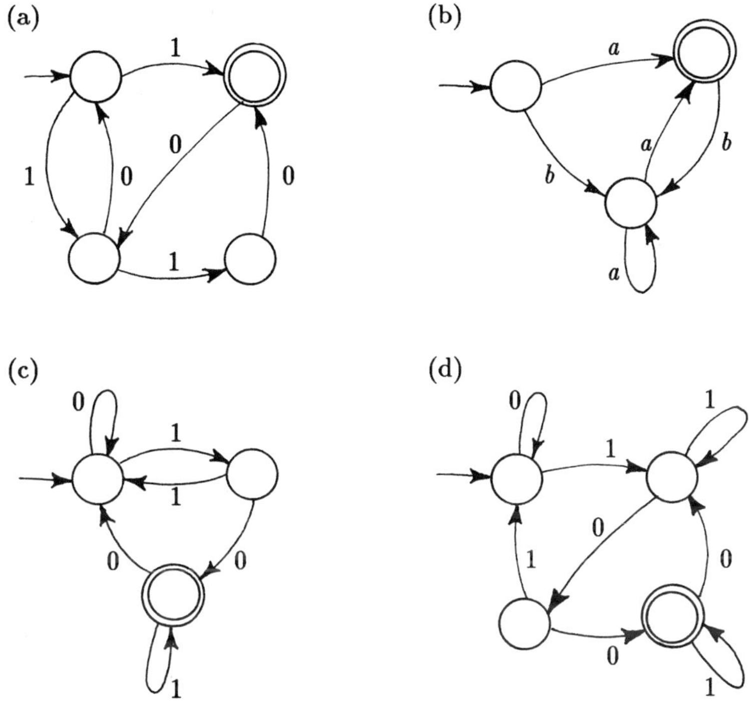

Figure 3.25. Finite state machines.

19. Construct a Moore machine equivalent to each one of the Mealy machines from Figure 3.26.

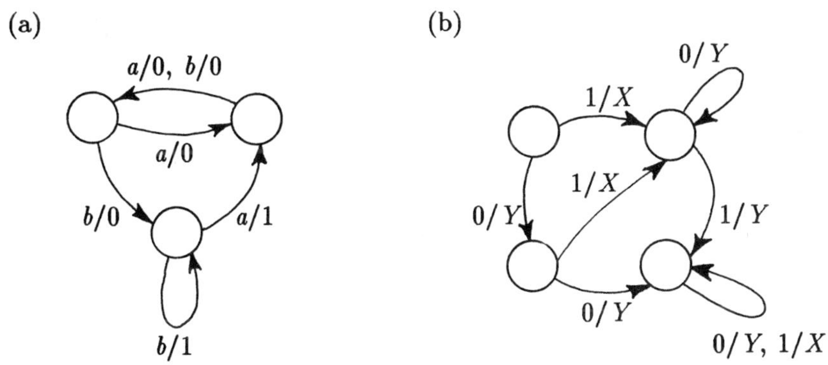

Figure 3.26. Some Mealy machines.

20. Construct a Mealy machine equivalent to each one of the Moore machines from Figure 3.27.

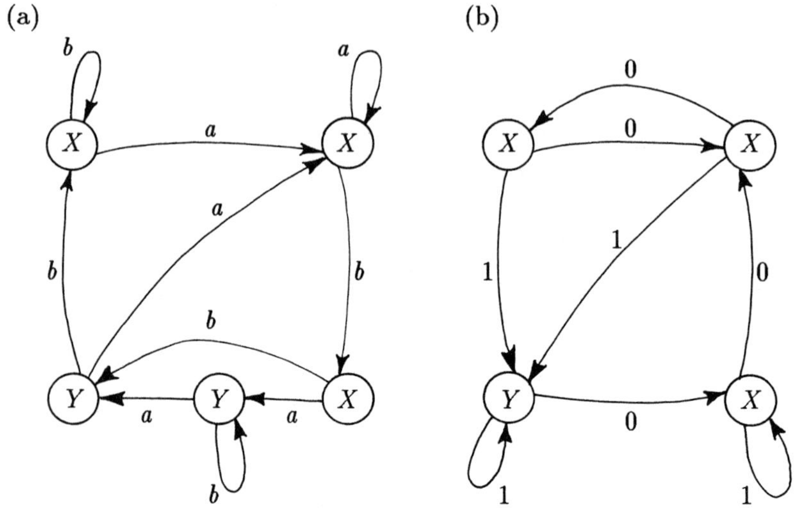

Figure 3.27. Some Moore machines.

CHAPTER 4

PUSH-DOWN AUTOMATA

4.1. DEFINITION OF A PUSH-DOWN AUTOMATON

We saw in Chapter 3 that there exist context-free grammars G for which it is impossible to construct a finite state machine that would recognize the language $L(G)$. The example given was the language $L = \{0^n 1^n \mid n = 1, 2, \ldots\}$, i.e., the language consisting of n 0's followed by n 1's. Heuristically, the reason that there is no FSM that can recognize L is that any finite state machine encountering a string from this language would have to "remember" how many 0's occur in front of the string, and then check that the number of 1's that follow is the same. Thus, any machine that recognizes L should have a "memory" capable of storing an arbitrarily large amount of information. Since by definition finite state machines possess only a finite number of states, they cannot recognize the language L. The precise proof is, of course, not couched in such vague terms as these, and is given in Section 3.1. We now introduce another kind of device, one that can remember the past inputs and its own past behavior. These devices are called the push-down automata; they have the advantage of being easily implemented on a computer. It turns out that any context-free language can be recognized by such a machine.

A push-down automaton consists of a finite number of states, an input device (together with an input pointer), and a stack together with a stack pointer. It may be schematically represented as in Figure 4.1. The push-down automaton operates as follows: At any given moment the machine is in some state Q, its ***input pointer*** (IP) points at some symbol a on the input tape, and its ***stack pointer*** (SP) points at a symbol Z in the ***stack***. The location of this symbol Z is called the ***top of the stack*** (TOS). The squares below the top of the stack are filled with various allowable stack symbols and the squares above the top are considered to be empty. There is no limit on how large this stack may be, but it is always finite.

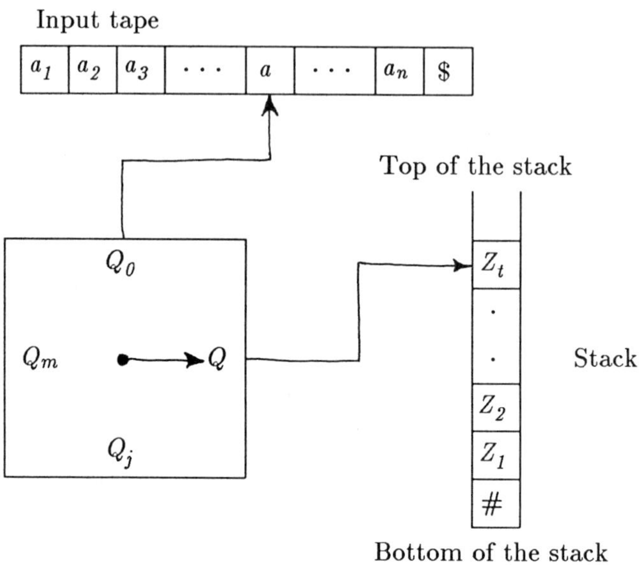

Figure 4.1. Push-down automaton.

Based on this information and this information only (i.e., on Q, a, and Z) the machine may take one or more of the following actions:

1. Change the state.
2. Move the input pointer one unit to the right.
3. Replace the symbol Z on top of the stack by a finite number (i.e., a string) of allowable stack symbols, and then readjust the stack pointer to point to the top of the stack.
4. Halt.

We emphasize once again that the decision of what is to be done is determined exclusively by Q, a, and Z. In the action of type 3 we are allowed to replace Z by the empty string λ. In that case, 3 is understood to consist of removing the symbol Z from the stack and adjusting the stack pointer one square downward. This sort of move is called a *POP*. After one or more of actions $1-3$ have taken place, the machine is (possibly) in some new state $\hat{Q}$, the input pointer points to the (possibly) new input symbol $\hat{a}$, and the stack pointer points to the (possibly) new symbol $\hat{Z}$ on top of the stack. The entire procedure is then repeated, until the machine halts. The symbols below the top of the stack are saved from move to move; they form the "memory" of the machine. The symbols of the input tape are lost once they are read—the input pointer can move only to the right. The stack pointer, however, can move up and down. The input symbols, of course, can be saved by inserting them into the stack when they are read. For a complete description of such a machine, we must, of course, specify the original configuration of the machine, that is, the initial state, the initial content of the input tape, and the initial content of the stack. For convenience, we introduce the following conventions regarding the push-down automata.

C.1. In the initial configuration the stack contains only one symbol—#. This symbol can never be removed from the stack (i.e., the stack is never empty), and it must not appear anywhere else on the stack. The location of # is called the bottom of the stack.

C.2. Any input string σ ends on the right side with the symbol \$, so that $\sigma = \sigma_1\$$, and this symbol \$ does not appear anywhere else in the input. The input pointer cannot move to the right of \$.

The reason for introducing these special symbols is so that the machine can detect the end of the input and the bottom of the stack.

As in the case of the finite state machines, the push-down automata may be deterministic or nondeterministic. In the deterministic case, given Q, a, and Z only one course of action is allowed; in the nondeterministic case at least two alternatives are exist for some situations. Each push-down automaton also has some of its states designated as accepting or final states.

Now let Σ be an alphabet not containing the symbol \$, and let L be a language over Σ. We say that a deterministic push-down automaton P ***accepts*** L if the following holds: Given a string σ, we set up the machine P in its initial state Q_0; we enter the string $\sigma\$$ on its input tape and point the input pointer to the leftmost symbol of $\sigma\$$. We also place the symbol # at the bottom of the stack and point the stack pointer to it. The machine P will then go through its motions and after a certain number of moves it will halt. If σ is in the language, then P will halt in one of the accepting states and the input pointer will point to the symbol \$ (indicating that the entire input \$ has been read). If σ is not in the language L, then P will halt in some other configuration, that is, either in a non-accepting state or without scanning the entire input σ (or both). Notice that we do not make any requirements regarding the content of the stack, for the acceptance of the string σ. The definition of acceptance of a language by a nondeterministic push-down automaton is similar to the definition of acceptance by a nondeterministic finite state machine. We say that a string σ is in the language generated by a nondeterministic push-down automaton P, if and only if, beginning from the initial configuration of P (as described above), it is possible for P, through a sequence of legal moves, to reach an accepting configuration (also as described above). Push-down automata will be abbreviated as PDA's. Before giving the formal definitions of the concepts under discussion, let us consider an example.

State Q_0		Input symbol: 0	1	$
Stack	A	Halt	Halt	Halt
	#	1. Change state to Q_1. 2. Put symbol A on the top of of the stack. 3. Move input pointer one square to the right.	Halt	Change state to Q_3, leave all pointers intact.

State Q_1		Input symbol: 0	1	$
Stack	A	1. Remain in the state Q_1. 2. Put the symbol A on the top of the stack. 3. Move input pointer right.	Change state to Q_2; leave pointers intact.	Halt
	#	Halt	Halt	Halt

State Q_2		Input symbol: 0	1	$
Stack	A	Halt	1. Remain in the state Q_2. 2. Remove A from the top of the stack. 3. Move input pointer right.	Halt
	#	Halt	Halt	Change state to Q_3, leave pointers intact.

State Q_3: Halt in all situations.

Figure 4.2. A push-down automata for the language $\{0^n1^n \mid n = 0, 1, \ldots\}$.

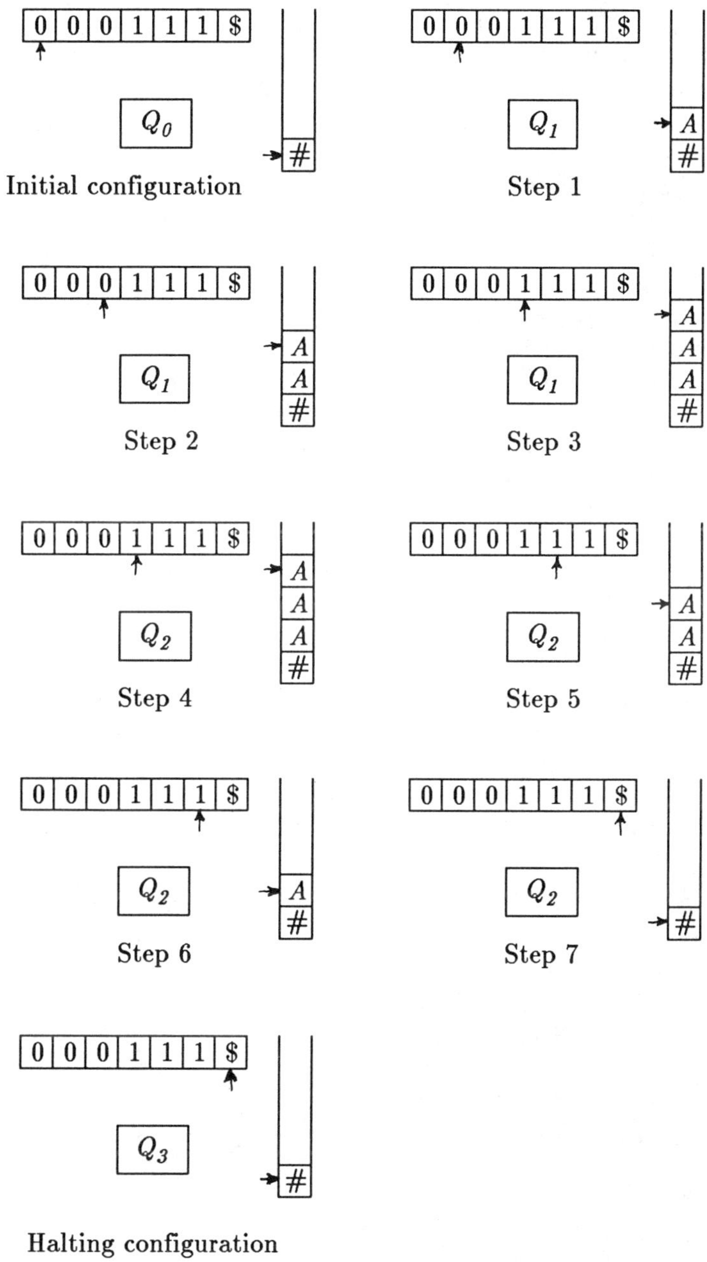

Figure 4.3. Movements of a PDA on the input 000111.

Example 4.1. Consider a push-down automaton P accepting the language $L = \{0^n 1^n \mid n = 0, 1, 2, \ldots\}$. This PDA will have four states Q_0 (= the initial state), Q_1, Q_2, and Q_3 (the accepting state). The input alphabet Σ is, of course, $\Sigma = \{0, 1\}$. The allowable stack symbol, in addition to #, will be A. Roughly speaking, the machine will operate as follows. Each time the input symbol is 0, the symbol A is added to the stack (from the top). Thus, when all the 0's are read the machine "knows" how many 0's were there in the input—there is one A saved on the stack for each 0 in the input. Next, when the symbol 1 is encountered, the machine proceeds to remove one A for each 1 encountered. When the symbol $ is finally reached on the input tape, the stack pointer should point to # on the bottom of the stack—the number of 1's should be the same as the number of saved A's. Any deviation from this indicates that the string σ is not in the language. The precise description of the movements of P is given in the tables in Figure 4.2, one table per state. The machine will halt in the state Q_3 with the input pointer reading $ if and only if the input string σ consists of a number of 0's followed by an equal number of 1's. In all other situations it will halt in some other state with (possibly) a portion of the input still unread. In Figure 4.3. we give the sequence of movements of this PDA on the input 000111.

It is clear that before proceeding with formal mathematical definitions, we need some notation to describe the configuration of a push-down automaton at any given time. Drawing schematic diagrams such as those in Figure 4.3. is very inconvenient. Thus, we describe a ***configuration*** of a PDA by a triple:

$$[\![\sigma\$, Q, \gamma\#]\!] = [\![x_k x_{k+1} \ldots x_p\$, \ Q, \ Z_t Z_{t-1} \ldots Z_1\#]\!]$$

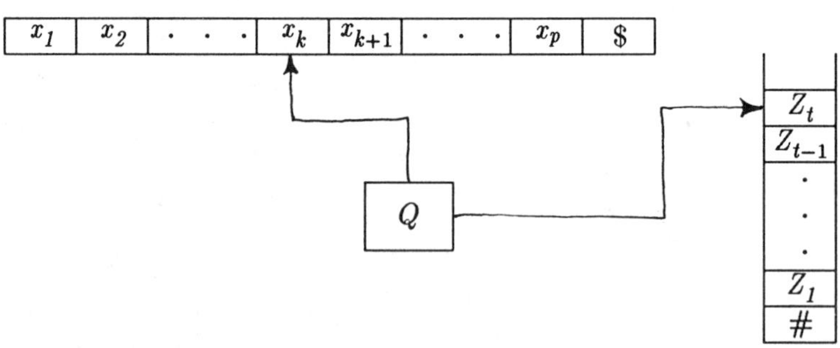

Figure 4.4. A PDA in a typical configuration $[\![x_k x_{k+1} \ldots x_p\$, Q, Z_t Z_{t-1} \ldots Z_1\#]\!]$.

The unread portion of the input is given by $\sigma\$ = x_k x_{k+1} \ldots x_p\$$, and the input pointer points to the symbol x_k. The present state is Q. The content of the stack is given by $\gamma\# = Z_t Z_{t-1} \ldots Z_1\#$, where Z_t is the top of the stack and $\#$ is the bottom of the stack. A machine in configuration (4.1) is given in Figure 4.4. With these conventions, the movements of the machine, given in Figure 4.3, can be described as follows:

$$\llbracket 000111\$,\ Q_0,\ \# \rrbracket \to \llbracket 00111\$,\ Q_1,\ A\# \rrbracket \to \llbracket 0111\$,\ Q_1,\ AA\# \rrbracket$$
$$\to \llbracket 111\$,\ Q_1,\ AAA\# \rrbracket \to \llbracket 111\$,\ Q_2,\ AAA\# \rrbracket \to \llbracket 11\$,\ Q_2,\ AA\# \rrbracket$$
$$\to \llbracket 1\$,\ Q_2,\ A\# \rrbracket \to \llbracket \$,\ Q_2,\ \# \rrbracket \to \llbracket \$,\ Q_3,\ \# \rrbracket \text{ — Halt}$$

We will also denote the input pointer by *IP* and the stack pointer by *SP*.

Definition 4.1. A ***push-down automaton***, abbreviated PDA, consists of the following six objects:

1. A nonempty set Σ of allowable input symbols. This set is called the ***input alphabet*** and it does not contain the symbol \$.
2. A nonempty set Γ of allowable stack symbols. This set is called the ***stack alphabet*** and it does not contain the symbol #.
3. A finite collection $\mathfrak{Q} = \{Q_0, Q_1, \ldots, Q_n\}$ of ***states.***
4. A distinguished state, denoted by Q_0 ($\in \mathfrak{Q}$), called the ***initial state.***
5. A nonempty collection $\mathfrak{F}$ of states, called final or ***accepting states.***
6. A ***transition function*** $\delta(Q, x, Z)$. The arguments of δ are: x—a symbol from either Σ or \$; Q—a state from $\mathfrak{Q}$, Z—a symbol from either Γ or #. The values of $\delta(Q, x, Z)$ are finite (possibly empty) collections of triples of the form $(N, \hat{Q}, \gamma)$ where
   a) N is one of the symbols $\uparrow$ or $\rightarrow$ (stay or move).
   b) $\hat{Q}$ is a state from $\mathfrak{Q}$.
   c) γ is a (possibly empty) string of characters from Γ, which may (but need not) be followed by the symbol #.

   Formally, we have of, course,

$$\delta : \mathfrak{Q} \times \left(\Sigma \cup \{\$\}\right) \times \left(\Gamma \cup \{\#\}\right) \mapsto \mathfrak{P}\left(\{\uparrow, \rightarrow\} \times \mathfrak{Q} \times \{\Gamma^* \{\# + \lambda\}\}\right)$$

   where $\mathfrak{P}(E)$ denotes the set of all possible finite subsets of a set E, and D^* denotes, as usual, the collection of all possible strings of symbols from D. Thus, $\Gamma^*\{\# + \lambda\}$, using the notation of regular expressions, is the set of strings of symbols from Γ followed either by the empty string λ or by #. The function δ satisfies, moreover, the following three conditions:

C1. For any $Q \in \mathfrak{Q}$ and any $Z \in \Gamma$, $\delta(Q, \$, Z)$ must contain only triples of the form $(\uparrow, \hat{Q}, \gamma)$. This corresponds to the requirement that the input pointer cannot move past the symbol $.

C2. For any $x \in \Sigma$ and any $Q \in \mathfrak{Q}$, $\delta(Q, x, \#)$ must contain only triples of the form $(N, \hat{Q}, \gamma\#)$, where γ is a string of elements from Γ. This corresponds to the requirement that the symbol # cannot be removed from the bottom of the stack: if we replace # by $\gamma\#$, the symbol # stays on the bottom of the stack.

C3. For any $x \in \Sigma$, any $Q \in \mathfrak{Q}$, and any $Z \in \Gamma (Z \neq \#)$, $\delta(Q, x, Z)$ must contain only triples of the form $(N, \hat{Q}, \gamma)$, where γ is a string from Γ^* that does not end with #. This corresponds to the requirement that # does not appear anywhere on the stack, except on the bottom.

A push-down automaton with Σ, Γ, $\mathfrak{Q}$, Q_0, $\mathfrak{F}$, and δ as above will be denoted by $P = \{\Sigma, \Gamma, \mathfrak{Q}, Q_0, \mathfrak{F}, \delta\}$.

The function δ in the above definition describes the possible movements of the machine. The arguments x, Q, and Z of δ are, respectively, the current input, the current state, and the content of the top of the stack. The machine defined by Definition 4.1 is nondeterministic, so the value of δ is the collection of possible moves from a given configuration (there may be more than one). Each such possible move is described by a triple $(N, \hat{Q}, \gamma)$. If $N = \uparrow$ then the input pointer does not change—the same input symbol is read again during the next move; if $N = \rightarrow$ then the input pointer moves one square to the right. $\hat{Q}$ denotes the next state of the machine. The meaning of γ is as follows: If $(N, \hat{Q}, \gamma)$ is one of the triples of $\delta(Q, x, \gamma)$, then the top of the stack Z is removed and replaced by the string γ. (The leftmost character of γ becomes the new top of the stack.) Condition C1 stipulates that the input pointer may not move past the symbol $. Condition C2 insures that # is never removed from the bottom of the stack and C3 guarantees that # does not appear anywhere on the stack except the bottom. The machine halts if $\delta(Q, x, Z) = \emptyset$—the empty set. A push-down automaton is said to be deterministic if, for each x, Q, and Z, the value of $\delta(Q, x, Z)$ either is empty, or contains only one triple. We now formally describe the movements of a push-down automaton.

Definition 4.2. Let P be a push-down automaton. A ***configuration*** of

P is a triple $[\![\sigma\$, Q, \gamma\#]\!]$, where σ is a string of characters from Σ and γ is a string of characters from Γ. (Both strings may be empty.) Let $[\![xy \ldots \$, Q, ZW \ldots \#]\!]$ be a configuration of P and let $(N, \hat{Q}, \gamma)$ be a triple from $\delta(Q, x, Z)$.

If $N = \uparrow$ then we say that $[\![xy \ldots \$, \hat{Q}, \gamma W \ldots \#]\!]$ is a ***next legal configuration*** and denote this by

$$[\![xy \ldots \$, Q, ZW \ldots \#]\!] \rightarrow [\![xy \ldots \$, \hat{Q}, \gamma W \ldots \#]\!]$$

and call it a ***legal move.***

If $N = \rightarrow$ then we say that $[\![y \ldots \$, \hat{Q}, \gamma W \ldots \#]\!]$ is a next legal configuration and denote this by

$$[\![xy \ldots \$, Q, ZW \ldots \#]\!] \rightarrow [\![y \ldots \$, \hat{Q}, \gamma W \ldots \#]\!]$$

and also call it a legal move.

If $\delta(Q, x, Z) = \emptyset$, we say that P halts. If $C_1 = [\![\sigma\$, Q, \gamma\#]\!]$ and $C_2 = [\![\hat{\sigma}\$, \hat{Q}, \hat{\gamma}\#]\!]$ are two configurations such that it is possible to move through a sequence of legal moves from C_1 to C_2, we denote this by

$$[\![\sigma\$, Q, \gamma\#]\!] \rightarrow^* [\![\hat{\sigma}\$, \hat{Q}, \hat{\gamma}\#]\!].$$

One special move of a PDA occurs quite often and has its own name. This move consists of placing a symbol, say A, on top of the stack without removing anything from the stack. The transition function for such a move has form $\delta(Q, x, Z) = (N, \hat{Q}, AZ)$: The symbol Z on top of the stack has been removed and replaced by the string AZ; the net effect is to place A on top of the stack. Such a move is called a ***push***—we say that we push A on TOS.

Example 4.2. Consider the PDA discussed above, which recognizes the language $L = \{0^n1^n: n = 0, 1, \ldots\}$. Its formal description is as follows: The set $\Sigma = \{0, 1\}$, the stack alphabet is $\Gamma = \{A\}$, the set $\mathcal{Q}$ of the states is $\{Q_0, Q_1, Q_2, Q_3\}$, and the set of accepting states is $\mathcal{F} = \{Q_3\}$. The initial state is Q_0 and the function δ is given by

For the state Q_0:

$\delta(Q_0, 0, A) = \delta(Q_0, 1, A) = \delta(Q_0, \$, A) = \emptyset$
$\delta(Q_0, 0, \#) = (\rightarrow, Q_1, A\#)$
$\delta(Q_0, 1, \#) = \emptyset$
$\delta(Q_0, \$, \#) = (\uparrow, Q_3, \#)$

For the state Q_1:
$\delta(Q_1, 0, A) = (\rightarrow, Q_1, AA)$
$\delta(Q_1, 1, A) = (\uparrow, Q_2, A)$
$\delta(Q_1, \$, A) = \emptyset$
$\delta(Q_1, 0, \#) = \delta(Q_1, 1, \#) = \delta(Q_1, \$, \#) = \emptyset$

For the state Q_2:
$\delta(Q_2, 0, A) = \delta(Q_2, \$, A) = \emptyset$
$\delta(Q_2, 1, A) = (\rightarrow, Q_2, \lambda)$
$\delta(Q_2, 0, \#) = \delta(Q_2, 1, \#) = \emptyset$
$\delta(Q_2, \$, \#) = (\uparrow, Q_3, \#)$

For the state Q_3: $\delta(Q_3, x, Z) = \emptyset$ for all values of $x \in \Sigma \cup \{\$\}$, and $Z \in \Gamma \cup \{\#\}$.

In the above example, for each x, Q, and Z the value of $\delta(Q, x, Z)$ either consists of exactly one triple, or is empty. Thus, the behavior of the machine is completely determined at each configuration. Such machines are called deterministic.

Definition 4.3. Let $P = \{\Sigma, \Gamma, \mathfrak{Q}, Q_0, \mathfrak{F}, \delta\}$ be a push-down automaton. If for each $x \in \Sigma \cup \{\$\}$, $Q \in \mathfrak{Q}$, and $Z \in \Gamma \cup \{\#\}$ the value of $\delta(Q, x, Z)$ is either a single triple or the empty set, we say that P is ***deterministic.*** If P is not deterministic, we say that P is ***nondeterministic.***

Given a push-down automaton P, the definition of the language $L(P)$ generated (or recognized, or accepted) by P is completely analogous to the one given for the finite state machines (Definition 2.2). A string σ is in the language $L(P)$ if and only if, when we start P in the initial configuration $[\![\sigma\$, Q_0, \#]\!]$, it is possible to go through a sequence of legal moves and halt in configuration $[\![\$, Q, \gamma]\!]$ for some accepting state $Q \in \mathfrak{Q}$. We require that the entire string σ be read and the last state be an accepting one, but we do not require, as some authors occasionally do, that the stack be empty. Formally, we have the following.

Definition 4.4. Let $P = (\Sigma, \Gamma, \mathfrak{Q}, Q_0, \mathfrak{F}, \delta)$ be a push-down automaton. The language $L(P)$ ***generated*** (or ***recognized,*** or ***accepted***) by P is defined by

$$L(P) = \{\sigma \mid \sigma \in \Sigma^*, [\![\sigma\$, Q_0, \#]\!] \rightarrow^* [\![\$, Q, Z\gamma]\!]\},$$

where $Q \in \mathfrak{F}$ and $\delta(Q, \$, Z) = \emptyset$.

Example 4.3. Let Σ be an alphabet; for each string $\sigma \in \Sigma^*$ let σ^R denote the reverse of σ. Thus if $\sigma = abcd$, $\sigma^R = dcba$, if $\sigma = aab$, $\sigma^R = baa$. A ***palindrome*** over Σ is a string of the form $\sigma\sigma^R$ where $\sigma \in \Sigma^*$. Examples of palindromes are $abcddcba$ ($\sigma = abcd$) and $aabbaa$ ($\sigma = aab$). Notice that this definition differs slightly from the one in common use—"a sentence that reads the same backward and forward." For example, $\sigma = abcba$ is not a palindrome according to our definition. We now show how to construct a push-down automaton P that will recognize the language of all palindromes over a given alphabet Σ. Roughly speaking, the machine P will begin to read the input string and push this input, character by character, on the stack. At some point, P "guesses" that it has reached the middle of the string; it then compares the content of the stack from top to bottom with the remainder of the input. If the guess was made correctly and the input is indeed a palindrome, the input pointer reaches the symbol \$ at the same as time the stack pointer reaches the bottom of the stack marker #. The exact definition of P is as follows:

1. Σ is a given nonempty finite set.
2. $\Gamma = \Sigma$ (the stack and the input alphabet are the same).
3. $\mathfrak{Q} = \{ Q_0, Q_1, Q_2, Q_3\}$.
4. The accepting state is Q_3 ($\mathfrak{F} = \{Q_3\}$).
5. The transition function δ is defined as :

   i. $\delta(Q_0, x, \#) = \{(\rightarrow, Q_1, x\#)\}$ for all $x \in \Sigma$.
   ii. $\delta(Q_0, \$, \#) = \{(\uparrow, Q_3, \#)\}$.
   iii. $\delta(Q_1, x, Z) = \{(\rightarrow, Q_1, xZ), (\uparrow, Q_2, Z)\}$ for all $x \in \Sigma$ and all $Z \in \Gamma$.
   iv. $\delta(Q_2, x, x) = \{(\rightarrow, Q_2, \lambda)\}$ for all $x \in \Sigma$.
   v. $\delta(Q_2, \$, \#) = \{(\uparrow, Q_3, \#)\}$.
   vi. $\delta(Q, x, Z) = \emptyset$ in all situations not defined by i–v.

The explanation of the moves is as follows:

i. P begins in the initial state Q_0 and starts to push the input characters on top of the stack. Most of this pushing is done while in the state Q_1.

ii. This insures that the empty string λ is in $L(P)$.

iii. P continues to push the input symbol on the stack, or it "guesses" that the middle of the word has been reached and it is time to compare the content of the stack with the remainder of the input. This is the part of the operation when the machine behaves nondeterministically.

iv. The symbols on the stack are compared, one by one, with the remainder of the input.

v. The word is found to be a palindrome, so P moves to the accepting state.

Notice that because of iii, the PDA is nondeterministic. Consider now, for example, the behavior of P on the input $\sigma = abccba$:

$$[\![abccba\$, Q_0, \#]\!] \rightarrow [\![bccba\$, Q_1, a\#]\!] \rightarrow [\![ccba\$, Q_1, ba\#]\!] \rightarrow$$
$$[\![cba, Q_1, cba\#]\!] \rightarrow [\![cba\$, Q_2, cba\#]\!] \rightarrow [\![ba\$, Q_2, ba\#]\!] \rightarrow$$
$$[\![a\$, Q_2, a\#]\!] \rightarrow [\![\$, Q_2, \#]\!] \rightarrow [\![\$, Q_3, \#]\!] \text{ — halt.} \tag{4.1}$$

We emphasize that the machine could have made "wrong guesses." For example, it could have waited too long for the middle of the string:

$$[\![abccba\$, Q_0, \#]\!] \rightarrow [\![bccba, Q_1, a\#]\!] \rightarrow [\![ccba\$, Q_1, ba\#]\!] \rightarrow$$
$$[\![cba\$, Q_1, cba\#]\!] \rightarrow [\![ba\$, Q_1, ccba\#]\!] \rightarrow [\![ba\$, Q_2, ccba\#]\!] \text{ — halt.}$$

Here the machine halts, since $\delta(Q_2, b, c) = \emptyset$, in a nonaccepting configuration. This does not mean that σ is not in $L(P)$; the criterion is that there should be a way for P to read through σ and end up in an accepting state. That such a way exists is demonstrated in (4.1).

It is clear that if the push-down automata are going to be used for recognizing the computer languages, this kind of behavior should not be allowed (or at least should be strictly controlled)—in other words, the PDA should be deterministic. In the case of finite state machines the deterministic and nondeterministic machines turn out to equivalent: Given a nondeterministic FSM M_1, there is a deterministic FSM M_2 such that $L(M_1) = L(M_2)$. This is not true, however, for the push-down automata. In fact, the language of the palindromes from the Example 4.3 cannot be generated by any deterministic PDA.

Theorem 4.1. Let L be the language $L = \{\sigma\sigma^R \mid \sigma \in \{0, 1\}^*\}$—that is, the collection of all palindromes composed of the symbols 0 and 1. There is no deterministic push-down automaton P such that $L = L(P)$.

Proof. The complete proof of this theorem is somewhat beyond the scope of this book. We will show only that L cannot be recognized by a deterministic PDA that satisfies the following three conditions:

1. The machine halts in all states whenever its input is empty, i.e.,

$\delta(Q, \$, Z) = \emptyset$ for all states Q and all stack symbols Z. In other words, the machine cannot make any moves after the input has been entirely read.

2. The machine accepts strings on empty stack only. This means that a string is accepted if and only if the machine halts in an accepting state and the stack contains only the symbol #.

3. The machine has only one accepting state.

Indeed, suppose a deterministic machine $P = \{\Sigma, \Gamma, \mathcal{Q}, Q_0, \mathcal{F}, \delta\}$ serves as an accepter for the language L in the hypothesis, and also assume that L satisfies conditions 1–3 above. By hypothesis, $\mathcal{F}$ contains only one accepting state—call it $\hat{Q}$. Let σ and τ be two strings from $\{0, 1\}^*$ such that $\sigma\sigma^R\tau\tau^R$ is not in L, for example $\sigma = 101$ and $\tau = 11$. The machine P accepts the strings $\sigma\sigma^R$, $\sigma\sigma^R\sigma\sigma^R$, $\tau\tau^R$, and $\tau\tau^R\tau\tau^R$, but not $\sigma\sigma^R\tau\tau^R$. After reading $\sigma\sigma^R$ the machine must be in the accepting state $\hat{Q}$ and its stack must be empty (i.e., containing only #). Thus, on the input $\sigma\sigma^R\sigma\sigma^R$ the machine moves through the following sequence of configurations:

$$[\![\sigma\sigma^R\sigma\sigma^R\$, Q_0, \#]\!] \to^* [\![\sigma\sigma^R, \hat{Q}, \#]\!] \to^* [\![\$, \hat{Q}, \#]\!] \tag{4.2}$$

Thus, if P is started in the state $\hat{Q}$ and is fed the input $\sigma\sigma^R$, it will end up in the accepting configuration. By exactly the same argument, on the input $\tau\tau^R\tau\tau^R$ the machine will execute the sequence of moves:

$$[\![\tau\tau^R\tau\tau^R\$, Q_0, \#]\!] \to^* [\![\tau\tau^R, \hat{Q}, \#]\!] \to^* [\![\$, \hat{Q}, \#]\!] \tag{4.3}$$

The state $\hat{Q}$ in the middle of the configurations (4.2) and (4.3) is the same since it is an accepting state, and we have assumed that there is only one of these. But now, consider what happens when the string $\sigma\sigma^R\tau\tau^R$ is fed into P. After reading the first part of the string, $\sigma\sigma^R$, the machine will be in the state $\hat{Q}$ and its stack will contain only #. (This follows from (4.2).) At this point, P is in configuration $[\![\tau\tau^R, \hat{Q}, \#]\!]$ and on account of (4.3) it proceeds to change to $[\![\$, \hat{Q}, \#]\!]$, i.e., it accepts $\sigma\sigma^R\tau\tau^R$, which we assumed was not in the language. Thus, $L \neq L(P)$.

For a complete proof, one should show that given a deterministic PDA P there is another deterministic PDA $\hat{P}$ such that $L(P) = L(\hat{P})$ and such that $\hat{P}$ has properties 1–3 above. We refer for the details to [13]. Q.E.D.

4.2. CONNECTIONS WITH CONTEXT-FREE LANGUAGES

We now take up the more detailed discussion of the role played by the push-down automata in recognizing the contex-free languages. In Chapters 2 and 3 we studied in some detail the concept of a finite state machine. These machines were quite simple to implement; however, they were able to recognize only simple kinds of languages—the regular languages. It was a straightforward exercise to give an example of a language not recognized by any of these machines. The push-down automata are in many ways similar to the finite state machines except for one crucial ingredient—the PDA's possess unlimited memory in the form of the stack. It is somewhat surprising that this one simple addition makes PDA's very powerful devices capable of generating arbitrary contex-free language. In fact, the contex-free languages turn out to be exactly those languages for which there is a PDA that recognizes them.

Theorem 4.2. Let L be a language, i.e., a collection of strings over some alphabet Σ. Then L is generated by some push-down automaton if and only if L has a contex-free grammar.

Proof. The completely rigorous proof of this theorem is not exceedingly difficult, but somewhat long. We will present only a fairly detailed sketch in one direction: Given a contex-free grammar $G = \{\Sigma, N, S, P\}$, we show how to construct a PDA P such that $L(P) = L$. For the complete proof and other details, the reader is invited to consult [13] or [7].

Recall that a grammar G is contex-free if all of its productions are of the form $X \rightarrow \gamma$, where X is a nonterminal and γ is a string, possibly empty, of terminals or nonterminals ($\gamma \in \{\Sigma \cup N\}^*$). The PDA P to be constructed will essentially simulate the leftmost derivation of any string in $L(G)$. The input alphabet of P will be Σ, the same as the alphabet of G, and the stack alphabet Γ of P will be $\Sigma \cup N$. We assume that the special symbols \$ and # do not belong to $\Sigma \cup N$. The machine will have three states: Q_0 (the initial state), Q_1, and Q_2 (the accepting state). Most of the time, the machine P will remain in Q_1. Heuristically, the operation of P is described as follows: Let σ be a string in $L(G)$ and let $S \Rightarrow \tau_1 \Rightarrow \tau_2 \Rightarrow \cdots \Rightarrow \sigma$ be the leftmost derivation of σ—the transition between the sentential forms $\tau_i \Rightarrow \tau_{i+1}$ being the result of replacing the leftmost nonterminal X of τ_i by the right-hand side of the production $X \rightarrow \gamma$. The machine will make a move during each such transition. Suppose the first few moves are

$$S \rightarrow \tau_1 \rightarrow \tau_2 \rightarrow \cdots \rightarrow x_1 x_2 \ldots x_k A \tau \rightarrow^* \sigma$$

where $x_1, x_2, \ldots, x_k$ are terminals and the next production in the derivation is $A \to \alpha$. It follows that the string σ is of the form $\sigma = x_1x_2 \ldots x_ky_1y_2 \ldots y_n$, since any further applications of production rules will not affect $x_1x_2 \ldots x_k$. At this instant, the machine P will be in configuration $[\![(y_1y_2 \ldots y_n\$, Q_1, A\tau\#]\!]$. (The input pointer points at y_1, the first symbol of the portion of σ still to be derived, and the stack pointer points to A, the next nonterminal to be replaced by in the left-most derivation of σ.) What the machine does now is replace the top of the stack, i.e., the symbol A, by the string α—the right hand side of the production $A \to \alpha$. If α begins with a nonterminal A', we are essentially back to the same situation, so we replace A' by α'—the right-hand side of the production $A' \to \alpha'$. We repeat the procedure until a terminal appears on top of the stack. Thus, we may assume that α already begins with a terminal. This terminal must be y_1, otherwise $A \to \alpha$ could not have been the correct production. Hence, after A is replaced by α, the input pointer and the stack pointer both point to the same symbol y_1. We then remove y_1 from the stack and move the input pointer to the right, and the procedure repeats. It should be reasonably clear that if we follow this procedure, then the machine P will move from the configuration $[\![\sigma\$, Q_1, \#]\!]$ to $[\![\$, Q_1, \#]\!]$, at which point we change the state to Q_2 and halt. The exact definition of the transition function δ is as follows:

1. $\delta(Q_0, x, \#) = \{(\uparrow, Q_1, S\#)\}$ for all terminals x. This has the effect of placing the start symbol S on top of the stack, and changing to the "working" state Q_1.
2. $\delta(Q_0, \$, \#) = \{(\uparrow, Q_1, S\#)\}$. This particular transition is needed in case the empty string λ is in the language $L(G)$. The starting symbol S will be placed on the stack; if $\lambda \in L(G)$ it will eventually "disappear."
3. $\delta(Q_1, x, x) = \{(\rightarrow, Q_1, \lambda)\}$ for all terminals x. The input and the stack pointers both point to the same symbol x. We pop x from the stack and read the next symbol.
4. If x is a terminal or the symbol \$, and if A is a nonterminal, then

$$\delta(Q_1, x, A) = \{(\uparrow, Q_1, \alpha_1), (\uparrow, Q_1, \alpha_2), \ldots, (\uparrow, Q_1, \alpha_p)\}$$

   where $A \to \alpha_1 | \alpha_2 | \ldots | \alpha_p$ are all the productions having A on the left-hand side. This rule applies when a nonterminal is on the top of the stack, and the machine makes a "guess" as to which production is to be applied next in order to match the current input symbol x (as well as the rest of the input).
5. $\delta(Q_1, \$, \#) = \{(\uparrow, Q_2, \#)\}$. All the input was read, the stack is

empty, so the machine moves to the accepting state.

6. $\delta(Q, x, Z) = \emptyset$ for all other x's, Q's, and Z's.

The machine P thus constructed is clearly nondeterministic: When rule 4 above is to be applied, P must "guess" the correct production to be used. It should be reasonably clear, however, that if the correct sequence of guesses exists (i.e., if the input σ is in the language), P will accept the input. It is also true that if P can move from the initial configuration to the accepting one, then σ can be derived in the grammar G. The rigorous proof along these lines can be easily constructed, and is based on the induction on the length of the string σ. Q.E.D.

Configuration of M	Corresponding sentential form (TOS) underlined	Comments
$[\![a * (a + a)\$, Q_0, \#]\!]$		Initial configuration
$[\![a * (a + a)\$, Q_1, E\#]\!]$	$\underline{E}$	E placed on TOS
$[\![a * (a + a)\$, Q_1, T\#]\!]$	$\underline{T}$	$E \rightarrow T$ applied
$[\![a * (a + a)\$, Q_1, T*F\#]\!]$	$\underline{T} * F$	$T \rightarrow T * F$ applied
$[\![a * (a + a)\$, Q_1, F * F\#]\!]$	$\underline{F} * F$	$T \rightarrow F$ applied
$[\![a * (a + a)\$, Q_1, a * F\#]\!]$	$\underline{a} * F$	$F \rightarrow a$ applied
$[\![* (a + a)\$, Q_1, * F\#]\!]$	$a \underline{*} F$	a removed from TOS
$[\![(a + a)\$, Q_1, F\#]\!]$	$a * \underline{F}$	$*$ removed from TOS
$[\![(a + a)\$, Q_1, (E)\#]\!]$	$a * \underline{(} E)$	$F \rightarrow (E)$ applied
$[\![a + a)\$, Q_1, E)\#]\!]$	$a * (\underline{E})$	(removed from TOS
$[\![a + a)\$, Q_1, E + T)\#]\!]$	$a * (\underline{E} + T)$	$E \rightarrow E + T$ applied
$[\![a + a)\$, Q_1, T + T)\#]\!]$	$a * (\underline{T} + T)$	$E \rightarrow T$ applied
$[\![a + a)\$, Q_1, F + T)\#]\!]$	$a * (\underline{F} + T)$	$T \rightarrow F$ applied
$[\![a + a)\$, Q_1, a + T)\#]\!]$	$a * (\underline{a} + T)$	$F \rightarrow$ a applied
$[\![+ a)\$, Q_1, + T)\#]\!]$	$a * (a \underline{+} T)$	a removed from TOS
$[\![a)\$, Q_1, T)\#]\!]$	$a * (a + \underline{T})$	+ removed from TOS
★$[\![a)\$, Q_1, F)\#]\!]$	$a * (a + \underline{F})$	$T \rightarrow F$ applied
$[\![a)\$, Q_1, a)\#]\!]$	$a * (a + \underline{a})$	$F \rightarrow a$ applied
$[\![ )\$, Q_1,)\#]\!]$	$a * (a + a\underline{)}$	a removed from TOS
$[\![\$, Q_1, \#]\!]$	$a * (a + a)$	) removed from TOS
$[\![\$, Q_2, \#]\!]$	halt and accept	Final configuration

Figure 4.5. Movements of a PDA.

Example 4.4. Consider the grammar of algebraic expressions:

$$E \to E + T \mid T \qquad T \to T * F \mid F \qquad F \to (E) \mid a$$

The transition rules for the corresponding push-down automaton are as follows:

$$\begin{aligned}
&\delta(Q_0, x, \#) = \{(\uparrow, Q_1, E\#)\} \text{ for all } x \in \Sigma = \{a, +, *, (,)\} \\
&\delta(Q_0, \$, \#) = \{(\uparrow, Q_1, E\#)\} \\
&\delta(Q_1, x, x) = \{(\rightarrow, Q_1, \lambda)\} \text{ for all } x \in \Sigma \\
&\delta(Q_1, x, E) = \{(\uparrow, Q_1, E + T), (\uparrow, Q_1, T)\} \text{ for all } x \in \Sigma \cup \{\$\} \\
&\delta(Q_1, x, T) = \{(\uparrow, Q_1, T * F), (\uparrow, Q_1, F)\} \text{ for all } x \in \Sigma \cup \{\$\} \\
&\delta(Q_1, x, F) = \{(\uparrow, Q_1, (E)), (\uparrow, Q_1, a)\} \text{ for all } x \in \Sigma \cup \{\$\} \\
&\delta(Q_1, \$, \#) = \{(\uparrow, Q_2, \#)\}
\end{aligned}$$

The sequence of moves of this PDA on the input $a * (a + a)$ is depicted in Figure 4.5. We re-emphasize the nondeterministic nature of this PDA. For example, when M was in configuration $[\![a)\$, Q_1, F)\#]\!]$ (marked by ★ in Figure 4.5), it chose the "correct" value of $\delta(Q_1, a, F)$, namely the triple $(\uparrow, Q_1, a)$. Should the other possibility, $(\uparrow, Q_1, (E))$, be taken, the PDA would immediately halt in a nonaccepting configuration: $[\![a)\$, Q_1, F)\#]\!] \to [\![a)\$, Q_1, (E))\#]\!]$ — halt.

Example 4.5. In this example we illustrate the construction and operation of a PDA arising from a grammar with an empty production. The grammar G is as follows:

$$\begin{aligned}
S &\to abA \mid B \mid baB \mid C \\
A &\to bS \mid b \\
B &\to aS \\
C &\to aA \mid \lambda
\end{aligned}$$

The resulting transition rules are as follows:

$$\begin{aligned}
&\delta(Q_0, x, \#) = \{(\uparrow, Q_1, S\#)\} \text{ for all } x \in \Sigma = \{a, b\} \\
&\delta(Q_0, \$, \#) = \{(\uparrow, Q_1, S\#)\} \\
&\delta(Q_1, x, x) = \{(\rightarrow, Q_1, \lambda)\} \text{ for all } x \in \Sigma \\
&\delta(Q_1, x, S) = \{(\uparrow, Q_1, abA), (\uparrow, Q_1, B), (\uparrow, Q_1, baB), (\uparrow, Q_1, C)\} \\
&\quad \text{for all } x \in \Sigma \cup \{\$\} \\
&\delta(Q_1, x, A) = \{(\uparrow, Q_1, bS), (\uparrow, Q_1, b)\} \text{ for all } x \in \Sigma \cup \{\$\} \\
&\delta(Q_1, x, B) = \{(\uparrow, Q_1, aS)\} \text{ for all } x \in \Sigma \cup \{\$\} \\
&\delta(Q_1, x, C) = \{(\uparrow, Q_1, aA), (\uparrow, Q_1, \lambda)\} \text{ for all } x \in \Sigma \cup \{\$\} \\
&\delta(\$, Q_1, \#) = \{(\uparrow, Q_2, \#)\}
\end{aligned}$$

As usual, Q_0 is the initial state and Q_2 is the accepting state. In this grammar the empty string λ is in the language $L(G)$, its derivation being $S \Rightarrow C \Rightarrow \lambda$. The PDA also accepts λ (as it should); the sequence of configurations is:

$$[\![\$, Q_0, \#]\!] \rightarrow [\![\$, Q_1, S\#]\!] \rightarrow [\![\$, Q_1, C\#]\!] \rightarrow$$
$$\rightarrow [\![\$, Q_1, \#]\!] \rightarrow [\![\$, Q_2, \#]\!] \text{ -- halts.}$$

The string $baaa$ is in $L(G)$; its leftmost derivation is $S \Rightarrow baB \Rightarrow baaS \Rightarrow baaaS \Rightarrow baaaC \Rightarrow baaa$. The corresponding movements of the PDA are:

$$[\![baaa\$, Q_0, \#]\!] \rightarrow [\![baaa\$, Q_1, S\#]\!] \rightarrow [\![baaa\$, Q_1, baB\#]\!]$$
$$\rightarrow [\![aaa\$, Q_1, aB\#]\!] \rightarrow [\![aa\$, Q_1, B\#]\!] \rightarrow [\![aa\$, Q_1, aS\#]\!]$$
$$\rightarrow [\![a\$, Q_1, S\#]\!] \rightarrow [\![a\$, Q_1, aS\#]\!] \rightarrow [\![\$, Q_1, S\#]\!] \rightarrow [\![\$, Q_1, C\#]\!]$$
$$\rightarrow [\![\$, Q_1, \#]\!] \rightarrow [\![\$, Q_2, \#]\!] \text{ — halt.}$$

Again, we emphasize the clairvoyance of P. On the same input $baaa$, the machine could have made the sequence of moves

$$[\![baaa\$, Q_0, \#]\!] \rightarrow [\![baaa\$, Q_1, S\#]\!] \rightarrow [\![baaa\$, Q_1, abA\#]\!] \text{ — halt}$$

since $\delta(Q_1, b, a) = \emptyset$. The point is that if σ is derivable in $L(G)$, then it is possible for the PDA to make a legal sequence of moves resulting in the acceptance of σ. We will discuss in Chapters 6–8 some of the methods of making such machines deterministic. This is clearly not always possible (see Theorem 4.1), but on occasion it can be done.

Thus, any contex-free language can be generated by a push-down automaton. The converse is also true: Given any push-down automaton P, there is a contex-free grammar G such that $L(P) = L(G)$; we will not give a proof of this result, however. It is not exceedingly difficult, but somewhat tedious and long (see [13] or [7]).

4.3. EVALUATION OF ARITHMETIC EXPRESSIONS

Push-down automata can also be used for automatic evaluation of arithmetic expressions. The problem is as follows: We wish to program a computer in such a way that when presented with an arithmetic expression, it will evaluate this expression correctly. For example, if the expression is, say $2 * (3 + 2 * 5) + 8 * 2$, the machine should perform first the multiplication $2 * 5$, add the result to 3, multiply that result by 2, etc. It should be programmed in such a way that it knows what to do in what order. We should remember that the machine receives the expression sequentially: It first reads the symbol 2, then the symbol $*$, then (, then 3, etc. When it reaches the end of the input, it should know the "meaning" of the input and perform the necessary operations in the right order. For the sake of simplicity, we restrict our attention to expressions involving only two binary operations, $*$ and $+$. Once the method is understood, it is quite easy to extend it to other operations as well (subtraction, division, and exponentiation, as well as unary operations such as $-a$). We first present the solution of the problem in case the expression is fed to the machine in what is called postfix notation (also called ***reverse Polish notation***). In this notation the operation is written not between the numbers, but after them. Thus $3 + 7$ is written as $3\ 7\ +$, $8 * 4$ as $8\ 4\ *$, etc. In general, if & denotes a binary operation (addition, multiplication, or whatever), then $a \& b$ *is* written as $a\, b \&$. Each operator is understood to act on the two immediately preceding operands. Thus, for example, the postfix notation $a\, b + c *$ is understood as $(ab+c)* = ((ab+)\, c)*$, so that $*$ acts on c and $ab+$. Notice that in the postfix notation we do not need the parentheses: The expression $ab + c*$ is deciphered uniquely since we require each operator to act on the two immediately preceding operands. It is quite easy now to construct a push-down automaton which will automatically evaluate any arithmetic expression σ, provided that expression is written in the postfix notation. The machine will have only one state and it will operate according to the following rules:

1. If the input symbol is a number, the PDA places (pushes) this number on top of the stack and moves the input pointer one unit to the right.
2. If the input is an operator, the machine removes the top two numbers from the stack, performs the indicated operation, and places the result on the top of the stack.
3. When the input marker \$ is reached, the stack will contain the correct value of the expression and nothing else (provided the input was grammatically correct).

Consider, for example, the expression $2*(3+2*5)+8*2$. The postfix translation of it is $2\,3\,2\,5**+*8\,2*+$. The movements of he PDA on this input are:

$$[\![2\,3\,2\,5*+*8\,2*+\$,\ \#]\!] \to [\![3\,2\,5*+*8\,2*+\$,\ 2\#]\!]$$

$$\to [\![25**+*82*+\$,\ 32\#]\!] \to [\![5*+*82*+\$,\ 232\#]\!]$$
$$\to [\![*+*82*+\$,\ 5232\#]\!] \to [\![+*82*+\$,\ \underline{10}\,32\#]\!]$$
$$\to [\![*82*+\$,\ \underline{13}\,2\#]\!] \to [\![82*+\$,\ \underline{26}\#]\!] \to [\![2*+\$,\ 8\,\underline{26}\,\#]\!]$$
$$\to [\![*+\$,\ 28\underline{26}\,\#]\!] \to [\![+\$,\ \underline{16}\,\underline{26}\,\#]\!] \to [\![\$,\ \underline{42}\#]\!]$$

We omitted the state symbol, since it is always the same. The underlining is to differentiate, in an obvious way, between, say, sixteen ($\underline{16}$), and 1 followed by 6. This method, while it works very nicely, does not completely solve our problem, since arithmetic expressions, as a rule, are not presented in the postfix notation, but rather in the "normal," way with the operator written between the operands—the infix notation. What we need is an automatic (deterministic) way of translating the arithmetic expressions from this usual notation to the postfix notation. The formal, precise description of the postfix notation is as follows:

Definition 4.5. Let Σ be the collection of operands (i.e., the numbers) and let Δ be the collection of operators (i.e., $+$, $*$, $-$, etc.). We have the following:

1. The postfix representation of each operand a is a itself.
2. If A is an expression written in the infix notation and $\hat{A}$ is its representation in the postfix notation, then the postfix representation of (A) is $\hat{A}$.
3. If A and B are expressions in the infix notation, and $\hat{A}$, $\hat{B}$ are the corresponding translations into the postfix notation, then for any operator &, the postfix translation of A & B is $\hat{A}\,\hat{B}\,\&$.

The meaning of 2 is as follows: Given the postfix notation $\hat{A}$ for A, the postfix notation for (A) is $\hat{A}$ (we omit the parentheses). Similarly, 3 says that if we know how to represent A and B in the postfix notation (as $\hat{A}$ and $\hat{B}$), then we know how to represent $A \,\&\, B$: namely as $\hat{A}\,\hat{B}\,\&$. What we want now is to construct a deterministic scheme that will convert a given infix notation into its postfix translation. It should convert the strings $a+b*c$, $a*(b+c)$ into $abc*+$, $abc+*$, etc. In general, if σ_1, σ_2, σ_3, and σ are arithmetic expressions in the infix notation, and their postfix representations are $\hat{\sigma}_1$, $\hat{\sigma}_2$, $\hat{\sigma}_3$, and $\hat{\sigma}$, then this scheme should perform translations indicated in (4.4). The first thing to notice about this scheme is that the operands in the postfix notation appear in the same order as in the infix notation, the only changes are that the parentheses are eliminated, and the operators $*$ and $+$ are shifted around.

$$\sigma \;\rightarrow\; \hat{\sigma}$$
$$\sigma_1 + \sigma_2 \;\rightarrow\; \hat{\sigma}_1\hat{\sigma}_2 +$$
$$(\sigma_1) * (\sigma_2) \;\rightarrow\; \hat{\sigma}_1\hat{\sigma}_2 *$$
$$\sigma_1 * (\sigma_2 + \sigma_3) \;\rightarrow\; \hat{\sigma}_1\hat{\sigma}_2\hat{\sigma}_3 + *$$
$$\sigma_1 + (\sigma_2) * (\sigma_3) \rightarrow \hat{\sigma}_1\hat{\sigma}_2\hat{\sigma}_3 * + \tag{4.4}$$

The scheme should also take into account the "priorities" of the operators. Thus, in the expression $a + b * c$, the multiplication $b * c$ should be performed before the addition, so that in the postfix notation the symbol $*$ should appear to the left of $+$. It should be clear that if such a scheme has all the properties listed in (4.4), then it will perform correctly in all situations. It turns out that such a scheme can be accomplished deterministically using a push-down automaton with an output. We first explain how such a machine works and then give an indication of the proof that it does work correctly. This push-down translator will be a push-down automaton as described in Section 4.1, together with an output device. Schematically it may be represented as in Figure 4.6.

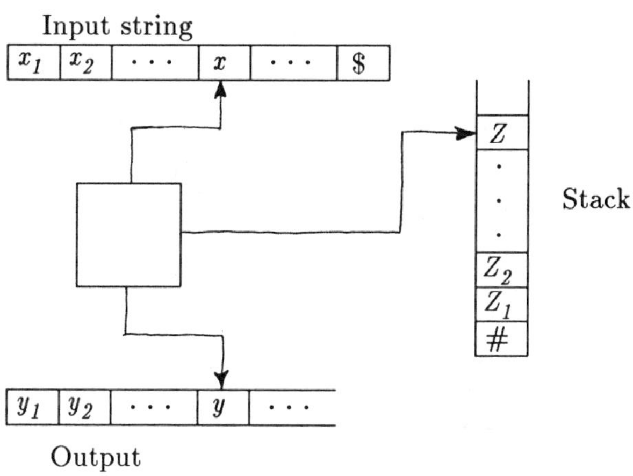

Figure 4.6. PDA translating infix into postfix notation.

The push-down automaton has only one state Q and operates as follows. Originally, the input contains an arithmetic expression in the infix notation; the stack is empty (i.e., it contains only the marker #); the output tape is blank; and the output pointer points to the leftmost square of the tape. We assume, as usual, that the input is delimited on the right by the symbol \$ so that T can detect the end of the input. At each instant of time the machine examines the current symbol on top of the stack and the current input symbol and may do one of the following:

1. Output one or more symbols to the output tape. These symbols may be taken either from the stack or from the input tape. The relevant pointers are then adjusted properly (the input pointer moves to the right and the stack pointer moves down). The output pointer moves right to the next available empty square.
2. Place the current input symbol on top of the stack, adjusting both pointers accordingly (This move is called ***push***.)

The allowable input symbols are the operands (i.e., the numbers) a, b, c, . . . , the operator symbols $*$, and $+$, the parentheses) and (, and the delimiting symbol \$. The allowable stack symbols are $+$, $*$, the left parenthesis (and the bottom of the stack symbol #. To each stack symbol Z we assign two numbers—the input priority $I(Z)$ and the stack priority $S(Z)$—according to a table in Figure 4.7.

Z	$I(Z)$	$S(Z)$
$*$	2	2
$+$	1	1
(	3	0
#	—	0

Figure 4.7. Priority functions.

The machine works as follows:

1. If the input symbol is one of the operands a, b, c, . . . , it is sent to the output and the next symbol is read in. The input and the output pointers are adjusted accordingly; the stack does not change.
2. If the input symbol x is either (, $+$, or $*$, i.e., it is also one of the stack symbols, the values of $I(x)$ and $S(Z)$, where Z is the current top of the stack, are compared. The following then takes place:

   i. If $I(x) > S(Z)$ the symbol x is pushed on top of the stack and the next symbol is read. The input and the stack pointers are adjusted accordingly and no output takes place.

ii. If $I(x) \leq S(Z)$ the symbol Z from the top of the stack is sent to the output, the stack and the output pointers are adjusted, and the symbol x is read again (input pointer stays put).

3. If the input symbol is the right parenthesis) the stack is sent to the output, one by one, until the left parenthesis (appears. Then this left parenthesis (is removed from the stack—it is not send to the output—the stack pointer is adjusted accordingly, and the input pointer moves to the right. The output pointer is also adjusted, of course.
4. If the input symbol x is \$, the contents of the stack are output one by one, from the top down, until the bottom marker # is reached.

We describe the configuration of the machine T at any given moment by a triple of strings as follows:

$$[\![\underset{\substack{\uparrow \\ C_{INP}}}{x_i}\ x_{i+1} \ldots x_n\$,\ \underset{\substack{\uparrow \\ C_{TOS}}}{Z_j}\ Z_{j-1} \ldots Z_1\#,\ y_1 y_2 \ldots \underset{\substack{\uparrow \\ C_{OUT}}}{y_k}\ ]\!] \tag{4.5}$$

where C_{INP} is the current input symbol, C_{TOS} is the current top of the stack, and C_{OUT} is the current output pointer. The PDA from Figure 4.6 is in the configuration (4.5). With this notation, we give some examples of movements of T on various inputs.

Example 4.6. Behavior of the machine T on various inputs.

On input $a + b * c$ the machine moves as follows:

$$[\![a + b * c\,\$,\ \#,\ \lambda]\!] \rightarrow [\![+\ b * c\$,\ \#,\ a]\!] \rightarrow [\![b * c\,\$,\ +\#,\ a]\!]$$
$$\rightarrow [\![*\ c\,\$,\ +\#,\ ab]\!] \rightarrow [\![\ c\,\$,\ * + \#,\ ab]\!] \rightarrow [\![\$,\ * + \#,\ abc]\!]$$
$$\rightarrow [\![\ \$,\ + \#,\ abc\ *]\!] \rightarrow [\![\ \$,\ \#,\ abc * +]\!]$$

On the input $(a + b) * c$ the movements of T are:

$$[\![(a + b) * c\,\$,\ \#,\ \lambda]\!] \rightarrow [\![a + b) * c\$,\ (\#,\ \lambda]\!] \rightarrow [\![+\ b) * c\,\$,\ (\#,\ a]\!]$$
$$\rightarrow [\![b) * c\,\$,\ +\ (\#,\ a]\!] \rightarrow [\![) * c\,\$,\ +\ (\#,\ ab]\!] \rightarrow [\![\ * c\,\$,\ \#,\ ab\ +]\!]$$
$$\rightarrow [\![c\,\$,\ *\#,\ ab\ +]\!] \rightarrow [\![\$,\ *\#,\ ab + c]\!] \rightarrow [\![\$,\ \#,\ ab + c\ *]\!]$$

If the input is $(a + b * c) * (d + e)$, the movements are:

$$[\![(a + b * c) * (d + e)\ \$,\ \#,\ \lambda]\!] \to [\![a + b * c) * (d + e)\ \$,\ (\#,\ \lambda]\!]$$
$$\to [\![+\ b * c) * (d + e)\ \$,\ (\#,\ a]\!] \to [\![b * c) * (d + e)\ \$,\ +\ (\ \#,\ a]\!]$$
$$\to [\![*\ c) * (d + e)\ \$,\ +\ (\#,\ ab]\!] \to [\![c) * (d + e)\ \$,\ \ * + (\ \#,\ ab]\!]$$
$$\to [\![) * (d + e)\ \$,\ * + (\ \#,\ abc]\!] \to [\![\ * (d + e)\ \$,\ \#,\ abc * +]\!]$$
$$\to [\![(d + e)\ \$,\ * \#,\ abc * +]\!] \to [\![d + e)\ \$,\ (\ * \#,\ abc * +]\!]$$
$$\to [\![+\ e\ )\ \$,\ (\ * \#,\ abc * +\ d]\!] \to [\![e\ )\ \$,\ +\ (\ * \#,\ abc * +\ d]\!]$$
$$\to [\![)\ \$,\ +\ (\ * \#,\ abc * +\ de]\!] \to [\![\$,\ * \#,\ abc * +\ de\ +]\!] \to$$
$$\to [\![\$,\ \#,\ abc * +\ de + *]\!]$$

It is evident that the machine worked correctly in all these examples. It actually does in all cases.

Theorem 4.3. Let T be the push-down automaton as described in Figures 4.5 and 4.6. If σ is any correctly formed arithmetic expression in the infix notation, then T will transform σ into $\hat{\sigma}$—the correct translation of σ into the postfix notation.

Proof. (An outline.) We use induction on the length of the input string. The only arithmetic expressions (in the infix notation) of length three or less are: a, (a), $a + b$, and $a * b$. It is easily seen that T will correctly translate all of these. Suppose now that T works correctly on all expressions of length at most $n \geq 3$ and let σ be an expression, written in the infix notation, that is of length $n + 1$. Then σ is in one of the following forms:

i. $\sigma = (\tau)$
ii. $\sigma = \tau_1 + \tau_2$
iii. $\sigma = \tau_1 * \tau_2$

where all the τ's are of length less than n. In each case T will correctly translate σ:

i. T will originally move from configuration $[\![(\tau)\$,\ \#,\ \lambda]\!]$ to $[\![\tau)\$,\ (\#,\ \lambda]\!]$. It will then operate on τ, producing the output $\hat{\tau}$—the postfix translation of τ—without disturbing the symbol (on the stack. Thus, at some point it will reach the configuration $[\![)\$,\ (\#,\ \hat{\tau}]\!]$, and it is seen that it will move from there to $[\![\$,\ \#,\ \hat{\tau}]\!]$, producing the correct result.

ii. T starts in configuration $[\![\tau_1 + \tau_2\$, \#, \lambda]\!]$. By the inductive hypothesis it translates τ_1 correctly, so after the last symbol of τ_1 has been read T will be in the configuration $[\![+\tau_2\$, \#, \hat{\tau}_1]\!]$. From there it will move to $[\![\tau_2\$, +\#, \hat{\tau}_1]\!]$ and, again by the inductive hypothesis, it will continue to change to $[\![\$, +\#, \hat{\tau}_1\hat{\tau}_2]\!]$. The symbol $+$ on the stack will be left undisturbed since τ_2 must begin with an operand x or a left parentheses (; in both cases $+$ remains on the stack. From this last configuration, T will proceed to $[\![\$, \#, \hat{\tau}_1\hat{\tau}_2+]\!]$, again producing the correct translation.

iii. The argument here is essentially the same as in part ii. Q.E.D.

It should be noted here that T does not detect mistakes in the original input. Thus, for example, if the input σ is $a + * b$, the output of T will be $ab * +$, both meaningless sequences. In Chapters 6 and 8 we will construct deterministic parsers that will not only evaluate these arithmetic expressions, but will also be able to decide if the input strings are correctly formed. The machine T given here is not a true parser since it does not reconstruct the derivation tree of the input.

4.4. PUMPING LEMMA FOR PDA'S

In Sections 4.1 and 4.2 we saw that the push-down automata were more versatile than the finite state machines. More precisely, we exhibited a language that was accepted by a PDA but not by any finite state machine (Example 4.1). It is reasonable to ask, therefore, if every language whatsoever is recognized by a PDA, or what amounts to the same thing (because of Theorem 4.2), does every language have a contex-free grammar? We will show in this section that such is not the case. The principal tool to be used is Theorem 4.4, which is analogous to the pumping lemma for finite state machines (Theorem 3.1).

Theorem 4.4. (Pumping lemma for push-down automata). Let $G = \{\Sigma, N, S, P\}$ be a contex-free grammar. Then there exists a number k, depending only on G, with the following property: Any sentence σ in $L(G)$ of length longer than k can be written as $\sigma = \alpha\tau_1\beta\tau_2\gamma$, where α, β, γ, τ_1, and τ_2 are strings from Σ^*, and such that for each $n = 0, 1, 2, 3, \ldots$, the string $\sigma = \alpha\tau_1^n\beta\tau_2^n\gamma$ also belongs to $L(G)$. Moreover one of the strings τ_1 or τ_2 (or both) is different from the empty string λ.

The reason for calling this a theorem about push-down automata is that the languages possessing a contex-free grammar are precisely those that are recognized by some push-down automaton (Theorem 4.2).

Before proceeding with the proof we illustrate how this theorem is applied.

Example 4.7. Let L_0 be the language $L_0 = \{a^n b^n c^n \mid n = 0, 1, 2, \ldots\}$. Thus, L consists of strings having equal number of a's, b's, and c's following each other in succession. We wish to show that L_0 is not accepted by any PDA, or, equivalently, that it has no contex-free grammar. Suppose to the contrary that L does have a contex-free grammar G such that $L_0 = L(G)$ and let k be the number corresponding to this G as in Theorem 4.4. If $m > k$, then the string $\sigma = a^m b^m c^m$ has length $3m > k$, so σ can be written as $a^m b^m c^m = \alpha\tau_1\beta\tau_2\gamma$, where either $\tau_1 \neq \lambda$ or $\tau \neq \lambda$, and for each $n = 1, 2, \ldots$ the string $\alpha\tau_1^n\beta\tau_2^n\gamma$ is in the language L. We show, however, that this is impossible. Suppose, say, that $\tau_1 \neq \lambda$. Then τ_1 must be a string consisting of only one kind of symbols, i.e., either all a's, or all b's, or all c's. Indeed if τ contained a's and b's, for example, then $\tau^2 = \tau\tau$ will have a's (in the second τ) that are to the right of b's (in the first τ). But this implies that $\alpha\tau_1^2\beta\tau_2^2\gamma$ is not in L_0—contrary to the choice of τ_1. A similar argument holds when τ_1 contains a's and c's, or b's and c's. In the same way we show that if $\tau_2 \neq \lambda$, then τ_2 must be a string consisting either only of a's, or only of b's, or only of c's. But then consider again the string $\rho = \alpha\tau_1^2\beta\tau_2^2\gamma$, which is guaranteed to be in L_0 by Theorem 4.4. If τ_1 consists only of a's and τ_2 only of b's, then ρ has too few c's. If τ_1 has only b's and τ_2 has only c's, then ρ has too few a's, etc. In all possible cases the string ρ cannot be a sentence from the language L. Thus, indeed, L cannot have a contex-free grammar.

We now proceed with the proof of Theorem 4.4. To simplify the arguments, we will make an additional hypothesis that G does not have empty productions, i.e., productions of the form $A \to \lambda$. Given a grammar G, we will construct a number $k = k(G)$ such that for any string σ in $L(G)$ of length greater than k, there is derivation of σ of the form

$$S \Rightarrow^* \alpha X\gamma \Rightarrow^* \alpha\tau_1 X\tau_2\gamma \Rightarrow^* \alpha\tau_1\beta\tau_2\gamma = \sigma, \tag{4.6}$$

where X is some nonterminal and either τ_1 or τ_2 is a nonempty string. Indeed, if (4.6) is true, then

$$X \Rightarrow^* \tau_1 X\tau_2 \quad \text{and} \quad X \Rightarrow^* \beta$$

are valid derivations in G. Thus, all of the following derivations can be made in G:

$$S \Rightarrow^* \alpha X\gamma \Rightarrow^* \alpha\beta\gamma$$

$$S \Rightarrow^* \alpha X\gamma \Rightarrow^* \alpha\tau_1 X\tau_2\gamma \Rightarrow^* \alpha\tau_1\beta\tau_2\gamma$$

$$S \Rightarrow^* \alpha X\gamma \Rightarrow^* \alpha\tau_1 X\tau_2\gamma \Rightarrow^* \alpha\tau_1^2 X\tau_2^2\gamma \Rightarrow^* \alpha\tau_1^2\beta\tau_2^2\gamma$$

$$\cdots\cdots\cdots\cdots\cdots\cdots\cdots\cdots\cdots$$

and the theorem will follow.

Let r be the length of the longest string appearing on the right-hand side of any of the productions of G, and let n be the number of nonterminals in G; put $n_0 = n + 1$. We set $k = r^{n_0} + 1$. Let now σ be any string in $L(G)$ whose length is larger than k and consider its derivation tree as in Figure 4.8. Define a path in such a tree to be the sequence of nodes and line segments joining them, originating from the root S and going down through nonterminals to some leaf (i.e., a terminal in σ). The length of such a path is the number of such line segments. We define the depth of the tree as the largest length of any of its paths.

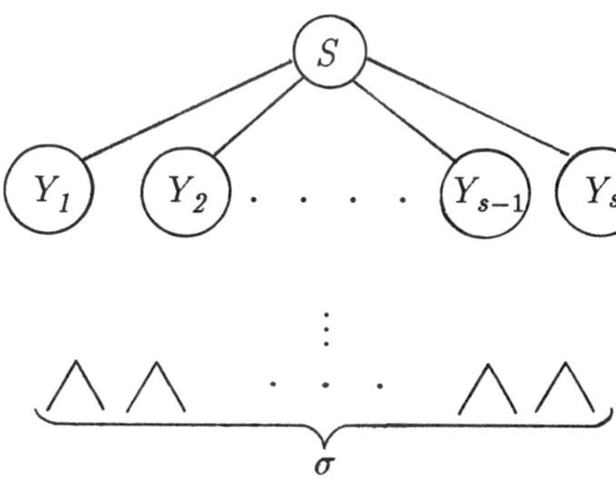

Figure 4.8. Schematic parse tree for σ.

Consider, for example, the grammar G_0 of arithmetic expressions (Example 1.3). The string $\sigma = (a + a) * a$ has the derivation tree depicted in Figure 4.9. Examples of paths in this tree are: $E{-}T{-}F{-}a$, (length 3), $E{-}T{-}T{-}F{-})$, (length 4), $E{-}T{-}T{-}F{-}E{-}E{-}T{-}F{-}a$ (length 8), etc. The depth of this tree is 8. It is easy to see that if the string σ has a parse tree of depth d, then σ cannot have more than r^d symbols (at every level, each node can have at most r children). Thus the root S can have at most r children, r^2 grandchildren, etc. In other words, if the number of leaves in a parse tree of some string σ is larger than r^d, then the derivation tree must contain a path of length greater than d.

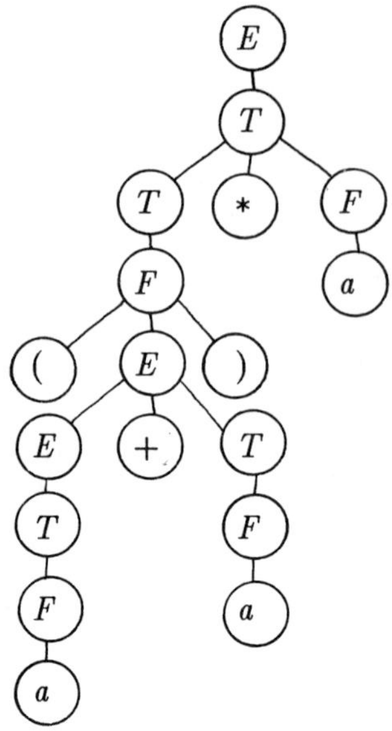

Figure 4.9. Example of a parse tree.

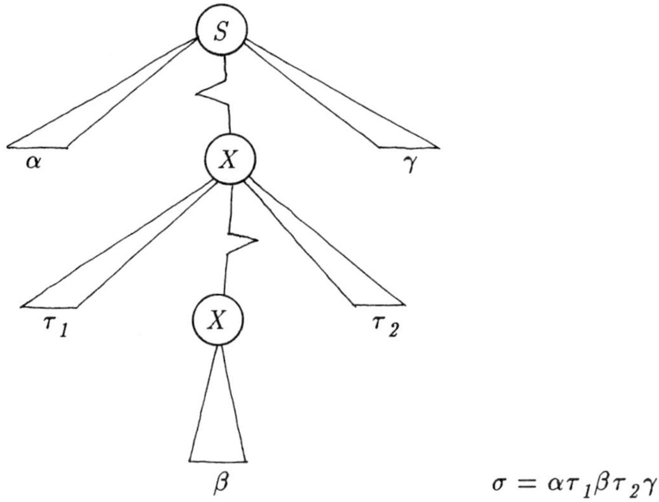

Figure 4.10. Proof of Theorem 4.4.

Suppose now that the string σ is longer than $k = r^{n_0} + 1$ and consider a derivation tree of σ that involves the fewest number of nodes. (σ may have more than one derivation tree. If there are several such minimal derivation trees, choose any one of them.) By preceding remarks, the derivation tree of σ must contain a path of length longer than n_0, i.e., of length $n_0 + 1 = n + 2$ or more (n is the number of nonterminals in G). This path contains exactly one terminal, all the other nodes (at least $n + 1$ of them) are nonterminals. Thus, there is a nonterminal X that appears twice in this path, and the derivation tree of σ has form as in Figure 4.10. One of the strings τ_1 or τ_2 must be different from λ, since otherwise we could remove the entire portion of the derivation tree between the upper X and the lower X and obtain a derivation tree with fewer symbols. But this shows that (4.6) is true, and we are done. Q.E.D.

4.5. CLOSURE PROPERTIES OF CONTEXT-FREE LANGUAGES

We saw in Chapter 3 (Theorem 3.6) that if L, L_1, and L_2 are regular languages then L^*, $\bar{L}$, $L_1 + L_2$, L_1L_2, and $L_1 \cap L_2$ are also regular. Some, but not all, of these properties are true for the contex-free languages. We recall that L^* is the language of all the strings of the form $\sigma_1\sigma_2 \ldots \sigma_n$, $\sigma_i \in L$; $\bar{L}$ is the set of strings not in L; $L_1 + L_2$ is the set theoretic union of L_1 and L_2; L_1L_2 is the set of strings of the form $\sigma_1\sigma_2$, $\sigma_i \in L_i$; and $L_1 \cap L_2$ is the set of strings in both L_1 and L_2.

Theorem 4.5. Let L, L_1, and L_2 be contex-free languages. Then the languages L^*, $L_1 + L_2$, and L_1L_2 are also contex-free.

Proof. Suppose L has a contex-free grammar $G = \{\Sigma, N, S, P\}$. Define a new grammar G^* as follows: The terminals Σ are the same as those of G. The nonterminals are also those of G, plus one new symbol S^*. The starting symbol is then S^*, and the productions are taken to be the productions of G, plus one more: $S^* \rightarrow S^*S \mid \lambda$. It is clear that $L(G^*) = (L(G))^*$, and that G^* is a contex-free grammar.

To show that the union and concatenation of two contex-free grammars is again contex-free we argue as follows. Let $G_i = \{\Sigma_i, N_i, S_i, P_i\}$ be a contex-free grammar for the language L_i, $i = 1, 2$. We may assume that the nonterminals of L_1 are disjoined from the nonterminals of L_2; $N_1 \cap N_2 = \emptyset$. To construct a grammar $G = \{\Sigma, N, S, P\}$ for the language $L_1 + L_2$ we take $\Sigma = \Sigma_1 \cup \Sigma_2$, $N = N_1 \cup N_2$ plus an additional new symbol S, which is also the new starting symbol of G, and the productions are $S \rightarrow S_1 \mid S_2$ plus all the productions from P_1 and P_2. Again it is clear that $L(G) = L(G_1) + L(G_2)$. To obtain a grammar for the language L_1L_2, we proceed in exactly the same way, except we introduce the production $S \rightarrow S_1S_2$, instead of $S \rightarrow S_1 \mid S_2$. Q.E.D.

Example 4.8. The intersection of two contex-free languages need not be contex-free. Indeed, the language $M_1 = \{a^n b^n \mid n = 0, 1, 2, \ldots\}$ is contex-free, its grammar may be taken to be $S \rightarrow aSb \mid \lambda$. The language $M_2 = \{c^k \mid k = 0, 1, 2, \ldots\}$ is also contex-free. Similarly, the languages $M_3 = \{a^i \mid i = 0, 1, \ldots\}$ and $M_4 = \{b^j c^j \mid j = 0, 1, 2, \ldots\}$ are contex-free. By Theorem 4.5 the languages $L_1 = M_1 M_2$ and $L_2 = M_3 M_4$ are contex-free. The language $L_1 \cap L_2$, however, is not context free. A moment of reflection shows that $L_1 \cap L_2$ is the language $L_0 = \{a^n b^n c^n \mid n = 0, 1, 2, \ldots\}$, which, as was shown in Example 4.7, is not contex-free.

The complement of a contex-free language need not be contex-free. Indeed, suppose the complement of every contex-free language were contex-free. Then, given two contex-free languages L_1 and L_2, the language $L_1 \cap L_2 = \overline{\overline{L_1} + \overline{L_2}}$ would be contex-free, which we just saw is not the case. This is a valid argument, but does not provide a concrete example. To construct such an example, we will show that the complement of the language L_0 above is contex-free. This clearly suffices, since any language is the complement of its complement: $\overline{\overline{L}} = L$. Consider now the language $\overline{L_0}$. A string σ will belong to $\overline{L_0}$ (i.e., not belong to L_0) if one of the two conditions hold:

1. σ is not of the form $a^i b^j c^k$.
2. σ is of the form $a^i b^j c^k$, but either $i \neq j$ or $j \neq k$.

Let K_1 be the set of strings from $\{a, b, c\}^*$ that satisfy 1, and let K_2 be the set of strings from $\{a, b, c\}^*$ that satisfy 2; evidently $\overline{L_0} = K_1 + K_2$. It is sufficient now to show that both K_1 and K_2 are contex-free, since the contex-free languages are closed with respect to the operation + (Theorem 4.5). The language K_1 is itself the complement of a regular language described by the regular expression $\boldsymbol{a^* b^* c^*}$. Since a complement of a regular language is again a regular language (Theorem 3.7), K_1 is a regular language, hence it is also contex-free. K_2 is a union of two languages, K_a and K_b, where $K_a = \{a^i b^j c^k \mid i \neq j\}$ and $K_b = \{a^i b^j c^k \mid j \neq k\}$: $K_2 = M_1 + M_2$. The argument will be completed if we can show that both K_a and K_b are contex-free: But we can produce a contex-free grammar for K_a:

$$
\begin{aligned}
S &\rightarrow AC \mid BC \\
A &\rightarrow aA \mid aP \\
B &\rightarrow Bb \mid Pb \\
C &\rightarrow cC \mid \lambda \\
P &\rightarrow aPb \mid \lambda
\end{aligned}
$$

The idea is quite simple: Nonterminal A will produce strings of the form $a^i b^j$ with $i > j$ and the nonterminal B will produce the strings of the form $a^i b^j$ with $i < j$. The nonterminal C produces strings consisting of c's alone, and the nonterminal P produces strings of the form $a^m b^m$. Hence, K_a is contex-free. The argument for K_b is completely analogous.

It is often said that one of the limitations of the push-down automata is that they cannot keep track of more that two infinite sequences. The fact that the above language L_0 is not a contex-free language and thus not accepted by any push-down automaton is the reason for that informal description. Any push-down automaton accepting L_0 would have to keep track of three arbitrarily long sequences: a's, b's, and c's.

PROBLEMS

In each of problems 1–7 construct a deterministic push-down automaton recognizing the given language. Give an informal verbal description and also provide all the formalities. In each problem show the movements of your machine on the indicated strings.

1. $L = \{a^{2n} b^n \mid n = 0, 1, 2, \ldots\}$; $\sigma_1 = aaaabb$, $\sigma_2 = aaabb$
2. $L = \{a^n bc^n \mid n = 0, 1, 2, \ldots\}$; $\sigma_1 = aaabccc$, $\sigma_2 = aabccc$
3. $L = \{\sigma \in \{0, 1\}^* \mid \sigma$ has more 0's than 1's$\}$; $\sigma_1 = 0110010$, $\sigma_2 = 110010$
4. $L = \{a^{2n} b^{3n} \mid n = 0, 1, 2, \ldots\}$; $\sigma_1 = aabbb$, $\sigma_2 = ababb$
5. $L = \{\sigma \in \{a, b\}^* \mid \sigma$ has the same number of a's as b's$\}$ $\sigma_1 = abbaab$, $\sigma_2 = bbaba$
6. $L = \{a^n b^m \mid n \neq m\}$; $\sigma_1 = aaabb$, $\sigma_2 = aaba$, $\sigma_3 = aabb$
7. $L = \{a^i b^j c^k \mid i + j = k\}$; $\sigma_1 = abbccc$, $\sigma_2 = aabbccc$

In each of problems 8–12 construct a nondetrministic PDA that accepts the languages with given grammar. Show the accepting movements of this PDA on the indicated string.

8. $S \to 0A1,\ A \to 00A1 \mid \lambda$; $\sigma = 00011$
9. $S \to 0AB \mid B1A,\ A \to BB \mid 0,\ B \to AA \mid 1$; $\sigma = 10001$
10. $S \to ABC,\ A \to BB \mid \lambda,\ B \to CC \mid a,\ C \to AA \mid b$; $\sigma = aaab$
11. $E \to E + T \mid T,\ T \to T * F \mid F,\ F \to (E) \mid a$; $\sigma = (a + a) * a$
12. $S \to Aa \mid bB,\ A \to aA \mid S,\ B \to b \mid Aa \mid \lambda$; $\sigma = aba$
13. Construct a PDA that will correctly translate arithmetic expressions from the infix notation to the postfix notation and that allows for exponentiation. Thus, a^b is denoted by $a \uparrow b$. The exponentiation

takes precedence over + and ∗, so that the expression (3 + 7) ∗ 5↑8 means in the usual notation $(3 + 7) * 5^8$ and should be translated to 3 7 + 5 8 ↑ ∗.

14. Write the following expressions in the postfix notation:
    a. (7 + 3 ∗ 5) ∗ (8 + 7 ∗ 2) + 1
    b. (3 + 2) ∗ (3 ∗ 7 + 8)
15. Convert the following expressions to the infix notation (all the numbers involved are single digits).
    a. 357 + ∗ 4 ∗ 5 +
    b. 12 + 3 ∗ 4 + 5 ∗
16. Show that the following languages have no contex-free grammars.
    a. $L = \{ a^{n^2} \mid n = 1, 2, 3, \ldots \}$
    b. $L = \{ a^n b^m c^k \mid 0 < n < m < k\}$
    c. $L = \{ a^p \mid p$ is a prime number$\}$
    d. $L = \{ a^n b^n c^m \mid m \leq n\}$
    e. $L = \{\sigma \in \{a, b, c\}^* \mid \sigma$ has equal number of a's, b's and c's$\}$
    f. $L = \{\sigma\sigma^R\sigma \mid \sigma \in \{0, 1\}^*\}$; σ^R means the reverse of σ
17. a. Show that the languages $L_1 = \{a^i b^{2j} c^j \mid i, j = 0, 1, 2, \ldots \}$ and $L_2 = \{a^j b^i c^{2i} \mid i, j = 0, 1, 2, \ldots \}$ are contex-free.
    b. Show that the language $L_1 \cap L_2$ is not contex-free.
18. Let L be a contex-free language and let $L^R = \{\sigma \mid \sigma^R \in L\}$. Show that L^R is also a contex-free language. (σ^R is the reverse of the string σ.)

CHAPTER 5

TURING MACHINES

5.1. INTRODUCTION AND DEFINITIONS

In previous chapters we introduced various kind of automatic devices, such as finite state machines and push-down automaton, that were designed to "recognize" languages generated by some grammar. The kinds of languages recognizable by finite state machines were quite restrictive—they were the languages possessing a regular grammar. The push-down automata turned out to be a more powerful devices; in fact, any context-ree language was recognized by some (possibly nondeterministic) PDA. However, even these machines have their limitations; for instance, a seemingly simple language $\{a^n b^n c^n |\ n = 0, 1, 2, \ldots\}$ is not recognized by any PDA. (See Example 4.6.) We have also discussed machines with output (Sections 3.4 and 4.3). These can be regarded as mathematical models of an intuitive concept of an algorithm: Given an input (presented as a finite sequence of symbols on a tape), the machine goes through the motions of performing computations on this input and produces certain output. The process of computation in these machines consisted of channging the internal states and adjusting various pointers (input, stack, and/or output). In this chapter we study another kind of device, called a Turing machine, that encompasses all of these capabilities, and is more powerful than any of the machines discussed so far. Curiously, the Turing machines seem to be the most powerful automatic devices possible—they are the very essence, in fact the precise mathematical definition, of the concept of an algorithm or an effective procedure. They were introduced for this very purpose in 1936 by Alan Turing, see [19]. We will discuss these ideas more precisely later on, but heuristically, the situation is as follows.

One thinks of an algorithm as a set of instructions, a "cookbook" if you will, issued to a machine that is supposed to operate on certain kinds of inputs. These inputs can be thought of as finite sequences of symbols that are to be read in by the machine (one by one), and the program or instructions that tell the machine what to do after reading each such symbol. The Turing machines essentially behave in this way, but what is interesting is that any reasonable, precise definition of an algorithm is equivalent to the concept of a Turing machine. As a matter of fact, an algorithm is defined as a Turing machine.

Heuristically, a Turing machine consists of a finite number of states and a tape. The tape is divided into an infinite (countable) number of cells. There is a leftmost cell, but the tape extends indefinitely to the right. Pictorially, Turing machines can be represented as in Figure 5.1.

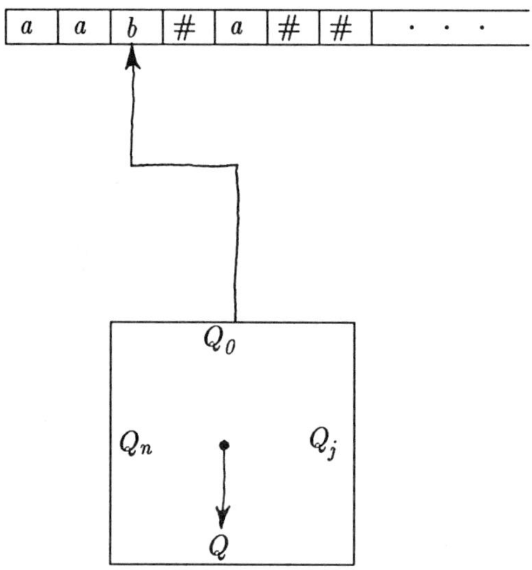

Figure 5.1. A Turing Machine.

The machine also has a read/write pointer (head) that at any given time points to one of the cells of the tape. There is also a finite collection Σ of symbols, called the tape alphabet. The elements of Σ are the symbols that are allowed to appear in the cells of the tape—one symbol per cell. One of these symbols is distinguished and is called the blank symbol, we will always denote it by #. When this symbol # appears in a cell, we say that the cell is blank. At any given moment there are only finitely many cells containing a non-blank symbol, all other cells are blank. Thus, all the cells to the right of certain cell are blank. The machine operates in discrete steps. At any given instant of time it is in some state Q, and its head points to a cell containing a symbol $x \in \Sigma$. Based on this information (x and Q), and this information only, the machine performs the following three operations:

1. Changes to a new state $\hat{Q}$.
2. Replaces the symbol x, presently scanned by the head, with another symbol $\hat{x}$ from Σ.
3. Moves the head one cell to the right or one cell to the left, or leaves the head where it is.

These three actions, when executed together, are called a move. After the machine executes a move it is in a new state and its head reads another symbol, so it executes another move and the procedure repeats. Initially, of course, the machine is in some specified initial state, which we will usually denote by Q_0, and the tape is filled with some sequence of symbols from Σ. The initial content of the tape will be called the input. We will always assume that the input contains only a finite number of non-blank cells. Thus, given the initial setup, the machine will start running. It will stop in the following three situations:

1. One of the states of the machine is designated as the halting state and will always be denoted by H. After the machine enters into this state H it ***halts*** and stops operating. We say in this case that the machine halts.

2. The read/write head of the machine points to the leftmost cell of the tape and the instructions call for the head to move one cell to the left. In this instance the machine also ceases to operate; when this happens we say that the machine ***hangs.***

3. There are no instruction in the program of the machine as to what to do in the present state and for the symbol presently under the head. When this happens, we also say that the machine ***hangs.***

Thus, given the initial input, the machine begins from the initial state Q_0 and then proceeds to go through the states while operating on the tape. It may operate indefinitely, it may halt, or it may hang. Formally we have the following:

Definition 5.1. A ***Turing machine*** T consists of the following four objects.

1. A finite set $\mathbb{Q}$ of ***states.*** One of the elements of $\mathbb{Q}$ is denoted by

H and is called the ***halting state.***

2. A finite set Σ of symbols, called the ***tape alphabet.*** One of the elements of Σ is #, it is called the ***blank symbol.*** It is also assumed that the symbols L, R, and S are not members of Σ.
3. A specified state Q_0 of $\mathbb{Q}$ called the ***initial state.***
4. A ***transition function*** $\delta(Q, x)$ defined for a collection of pairs (Q, x) where $Q \in \mathbb{Q}$ $(Q \neq H)$ and $x \in \Sigma$. The value of $\delta(Q, x)$ is a triple $(\hat{Q}, \hat{x}, N)$ where $Q \in \mathbb{Q}$, $x \in \Sigma$, and $N = L$, R, or S. Formally,

$$\delta\colon (\mathbb{Q}\backslash\{H\}) \times \Sigma \mapsto \mathbb{Q} \times \Sigma \times \{L, R, S\},$$

with the understanding that the function δ need not be defined for all values of Q and x.

Such a Turing machine will be denoted by $T = \{\mathbb{Q}, \Sigma, Q_0, \delta\}$. The interpretation of the transition function $\delta(Q, x) = (\hat{Q}, \hat{x}, N)$ is this: If the machine is in the state Q and its read/write head points at the symbol x, then T changes to state $\hat{Q}$, replaces x with $\hat{x}$, and moves the head one cell to the right (if $N = R$), one cell to one cell to the left (if $N = L$), or stays put (if $N = S$).

Before presenting some examples, we will develop a notation for describing configurations of Turing machines. Since at any given moment the tape of the machine contains only a finite number of non-blank symbols, the content of such a tape is completely described by listing the left-most portion of the tape up to and including the last non-blank symbol. To avoid certain ambiguities—for instance, when the tape is completely blank—we actually describe the content of the tape by three strings: σ_1, x, and σ_2, where σ_1 is the content of the tape to the left of the head, x is the symbol under the head, and σ_2 is the portion of the tape to the right of the head, up to and including the last non–blank symbols. Each of the strings σ_1 and σ_2 is allowed to be the empty string λ: If $\sigma_1 = \lambda$, the head points to the leftmost cell of the tape, if $\sigma_2 = \lambda$, all the cells to the right of the head are blank (i.e., contain the symbol #). The configuration of a Turing machine T is then defined to be a quadruple $[\![Q, \sigma_1, x, \sigma_2]\!]$, where Q is the present state and σ_1, x, and σ_2 are as described above. Thus, for instance, the configurations (i) and (ii) from Figure 5.2 are $[\![Q_4, a\#ba, \#, a]\!]$ and $[\![Q_5, aba, \#, \lambda]\!]$, respectively. When there is no danger of confusion, it is convenient to combine the strings σ_1, x, and σ_2 into one string $\sigma_1 x \sigma_2$ and underline the position of the head (i.e., the symbol x). Thus, $[\![Q, \sigma_1, x, \sigma_2]\!]$ is written as $[\![Q, \sigma_1\underline{x}\,\sigma_2]\!]$. The configurations from Figure 5.2 are then $[\![Q_4, a\#ba\underline{\#}a]\!]$ and $[\![Q_5, aba\underline{\#}]\!]$. The configuration of a machine in a state Q, whose tape is totally blank and whose head points to the leftmost cell is then $[\![Q, \underline{\#}]\!]$.

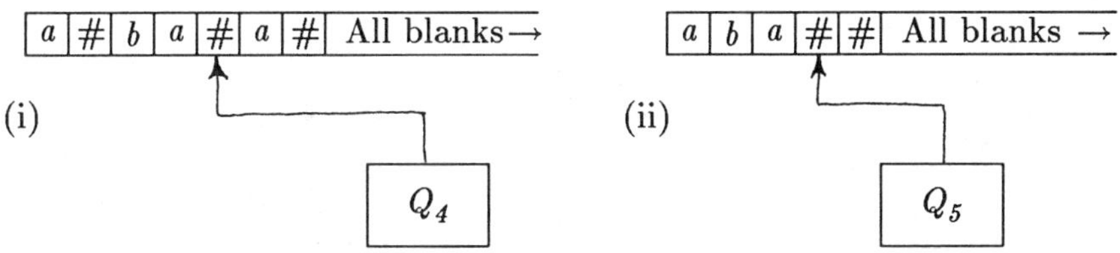

Figure 5.2. Configurations of a Turing machine.

Suppose now a Turing machine is in configuration $[\![Q, \sigma_1\underline{x}\sigma_2]\!]$ and as a result of application of a transition function δ it moves to configuration $[\![\hat{Q}, \hat{\sigma}_1\underline{\hat{x}}\ \hat{\sigma}_2]\!]$. We denote this by

$$[\![Q, \sigma_1\underline{x}\sigma_2]\!] \quad \rightarrow \quad [\![\hat{Q}, \hat{\sigma}_1\underline{\hat{x}}\ \hat{\sigma}_2]\!]$$

If the machine T goes from configuration $[\![Q, \sigma_1\underline{x}\sigma_2]\!]$ to $[\![\hat{Q}, \hat{\sigma}_1\underline{\hat{x}}\ \hat{\sigma}_2]\!]$ through a sequence of several moves, we denote this by

$$[\![Q, \sigma_1\underline{x}\sigma_2]\!] \quad \rightarrow^* \quad [\![\hat{Q}, \hat{\sigma}_1\underline{\hat{x}}\ \hat{\sigma}_2]\!].$$

This notation is completely analogous to the one used to describe the movements of finite state machines and push-down automata. In the same spirit, Turing machines may be represented by diagrams similar to those of finite state machines. If $T = \{\mathfrak{Q}, \Sigma, Q_0, \delta\}$ is a Turing machine, for each value $\delta(Q, x) = (\hat{Q}, \hat{x}, N)$ we draw an arrow between the states Q and $\hat{Q}$, as depicted in Figure 5.3.

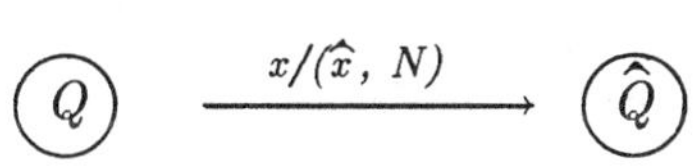

where $N = L$, R, or S

Figure 5.3. Transition of a Turing machine.

5.2. TURING MACHINES AS DECISION PROCEDURES

Turing machines may be used as recognizers of languages. What we mean by this is that given a language L, a Turing machine $T = T_L$ is said to recognize L if T is able to determine whether or not any given string σ is in L. Such a Turing machine can be viewed as a "decision procedure" for membership in the language. This is analogous to the situation for finite state machines. In that case, given a language L and a FSM M recognizing L, we were able to determine for any string σ whether or not σ is in L. The procedure was quite simple: We started M in the initial state with input σ and observed the behavior of M. If M halted in an accepting state σ was in L, if M halted in a nonaccepting state σ was not in L. In the case of Turing machines, the information whether or not given string σ is in the language is displayed on the tape. Formally, we have the following.

Definition 5.2. Suppose L is a language over some alphabet Σ; for simplicity we assume that Σ does not contain the symbols # and \$. We say that L is ***Turing recognizable***, if there exists a Turing machine $T = T_L$ with the following properties:

1. The tape alphabet of T contains $\Sigma \cup \{\$, \#\}$ (it may contain other symbols as well);
2. Suppose σ is a string of symbols in Σ ($\sigma \in \Sigma^*$) and consider the machine T in the initial configuration $[\![Q_0, \underline{\$}\sigma]\!]$. If σ is in L, the machine T will halt in configuration $[\![H, \underline{\$}Y]\!]$:

$$[\![Q_0, \underline{\$}\sigma]\!] \quad \rightarrow^* \ [\![H, \underline{\$}Y]\!] \ \text{ for } \sigma \in L;$$

   If, however, σ is not in L, the machine T will end up in configuration $[\![H, \underline{\$}N]\!]$:

$$[\![Q_0, \underline{\$}\sigma]\!] \quad \rightarrow^* \quad [\![H, \underline{\$}N]\!] \quad \text{for } \sigma \notin L.$$

Notice that the Turing machine T is required to halt on all valid inputs, i.e., whenever it is started in configuration $[\![Q_0, \underline{\$}\sigma]\!]$ for any $\sigma \in \Sigma^*$. This means that T can decide the membership question for ***any*** string $\sigma \in \Sigma^*$. For this reason, the languages recognized by a Turing machine are also called ***Turing decidable.*** A language can also be described by a Turing machine based on whether or not the machine halts on a given string. We say that a language L is ***accepted*** by a Turing machine $T = T_L$ if L consists of those σ's for which T, when started in configuration $[\![Q_0, \underline{\$}\sigma]\!]$, will eventually halt (the content of the tape when entering the halting state is immaterial). If a language L is accepted by some Turing machine, we say that L is ***Turing acceptable.*** This method of describing a language is profoundly different from the one just given and we will discuss it in more detail in Chapter 9.To clarify all these concepts, let us consider some examples.

Example 5.1. We will design a Turing machine that will recognize the language

$$L = \{1^n \mid n = 1, 3, 5, \ldots\}$$

i.e., the language consisting of all possible strings of odd number of 1's. The basic idea of such a machine T is as follows: Starting in configuration $[\![Q_0, \underline{\$}11 \ldots 1]\!]$ it will move the head to the right, alternating between two states to keep track of how many 1's have been encountered, until # is detected. It will then move left, replacing all tape symbols by #, until the left end of the tape is encountered; then either Y or N is placed on tape and the machine halts. The formal description of this machine is as follows:

1. The alphabet Σ is $\{\$, 1, Y, N, \#\}$.
2. The states are: Q_0, the initial state; Q_1, even number of 1's so far; Q_2, odd number of 1's so far; Q_3, the number of 1's in σ is even, move the head back to \$; Q_4, the number of 1's in σ is odd, move the head back to \$; Q_5, write Y and halt; Q_6, write N and halt; H, halting state.
3. The transition function δ is given by the diagram in Figure 5.4.

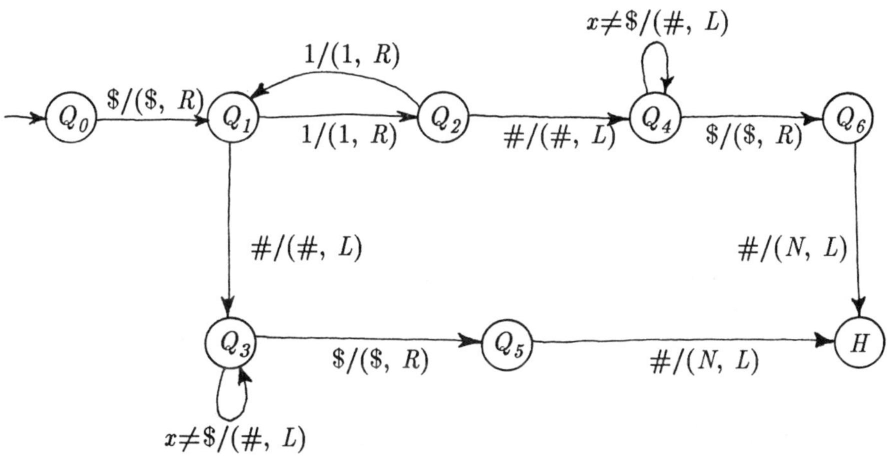

Figure 5.4. Turing machine recognizing a language.

In tabular form, the values of the transition function are given in Figure 5.5. The function δ is undefined for all the remaining values of Q and x. Consider now, for example, the movements of the machine on inputs $\sigma_1 = 111$ and $\sigma_2 = 1111$. On input σ_1 we have

$$\llbracket Q_0, \underline{\$}111\rrbracket \to \llbracket Q_1, \$\underline{1}11\rrbracket \to \llbracket Q_2, \$1\underline{1}1\rrbracket \to \llbracket Q_1, \$11\underline{1}\rrbracket$$
$$\to \llbracket Q_2, \$111\underline{\#}\rrbracket \to \llbracket Q_4, \$11\underline{1}\rrbracket \to \llbracket Q_4, \$1\underline{1}\rrbracket \to \llbracket Q_4, \$\underline{1}\rrbracket$$
$$\to \llbracket Q_4, \underline{\$}\rrbracket \to \llbracket Q_6, \$\underline{\#}\rrbracket \to \llbracket H, \underline{\$}Y\rrbracket$$ — Halts, the input string is in L.

		Tape symbol x				
		1	\$	#	Y	N
	Q_0		$(Q_1,\$,R)$			
S	Q_1	$(Q_2,1,R)$		$(Q_3,\#,L)$		
t	Q_2	$(Q_1,1,R)$		$(Q_4,\#,L)$		
a	Q_3	$(Q_3,\#,L)$	$(Q_5,\$,L)$	$(Q_3,\#,L)$		
t	Q_4	$(Q_4,\#,L)$	$(Q_6,\$,R)$	$(Q_4,\#,L)$		
e	Q_5			(H,N,L)		
	Q_6			(H,N,L)		
	H					

Figure 5.5. Values of the transition function δ.

On input σ_2 we have

$$\llbracket Q_0, \underline{\$}1111\rrbracket \to \llbracket Q_1, \$\underline{1}111\rrbracket \to \llbracket Q_2, \$1\underline{1}11\rrbracket \to \llbracket Q_1, \$11\underline{1}1\rrbracket$$
$$\to \llbracket Q_2, \$111\underline{1}\rrbracket \to \llbracket Q_1, \$1111\underline{\#}\rrbracket \to \llbracket Q_3, \$111\underline{1}\rrbracket \to \llbracket Q_3, \$11\underline{1}\rrbracket$$
$$\to \llbracket Q_3, \$1\underline{1}\rrbracket \to \llbracket Q_3, \$\underline{1}\rrbracket \to \llbracket Q_3, \underline{\$}\rrbracket \to \llbracket Q_5, \$\underline{\#}\rrbracket \to \llbracket \text{H}, \underline{\$}N\rrbracket$$
— Halts, the input string is not in L.

This machine, while quite simple and straightforward, is not all that interesting. The language in question was already recognized by finite automata. We now give an example of a Turing machine that will recognize the language $L = \{a^n b^n c^n \mid n = 0, 1, 2, \ldots\}$, which we know is not accepted by any push-down automaton, see Example 4.7.

Example 5.2. We construct a Turing machine T that recognizes the language $L = \{a^n b^n c^n \mid n = 0, 1, 2, \ldots\}$. The machine T will perform as follows: Given a string σ of a's, b's, and c's ($\sigma \in (a + b + c)^*$), the machine, once started in configuration $\llbracket Q_0, \underline{\$}\sigma\rrbracket$, will end in configuration $\llbracket H, \underline{\$}Y)\rrbracket$ if σ is in the language, and will end in configuration $\llbracket H, \underline{\$}N\rrbracket$ if σ is not in the language. A rough overview of the operation of T is as follows:

1. It will have states C_1, C_2, C_3. When T decides that σ is in the language, it will enter the state C_1 and then move to "clean up the tape" and end up in configuration $[\![H, \underline{\$}Y]\!]$.

2. It will have states D_1, D_2, D_3. When T decides that σ is not in the language, it will enter the state D_1 and proceed to the configuration $[\![H, \underline{\$}N]\!]$.

3. It will use states $E_1 - E_5$ to determine whether σ is of the form $a^i b^j c^k$, i.e., if $\sigma \in \boldsymbol{a}^* \boldsymbol{b}^* \boldsymbol{c}^*$. This will be done, beginning from configuration $[\![E_1, \underline{\$}\sigma]\!]$, by moving the head to the right and entering state E_2. If a is encountered, the head continues to move to the right waiting for b to appear, upon which T enters state E_3. The head is then moved right again, until c is encountered and the state is changed to E_4. The head continues to move right until # is found and it is determined that, indeed, $\sigma \in \boldsymbol{a}^* \boldsymbol{b}^* \boldsymbol{c}^*$. If anything goes wrong along the way, the machine enters the state D_1.

4. Next, it is determined if the number of a's, b's, and c's is the same. At this point it is already known that the string σ is of the form $a^i b^j c^k$, so what has to be checked is that $i = j$ and $j = k$. To verify that there are the same number of a's as b's, the head is positioned at the beginning of the string and is shuttled back and forth between a's and b's. Each time an a is detected, it is changed to p, and the head moves right to find a b. When one is found, it is changed to q, and the head moves back to find another a. If none is found, the machine checks that there are no unmarked b's, i.e., that all the b's have been changed to q's. Again, if anything goes wrong along the way, the machine moves to the state D_1. All this is done while the machine remains in one of the states F_1, F_2, F_3, F_4. What remains now is to determine if the number of p's is the same as the number of c's (each a was changed to a p, so there are as many p's as there were a's). This is done while the machine moves between states G_1, G_2, G_3; the idea is pretty much the same as in comparing a's and b's.

This may not be the most efficient way to construct the machine in question; the scheme was chosen for sake of clarity of exposition. The formalities of the construction are as follows:

1. The machine has the following states:
   Q_0, Q_1—to start the operation; (it will also be determined here if $\sigma = \lambda$)
   C_1, C_2, C_3—to clean up after it has been determined that $\sigma \in L$
   D_1, D_2, D_3—to clean up after it has been determine that $\sigma \notin L$
   E_1, E_2, E_3, E_4, E_5—to determine if $\sigma \in \boldsymbol{a}^* \boldsymbol{b}^* \boldsymbol{c}^*$
   F_1, F_2, F_3, F_4 —to determine if the number of a's and b's is the same

G_1, G_2, G_3—to determine if the number of a's and c's is the same

2. The tape alphabet is $\Sigma = \{\$, a, b, c, p, q, r, s, Y, N, \#\}$.
3. The initial state is Q_0.
4. The transition function δ is given as follows:

States C_1, C_2, and C_3: When the machine enters state C_1, it has determined that the string σ is in the language, and all that has to be done is to perform some housecleaning operations:

$\delta(C_1, x) = (C_1, x, R)$ for all $x \neq \#$ (This locates the first symbol
$\delta(C_1, \#) = (C_2, \#, L)$ on the right)

$\delta(C_2, x) = (C_2, \#, L)$ for all $x \neq \$$ (This erases all the symbols
$\delta(C_2, \$) = (C_3, \$, R)$ on the tape except \$)

$\delta(C_3, \#) = (H, Y, L)$ —Write Y on the tape and halt.

States D_1, D_2, and D_3: The movements here are almost the same as above, except that the symbol N has to be written at the end:

$\delta(D_1, x) = (D_1, x, R)$ for all $x \neq \#$, $\delta(D_1, \#) = (D_2, \#, L)$
$\delta(D_2, x) = (D_2, \#, L)$ for all $x \neq \$$, $\delta(D_2, \$) = (D_3, \$, R)$
$\delta(D_3, \#) = (H, N, L)$

States E_1—E_5. We start in configuration $[\![E_1, \underline{\$}\sigma]\!]$, then move to the right, expecting to find a string of a's, followed by a sequence of b's, followed by c's, and finally expect to find #. When this happens, we return the head back to \$ and proceed with the next stage. Any deviation from expected results in changing to the state D_1. We have:

$\delta(E_1, \$) = (E_2, \$, R)$ $\delta(E_2, a) = (E_2, a, R)$
$\delta(E_2, b) = (E_3, b, R)$ $\delta(E_3, b) = (E_3, b, R)$
$\delta(E_3, c) = (E_4, c, R)$ $\delta(E_4, c) = (E_4, c, R)$
$\delta(E_4, \#) = (E_5, \#, L)$

At this point, the machine has determined that $\sigma \in a^* b^* c^*$, so it must move the head back to \$ and proceed with the next set of tests:

$\delta(E_5, x) = (E_5, x, L)$ for all $x \neq \$$, $\delta(E_5, \$) = (F_1, \$, S)$. In all other cases, $\delta(E_j, x) = (D_1, x, R)$. (Proceed with rejection.)

States F_1—F_4: The object here is to determine if the number of a's is the same as the number of b's. Since we reached the configuration $[\![F_1, \underline{\$}\sigma]\!]$, we are guaranteed that σ is of the form $a^i b^j c^k$. We begin by moving the head to the right until a is found. The state will then be changed to F_2 and a replaced by p. The head will continue to move to the right (expecting only a's and q's along the way) until a b is encountered. When a b is indeed encountered, it is changed to q, the head moves back to the leftmost cell (\$), and the process starts again. The string σ passes this test of belonging to L if the machine, starting at \$ and moving right, does not find an a and also does not encounter any b's—all it sees are p's and q's and then stumbles on a c. The details are as follows:

$\delta(F_1, x) = (F_1, x, R)$ for $x = \$, p, q$; $\delta(F_1, a) = (F_2, p, R)$
(Find and mark an a)
$\delta(F_2, x) = (F_2, x, R)$ for $x = a, q$; $\delta(F_2, b) = (F_3, q, L)$
(Find and mark a b)
$\delta(F_3, x) = (F_3, x, L)$ for $x \neq \$$; $\delta(F_3, \$) = (F_1, \$, R)$
(Start searching for an a again)
$\delta(F_1, c) = (F_4, c, L)$; (All the a's and b's are matched, time to see if the number of p's is the same as the number of c's.)
$\delta(F_4, x) = (F_4, x, L)$ for all $x \neq \$$; $\delta(F_4, \$) = (G_1, \$, S)$
In all other situations $\delta(F_j, x) = (D_1, x, R)$ (the string is not in L).

States $G_1 - G_3$. It is determined here if the number of a's (p's at this stage) is equal to the number of c's. The main idea is completely analogous to the behavior in the states F; the exact formulation is as follows:

$\delta(G_1, x) = (G_1, x, R)$ for $x = \$, r, q, s$; $\delta(G_1, p) = (G_2, r, R)$
(Find and mark a p)
$\delta(G_2, x) = (G_2, x, R)$ for $x = p, q, s$; $\delta(G_2, c) = (G_3, s, L)$
(Find and mark a c)
$\delta(G_3, x) = (G_3, x, L)$ for $x \neq \$$; $\delta(G_3, \$) = (G_1, \$, R)$
(Start searching for a p again)
$\delta(G_1, \#) = (C_1, \#, L)$
(The number of p's is the same as the number of c's so $\sigma \in L$)
In all other situations $\delta(G_j, x) = (D_1, x, R)$.

Finally, the entire operation begins in the configuration $[\![Q_0, \underline{\$}\sigma]\!]$. Thus:

$$\delta(Q_0, \$) = (Q_1, \$, R);\ \delta(Q_1, \#) = (C_1, \#, R)$$
(the string $\sigma = \lambda$, proceed to accept)
$$\delta(Q_1, x) = (E_1, x, L) \text{ for all other } x\text{'s. (Begin with testing)}$$

We illustrate the behavior of T on the input $\sigma = aabbcc$. The movements are:

$$[\![Q_0, \underline{\$}aabbcc]\!] \to [\![Q_1, \$\underline{a}abbcc]\!] \to [\![E_1, \underline{\$}aabbcc]\!] \to [\![E_2, \$\underline{a}abbc]\!]$$
$$\to [\![E_2, \$a\underline{a}bbcc]\!] \to [\![E_2, \$aa\underline{b}bcc]\!] \to [\![E_3, \$aab\underline{b}cc]\!] \to [\![E_3, \$aabb\underline{c}c]\!]$$
$$\to [\![E_4, \$aabbc\underline{c}]\!] \to [\![E_4, \$aabbcc\underline{\#}]\!] \to [\![E_5, \$aabbc\underline{c}]\!] \to [\![E_5, \$aabb\underline{c}c]\!]$$
$$\to [\![E_5, \$aab\underline{b}cc]\!] \to [\![E_5, \$aa\underline{b}bcc]\!] \to [\![E_5, \$a\underline{a}bbcc]\!] \to [\![E_5, \$\underline{a}abbcc]\!]$$
$$\to [\![E_5, \underline{\$}aabbcc]\!] \to [\![F_1, \underline{\$}aabbcc]\!] \to [\![F_1, \$\underline{a}abbcc]\!] \to [\![F_2, \$p\underline{a}bbcc]\!]$$
$$\to [\![F_2, \$pa\underline{b}bcc]\!] \to [\![F_3, \$p\underline{a}qbcc]\!] \to [\![F_3, \$\underline{p}aqbcc]\!] \to [\![F_3, \underline{\$}paqbcc]\!]$$
$$\to [\![F_1, \$\underline{p}aqbcc]\!] \to [\![F_1, \$p\underline{a}qbcc]\!] \to [\![F_2, \$pp\underline{q}bcc]\!] \to [\![F_2, \$ppq\underline{b}cc]\!]$$
$$\to [\![F_3, \$pp\underline{q}qcc]\!] \to [\![F_3, \$p\underline{p}qqcc]\!] \to [\![F_3, \$\underline{p}pqqcc]\!] \to [\![F_3, \underline{\$}ppqqcc]\!]$$
$$\to [\![F_1, \$\underline{p}pqqcc]\!] \to [\![F_1, \$p\underline{p}qqcc]\!] \to [\![F_1, \$pp\underline{q}qcc]\!] \to [\![F_1, \$ppq\underline{q}cc]\!]$$
$$\to [\![F_1, \$ppqq\underline{c}c]\!] \to [\![F_4, \$ppq\underline{q}cc]\!] \to [\![F_4, \$pp\underline{q}qcc]\!] \to [\![F_4, \$p\underline{p}qqcc]\!]$$
$$\to [\![F_4, \$\underline{p}pqqcc]\!] \to [\![F_4, \underline{\$}ppqqcc]\!] \to [\![G_1, \underline{\$}ppqqcc]\!] \to [\![G_1, \$\underline{p}pqqcc]\!]$$
$$\to [\![G_2, \$r\underline{p}qqcc]\!] \to [\![G_2, \$rp\underline{q}qcc]\!] \to [\![G_2, \$rpq\underline{q}cc]\!] \to [\![G_2, \$rpqq\underline{c}c]\!]$$
$$\to [\![G_3, \$rpq\underline{q}sc]\!] \to [\![G_3, \$rp\underline{q}qsc]\!] \to [\![G_3, \$r\underline{p}qqsc]\!] \to [\![G_3, \$\underline{r}pqqsc]\!]$$
$$\to [\![G_3, \underline{\$}rpqqsc]\!] \to [\![G_1, \$\underline{r}pqqsc]\!] \to [\![G_1, \$r\underline{p}qqsc]\!] \to [\![G_2, \$rr\underline{q}qsc]\!]$$
$$\to [\![G_2, \$rrq\underline{q}sc]\!] \to [\![G_2, \$rrqq\underline{s}c]\!] \to [\![G_2, \$rrqqs\underline{c}]\!] \to [\![G_3, \$rrqq\underline{s}s]\!]$$
$$\to [\![G_3, \$rrq\underline{q}ss]\!] \to [\![G_3, \$rr\underline{q}qss]\!] \to [\![G_3, \$r\underline{r}qqss]\!] \to [\![G_3, \$\underline{r}rqqss]\!]$$
$$\to [\![G_3, \underline{\$}rrqqss]\!] \to [\![G_1, \$\underline{r}rqqss]\!] \to [\![G_1, \$r\underline{r}qqss]\!] \to [\![G_1, \$rr\underline{q}qss]\!]$$
$$\to [\![G_1, \$rrq\underline{q}ss]\!] \to [\![G_1, \$rrqq\underline{s}s]\!] \to [\![G_1, \$rrqqs\underline{s}]\!] \to [\![G_1, \$rrqqss\underline{\#}]\!]$$
$$\to [\![C_1, \$rrqqs\underline{s}]\!] \to [\![C_1, \$rrqqss\underline{\#}]\!] \to [\![C_2, \$rrqqs\underline{s}]\!] \to [\![C_2, \$rrqq\underline{s}]\!]$$
$$\to [\![C_2, \$rrq\underline{q}]\!] \to [\![C_2, \$rr\underline{q}]\!] \to [\![C_2, \$r\underline{r}]\!] \to [\![C_2, \$\underline{r}]\!] \to [\![C_2, \underline{\$}]\!]$$
$$\to [\![C_3, \$\underline{\#}]\!] \to [\![H, \underline{\$}Y]\!]$$ — the string is in the language.

5.3. COMPUTATIONS WITH TURING MACHINES

In Examples 5.1 and 5.2 we constructed Turing machines that served the role of recognizers of certain kind of languages. These machine decided if a given input string was "valid" or not, that is, they made a decision whether the given string belonged to certain languages. Turing machines can also serve a role of "calculators" or "computers." More precisely, suppose $f(n)$ is a function of one variable n which we restrict to be a positive integer, and suppose that the values of f are also positive integers ($f\colon \mathbb{N}^+ \mapsto \mathbb{N}^+$). We say that f is ***Turing computable*** if there is a Turing machine T_f with the following property: Given any initial input consisting of n 1's, the machine T_f will move from the initial configuration

$$[\![Q_0,\ \underline{\$}\ \underbrace{111\ldots1}_{n\ 1\text{'s}}]\!]$$

to the halting configuration

$$[\![H,\ \underline{\$}\ \underbrace{111\ldots1}_{f(n)\ 1\text{'s}}]\!]$$

Example 5.3. We will construct an example of a Turing machine T for the function $f(n) = 2n$. Heuristically, such a machine will operate as follows:

1. Starting from the leftmost cell of the tape, the machine moves right until it finds symbol 1. When that occurs, 1 is replaced by a, and the head continues to move right until the first blank symbol # is encountered and is replaced by b.

2. The head moves back to the leftmost cell and proceeds to seek another 1. When found, this 1 is again replaced by a and the first available blank symbol is replaced by b.

3. Step 2 is repeated as many times as there are 1's in the original input. When there are no more 1's left, the tape will contain n a's and n b's. All these are again replaced by 1's and the machine halts.

Formally, this machine is depicted by the diagram in Figure 5.6. The state Q_1 is used to seek the next 1 and replace it by a, Q_2 finds the first available # and replaces it by b, Q_3 moves the head back to the leftmost cell, Q_4 replaces a's and b's by 1's and changes to the halting state when \$ is reached. The tape alphabet is $\Sigma = \{1, a, b, \$, \#\}$. The symbol \$ is introduced here, and in the previous examples, strictly for convenience—it is used to mark the leftmost cell of the tape but it actually could be dispensed with, at the cost of making the machine more complicated. Consider, for example, the movements of this machine on the input $\sigma = 11$:

$$[\![Q_0, \underline{\$}11]\!] \to [\![Q_1, \$\underline{1}1]\!] \to [\![Q_2, \$a\underline{1}]\!] \to [\![Q_2, \$a1\underline{\#}]\!]$$
$$\to [\![Q_3, \$a\underline{1}b]\!] \to [\![Q_3, \$\underline{a}1b]\!] \to [\![Q_3, \underline{\$}a1b]\!] \to [\![Q_1, \$\underline{a}1b]\!]$$

$\rightarrow [\![Q_1, \$a\underline{1}b]\!] \rightarrow [\![Q_2, \$aa\underline{b}]\!] \rightarrow [\![Q_2, \$aab\underline{\#}]\!] \rightarrow [\![Q_3, \$aa\underline{b}b]\!]$

$\rightarrow [\![Q_3, \$a\underline{a}bb]\!] \rightarrow [\![Q_3, \$\underline{a}abb]\!] \rightarrow [\![Q_3, \underline{\$}aabb]\!] \rightarrow [\![Q_1, \$\underline{a}abb]\!]$

$\rightarrow [\![Q_1, \$a\underline{a}bb]\!] \rightarrow [\![Q_1, \$aa\underline{b}b]\!] \rightarrow [\![Q_1, \$aab\underline{b}]\!] \rightarrow [\![Q_1, \$aabb\underline{\#}]\!]$

$\rightarrow [\![Q_4, \$aab\underline{b}]\!] \rightarrow [\![Q_4, \$aa\underline{b}1]\!] \rightarrow [\![Q_4, \$a\underline{a}11]\!] \rightarrow [\![Q_4, \$\underline{a}111]\!]$

$\rightarrow [\![Q_4, \underline{\$}1111]\!] \rightarrow [\![H, \underline{\$}1111]\!]$—Yet another proof that $2 * 2 = 4$.

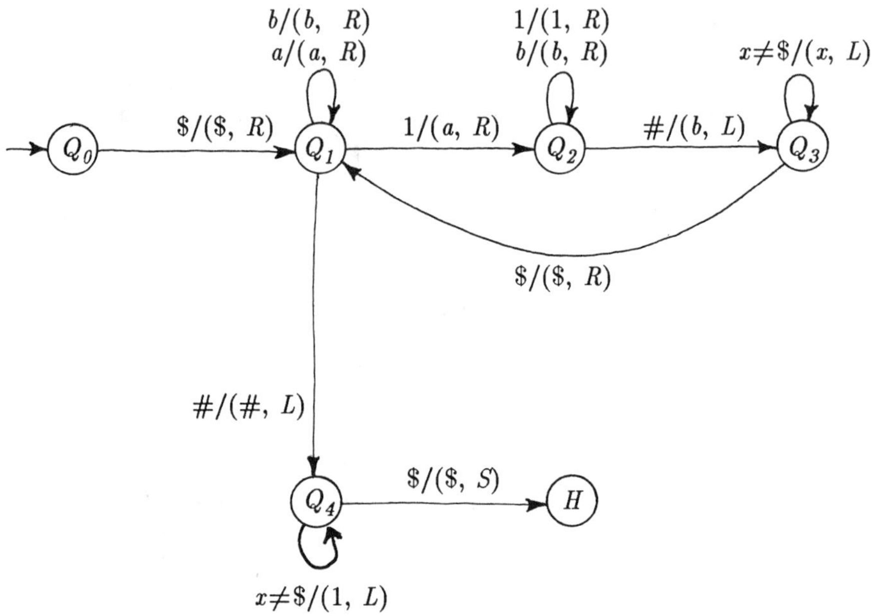

Figure 5.6. A calculating Turing machine.

The idea of computable functions need not be restricted to functions between the integers. One thinks of a computable function as an "algorithm," or a "set of rules" that, given an argument (input) consisting of a finite string of symbols, produces a value (output), also consisting of a finite string of (possibly different) symbols.

Definition 5.3. Let Δ_1 and Δ_2 be two alphabets (finite, nonempty set of symbols), which, for convenience, we assume do not contain the symbols \$ and #. Let $f(\sigma)$ be a function whose arguments are strings σ of symbols from Δ_1, and whose values are strings ρ of symbols from Δ_2. We assume that f is defined for all strings σ as above—$f\colon \Delta_1^* \mapsto \Delta_2^*$. We say that f is ***Turing computable*** if there exists a Turing machine T_f such that whenever $f(\sigma) = \rho$, the machine T_f will move from the initial configuration $[\![Q_0, \underline{\$}\sigma]\!]$ to the halting configuration $[\![H, \underline{\$}\rho]\!]$. In other words, T_f will transform the input σ to the output $f(\sigma)$.

This definition covers all kind of situations. For example, an integer valued function of three variables $w = f(x, y, z)$ is Turing computable if there is a Turing machine T_f that will transform an input

$$e_1\underbrace{11\ldots1}_{x\ 1\text{'s}} \mid e_2\underbrace{11\ldots1}_{y\ 1\text{'s}} \mid e_3\underbrace{11\ldots1}_{z\ 1\text{'s}}$$

into

$$e\underbrace{11\ldots1}_{f(x,y,z)\ 1\text{'s}}$$

The e's are either empty strings λ or $+$ or $-$, and $|$ is a delimiter. Thus, if $w = f(x, y, z) = 3x - 4y - z$, so that $f(1, 2, -3) = -2$, the Turing machine for f would have to transform the string $1|11|-111$ into -11, i.e., move from configuration $[\![Q_0, \underline{\$}1|11|-111]\!]$ to $[\![H, \underline{\$}-11]\!]$.

Turing machines are generally accepted to be precise notions of vague concepts of "***algorithm***" or "***effective procedure***." Thus, to say that there exists an algorithm to solve a certain problem is to say that there exists a Turing machine which, when presented with a tape containing the description of this problem, will perform a finite sequence of moves and will halt with its tape containing the solution of the problem. There are other definitions of algorithms and effectively computable functions, but they are equivalent to the one just given. The assertion that any computationally effective procedure, or any algorithm, can be implemented by a Turing machine is known as the Church-Turing thesis (see [6] and [19]). It cannot, of course be proved, but it is almost universally accepted. This, naturally, brings a question whether every function is computable and whether every problem has an algorithm to solve it. Precisely what is meant by this is the following:

1. Is it true that given any function $f\colon \mathbb{N} \mapsto \mathbb{N}$, say, there exists a Turing machine T_f which for any n will execute the following sequence of moves:

$$[\![Q_0, \underline{\$}\underbrace{1\,1\ldots1}_{n\ 1\text{'s}}]\!] \to^* [\![H, \underline{\$}\underbrace{1\,1\ldots1}_{f(n)\ 1\text{'s}}]\!]$$

2. The question "Does every problem have an algorithm which will solve it?" is of course too vague and imprecise for any sensible mathematical analysis. We will formulate it as follows: Suppose $\mathcal{C}$ is a class of problems, each one of which can be completely described by a finite number of symbols from a fixed alphabet Δ. Suppose also that each problem from $\mathcal{C}$ is well posed, i.e., can be answered Yes or No. To ask for the existence of an algorithm to solve all the problems from $\mathcal{C}$ is to ask the following: Does there exist a Turing machine $T_{\mathcal{C}}$ that, when started in configuration $[\![Q_0, \underline{\$}\sigma]\!]$, where σ is the description of a problem from $\mathcal{C}$, will halt in configuration $[\![H, \underline{\$}Y]\!]$ if the answer to σ is Yes, and it will halt in configuration $[\![H, \underline{\$}N]\!]$ if the answer to σ is No. When expressed in these terms, an algorithm is then just another effectively computable function $f\colon \Delta^* \mapsto \{Y, N\}$.

The surprising answer to both of these questions is no. Uuncomputable functions and unsolvable problems do exist. This asserton, of course, has a variety of philosophical implications, which we will not touch upon here. Instead, the remainder of the chapter will be devoted to explicitly exhibiting such problems and such functions.

5.4. EXTENSIONS OF TURING MACHINES

A curious, and essential, property of Turing machines is that their power in terms of computation cannot be readily increased. We may, for instance, consider Turing machines with more than one tape, the precise definition being more or less obvious. It turns out that any function that can be computed by such a machine can also be computed by a standard (one tape) machine. Another possibility is to allow the Turing machine to have more than one head on its tape—again nothing is gained by this. Anything that can be computed by these seemingly more powerful machines can also be computed by a standard Turing machine.

The situation is similar when we consider nondeterministic Turing machines. The precise definition of these is exactly as before, except that we allow the transition function $\delta(Q, x)$ to be multiple valued: Given that the machine is in the state Q and its head points to symbol x on the tape, $\delta(Q, x)$ gives the list of possible legal moves. It is difficult to speak of a language being recognized by a nondeterministic Turing machine, since, depending on the initial input, different choices of moves may produce different results. We may, however, talk of a language L being accepted by a nondeterministic Turing machine. Given such a Turing machine T, the language L_T accepted by L consists of those strings σ for which there is ***some*** sequence of legal moves, beginning with the configuration $[\![Q_0, \underline{\$}\sigma]\!]$, that will cause T to halt. (We do not require that T is able to ***decide*** whether or not given string σ is in L.) As far as acceptance of languages goes, the nondeterministic machines are no more powerful than the deterministic: If a language L is accepted by some nondeterministic Turing machine T_1, it is also accepted by some other, deterministic Turing machine T_2. The situation is thus quite analogous to the case of finite automata, but different from push-down automata.

We will not prove all of these results—the arguments are quite tedious and do not give any additional insight into the structure of the subject matter. We refer the reader to any one of the more detailed treatises on the subject, see [15] or [8]. We shall give only one illustration of a theorem of this kind, namely, that any Turing machine with two tapes is equivalent to a standard, one-tape machine. We should make things a bit more precise. A Turing machine with two tapes will, of course, have two heads. Thus a transition function δ of such a machine has the form

$$\delta(Q, x_1, x_2) = (\hat{Q}, \hat{x}_1, N_1, \hat{x}_2, N_2)$$

where Q is the present state, x_1 is the tape symbol under the head on the first tape, x_2 is the symbol read by the second head, $\hat{Q}$ is the new state, $\hat{x}_1$ and $\hat{x}_2$ are the symbols replacing x_1 and x_2, and N_1 and N_2 are the instructions for the respective heads to move right ($N_i = R$), left ($N_i = L$), or stay put ($N_i = S$). A configuration of such a machine will be described by

$$[\![Q, \alpha_1 \underline{x_1} \beta_1, \alpha_2 \underline{x_2} \beta_2]\!]$$

where Q is the present state and $\alpha_i \underline{x_i} \beta_i$ is the content of the ith tape, $i = 1, 2$ (the location of the head is underlined).

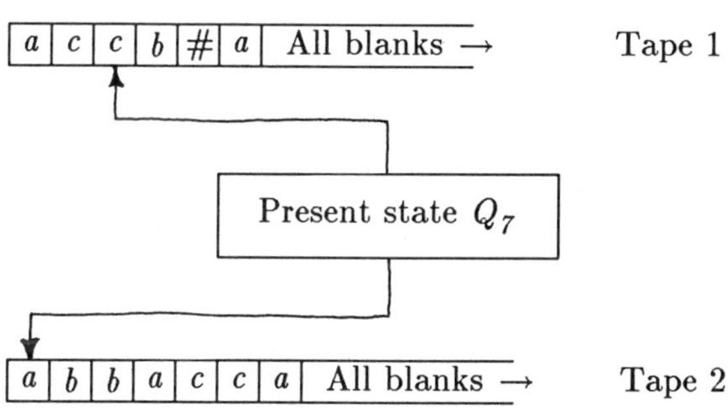

Figure 5.7. A two-tape Turing machine.

For example, the two-tape Turing machine from Figure 5.7 is in configuration $[\![Q_7,\ ac\underline{c}b\#a,\ \underline{a}bbacca]\!]$. If, for instance, $\delta(Q_7, c, a) = (Q_3, b, L, b, R)$, the next configuration of this machine will be $[\![Q_3,\ a\underline{c}cb\#a,\ b\underline{b}bacca]\!]$.

Let L be a language over an alphabet Σ. We say that L is ***recognized*** by a two-tape Turing machine T_2 if for any σ in Σ^* the following is true:

$$\sigma \in L \quad \text{implies } [\![Q_0,\ \underline{\$}\sigma,\ \underline{\$}]\!] \quad \to^* \quad [\![H,\ \underline{\$}Y,\ \underline{\$}]\!]$$
$$\sigma \notin L \quad \text{implies } [\![Q_0,\ \underline{\$}\sigma,\ \underline{\$}]\!] \quad \to^* \quad [\![H,\ \underline{\$}Y,\ \underline{\$}]\!]$$

With this notation we have the following:

Theorem 5.1. Let L be a language over an alphabet Σ. Then L is recognized by a two-tape Turing machine T_2 if and only if it is recognized by a standard, one-tape machine T_1 (as in Definition 5.2).

Proof. If a language is recognized by a one-tape machine T_1, it is clearly recognized by a two-tape machine T_2: we do not move the second head. Formally, given $T_1 = \{\mathfrak{Q}, \Sigma, Q_0, \delta\}$, the machine T_2 will have the same states and the same alphabet as T_1, and its transition function will be given by

$$\delta_2(Q, x, y) \quad = \quad (\hat{Q}, \hat{x}_1, \hat{N}, y, S)$$

where $\delta_1(Q, x) = (\hat{Q}, \hat{x}, \hat{N})$—we move the first head of T_2 in the same way as the single head of T_1 moves, and keep the second head always pointing to the leftmost cell. A moment of reflection shows that everything works out fine. The more difficult (and interesting) part of the proof is to show that if a language L is recognized by a two-tape machine, it is also recognized by a standard, one-tape machine. After all, it may seem at first sight that having a second tape at our disposal allows for more powerful computations: We may store some information on one tape while massaging the other. It turns out that this is not the case. A completely formal proof of this is quite tedious and involved, and somewhat beyond the scope of this book. We will present a fairly detailed sketch of the main idea.

Let T_2 be a two-tape Turing machine recognizing a language L. Denote its heads by h_1 and h_2. We will first construct an auxiliary one-tape machine U that will simulate the movements of T_2 as follows. Each cell of the tape of the machine U will contain one of the following: the symbol £, the blank symbol % (to distinguish it from the blank symbol

of the machine T_2), or a quadruple $(a_1, \epsilon_1, a_2, \epsilon_2)$. The symbol £ will always be in the leftmost cell and will never be removed. The quadruple $(a_1, \epsilon_1, a_2, \epsilon_2)$ in the ith cell of U will contain the information about the ith cells of the tapes of the machine T_2. (We number the cells of U beginning with 0th cell: the leftmost cell of U is the 0th cell, the next one is the first cell, etc. The cells of T_2 will be numbered beginning with 1: the leftmost cell of each of the tapes of T_2 is referred to as cell number 1, followed by cell number 2, etc.).

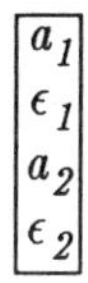

Figure 5.8. A cell of the Turing machine U.

If the ith cells of the tapes of T_2 contain symbols x and y, respectively, then the ith cell of U contains the quadruple $(x, \epsilon_1, y, \epsilon_2)$. The symbols ϵ_1 and ϵ_2 are determined as follows: If the head h_1 points at the ith cell of the first tape of T_2, we set $\epsilon_1 = 1$, otherwise $\epsilon_1 = 0$; the same rule applies to the symbol ϵ_2—it is equal to 1 or 0 depending whether or not the head h_2 points to the ith cell of the second tape of T_2. We will depict such a quadruple in a vertical form as in Figure 5.8. Thus, if the tapes of the machine T_2 are in configuration depicted in Figure 5.9, the tape of the machine U will be of the form given in Figure 5.10.

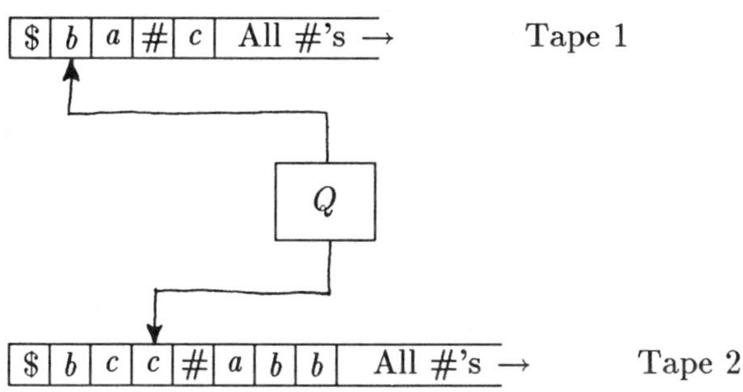

Figure 5.9. Tapes of a two-tape Turing machine.

The behavior of the machine U should now be evident: A single move of the machine T_2 will result in changing the state of the machine, the content of two of the cells (one on each tape), and readjusting of the positions of the heads h_1 and h_2. Each such move by T_2 will precipitate a sequence of moves by U, resulting in an adjustment of its cells—the relevant values of a_i's and ϵ_i will have to be changed to reflect the new configuration of the machine T_2.

<table>
<tr><td rowspan="4">£</td><td>$</td><td>b</td><td>a</td><td>#</td><td>c</td><td>#</td><td>#</td><td>#</td><td rowspan="4">%</td><td rowspan="4">All %'s →</td></tr>
<tr><td>0</td><td>1</td><td>0</td><td>0</td><td>0</td><td>0</td><td>0</td><td>0</td></tr>
<tr><td>$</td><td>b</td><td>c</td><td>c</td><td>#</td><td>a</td><td>b</td><td>b</td></tr>
<tr><td>0</td><td>0</td><td>0</td><td>1</td><td>0</td><td>0</td><td>0</td><td>0</td></tr>
</table>

Figure 5.10. A single tape of a Turing machine.

Formally, the alphabet Σ_U of the machine U is given by a finite set

$$\Sigma_U = \{£, \%\} \cup (\Sigma \times \{0, 1\} \times \Sigma \times \{0, 1\})$$

The machine U will start operating with its head pointing to the leftmost cell (containing symbol £). After each move of T_2 its head will move to the right, making whatever adjustment are necessary, and return back to the leftmost cell awaiting the next move by T_2. This can be accomplished by having the states of U be essentially expressions of the form

$$(Q, x, y, \delta(Q, x, y))$$

where Q is the present state of T_2, and x and y are the symbols from Σ under the heads h_1 and h_2, respectively. The instructions of the machine U can be made now quite explicit:

1. Start in the state $(Q_0, x_0, y_0, \delta(Q_0, x_0, y_0))$ with the head pointing to the leftmost cell (containing the symbol £). The symbols x_0 and y_0 as well as the initial content of the tape of U will reflect the initial configuration of the machine T_2.

2. Move the head to the right until both occurrences of $\epsilon_i = 1$ are encountered. At each such occurrence, change the values of the relevant a's and ϵ's. (The information of what to do when $\epsilon = 1$ is encountered is contained in the value of $\delta(Q_0, x_0, y_0)$.) Make note of these new values, say $\hat{Q}$, $\hat{x}$, and $\hat{y}$; return to the leftmost cell (which can be detected by the presence of £); and change to a new state $(\hat{Q}, \hat{x}, \hat{y}, \delta(\hat{Q}, \hat{x}, \hat{y}))$.

3. Repeat step 2 until the new state $\hat{Q}$ is the halting state H of T_2.

4. "Clean up" by ending with the head at the leftmost cell and halt.

It should be quite clear that the one-tape machine U will simulate the movements of the two-tape machine T_2—whatever decisions are made by T_2 will be also made by U. It is also clear that, by adding some additional states to U, one can transform the final content of its tape to the form required in the enunciation of Theorem 5.1 . Q.E.D.

We should remark here that while adding an additional tape to a Turing machine has no effect on the computational power of such a machine, it does have a definite effect on its efficiency. Suppose T_2 is a two-tape Turing machine being simulated by a one-tape machine T_1, as in Theorem 5.1. If one of the heads of T_2 is m cells away from the beginning of the tape and T_2 makes a move, it takes at least m moves by T_1 to simulate that single move. If T_2 starts its operation with both heads at the left-most cells and at each move both heads move to the right, then it takes at least $1 + 2 + \cdots + k \approx \frac{1}{2}k^2$ moves by T_1 to simulate the first k moves of T_2. Hence, very loosely speaking, if a one-tape Turing machine takes n moves to complete certain task, one may expect that adding an additional tape will result in the task being performed in $\sqrt{n}$ steps. These ideas can be made considerably more precise, and the subject of computational complexity deals with questions of this kind. We refer an interested reader to [13].

5.5. ENCODINGS

It is clear that the concept of a Turing machine is independent of the way one describes such machines. Thus, it does not matter if we denote the states of a machine by $Q_0, Q_1, \ldots$, or by $P_0, P_1, \ldots$. What matters only are the "internal works" of the device—i.e., the number of states, the number of tape symbols, the transition relations, and the designation of certain states as initial and/or halting. We will now present a scheme that uniformly describes any and all Turing machines. More precisely, given a Turing machine T, we will show how to give a complete and unambiguous description of T using only a finite number of fixed symbols. In fact, any Turing machine can be so described using only the symbols B, A, E, P, X, Y, R, L, S, 0, and 1. This is done as follows: Any Turing machine, by definition, consists of a ***finite*** number of states, a ***finite*** tape alphabet, and a ***finite*** number of transition relations involving only the states and the tape symbols. Thus, any Turing machine may be described by a sequence of symbols

$$B\epsilon_1 A\epsilon_2 PT_1T_2 \ldots T_mE \tag{5.1}$$

where

1. ϵ_1 is the number of states of T written in binary notation (i.e., using only 0's and 1's). The initial state is assigned number 1 and the halting state the number ϵ_1.
2. ϵ_2 is the number of tape symbols of T, again written in binary notation. The blank symbol, which is a tape symbol for any Turing machine, will be assigned number 1.
3. $T_1, T_2, \ldots, T_k$ are encoded transition relations of T as follows. Each state and each tape symbol of T are assigned a unique number—the states have numbers between 1 and ϵ_1 and the tape symbols numbers between 1 and ϵ_2. Each transition relation $\delta(Q, x) = (\hat{Q}, \hat{x}, N)$ is then encoded as

$$\eta_1 X \eta_2 X \eta_3 X \eta_4 X N Y$$

where η_1 and η_2 are the numbers assigned to Q and x, respectively, η_3 and η_4 are the numbers assigned to $\hat{Q}$ and $\hat{x}$, and $N = R$, L, or S. The symbols B, A, P, X, Y, and E are used as delimiters.

If T is a Turing machine, we denote by $D_1(T)$ the description of T given by (5.1):

$$D_1(T) = B\epsilon_1 A\epsilon_2 P T_1 T_2 \ldots T_m E \tag{5.2}$$

In a similar way, any initial (finite) segment of the tape of any Turing machine T can be encoded using only symbols A, F, W, Z, 0, and 1. The encoding of such a tape has form

$$W\epsilon_2 A\psi_1 Z\psi_2 Z\psi_2 \ldots Z\psi_k F \tag{5.3}$$

Here ϵ_2 is the number of tape symbols of T and $\psi_1, \psi_2, \ldots, \psi_k$ are the numbers of these symbols actually appearing on the tape: ψ_1 is the number of the tape symbol appearing in the first (leftmost) cell, ψ_2 is the number of symbol appearing in the second cell, etc. These numbers ϵ_2, $\eta_1, \eta_2, \ldots, \eta_k$ are expressed in binary notation and W, A, Z, and F serve as delimiters. It is understood that the symbol appearing in the cells to the right of the kth cell is the blank symbol, whose number is 1. The encoding of the initial portion σ of the tape just described will be denoted by $D_2(\sigma)$:

$$D_2(\sigma) = W\epsilon_2 A\psi_1 Z\psi_2 Z\psi_2 \ldots Z\psi_k F \tag{5.4}$$

Example 5.4. Consider the Turing machine given by the diagram in Figure 5.11.

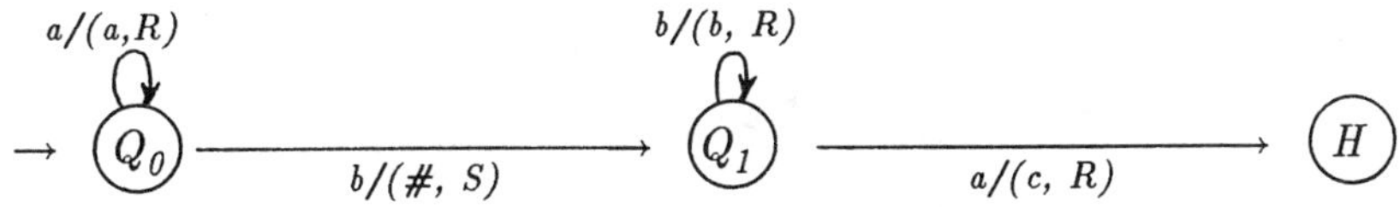

Figure 5.11. A Turing machine T.

This machine has three states, so $\epsilon_1 = 11$ (binary, $= 3$ in decimal). By convention, the initial state Q_0 is assigned number 1 and the halting state H the number $\epsilon_1 = 11$; thus, Q_1 is assigned number 10. There are 4 tape symbols: a, b, c, and #, so $\epsilon_2 = 100$(in binary); by convention # is assigned number 1, and we arbitrarily assign 10 to a, 11 to b, and 100 to c. The transitions of T are encoded as follows:

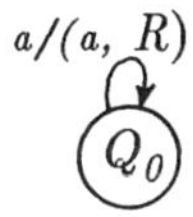

stands for $\delta(Q_0, a) = (Q_0, a, R)$ and is encoded as

$$\underbrace{1}_{Q_0}\ X\ \underbrace{10}_{a}\ X\ \underbrace{1}_{Q_0}\ X\ \underbrace{10}_{a}\ X\ R\ Y$$

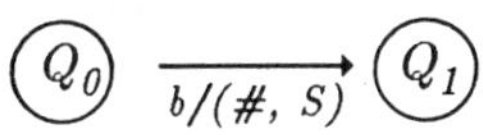

stands for $\delta(Q_0, b) = (Q_1, \#, S)$ and is encoded as

$$\underbrace{1}_{Q_0}\ X\ \underbrace{11}_{b}\ X\ \underbrace{10}_{Q_1}\ X\ \underbrace{1}_{\#}\ X\ S\ Y$$

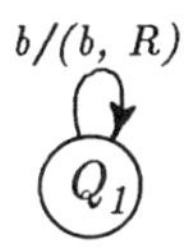

stands for $\delta(Q_1, b) = (Q_1, b, R)$ and is encoded as

$$\underbrace{10}_{Q_1}\ X\ \underbrace{11}_{b}\ X\ \underbrace{10}_{Q_1}\ X\ \underbrace{11}_{b}\ X\ R\ Y$$

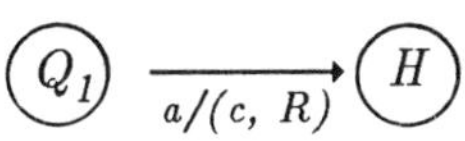

stands for $\delta(Q_1, a) = (H, c, R)$ and is encoded as

$$\underbrace{10}_{Q_1}\ X\ \underbrace{10}_{a}\ X\ \underbrace{11}_{H}\ X\ \underbrace{100}_{c}\ X\ R\ Y$$

The entire machine T is then encoded as

$$D_1(T) =$$

$$B\,\underbrace{11}_{\epsilon_1}\,A\,\underbrace{100}_{\epsilon_2}\,P\,\underbrace{1X10X1X10XRY}_{T_1}\,\underbrace{1X11X10X1XSY}_{T_2}$$

$$\underbrace{10X11X10X11XRY}_{T_3}\,\underbrace{10X10X11X100XRY}_{T_4}E$$

In a similar way, if the leftmost portion of the tape of T were $\sigma = ab\#ac$, say, the content of this tape would be encoded as

$$D_2(\sigma) = W\underbrace{1\ 0\ 0}_{\epsilon_2}\ A\underbrace{1\ 0}_{a}\ Z\underbrace{1\ 1}_{b}\ Z\underbrace{1}_{\#}Z\underbrace{1\ 0}_{a}\ Z\underbrace{1\ 0\ 0}_{c}\ F$$

It is clear from this example that more complicated machines will have considerably longer encodings, but it should also be clear that, in principle, any Turing machine and any finite portion of the tape can be encoded by this scheme.

The possibility of complete and unambiguous encoding of an arbitrary Turing machine and its input allows us to construct the so-called universal Turing machine U_0. Such a machine essentially simulates any other Turing machine in the following way: Let T be any Turing machine and let σ be the initial content of the tape of T. Let the encodings of T and σ be $D_1(T)$ and $D_2(\sigma)$ as described above. We set the machine T in the initial configuration $[\![Q_0, \sigma]\!]$ and the machine U_0 in the configuration $[\![\overline{Q}_0, D_1(T)\$D_2(\sigma)]\!]$. In other words, we feed the description of T and the initial content σ of the tape of T to the machine U_0. The "universality" of U_0 consists of the following description of the behavior of U_0:

1. If, starting from the initial configuration $[\![Q_0, \sigma]\!]$, T halts with its tape containing string τ, then U_0, starting from the configuration $[\![\overline{Q}_0, D_1(T)\$D_2(\sigma)]\!]$, will also halt, with its tape containing the string $D_2(\tau)$. Formally,

$$[\![Q_0, \sigma]\!] \ \to^* \ [\![H, \tau]\!] \text{ implies } [\![\overline{Q}_0, D_1(T)\$D_2(\sigma)]\!] \ \to^* \ [\![\overline{H}, D_2(\tau)]\!]$$

The precise location of the heads of either of the machines is immaterial.

2. If T does not halt on the indicated input, U_0 will not halt either.

The exact, formal construction of the machine U_0 is tedious and cumbersome, and somewhat beyond the scope of this book. We will only present the main idea; for full details the reader is invited to consult [13]. The universal Turing machine U_0 will have three tapes $T1$, $T2$, and $T3$, with respective heads $h1$, $h2$, and $h3$. The tape $T1$ will contain the encoded description of the Turing machine T that is being simulated, and the tape $T2$ will contain the initial input to T. The tape $T3$ will contain the current state and the current location of the head of the machine T. The instructions to the machine U_0 are as follows:

1. Enter the encoding $D_1(T)$ of the machine T on tape $T1$, the encoding $D_2(\sigma)$ of the initial input σ to T on tape $T2$, and the initial state of T, together with the initial location of the head of T, on tape $T3$. Place all the heads $h1$, $h2$, and $h3$ at the left end of their respective tapes.
2. Move the head $h3$ to the right until the description of the present state of T and the present location of the head of T is found.
3. Using the information obtained in step 2, move the head $h1$ until the appropriate description of the transition function δ is found.
4. Using the information from steps 1 and 2, adjust the content of tapes $T2$ and $T3$ to reflect the new state and the new tape of T.
5. If the new state of T is the halting state then "clean up," otherwise move all the heads to the leftmost cells and go back to step 2.

The fact that U_0 has three states presents no problem; it can now be replaced by a standard one-tape Turing machine along the lines indicated in Theorem 5.1. These ideas can be formalized as follows.

Definition 5.4. A Turing machine $U_0 = \{\overline{\mathbb{Q}}, \overline{\Sigma}, \overline{Q}_0, \overline{\delta}_0\}$ is said to be ***universal*** if it has the following property. Let $T = \{\mathbb{Q}, \Sigma, Q_0, \delta\}$ be any Turing machine and let σ be a string from Σ^*. Let $D_1(T)$ be the encoding of T and let $D_2(\delta)$ be the encoding of σ. Then the machine T will execute the sequence of moves $[\![Q_0, \sigma]\!] \to^* [\![H, \tau]\!]$ if and only the machine U_0 will execute the sequence of moves

$$[\![\overline{Q}_0, D_1(T)\$D_2(\sigma)]\!] \to^* [\![\overline{H}, D_2(\tau)]\!]$$

Both of the above machines are assumed to begin and end their operations with the head placed at the leftmost cell.

Theorem 5.2. There exists a universal Turing machine.

We should point out that actually there exists a universal Turing machine with only two states. Its construction was given by C. E. Shannon in [18].

The possibility of uniform encoding of every Turing machine has another important consequence: It is possible to list all Turing machines in a single sequence

$$T_1, T_2, T_3, T_4, \ldots \tag{5.5}$$

Every conceivable Turing machine is going to be somewhere on this list. This enumeration of Turing machines is accomplished as follows: We saw that each Turing machine can be uniquely described by a finite sequence of symbols each one of which is one of the 11 characters: B, A, E, P, X, Y, R, L, S, 0, and 1. Given any integer n, there is only a finite number of distinct strings of length n—in fact there are exactly 11^n of them. Thus, we can list all Turing machines in a sequence as follows: First we list all Turing machines whose description requires only one symbol (if there are any such), then all machines describable by 2 symbols (if there are any), etc. To be sure, the "smallest" Turing machine is

which has only one tape symbol #. (This is the minimum that any Turing machine can have.) Its description is $B10A1PE$, requiring a string of length 7, and it stands at the beginning of the sequence (5.5) of all Turing machines. Thus, we have the following:

Theorem 5.3. The number of distinct Turing machines is countable.

In exactly the same way, all possible inputs to all possible Turing machines can be ordered in a single sequence. This follows from the fact that any finite portion of a tape can be described using only a finite string of symbols A, W, Z, F, 0, and 1. The rest of the argument is as before.

5.6. UNDECIDABLE PROBLEMS

In this section we will give a precise formulation (and the solution) of the questions discussed briefly in Sec. 5.3:

1. Does every problem have an algorithm that will solve it?
2. Is every function computable?

These two questions are actually one and the same, since the "solution of a problem" can be viewed as a function of the description of the problem. To demonstrate only that there are uncomputable functions is fairly easy. By Theorem 5.3 there are only countably many Turing machines. There are, however, uncountably many functions $f\colon \mathbb{N} \mapsto \{0, 1\}$, see Appendix 1. Thus, some of these functions (in fact, most of them) will not be Turing computable. This argument, while perfectly correct, is somewhat unsatisfactory, since it does not give a specific example of an unsolvable problem or an uncomputable function. In this section we will provide two specific example of this kind.

We take up the question of an algorithm to solve a given problem. Recall that it has been postulated that to say that an algorithm exists to solve a problem is to say that a Turing machine exists that will solve that problem (Church-Turing thesis). We will show that there exists no algorithm that, given the description of a Turing machine T and the description of the input σ of T, will determine whether T will halt or not. Thus, we say that the halting problem for the Turing machines is undecidable. In terms of Turing machines this can be formulated as follows:

Theorem 5.4. The halting problem for Turing machines is undecidable. More precisely, there does ***not*** exist a Turing machine $A = \{\mathcal{Q}, \Sigma, Q_0, \delta\}$ with the following properties: Let $T = \{\hat{\mathcal{Q}}, \hat{\Sigma}, \hat{Q}_0, \hat{\delta}_0)$ be any Turing machine and let σ be any string from $\hat{\Sigma}^*$. Let $D_1(T)$ and $D_2(\sigma)$ be the encoding of T and σ as described in Section 5.4, and consider the behavior of T on the input σ (i.e., the behavior of T when started in configuration $[\![\hat{Q}_0, \sigma]\!]$, with the head pointing to the leftmost cell). Consider also the behavior of A on the input $\$D_1(T)\pounds D_2(\sigma)$, i.e., the behavior of A when started in the initial configuration $[\![Q_0, \underline{\$}D_1(T)\pounds D_2(\sigma)]\!]$. If T eventually halts, then A will halt in configuration $[\![H, \underline{1}]\!]$, if T does not halt, then A will halt in configuration $[\![H, \underline{0}]\!]$.

Notice that T need not halt—it may go into an infinite loop or it may hang; the machine A is, however, always required to halt, provided it is given a properly formatted input. We need a couple of preliminary results before proving this theorem. Let $T_1, T_2, T_3, \ldots$ be the enumeration of all possible Turing machines and let $\sigma_1, \sigma_2, \sigma_3, \ldots$ be the sequence of all possible inputs on these machines. T's and σ's are encoded as in Section 5.5. Let L_0 be the set of those σ_i's for which the machine T_i does ***not*** halt in configuration $[\![H, \underline{1}]\!]$. Thus, an input sequence σ_i is in the language L_0 if and only if the machine T_i, when started in the initial configuration $[\![Q_0^{(i)}, \sigma_i]\!]$, will either not halt at all, or will halt in a configuration other than $[\![H, \underline{1}]\!]$.

Lemma 5.1. There is no Turing machine T_0 that will decide for every σ_i whether or not σ_i is in the language L_0. More precisely, there is no

Turing machine $T_0 = \{Q_0, \Sigma_0, Q_0, \delta_0\}$ with the property that for each $i = 1, 2, 3, \ldots$

$$1.\ [\![Q_0, \underline{\$}\sigma_i]\!] \to^* [\![H, \underline{1}]\!] \quad \text{if } \sigma_i \text{ is in } L_0$$
$$2.\ [\![Q_0, \underline{\$}\ \sigma_i]\!] \to^* [\![H, \underline{0}]\!] \quad \text{if } \sigma_i \text{ is not in } L_0$$

Proof. Suppose such a machine T_0 existed; then it must have been one of the machines $T_1, T_2, \ldots$ in (5.5). Every conceivable Turing machine appears on this list. Let then $T_0 = T_{i_0}$ and consider what happens when we start $T_0 = T_{i_0}$ on the input σ_{i_0}. By hypothesis, T_0 ($= T_{i_0}$) will halt either in configuration $[\![H, \underline{1}]\!]$ or $[\![H, \underline{0}]\!]$. If the former is the case, then σ_{i_0} is in the language L_0, which means that T_{i_0} does ***not*** halt in configuration $[\![H, \underline{1}]\!]$; that is clearly impossible. If $T_0 = T_{i_0}$ halts in configuration $[\![H, \underline{0}]\!] \neq [\![H, \underline{1}]\!]$, this means that σ_{i_0} is in the language L_0, thus T_0—and hence T_{i_0}—should halt in configuration $[\![H, \underline{1}]\!]$, but we assumed that this does not happen. Thus T_0 cannot correctly decide if σ_{i_0} is in the language L_0. Q.E.D.

We are now ready to prove Theorem 5.4. The idea of the proof is to show that if a Turing machine A, as described in Theorem 5.4, existed, then one could construct a machine T_0 recognizing the language L_0 as in Lemma 5.1. That, however, is impossible. The construction of T_0, assuming that A exists, is as follows. Given a string σ_i, the machine T_0 feeds the encoding $D_2(\sigma_i)$ and the encoding $D_1(T_i)$ to the machine A. If A halts with "0" on its tape (in configuration $[\![H, \underline{0}]\!]$), then T_0 prints 1 on its tape and halts in configuration $[\![H, \underline{1}]\!]$. (It may have to do some cleaning up beforehand.) If A halts with 1 on its tape (in configuration $[\![H, \underline{1}]\!]$), then T_0 feeds the descriptions $D_1(T_i)$ and $D_2(\sigma_i)$ to the universal machine U_0 from Theorem 5.2. By its definition, the machine U_0 will behave on this input in the same way as the machine T_i will behave on the input σ_i, in particular it will halt. (Since A predicted, presumably correctly, that T_i will halt.) If U halts with 1 on its tape, T_0 will print 0 on its tape and halt in configuration $[\![H, \underline{0}]\!]$. If U halts with the tape containing anything other than 1, then T_0 will print 1 on its tape and halt in configuration $[\![H, \underline{1}]\!]$. It is now quite straightforward to show that the machine T_0 will correctly predict whether a given string σ_i is in the language L_0 or not. Indeed, suppose σ_i is in L_0. This means that T_i, on input σ_i, will not halt in configuration $[\![H, \underline{1}]\!]$. There are two possibilities: i) T_i will not halt at all, or ii) T_i will halt, but in a configuration other than $[\![H, \underline{1}]\!]$. In case i), machine A will halt in configuration $[\![H, \underline{0}]\!]$ so, by construction, T_0 will halt in configuration $[\![H, \underline{1}]\!]$, correctly predicting that $\sigma_i \in L_0$. In case ii), A will halt in configuration $[\![H, \underline{1}]\!]$, and the string σ_i, together with the description of T_i will be fed to the universal machine U_0, which, in turn, halts in a configuration other than $[\![H, \underline{1}]\!]$. Again, by construction, T_0 will halt in configuration $[\![H, \underline{1}]\!]$, correctly predicting that $\sigma_i \in L_0$. It is also easily seen that T_0 will behave correctly when $\sigma_i \notin L_0$, we leave the proof of which as an exercise. Q.E.D.

We now turn our attention to uncomputable functions. Recall that a function $f(n) = m$ (n, m positive integers) is said to be computable if there exists a Turing machine T_f which, on input \$111 . . . 1 (n 1's) will produce an output \$111 . . . 1 ($f(n)$ 1's). A function f which is not computable is called uncomputable.

Theorem 5.5. There exists an uncomputable function.

Proof. We have seen in Secion 5.5 that there exists a finite set Δ_1 such that any Turing machine can be described by a finite string of elements (characters) from Δ_1. As a matter of fact, this set could be taken to consist of 11 distinct characters. In a similar way, any input to any Turing machine can be described by a finite string of symbols from some set Δ_2, where Δ_2 is again finite. (In Section 5.5 the set Δ_2 had six elements.) Let T be a Turing machine and let σ be an input to T (i.e., the initial content of the tape of T). Let $D_1(T)$ and $D_2(\sigma)$ be, respectively, the descriptions of T and σ as indicated above. Let $p(T)$ be the length of the string $D_1(T)$ and let $q(\sigma)$ be the length of the string σ. Given a positive integer n, there is only a finite number of pairs (T, σ), where T is a Turing machine and σ is its initial input, such that $p(T) + q(\sigma) \leq n$. Let $\mathcal{A}_n$ be the collection of all such pairs. If (T, σ) is a pair from $\mathcal{A}_n$ then T, on the input σ, may or may not halt. Let $\mathcal{B}_n$ be the collection of all those pairs from $\mathcal{A}_n$ having the property that T will halt on the input σ. Again, $\mathcal{B}_n$ clearly consists of only a finite number of pairs. If (T, σ) is a pair from $\mathcal{B}_n$, let $\beta(T, \sigma)$ denote the number of moves T makes before it halts in the halting state. Now define a function $b(n)$

$$b(n) = Max\{\beta(T, \sigma) \mid (T, \sigma) \in \mathcal{B}_n\}$$

Loosely speaking, $b(n)$ is the largest number of moves that a Turing machine can make on input σ, if the descriptions of T and σ taken together do not exceed n symbols. The function $b(n)$ so defined is called a ***busy beaver*** function and is uncomputable. Indeed, suppose there is a Turing machine B which computes $b(n)$. We will show this implies that one can construct a Turing machine A that will solve the halting problem. That, however, is impossible, as Theorem 5.4 showed. To construct A we proceed as follows: Given a Turing machine T and its input σ, the machine A encodes T and σ as $D_1(T)$ and $D_2(\sigma)$ and calculates $n = p(T) + q(\sigma)$. When this is done, the machine A passes this number n to the machine B and obtains $b(n)$ back. Having done that, it passes the descriptions $D_1(T)$ and $D_2(\sigma)$ of T and σ to the universal machine U_0 and begins to count the moves of U_0. If U_0 halts before $b(n)^{th}$ move, A prints 1 on its tape and halts in configuration $\llbracket H, \underline{1} \rrbracket$. If U_0 does not halt by the $b(n)^{th}$ move, A prints 0 on the tape and halts in configuration $\llbracket H, \underline{0} \rrbracket$. It is clear that A will behave correctly: If U_0 does not halt by the $b(n)^{th}$ move, neither will T, since U_0 simulates T move by move and $p(T) + q(\sigma) \leq n$. Q.E.D.

Some comments should be made about the last two theorems. When Theorem 5.4 asserts that the halting problem for Turing machines is undecidable, it does ***not*** mean that we cannot decide in some specific cases whether or not a given Turing machine will halt on some fixed input. Consider, for example the Turing machine described in Figure 5.12. It is clear by inspection that if the machine T is started in configuration $\llbracket Q_0, \underline{a}b \rrbracket$ it will never halt; if, however if it is started in configuration $\llbracket Q_0, \underline{b}aab \rrbracket$ it will halt. What the theorem asserts is that there is no uniform procedure that will decide such a question in all possible cases.

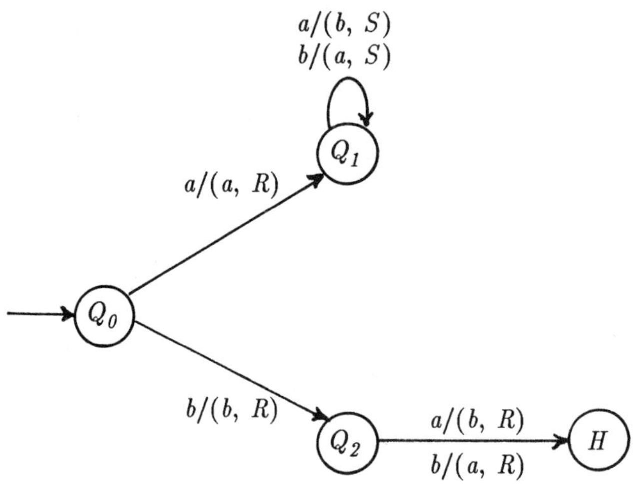

Figure 5.12. A Turing machine that sometime halts and sometime does not.

Many concrete questions about formal languages are undecidable. We list some of them here. Their proofs would, however, would take us too far afield. An interested reader is invited to consult many excellent treatises on the subject, e.g., [13] or [15].

Theorem 5.6. It is undecidable whether an arbitrary context free grammar is ambiguous.

Again, this does not mean that we cannot decide this question in some specific cases. A grammar $S \to a \mid b \mid \lambda$ is clearly unambiguous. What the theorem asserts is that there is no Turing machine that will, given an input describing a grammar, decide if this grammar is ambiguous or not. It is clearly possible to describe a grammar by a finite sequence of symbols, so the question of the existence of such a Turing machine makes perfect sense.

Theorem 5.7. It is undecidable whether two context free languages have a common sentence.

Thus, there is no Turing machine that will, given any two context free grammars G_1 and G_2, decide whether $L(G_1) \cap L(G_2) = \emptyset$. We will show in Chapter 6, however, that there is an effective procedure, i.e., a Turing machine, that, when it is given a context free grammar $G = \{\Sigma, N, S, P\}$ and a specific string σ in Σ^*, will decide whether or not $\sigma \in L(G)$.

Theorem 5.8. It is undecidable whether an arbitrary context-free grammar is inherently ambiguous.

Even more surprisingly, we have the following:

Theorem 5.9. It is undecidable whether an arbitrary context-free language has a regular grammar.

PROBLEMS

1. Construct a Turing machine recognizing the language

$$L = \{1^{2n} \mid n = 0, 1, 2, \ldots\}$$

   Show the movements of your machine on inputs 111 and 1111.
2. Construct a Turing machine that will compute the function $f(n) = 3n$. Show the movements of your machine on the input 11.

3. Consider the following Turing machine given below in tabular form

		Input symbol			
		a	b	c	$\#$
State	Q_0	(Q_1, a, S)	(Q_1, b, S)	(H, c, S)	$(Q_0, \#, R)$
	Q_1	(Q_1, b, R)	(Q_1, a, R)	(Q_2, c, S)	$(Q_2, \#, S)$
	Q_2	(Q_2, a, L)	(Q_2, b, L)	(Q_2, c, L)	$(H, \#, S)$

a. Show the movements of this machine beginning from configurations $[\![Q_0, \#abbaacaa]\!]$, $[\![Q_0, \#bbaaca]\!]$ and $[\![Q_0, \#abbcaab]\!]$.
b. Give a state diagram of this machine.
c. Describe informally what does this machine do.

4. Consider the following Turing machine

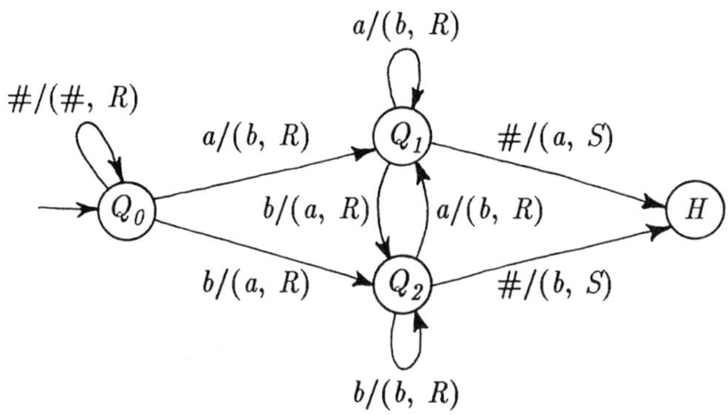

a. Show the movements of this machine on the input $\sigma = ababbba$ beginning with the configuration $[\![Q_0, \underline{a}babbba]\!]$.
b. Give a tabular description of this machine.
c. Describe informally what this machine does.

5. Construct a Turing machine that compares two numbers m and n. Specifically, such a machine should move from the configuration

$$[\![Q_0, \#\underbrace{11\ldots1}_{n}\#\underbrace{11\ldots1}_{m}]\!] \text{ to } [\![H, \#x]\!],$$

where $x = f$, s, or e depending on whether $n > m$, $n < m$ or $n = m$.

6. Construct a Turing machine with a two way infinite tape that will halt if and only if the initial input will contain the symbol a. This symbol may appear anywhere on the tape, not necessarily to the

right of the initial position of the head.

7. Construct a Turing machine recognizing the language

$$L = \{\sigma\sigma^R \mid \sigma \in \{a, b\}^*\}$$

Here σ^R, as usual, denotes the reverse of the string σ.

8. Give encodings of the Turing machines from problems 1 and 2, as described in Section 5.5. Also give the encodings of the initial content of the tape of each of the initial configuration mentioned in these problems.
9. Prove that there is no algorithm that will decide whether or not any given Turing machine with a given initial input will ever return to the initial state Q_0.
10. Prove that there is no algorithm that will decide whether or not any given Turing machine with a given initial input will ever write the symbol a on its tape.

CHAPTER 6

TOP-DOWN PARSING

6.1. PRELIMINARIES

We saw in Chapter 1 that one of the primary tasks of a compiler is parsing. More precisely, this task is as follows. Given a grammar $G = \{\Sigma, N, S, P\}$ and a string $\sigma = x_1 x_2 x_3 \ldots x_n$ of symbols from Σ, the job of a parser is to reconstruct a derivation of σ from the start symbol S, or to ascertain that σ cannot be so derived, i.e., that σ is not in $L(G)$. The reconstruction of a derivation tree of σ is equivalent to reconstructing the "meaning" of σ. Given a string σ, there may be many ways to derive it from the start symbol S; in this chapter we will restrict our attention to finding a leftmost derivation (at each stage of the derivation we replace the leftmost nonterminal by the corresponding right-hand side of the production). Even this need not guarantee the uniqueness of the derivation, as we saw Chapter 1. Thus, we seek an algorithm that, when given an input $\sigma = x_1 x_2 \ldots x_n$, will produce a sequence of productions used in the leftmost derivation of σ. This algorithm should be completely deterministic with no "clairvoyance" in the process. The method of accomplishing this presented in this section consists of reconstructing the derivation tree from the top down. We know that the derivation of σ begins with the symbol S; equivalently, the derivation tree of σ has S as its root. The first question we ask in the top-down method of parsing is this: What was the first production used in deriving σ, or, equivalently, what are the children of the root S in the derivation tree of σ? Having answered that question we can isolate the leftmost terminal X and then ask again: What is the second production used in this derivation, or, equivalently, what are the children of X in this derivation tree? We continue in this manner until the entire tree is reconstructed. Such top-down parsers are also called *LL* parsers. Before proceeding with a general discussion let us consider an example.

Example 6.1. Let G be the grammar given by

$$\begin{array}{lllll} 1. & S & \rightarrow & aAS \\ 2. & S & \rightarrow & b \\ 3. & A & \rightarrow & bSA \\ 4. & A & \rightarrow & a \end{array}$$

and let $\sigma = abbab$. We know that the first production used, to derive σ is either 1 or 2. However, 2 is ruled out since after it is used, the sentential form at hand is b and no further derivation is possible (there are no nonterminals left). Thus, the first production used is 1 and the derivation of σ must begin as $S \Rightarrow aAS$. Equivalently, the derivation tree of σ must have its top as in Figure 6.1(b). We now inquire about the second production used. Since we seek the leftmost derivation, the nonterminal to be replaced is A. Again, there is a choice of productions: 3 ($A \rightarrow bSA$) or 4 ($A \rightarrow a$). Here production 4 is ruled out, since if it were applied the final string would begin with aa. Thus, production 3 is called for, and we know that the leftmost derivation of σ begins with the sequence $S \Rightarrow aAS \Rightarrow abSAS$. Notice this point that the first two symbols (ab) are fixed—further substitutions will have no effect on this part of the sentential form. We may conceptualize at this point that the sentential form $abSAS$ and the target string $\sigma = abbab$ are divided into two parts as follows:

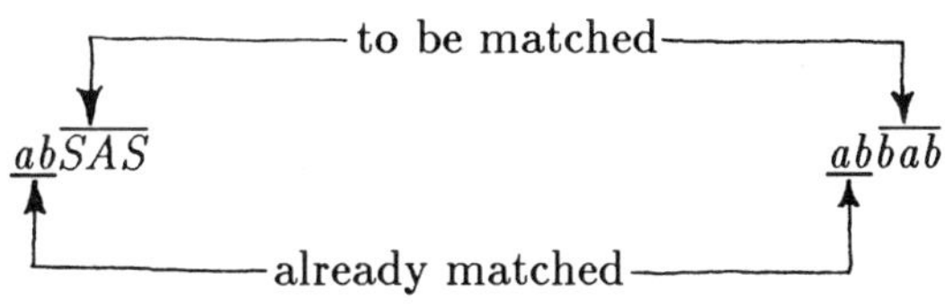

The remaining problem thus becomes of deriving the unmatched portion of σ (i.e., bab) from the unmatched portion of the sentential form (i.e., SAS). Again, since the leftmost S must be substituted, there a choice of two productions: 1 ($S \rightarrow aAS$) and 2 ($S \rightarrow b$). Since the first symbol of the unmatched portion of σ is b, the production to be applied is $S \rightarrow b$. Continuing in this way, we obtain the following derivation of σ:

$$\underline{S} \stackrel{1}{\Rightarrow} a\underline{A}S \stackrel{3}{\Rightarrow} ab\underline{S}AS \stackrel{2}{\Rightarrow} abb\underline{A}S \stackrel{4}{\Rightarrow} abba\underline{S} \stackrel{2}{\Rightarrow} abbab$$

At each stage we underlined the nonterminal being replaced. The corresponding growth of the derivation tree is pictured in Figure 6.1.

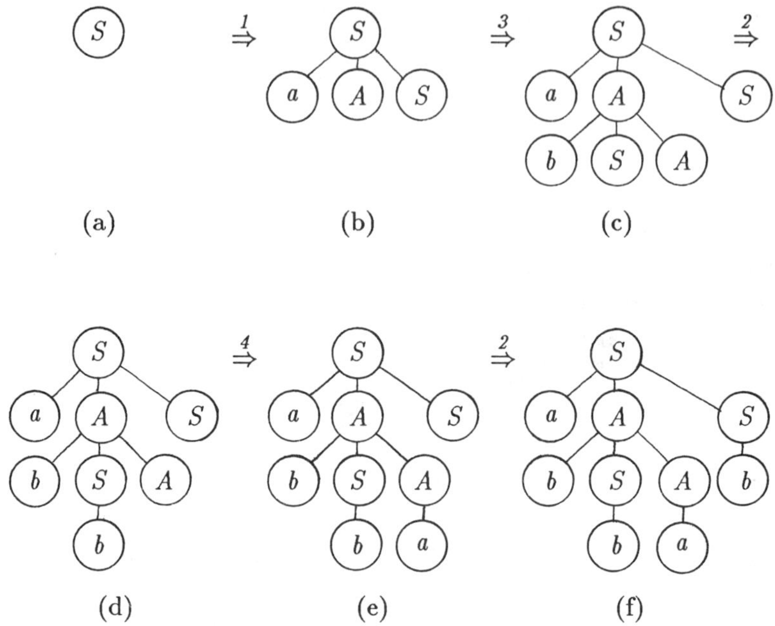

Figure 6.1. Derivation tree of *abbab*.

6.2. DESCRIPTION OF A TOP-DOWN PARSER

We now present the mechanics of a top-down parser. How such a parser is constructed from a given grammar will be discussed later in the chapter. Right now, we are only interested in how such a device works. We make one simplifying assumption about the form of the strings to be parsed: Every such string ends with the symbol \$, which does not appear anywhere else in σ. The effect of this hypothesis is that if we go through the string σ from left to right, we can detect the end of the input. It is quite clear that this extra hypothesis does not put any serious restrictions on the types of strings to be parsed.

The top-down parser for a grammar $G = \{\Sigma, N, S, P\}$ will be a nondeterministic push-down automaton with an output. Schematically, it may be pictured as in Figure 6.2. The parser in this scheme will have only one state Q. The input alphabet of this push-down automaton is the alphabet Σ of the grammar together with the symbol \$ (which is assumed ***not*** to be in Σ). The stack alphabet Γ consists of all the terminals and all the nonterminals of the grammar G, together with the bottom of the stack symbol # (which is assumed ***not*** to be in either Σ or N). As usual, the stack pointer is allowed to move up and down, while the input and output pointers can move only to the right. The configuration of the parser in Figure 6.2 will be denoted by

$$[\![a_i a_{i+1} \ldots a_n\$,\ \gamma_j\,\gamma_{j-1} \ldots \gamma_2\gamma_1\#,\ n_1 n_2 \ldots n_k]\!]$$

This notation differs slightly from the one used in Chapter 4, but should cause no confusion. We do not indicate the current state of the parser because it is always the same. We do, however, indicate the content of the output tape.

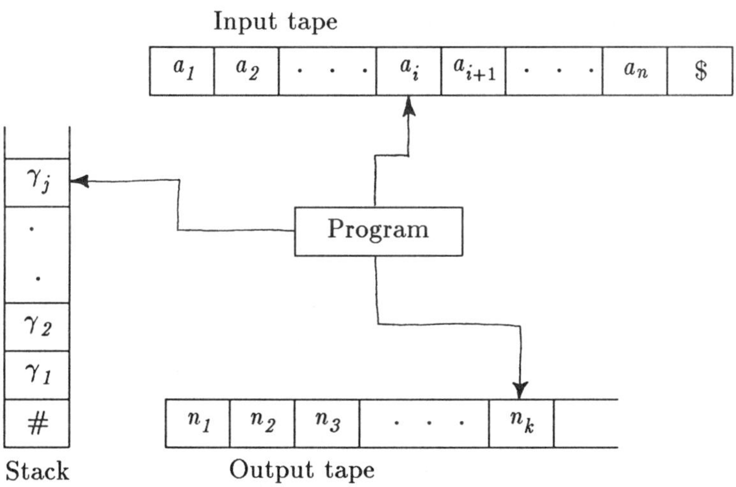

Figure 6.2. Top-down parser as a push-down automaton.

The initial configuration of the parser is

$$[\![a_1 a_2 \ldots a_n\$,\ S\#,\ \lambda]\!]$$

where $a_1 a_2 \ldots a_n$ is the string σ to be parsed and S is the start symbol of the grammar G. Thus, the input tape initially contains the string $a_1 a_2 \ldots a_n\$$ with the input pointer pointing to the leftmost symbol a_1; the stack contains two symbols: # on the bottom and S on the top. At any given instant of time the parser may do one, and only one, of the following:

1. If the top of the stack contains a nonterminal X, the parser replaces X by the string $\alpha_1\alpha_2 \ldots \alpha_t$, where $X \rightarrow \alpha_1\alpha_2 \ldots \alpha_t$ is a production of the grammar G. (α_1 becomes the new top of the stack.) At the same time, the parser notes on the output tape the number of this production. Notice that in general there will be several productions with X on the left-hand side; the parser should be able to choose the right one. This kind of move is called an application of the production $X \rightarrow \alpha_1\alpha_2 \ldots \alpha_t$, and it will be denoted by $APPLY(X \rightarrow \alpha_1\alpha_2 \ldots \alpha_t)$. The input pointer does not move in this situation, the same symbol is read again.

2. If the top of the stack contains a terminal x, this x is compared with the present input symbol a. If $x = a$, then x is removed from the top of the stack and the input pointer moves one cell to the right. This kind of move is called *POP*. We say that the terminal x was *POPPED* from the stack and the input tape. If $x \neq a$ the parser writes *REJECT* on the output tape and halts. It has been determined that σ is not in the language $L(G)$.

3. If the stack contains only the symbol # and the input pointer points to \$, the parser writes *ACCEPT* on the output tape and halts. When this happens the output tape will contain the left parse of the original input $\sigma = a_1a_2 \ldots a_n$.

The decision of what to do in each situation depends only on the symbol γ on top of the stack and the current input symbol a. Thus, the operation of the parser is completely described by the function

$$M[\gamma, x] = \text{What to do}$$

where γ is one of the stack symbols and x is one of the tape symbols.

Heuristically, this parser reconstructs the derivation of a string $\sigma = a_1a_2 \ldots a_n$ as follows: Suppose the leftmost derivation of σ is

$$S = \tau_1 \Rightarrow \tau_2 \Rightarrow \cdots \Rightarrow \tau_j \Rightarrow \tau_{j+1} \Rightarrow \cdots \Rightarrow \tau_m = \sigma$$

where each τ is a sentential form (i.e., a string of terminals and nonterminals). Suppose, moreover, that the transition $\tau_j \Rightarrow \tau_{j+1}$ is the result of applying a production $X \rightarrow \alpha_1\alpha_2 \ldots \alpha_t$. This means that τ_j is of the form $\tau_j = \rho X\beta$, where ρ is a string of terminals, X is the nonterminal in question, and β is a string of terminals or nonterminals. Since any further derivation will not change ρ, this string must be identical with a beginning portion of $\sigma = a_1a_2 \ldots a_n$. In other words, $\tau_j = a_1a_2 \ldots a_iX\beta$, and $\tau_{j+1} = a_1a_2 \ldots a_i\alpha_1\alpha_2 \ldots \alpha_t\beta$. To complete the derivation we must transform the tail end of τ_j, i.e., the string $X\beta$ into $a_{i+1}a_{i+2} \ldots a_n$. Thus, the parser keeps the string $X\beta$ on the stack and continues to replace the top of the stack (i.e., substitute the leftmost nonterminal) until a_{i+1} appears on top. At this point a_{i+1} is removed from the stack (*POPPED*), and what is left has to be transformed to match $a_{i+2}a_{i+3} \ldots a_n$. The procedure is repeated until all the input symbols are matched. We illustrate this by example.

Example 6.2. We consider the grammar

$$1.\ S \rightarrow aAS \qquad 2.\ S \rightarrow b$$
$$3.\ A \rightarrow bSA \qquad 4.\ A \rightarrow a$$

The parsing function is then given as follows:

$M[x, x] = POP$ for all terminals x ($= a$ or b)
$M[x, y] = REJECT$ if x, y are terminals and $x \neq y$
$M[\#, \$] = ACCEPT$ $\qquad$ $M[\#, x] = REJECT$ for $x \neq \$$
$M[\#, \gamma] = REJECT$ for $\gamma \neq \#$ $\qquad$ $M[S, a] = APPLY(S \rightarrow aAS)$
$M[A, a] = APPLY(A \rightarrow a)$ $\qquad$ $M[S, b] = APPLY(S \rightarrow b)$
$M[A, b] = APPLY(A \rightarrow bSA)$

This can be conveniently represented in a self-explanatory way by the table in Figure 6.3. The numbers in parenthesis refer to the production number.

		Input symbol x		
		a	b	$
S	S	$S \rightarrow aAS(1)$	$S \rightarrow b(2)$	*REJECT*
t	A	$A \rightarrow a(4)$	$A \rightarrow bSA(3)$	*REJECT*
a	a	*POP*	*REJECT*	*REJECT*
c	b	*REJECT*	*POP*	*REJECT*
k	#	*REJECT*	*REJECT*	*ACCEPT*

Figure 6.3. A parsing table.

Now, consider movements of this parser on the input $\sigma = abbab$. We have

$$[\![abbab\$, S\#, \lambda]\!] \rightarrow [\![abbab\$, aAS\#, 1]\!] \rightarrow [\![bbab\$, AS\#, 1]\!]$$
$$\rightarrow [\![bbab\$, bSAS\#, 13]\!] \rightarrow [\![bab\$, SAS\#, 13]\!] \rightarrow [\![bab\$, bAS\#, 132]\!]$$
$$\rightarrow [\![ab\$, AS\#, 132]\!] \rightarrow [\![ab\$, aS\#, 1324]\!] \rightarrow [\![b\$, S\#, 1324]\!]$$
$$\rightarrow [\![b\$, b\#, 13242]\!] \rightarrow [\![\$, \#, 13242]\!] \rightarrow ACCEPT$$

Notice that at each step the stack contains a sentential form that has to be transformed into the "as yet unmatched" part of the input. When the parser accepts σ it halts and the output contains the sequence 1, 3, 2, 4, 2 which is exactly the left parse of σ.

6.3. CONSTRUCTION OF PARSING TABLES

Now that we know how a top-down parser should operate, we turn to the question of how to construct one from a given grammar $G = \{\Sigma, N, S, P\}$. Specifically, we wish to construct the function $M[\gamma, x]$ as described in Section 6.2. This function should be defined for all stack symbols $\gamma \in \Sigma \cup N \cup \{\#\}$ and all $x \in \Sigma \cup \{\$\}$. The function M should uniquely define the course of action the parser is to take if the current input symbol is x and the top of the stack contains γ. It turns out that such a function does not exist for every context-free grammar G. Let us, however, define a class of grammars for which such a function M does exist and, thus, for which a deterministic top-down parser is possible.

Definition 6.1. A grammar $G = \{\Sigma, N, S, P\}$ is called ***simple*** if it satisfies the following two conditions:

1. Each production of G is of the form $A \to x\beta$, where x is a terminal and β is a (possibly empty) string of terminals and/or nonterminals.
2. If $A \to x_1\beta_1$ and $A \to x_2\beta_2$ are two distinct productions of G then $x_1 \neq x_2$.

Notice that condition 1 implies that G has no empty productions ($A \to \lambda$). For simple grammars the construction of a top-down parser is quite easy.

Theorem 6.1. If $G = \{\Sigma, N, S, P\}$ is a simple grammar, then G has a deterministic top-down parser defined by the function $M[\gamma, x]$ as follows:

1. $M[x, x] = POP$ for all $x \in \Sigma$
2. $M[\#, \$] = ACCEPT$
3. For each production $A \to x\beta$ set $M[A, x] = APPLY(A \to x\beta)$
4. $M[\gamma, x] = REJECT$ in all other cases

Proof. First of all, notice that the values $M[A, x]$ defined by condition 3 are unique: By hypothesis, for each nonterminal A and each terminal x there is at most one production of the form $A \to x\beta$. What we have to show is that the parser defined by the function M as above acts correctly. This means that if $\sigma = b_1 b_2 \ldots b_k \in L(G)$, then the parser will correctly reconstruct the derivation of σ. Since the grammar G is simple, the first production used in deriving σ is of the form $S \to b_1\beta_1$ and, moreover, this identifies the production uniquely, say it number is n_1. The parser defined by M, on input σ, starts in configuration $[\![b_1 b_2 \ldots b_k\$, S\#, \lambda]\!]$. By definition of the parser and the fact that G is simple, the value of $M[S, b_1]$ is $APPLY(S \to b_1\beta_1)$. Thus the parser reconstructs correctly the first production. Suppose that the parser correctly reconstructed the first m productions used in the derivation of σ, and that after applying these m productions we arrive at the sentential form

$$b_1 b_2 \ldots b_j A X_1 X_2 \ldots X_i$$

where A is a nonterminal and X's are either terminals or nonterminals. By the same argument as in the case of the first production, the next production used must be of the form $A \to b_{j+1}\beta$ and, moreover, this uniquely identifies the production, say its number is n_{j+1}. By inductive hypothesis, after correctly determining the first m productions, the parser arrives at configuration

$$[\![b_{j+1} b_{j+2} \ldots b_k\$, \; AX_1X_2 \ldots X_i\#, \; n_1 n_2 \ldots n_m]\!]$$

By construction and the property of simple grammars, the $M[A, b_{j+1}] = APPLY(A \to b_{j+1}\beta)$, thus the parser correctly determines the next production. Q.E.D.

Example 6.3. Consider the grammar given by

1. $S \to 0A$
2. $A \to 0AB$
3. $A \to 1$
4. $B \to 1$

It can be seen by inspection that G is simple. The parsing table described by Theorem 6.1. in given in Figure 6.4. The empty spaces in the table indicate the value *REJECT*; this is a common convention, which we shall follow.

The conditions that must be imposed on a grammar in order that it be simple are obviously quite restrictive and very few languages have simple grammars. We now present an algorithm for constructing a deterministic parser for a considerably larger class of grammars (but by no means all). In order to do this we must introduce two functions: $FIRST(\alpha)$, defined for any sentential form α, and $FOLLOW(A)$, defined for all nonterminals A. The values of both of these functions will be sets of symbols.

		Input symbol x		
		0	1	$
S	S	$S \to 0A$		
t	A	$A \to 0AB$	$A \to 1$	
a	B		$B \to 1$	
c	0	*POP*		
k	1		*POP*	
	#			*ACCEPT*

Figure 6.4. Parsing table for a simple grammar.

Let $G = \{\Sigma, N, S, P\}$ be a grammar. Intuitively, given a sentential form α, $FIRST(\alpha)$ will consist of all terminals x such that there exists a derivation of the form $\alpha \Rightarrow^* x\beta$. In other words, if it is possible to derive from α a sentential form beginning with x, then x will be in $FIRST(\alpha)$. If the empty string λ is derivable from α, we also include the symbol λ in $FIRST(\alpha)$.

The heuristic description of $FOLLOW(A)$ is as follows. Given a nonterminal A, the set $FOLLOW(A)$ consists of all terminals x that can appear immediately following A in all possible sentential forms derivable from S. Thus, x is in $FOLLOW(A)$ if and only if there is a legal derivation in the grammar G of the form $S \Rightarrow^* \alpha A x \beta$ for some strings α and β. Moreover, if A can appear at the end of some sentential form derivable from S, that is, if there is a legal derivation of the form $S \Rightarrow^* \alpha A$, we then include the symbol \$ in $FOLLOW(A)$. Formally, we have the following ($\mathfrak{P}(E)$ denotes the power set of E—the set of all possible subsets of E):

***Definition** 6.2.* Let $G = \{\Sigma, N, S, P\}$ be a context-free grammar such that $\$ \notin \Sigma \cup N$. For each sentential form $\alpha \in (\Sigma \cup N)^+$ define $FIRST$: $(\Sigma \cup N)^+ \mapsto \mathfrak{P}(\Sigma \cup \{\lambda\})$ to be

$$FIRST(\alpha) = \{x \in \Sigma \mid \text{There is a legal derivation of the form } \alpha \Rightarrow^* x\beta\} \cup \{\lambda \mid \text{The derivation } \alpha \Rightarrow^* \lambda \text{ is legal}\}$$

For each $A \in N$ define $FOLLOW$: $N \mapsto \mathfrak{P}(\Sigma \cup \{\$\})$ by

$FOLLOW(A) =$

$$\{x \in \Sigma \mid \text{There is a legal derivation of the form } S \Rightarrow^* \alpha A x \beta\}$$
$$\cup \ \{\ \$ \mid \text{There is a legal derivation of the form } S \Rightarrow^* \alpha A\}$$

Given a context-free grammar G there is a deterministic algorithm for computing the functions *FIRST* and *FOLLOW*. We will present these algorithms in Section 6.4; now we will only give a heuristic example.

Example 6.4. Let G be the grammar given by

$$\begin{array}{lcl} S & \rightarrow & BA \\ A & \rightarrow & aBA \mid \lambda \\ B & \rightarrow & DC \\ C & \rightarrow & bDC \mid \lambda \\ D & \rightarrow & cSc \mid d \end{array}$$

In an ad hoc way we will calculate $FIRST(\alpha)$ for all α's appearing on the right-hand sides of the above productions and $FOLLOW(X)$ for all nonterminals X. We have

$$FIRST(BA) = \{c, d\} \tag{6.1}$$

Indeed,

$$BA \Rightarrow DCA \Rightarrow cScCA \quad \text{so } c \in FIRST(BA)$$
$$BA \Rightarrow DCA \Rightarrow dCA \quad \text{so } d \in FIRST(BA)$$

By inspection, it should be reasonably clear that starting from the sentential form BA it is impossible to derive a string beginning with a or b. It is also impossible to derive λ from BA, so (6.1) follows. Next,

$$FIRST(aBA) = \{a\} \tag{6.2}$$

This follows from a general observation that if α begins with a terminal x, then $FIRST(\alpha) = \{x\}$: Whatever we do with the string aBA, the symbol a will stay up front. By similar arguments we get

$$\begin{array}{lll} FIRST(\lambda) = \{\lambda\} & FIRST(DC) = \{c, d\} & FIRST(d) = \{d\} \\ FIRST(bDC) = \{b\} & FIRST(cSc) = \{c\} & \end{array} \tag{6.3}$$

We next turn to the function *FOLLOW*. We have

$$FOLLOW(S) = \{\$, c\} \tag{6.4}$$

Indeed, S can stand at the end of a sentential form derivable from S—namely, S itself. Thus $\$ \in FOLLOW(S)$. Similarly, the derivation

$$S \Rightarrow BA \Rightarrow DCA \Rightarrow cScCA$$

shows that c can follow S. Thus, $c \in FOLLOW(S)$. By inspection, no other terminal is included in $FOLLOW(S)$. Next, we have

$$FOLLOW(A) = \{\$, c\} \tag{6.5}$$

This is a consequence of the derivations $S \Rightarrow BA$ and $S \Rightarrow BA \Rightarrow DCA \Rightarrow cScCA \Rightarrow cBAcCA$. Intuitively, it should be clear that no other terminal can follow A in a sentential form derivable from S. Using the same ad hoc techniques we establish that

$$FOLLOW(B) = \{\$, a, c\} \tag{6.6}$$

$$FOLLOW(C) = \{\$, a, c\} \tag{6.7}$$

$$FOLLOW(D) = \{\$, a, b, c\} \tag{6.8}$$

The reason, for instance, for including \$ in $FOLLOW(B)$ is the derivation $S \Rightarrow BA \Rightarrow B$ ($A \rightarrow \lambda$ is a production of the grammar G).

Using the functions *FIRST* and *FOLLOW* it is possible to construct a top-down parser for any context-free grammar G. We emphasize that the ability to do this depends very strongly on being able to deterministically compute the functions *FIRST* and *FOLLOW*. How this can be done will be shown in the next section; assume for now that indeed it can be accomplished. The parser construction is then as follows:

Algorithm 6.1. Top-down, also called LL, parser.
Input: Context-free grammar $G = \{\Sigma, N, S, P\}$.
Output: Parsing table $M[\gamma, x]$ for a top-down parser.

If $\gamma \in \Sigma \cup N \cup \{\#\}$ is a stack symbol and $x \in \Sigma \cup \{\$\}$ is an input symbol then the entries $M[\gamma, x]$ of the parsing table are defined by the following rules:

1. $M[x, x] = POP$ for every terminal $x \in \Sigma$.
2. $M[\#, \$] = ACCEPT$.
3. For each production $X \rightarrow \alpha$ of G do the following:
   (a) For every terminal y in $FIRST(\alpha)$ set

$$M[X, y] = APPLY(X \to \alpha)$$

(b) If $\lambda \in FIRST(\alpha)$, set

$$M[X, y] = APPLY(X \to \alpha) \text{ for each } y \in FOLLOW(X)$$

4. $M[X, y] = REJECT$ in all cases not defined in steps 1–3 above.

Before discussing this algorithm in detail and demonstrating its correctness, let us give an illustration of how it works.

Example 6.5. Let $G = \{\Sigma, N, S, P\}$ be the grammar from Example 6.4:

$$\begin{array}{lll} S & \to & BA \\ A & \to & aBA \mid \lambda \\ B & \to & DC \end{array} \qquad \begin{array}{lll} C & \to & bDC \mid \lambda \\ D & \to & cSc \mid d \end{array}$$

The values of $FIRST(\alpha)$ needed for Algorithm 6.1. were calculated in (6.1)–(6.3):

$$\begin{array}{lll} FIRST(BA) = \{c, d\} & FIRST(aBA) = \{a\} & FIRST(\lambda) = \{\lambda\} \\ FIRST(DC) = \{c, d\} & FIRST(bDC) = \{b\} & \\ FIRST(cSc) = \{c\} & FIRST(d) = \{d\} & \end{array}$$

The relevant values of $FOLLOW$ are given by (6.4)–(6.8):

$$FOLLOW(S) = FOLLOW(A) = \{\$, c\}$$

$$FOLLOW(B) = FOLLOW(C) = \{\$, a, c\}$$

$$FOLLOW(D) = \{\$, a, b, c\}$$

The parsing table is then given by the table in Figure 6.5. As usual, the empty spaces in this table indicate the value $M[\gamma, x] = REJECT$. We now explain some of the entries. $M[a, a] = M[b, b] = M[c, c] = M[d, d] = POP$ because of step 1 of the algorithm, and $M[\#, \$] = ACCEPT$ is just step 2. We now proceed with the entries defined in step 3. Consider the production $S \to BA$. Since $FIRST(BA) = \{c, d\}$, we have $M[S, c] = M[S, d] = APPLY(S \to BA)$ by step 3(a). Since $\lambda \in FIRST(BA)$, step 3(b) is not applied to this production. In a similar way, production $A \to aBA$ produces entry $M[A, a] = APPLY(A \to aBA)$; production

$B \to DC$ produces entries $M[B, c] = M[B, d] = APPLY(B \to DC)$ (because $FIRST(DC) = \{c, d\}$); $C \to bDC$ defines $M[C, b]$; $D \to cSc$ and $D \to d$ lead to definitions of $M[D, c]$ and $M[D, d]$. In none of these cases was part (b) of step 3 applied. Consider now the production $A \to \lambda$. Since $FIRST(\lambda) = \{\lambda\}$, step 3(a) is not applicable (there are no terminals in $FIRST(\lambda)$), but step 3(b) requires that $M[A, x] = APPLY(A \to \lambda)$ for every symbol x in $FOLLOW(A)$. Since $FOLLOW(A) = \{\$, c\}$ we get $M[A, \$] = M[A, c] = APPLY(A \to \lambda)$. Similarly, the production $C \to \lambda$ leads to $M[C, \$] = M[C, a] = M[C, c] = APPLY(C \to \lambda)$, because $FOLLOW(C) = \{\$, a, c\}$. This pretty much explains all the entries in Figure 6.5.

		Input symbol x				
		a	b	c	d	$\$$
Stack	a	POP				
	b		POP			
	c			POP		
	d				POP	
	S			$S \to BA$	$S \to BA$	
	A	$A \to aBA$		$A \to \lambda$		$A \to \lambda$
	B			$B \to DC$	$B \to DC$	
	C	$C \to \lambda$	$C \to bDC$	$C \to \lambda$		$C \to \lambda$
	D			$D \to cSc$	$D \to d$	
	$\#$					$ACCEPT$

Figure 6.5. Parsing table for Example 6.5.

We now take up discussion of Algorithm 6.1. The first thing to notice is that the function $M[\gamma, x]$ may turn out to be multiply defined, i.e., nondeterministic. More precisely, it may happen that for some stack symbol γ and some input x, application of step 3 will produce two distinct values for $M[\gamma, x]$. Consider, for example, the grammar

$$S \to aA \mid aB \qquad A \to a \qquad B \to b$$

By inspection, $FIRST(aA) = \{a\}$, so $M[S, a] = APPLY(S \to aA)$. But $FIRST(aB) = \{a\}$; this requires $M[S, a] = APPLY(S \to aB)$. When this happens, we say that the parsing table contains a ***conflict***. (Strictly speaking, we should define $M[\gamma, x]$ to be set-valued, the conflict is then defined as an occurrence of some $M[\gamma, x]$ with two or more elements. We will forgo this set-theoretic etiquette here.) If a conflict occurs, we may still consider Algorithm 6.1 as generating a top-down parser, except that the parser is now nondeterministic. The value $M[\gamma, x]$ describes the course of action of the parser (a push-down automaton) when the top of the stack contains the symbol γ and the current input is x. If $M[\gamma, x]$ contains more than one entry, the parser has a choice of action. Given a string σ, such a parser will accept σ if it is possible to go from the initial configuration $[\![\sigma\$, S\#, \lambda]\!]$ to $[\![\$, \#, n_1 n_2 \ldots n_k, ACCEPT]\!]$. (Not every sequence of choices will cause this transition, of course.) From the point of view of applications, it is preferable to have parsers that are deterministic, that is, for which $M[\gamma, x]$ is uniquely defined for each γ and x.

Definition 6.3. Let $G = \{\Sigma, N, S, P\}$ be a context-free grammar and let $M[\gamma, x]$ be the parsing function defined by Algorithm 6.1. If $M[\gamma, x]$ is single valued, we say that G is $LL(1)$. If $M[\gamma, x]$ is not single valued, we say that the parsing table for G contains conflicts and G is not $LL(1)$.

Theorem 6.2. If $G = \{\Sigma, N, S, P\}$ is an $LL(1)$ grammar then G has a deterministic top-down parser, namely the one defined by the function $M[\gamma, x]$ from Algorithm 6.1.

Proof. We must show that if $\sigma \in L(G)$ then the parser will correctly reconstruct the leftmost derivation of σ, and if $\sigma \notin L(G)$ the parser will reject σ. Let $\sigma = a_1 a_2 a_3 \ldots a_n$. When σ is fed into the parser, the initial configuration of the parser is $[\![a_1 a_2 \ldots a_n\$, S\#, \lambda]\!]$ and the program looks at the value of $M[a_1, S]$. If that entry is $REJECT$, this means that $a_1 \notin FIRST(\alpha)$ for any α such that $S \rightarrow \alpha$ is a production of G. But this means that, starting with S, it is impossible to derive any string beginning with a_1, hence $\sigma \notin L(G)$. If, on the other hand, $M[a_1, S]$ does contain a production, it can contain only one. (By hypothesis, the parsing table has no conflicts.) This production is of the form $S \rightarrow \alpha$ and could have entered the table either from application of step 3(a) or step 3(b). If 3(a) was used then $a_1 \in FIRST(\alpha)$ and if $S \rightarrow \beta$ is any other production with S on the left-hand side, then a_1 is not in $FIRST(\beta)$. Thus the parser determines the first production correctly. If the step 3(b) was used, this means that $\lambda \in FIRST(\alpha)$ and $a_1 \notin FIRST(\beta)$ for any production of the form $S \rightarrow \beta$. A moment of reflection shows that in this case the string σ must be the empty string λ, a_1 is actually the delimiter \$, and the first production to be used in transforming S into λ must be $S \rightarrow \alpha$.

Thus, if σ is derivable from the start symbol S, our parser correctly determines the first production to be used. In a similar way, suppose that after several moves the parser reaches configuration $[\![a_k a_{k+1} \ldots a_n\$, AX_1X_2 \ldots X_p\#, s]\!]$. This means that the parser correctly guessed the sequence s of productions that transform S into $a_1 a_2 \ldots a_{k-1} AX_1X_2$

$\ldots X_p$ and it must correctly determine the next production. Again, the parser looks at the entry $M[A, a_k]$ of the parsing table. If that entry is *REJECT*, then it is impossible to derive a string beginning with a_k from the sentential form $AX_1X_2 \ldots X_p$. Indeed, $a_k \notin FIRST(\alpha)$ for any α that is on the right-hand side of a production of the form $A \rightarrow \alpha$. It could happen, however, that the nonterminal A can be transformed to λ and a_k will be the first symbol of a string derivable from $X_1X_2 \ldots X_p$. In that case, however, $a_k \in FOLLOW(A)$, which would cause, by step 3(b), $M[a_k, A] \neq REJECT$. Suppose now that $M[a_k, A]$ does contain a production, it contains only one and the production must be of the form $A \rightarrow \alpha$. If that production was included as a result of step 3(a), then $a_k \in FIRST(\alpha)$ and the production must be applied in order to derive $a_k a_{k+1} \ldots a_n$. Moreover, no other production of the form $A \rightarrow \beta$ will accomplish this derivation, since $a_k \notin FIRST(\beta)$ for such β. If $A \rightarrow \alpha$ is included because of step 3(b), this means that $\lambda \in FIRST(\alpha)$, $a_k \notin FIRST(\alpha)$, and in order to derive $a_k a_{k+1} \ldots a_k$ from $AX_1X_2 \ldots X_p$ we must first transform A into the empty string λ (beginning with the production $A \rightarrow \alpha$) and then derive $a_k a_{k+1} \ldots a_n$ from $X_1X_2 \ldots X_p$. Hence, the parser acts correctly in this situation also. The completely pedantic proof can be made by induction on the length of the string σ using the above ideas. Q.E.D.

Now suppose we have a language for which we wish to construct a parser. We may write a grammar G of L and then apply Algorithm 6.1. If this results in a deterministic parser we are done. If not, several options are open. First of all, we may try to find another grammar G', equivalent to G, such that parser generated by G' is deterministic. After all, we are interested in parsing a language, and not a particular grammar generating it. We will discuss various grammar transformations which may accomplish this in Chapter 7. Another possibility is to use the parser as is, in the following way. When a conflict arises, that is, when the parsing table does not prescribe the next production uniquely but gives two or more alternatives, we may try all these alternatives one by one. More precisely, suppose $M[A, a]$ contains two productions $A \rightarrow \alpha_1$ and $A \rightarrow \alpha_2$, and the parser reaches configuration $[\![a \ldots \$, \quad A \ldots \#, s]\!]$. We may try to apply the production $A \rightarrow \alpha_1$ and see what happens. If the rest of the parse goes smoothly and we arrive at *ACCEPT*, we know that the string σ is in the language and we have generated a left parse of it. If, on the other hand, we arrive at *REJECT*, we know that the choice $A \rightarrow \alpha_1$ was not a correct one and we try applying $A \rightarrow \alpha_2$ and see what happens then. This kind of parsing is called ***back-track*** or ***recursive descent*** parsing. It is clear that such a parser may be very time-consuming as well as complicated to implement, especially if the parsing table contains many conflicts. Indeed, after encountering one conflict and making a guess as to which production should be used, we may run into another conflict and be forced another choice and so forth. One has to keep track of choices already made as well as the places in the parsing process where these choices have been made. For a detailed description of these parsing techniques see [2] or [3].

There is still another way to deal with parsing tables containing conflicts. Suppose at each instant of the parse we make a decision (on the next production to be applied) based not only on the value of the top of the stack and the current input symbol, but also on the next input symbol. In other words, at each step of parsing we look at two inputs symbols at a time. In this case the parsing function M is a function of three variables: $M = M[\gamma, x, y]$ where γ is the content of the top of the stack, x is the present input symbol, and y is the next input symbol. Consider, for example, the grammar

$$\begin{aligned} S &\rightarrow aA \\ S &\rightarrow aB \\ A &\rightarrow a \\ B &\rightarrow b \end{aligned}$$

It is easy to see that $M[S, a]$ contains two productions: $S \rightarrow aA$ and $S \rightarrow aB$. However, if we consider M as a function of three variables, $M[S, a, a] = APPLY(S \rightarrow aA)$ and $M[S, a, b] = APPLY(S \rightarrow aB)$, the conflict is resolved. The grammars for which it is possible to construct a deterministic top-down parser along the lines indicated here (that is, a parser that operates by looking at two symbols at each step) are called $LL(2)$ grammars. Clearly, the procedure can be generalized to considering k lookahead symbols, and leads to a concept of an $LL(k)$ grammar. For detailed exposition of these questions we refer the reader to [2] and [3].

Finally, a word of explanation about the letters LL in $LL(k)$. The first L means that the parser goes through the string from left (to right). The second L means that the parser produces the left parse of a string. In Chapter 8 we will discuss LR parsers. These also read the input from left to right, but produce the right parse.

6.4. *FIRST* AND *FOLLOW* FUNCTIONS

All the results and constructions of Section 6.3 hinge on the ability to compute deterministically the functions *FIRST* and *FOLLOW*. We begin with the function *FIRST*. Recall that if α is a sentential form, then $FIRST(\alpha)$ consists of all terminals x such that, starting from α, a sentential form beginning with x can be derived (see Definition 6.2.) The basic idea of an algorithm to calculate $FIRST(\alpha)$ is as follows: Given a sentential form α, we first determine all the terminals that can appear in front after making one substitution of the leftmost nonterminal. Next we determine the terminals that can appear in front of a sentential form that results from making two substitutions, etc. We will see that this procedure will end in a finite number of steps and produce the correct result. The precise algorithm is as follows.

Algorithm 6.2. Function $FIRST(\alpha)$.
Input: Context-free grammar $G = \{\Sigma, N, S, P\}$ and a sentential form α.
Output: The set $FIRST(\alpha)$.

Part I. Calculate $FIRST(X)$ for all grammatical symbols of G (i.e., for all $x \in \Sigma \cup N \cup \{\lambda\}$) according to the procedure below:

1. $FIRST(\lambda) = \{\lambda\}$
2. $FIRST(x) = \{x\}$ for all terminals $x \in \Sigma$
3. Let $A_1, A_2, \ldots, A_p$ be all the nonterminals of the grammar G
   (a) Define sets $N(A_1) = N(A_2) = N(A_3) = \cdots = N(A_p) = \emptyset$ and $N(x) = \{x\}$ for $x \in \Sigma$.
   (b) Go through all the productions of G in some arbitrary but fixed order and for each production modify the sets $N(A_1)$, $N(A_2)$, $N(A_3), \ldots, N(A_p)$ as follows:
   i) If the production is of the form $A \rightarrow x\alpha$ for some terminal x, add x to $N(A)$.
   ii) If the production is of the form $A \rightarrow \lambda$, add λ to $N(A)$.
   iii) If the production is of the form $A \rightarrow Y_1 Y_2 \ldots Y_k$ where the Y's are single grammatical symbols (Y_1 is a nonterminal, since otherwise case i holds, and $n \geq 2$, since otherwise case ii holds), there are two cases:
   (*) There is a smallest index $1 \leq j \leq k$ such that $\lambda \notin N(Y_j)$. In this case, add all the nonterminals of $N(Y_1), N(Y_2), \ldots, N(Y_j)$ to the set $N(A)$
   (**) There is no such index j, i.e., each one of the sets $N(Y_1)$, $N(Y_2), \ldots, N(Y_k)$ contains λ. In this case, add all the elements of $N(Y_1), \ldots, N(Y_k)$ to $N(A)$.
   (c) If any of the sets $N(A_1)$, $N(A_2)$, $N(A_3), \ldots, N(A_p)$ were modified during the execution of the step 3(b), go back and execute the step again. If, on the other hand, none of the sets $N(A_1), N(A_2), \ldots, N(A_p)$ were modified (i.e., no new elements were added to any of them), we set

$$FIRST(A_1) = N(A_1),\ FIRST(A_2) = N(A_2), \ldots, \\ FIRST(A_p) = N(A_p)$$

Part II. When Part I is completed, all the values of $FIRST(X)$ are known for $X \in \Sigma \cup N \cup \{\lambda\}$. Suppose now α is a sentential form given by $\alpha = Z_1Z_2 \ldots Z_m$, where each Z_m is either a terminal or a nonterminal. We may assume that $m \geq 2$, since otherwise $\alpha = \lambda$ ($m = 0$) or a single grammatical symbol ($m = 1$), in either case the value of $FIRST(\alpha)$ is already known from Part I. There are two possibilities:

1) There is a smallest index $1 \leq j \leq m$ such that $\lambda \notin FIRST(Z_j)$. In this case set

$$FIRST(\alpha) = \{FIRST(Z_1) \cup FIRST(Z_2) \cup \cdots \cup FIRST(Z_j)\} - \{\lambda\}$$

This means that $FIRST(\alpha)$ consists of all terminals from $FIRST(Z_1)$, $FIRST(Z_2), \ldots$, and $FIRST(Z_j)$; λ is not in $FIRST(\alpha)$.

2) There is no such index j, that is, $\lambda \in FIRST(Z_j)$ for all $j = 1, 2, \ldots, m$. In this case

$$FIRST(\alpha) = FIRST(Z_1) \cup FIRST(Z_2) \cup \cdots \cup FIRST(Z_m)$$

Thus, $FIRST(\alpha)$ is the union of all the symbols, including λ, from $FIRST(Z_1)$, $FIRST(Z_2), \ldots, FIRST(Z_m)$.

It should be quite clear that the above algorithm is completely deterministic and can be implemented on a machine. The only possibly troublesome point is step 3(b) of Part I. The algorithm calls for repeated application of this step until none of the sets $N(A_1), N(A_2), \ldots, N(A_p)$ are changed; the question is whether this will occur in a finite number of steps. Notice, however, that each modification consists of adding one or more terminals to these sets. Since there is only a finite number of terminals, each set can be modified only a finite number of times. Thus, the Algorithm 6.2 will terminate in a finite number of steps. Before giving the proof that this algorithm does indeed calculate the function *FIRST* correctly, we work out an example.

Example 6.6. Consider the grammar, discussed already in Examples 6.4 and 6.5, given by

$$\begin{array}{llll} S \rightarrow BA & B \rightarrow DC & D \rightarrow cSc & D \rightarrow d \\ A \rightarrow aBA & A \rightarrow \lambda & C \rightarrow bDC & C \rightarrow \lambda \end{array}$$

The values $FIRST(\alpha)$ were heuristically computed for all α's on the right-hand sides of the productions of G. We now derive these values using Algorithm 6.2. Part I, steps 1 and 2, gives

$$\begin{array}{lll} FIRST(\lambda) = \{\lambda\} & FIRST(a) = \{a\} & FIRST(B) = \{b\} \\ FIRST(c) = \{c\} & FIRST(d) = \{d\} & \end{array} \tag{6.9}$$

We now proceed with step 3. As required by (a), we originally put

$$N(S) = N(A) = N(B) = N(C) = N(D) = \emptyset \tag{6.10}$$

The first pass through the productions goes as follows:

$S \to BA$: Case iii applies here. Since $\lambda \notin N(B)$ $(= \emptyset)$ we use subcase $(*)$ with $j = 1$, i.e., one must add all the elements of $N(B)$ to $N(S)$. Since $N(B) = \emptyset$, no changes occur.
$A \to aBA$: The relevant case here is i, so we add terminal a to $N(A)$ so that $N(A) = \{a\}$ at this point.
$A \to \lambda$: This is covered by case ii, so we add λ to $N(A)$; thus $N(A)$ becomes $\{\lambda, a\}$.
$B \to DC$: Case iii applies. Since $\lambda \notin N(D)$ $(= \emptyset)$, we add all the terminals of $N(D)$ to $N(B)$. However, $N(D) = \emptyset$, so no changes take place.
$C \to bDC$: From case i we obtain $N(C) = \{b\}$.
$C \to \lambda$: Case ii causes λ to be added to $N(C)$, which becomes $\{\lambda, b\}$.
$D \to cSc$: Here, $N(D)$ becomes $\{c\}$ by case i.
$D \to d$: $N(D)$ increases to $\{c, d\}$, again on account of case i.

The values of N at the end of the first pass are

$$\begin{array}{lll} N(S) = \emptyset & N(A) = \{\lambda, a\} & N(B) = \emptyset \\ N(C) = \{\lambda, b\} & N(D) = \{c, d\} & \end{array} \tag{6.11}$$

Since these values differ from the values of N in (6.10), we execute step 3(b) again.

$S \to BA$: $\lambda \notin N(B) = \emptyset$, so no changes are made here.

$\left.\begin{array}{l} A \to aBA \\ A \to \lambda \end{array}\right\}$ Add a and λ to $N(A)$, but $N(A) = \{\lambda, a\}$ already, so no changes take place.

$B \to DC$: Since $\lambda \notin N(D) = \{c, d\}$, case iii$(*)$ gives $N(B) = \emptyset \cup N(D) = \{c, d\}$

$\left.\begin{array}{l} C \to bDC \\ C \to \lambda \end{array}\right\}$ Add b and λ to $N(C)$, but $N(C) = \{\lambda, b\}$ already, so no changes.

$\left.\begin{array}{l} D \to cSc \\ D \to d \end{array}\right\}$ Add c and d to $N(D)$, but $N(D) = \{c, d\}$ here, hence no change

At the end of the second pass we have

$$\begin{array}{lll} N(S) = \emptyset & N(A) = \{\lambda, a\} & N(B) = \{c, d\}, \\ N(C) = \{\lambda, b\} & N(D) = \{c, d\} & \end{array} \tag{6.12}$$

These are different from the values in (6.11) so we execute step 3a again.

$S \to BA$: This is case iii(*) with $j = 1$, resulting in $N(S) = \emptyset \cup N(B) = \{c, d\}$

One can easily check that the remaining productions do not alter any of the sets N. Thus we obtain

$$\begin{array}{lll} N(S) = \{c, d\} & N(A) = \{\lambda, a\} & N(B) = \{c, d\} \\ N(C) = \{\lambda, b\} & N(D) = \{c, d\} & \end{array} \tag{6.13}$$

These values are different from (6.12), so the fourth pass through step 3(b) is called for. One can easily check, however, that this fourth pass leaves all the sets N intact. Thus, at the end of Part I we have:

$$\begin{array}{lll} FIRST(S) = \{c, d\} & FIRST(A) = \{\lambda, a\} & FIRST(B) = \{c, d\} \\ FIRST(C) = \{\lambda, b\} & FIRST(D) = \{c, d\} & \end{array}$$

We now proceed with Part II.

$\alpha = BA$. Case 1 applies with $j = 1$ ($\lambda \notin FIRST(B)$) so $FIRST(BA) = FIRST(B) = \{c, d\}$

$\alpha = aBA$. Case 1 applies with $j = 1$ ($\lambda \notin FIRST(a)$) so $FIRST(aBA) = FIRST(a) = \{a\}$.

$\alpha = \lambda$. $FIRST(\lambda) = \{\lambda\}$ from Part I.

$\alpha = DC$. Case 1 with $j = 1$ gives $FIRST(DC) = FIRST(D) = \{c, d\}$.

$\alpha = bDC$. Case 1 with $j = 1$ yields $FIRST(bDC) = FIRST(b) = \{b\}$.

$\alpha = cSc$. $FIRST(cSc) = \{c\}$ as above.

$\alpha = d$. $FIRST(d) = \{d\}$ from Part I.

These values are identical to the ones in (6.3) which were obtained in a somewhat ad hoc and heuristic way.

Theorem 6.3. Algorithm 6.2 correctly computes the function *FIRST*.

Proof. First we show that Algorithm 6.2 for computing $FIRST(\alpha)$ works correctly when α consists of one symbol (Part I). By inspection, Algorithm 6.2 correctly determines the values of $FIRST(\alpha)$ when α is a terminal or $\alpha = \lambda$. Suppose now α is a single nonterminal, say $\alpha = A$. We claim that at each iteration of step 3(b) every one of the sets $N(A_i)$ contains only symbols from $FIRST(A_i)$. This is clearly true at the iteration 0—all these sets are empty. Assume now that the assertion is true at the end of the qth iteration. During the $(q+1)^{th}$ iteration, a symbol x is going to be added to $N(A_i)$ only as a result of an application of case i, ii, or iii. In case i, x is added to the set $N(A_i)$ if and only if there is production of the form $A_i \rightarrow x\beta$. Clearly such $x \in FIRST(A_i)$. In case ii, the symbol λ is added to $N(A_i)$ provided there is a production of the form $A_i \rightarrow \lambda$, but this mean that λ is in $FIRST(A_i)$. In case iii there are two possibilities: possibility (*), there is a production of the form $A_i \rightarrow Y_1 Y_2 \ldots Y_k$, and $1 \leq j \leq k$ such that $\lambda \notin N(A_j)$, but $\lambda \in N(Y_1), \ldots, N(Y_{j-1})$. In this situation we add all the terminals in $N(Y_1), N(Y_2), \ldots, N(Y_j)$ to $N(A_i)$. Since by inductive hypothesis each one of the nonterminals $Y_1, Y_2, \ldots, Y_j$ can be transformed into the empty string (λ is in each one of the sets $N(Y_1), \ldots, N(Y_{j-1})$), we see that any terminal added to $N(A_i)$ at this stage will also be in $FIRST(A_i)$. Completely analogous reasoning shows that the assertion is true if possibility (**) holds (λ is in each one of the sets $N(Y_1), \ldots, N(Y_k)$).

We must show next that if a symbol belongs to $FIRST(A)$, then this symbol will be added to $N(A)$ at some iteration of the step 3(b). Now choose $x \in FIRST(A)$; assume for a moment that $x \neq \lambda$. This means that there is a legal derivation in the grammar G of the form $A \Rightarrow^* x\beta$ for some string β. Let

$$A \Rightarrow \gamma_1 \Rightarrow \gamma_2 \Rightarrow \cdots \Rightarrow \gamma_{q-1} \Rightarrow \gamma_q = x\beta \tag{6.14}$$

be the shortest leftmost derivation that accomplishes this. (Such a derivation need not be unique, if the grammar is ambiguous, but it does not matter.) Define a function $\psi(A, x)$ to be the length of such a shortest derivation: In (6.14), $\psi(A, x) = q$. We show that for each nonterminal A_i, if $x \in FIRST(A_i)$ then x will be included in $N(A_i)$ before or during the $\psi(A_i, x)^{th}$ iteration. The assertion is certainly true if $\psi(A_i, x) = 1$, since in this case the shortest derivation is a result of a single production of the form $A_i \rightarrow x\beta$, so x is included in the set $N(A_i)$ during the first iteration. Suppose now the assertion is true for all A_r's and all x's for which $\psi(A_r, x) < q$. Let A_i and x be such that $x \in FIRST(A_i)$ and $\psi(A_i, x) = q$. Let the relevant derivation be as in (6.14). The sentential form γ_1 must have form $\gamma_1 = Y_1Y_2 \ldots Y_s$, where Y's are single grammatical symbols (terminals or nonterminals). Thus the derivation $A \Rightarrow^* x\beta$ must have form

$$A \Rightarrow Y_1Y_2 \ldots Y_s \Rightarrow^* x\beta$$

In order for this to happen, the first j_0 of the Y's $(0 \leq j_0 \leq s - 1)$ must be transformed into λ, and Y_{j_0+1} is transformed into a string beginning with x. All of these derivations are of length $< q$. By inductive hypothesis, $j_0 + 1$ is the first index such that $\lambda \notin N(Y_j)$ and $x \in N(Y_{j_0+1})$. This shows that x is added to $N(A_i)$ at the qth stage (step 3(b) iii(*)). The case when $x = \lambda$ is quite similar. This shows that the algorithm performs correctly during Part I, i.e., it correctly evaluates $FIRST(Y)$ for any single grammatical symbol Y. The proof that Algorithm 6.2 also works correctly during Part II is completely analogous, and is left as an exercise. Q.E.D.

We next take up the function *FOLLOW*. The algorithm is again inductive: We initially define sets $M(X)$ for all nonterminals X, then go through the productions one by one, adding some elements to these sets until no changes occur. As in the case of *FIRST*, during the qth iteration we add those symbols to $M(X)$ that can occur after X after making at most q substitutions. The algorithm for *FOLLOW* requires the ability to evaluate $FIRST(\alpha)$ for various sentential forms α.

Algorithm 6.3. Function $FOLLOW(X)$.
Input: Context-free grammar $G = \{\Sigma, N, S, P\}$. We assume that the symbol \$ is not in $\Sigma \cup N$.
Output: Values of $FOLLOW(X)$ for all nonterminals X.

1. Let the nonterminals of G be $S = A_1, A_2, A_3, \ldots, A_n$, where S is the start symbol. Define sets $M(A_i)$ for each A_i by

$$M(S) = M(A_1) = \{\$\} \quad M(A_2) = M(A_3) = \ldots = M(A_n) = \emptyset$$

2. Go through all the productions of G in some arbitrary but fixed order and for each one perform the following operations on the sets M:

(a) If the production has only terminals (or λ) on its right-hand side, do nothing.

(b) If the production has nonterminals on its right-hand side, then for each such nonterminal X express the production as $A_i \to \alpha X \beta$, and do the following:

i) Add all the terminals of $FIRST(\beta)$ to $M(X)$ (do not add λ, only the terminals).

ii) If $\lambda \in FIRST(\beta)$, add all the symbols of $M(A_i)$ to $M(X)$.

3. If any of the sets M were changed during the execution of step 2, go back and execute step 2 again. If none of the sets were changed, set $FOLLOW(A_i) = M(A_i)$, $i = 1, 2, \ldots, n$.

As in the case of the function *FIRST*, the algorithm does halt after a finite number of steps. Step 2 calls for (possibly) modifying the sets $M(A_i)$ by adding some terminals to them. Since there is only a finite number of the terminals, the procedure must stop after a finite number of iterations.

Example 6.7. We again consider the grammar G from Example 6.6:

$S \to BA$	$B \to DC$	$D \to cSc$
$A \to aBA$	$C \to bDC$	$D \to d$
$A \to \lambda$	$C \to \lambda$	

We will compute the sets $FOLLOW(S)$, $FOLLOW(A)$, $FOLLOW(B)$, $FOLLOW(C)$, and $FOLLOW(D)$ using Algorithm 6.3. Step 1 gives

$$M(S) = \{\$\} \qquad M(A) = M(B) = M(C) = M(D) = \emptyset \tag{6.15}$$

We now proceed with the first iteration of step 2.

$S \to BA$. Here $X = B$ or $X = A$ and we have to consider both cases. If $X = B$, then $\alpha = \lambda$, $\beta = A$. Since $FIRST(A) = \{\lambda, a\}$ (see Example 6.6), step 2(b)i calls for adding terminal a to $M(B)$ and step 2(b)ii calls for adding all the symbols from $M(S)$ to $M(B)$. Thus, $M(B)$ becomes $\{a, \$\}$. If $X = A$, then $\alpha = B$ and $\beta = \lambda$. In this case $FIRST(\beta) = \{\lambda\}$ so only step 2(b)ii applies: All the symbols from $M(S)$ are added to $M(A)$, which becomes $\{\$\}$.

$A \to aBA$. Again $X = B$ or $X = A$, and we consider both cases. If we take $X = B$, then $\alpha = a$ and $\beta = A$. This calls for adding a from $FIRST(A)$ to $M(B)$—no change, a is already there—and for adding $M(S)$ to $M(B)$ (because $\lambda \in FIRST(A)$)—again no change. If $X = A$, then $\alpha = aB$ and $\beta = \lambda$. This calls (step 2(b)ii) for adding elements of $M(A)$ to itself—no change.

$A \to \lambda$. No action taken because of step 2(a).

$B \to DC$. If we set $X = D$ then $\beta = C$ and $FIRST(C) = \{\lambda, b\}$. This calls for adding b to $M(D)$ (step 2(b)i) and all of $M(B)$ to $M(D)$ (step 2(b)ii). Hence $M(D)$ becomes $\{\$, a, b\}$. If $X = C$ then this causes $M(C) = M(B) = \{\$, a\}$.

$C \to \lambda$. No action here.

$D \to cSc$. $M(S)$ becomes $\{\$, c\}$.

$D \to d$. Nothing happens here.

At the end of the first pass we have

$$M(S) = \{\$, c\} \qquad M(A) = \{\$\} \qquad M(B) = \{\$, a\}$$
$$M(C) = \{\$, a\} \qquad M(D) = \{\$, a, b\} \tag{6.16}$$

These values of M's differ from the ones given in (6.15), so we execute step 2 again.

$S \to BA$. Setting $X = B$ causes c to be added to $M(B)$. This is because $\lambda \in FIRST(A)$ and $c \in M(S)$. Thus, $M(B)$ becomes $\{\$, a, c\}$. Letting $X = A$ causes c to be added to $M(A)$, which is now $\{\$, c\}$. Both additions are a result of step 2(b)ii.

$A \to aBA$. No changes occur here.

$B \to DC$. If $X = D$ then $M(B)$ must be added to $M(D)$ (because $\lambda \in FIRST(C)$), thus, $M(D)$ becomes $\{\$, a, b, c\}$. If $X = C$, then $M(B)$ must be added to $M(C)$, transforming it to $\{\$, a, c\}$.

The remaining productions produce no changes. Thus, at the end of the second iteration of step 2 we have

$$M(S) = \{\$, c\} \qquad M(A) = \{\$, c\} \qquad M(B) = \{\$, a, c\}$$
$$M(C) = \{\$, a, c\} \qquad M(D) = \{\$, a, b, c\}.$$

These values are different from those in (6.16), so we should repeat step 2 again. One can check, however, that the next iteration produces no changes. We finally have

$$FOLLOW(S) = FOLLOW(A) = \{\$, c\} \qquad FOLLOW(D) = \{\$, a, b, c\}$$
$$FOLLOW(B) = FOLLOW(C) = \{\$, a, c\}$$

This agrees with our heuristic derivation of the values of $FOLLOW$ in Example 6.4. The Algorithms 6.1–6.3 give a completely deterministic way of constructing a top-down parser for any context-free grammar G. (This parser may turn out to be nondeterministic.)

Theorem 6.4. Algorithm 6.3 correctly evaluates the values of $FOLLOW$.

The proof of this theorem is very similar to the proof of Theorem 6.3. We show first that at each iteration of step 2, only the symbols from $FOLLOW(A_i)$ are added to the set $M(A_i)$, and then prove that every symbol from $FOLLOW(A_i)$ will eventually be included in $M(A_i)$. In both instances the formal proof uses induction. We will not present this proof (it is a bit tedious), instead we will informally discuss why one needs step 2(b)ii in the iterative process. (It is fairly clear that step 2(b)i is needed.) Step 2(b)ii says, essentially, that if $Y \to \alpha X \beta$ is a production and $FIRST(\beta)$ contains λ, then every symbol from $FOLLOW(Y)$ should be included in $FOLLOW(X)$. Indeed, suppose $x_0 \in FOLLOW(Y)$; thus, there is a legal derivation of the form $S \Rightarrow^* \gamma Y x_0 \delta$. Since $Y \to \alpha X \beta$ is a production of G, the derivation $S \Rightarrow^* \gamma Y x_0 \delta \Rightarrow \gamma \alpha X \beta x_0 \delta$ is also legal. Because $\lambda \in FIRST(\beta)$, there is a derivation $\beta \Rightarrow \lambda$, so, finally, the derivation

$$S \Rightarrow^* \gamma Y x_0 \delta \Rightarrow \gamma \alpha X \beta x_0 \delta \Rightarrow^* \gamma \alpha X x_0 \delta$$

is also legal, i.e., x_0 must be included in $FOLLOW(X)$.

PROBLEMS

In each of problems 1–4 construct an LL parser for each given grammar. Do not formally evaluate the functions $FIRST$ and $FOLLOW$, just make an "educated guess" of what they are. Which of these grammars are $LL(1)$?

1. $S \to aA,\ A \to S \mid \lambda.$
2. $S \to AB,\ A \to a,\ B \to CD \mid aE,\ C \to ab,\ D \to bb,\ E \to bba.$
3. $S \to aAaB \mid bAbB,\ A \to a \mid ab,\ B \to aB \mid a$
4. $S \to BA,\ A \to +BA \mid \lambda,\ B \to DC,\ C \to *DC \mid \lambda,\ D \to (S) \mid a$

In each of problems 5–8 calculate the $FIRST$ and $FOLLOW$ of all the nonterminals in the given grammar. Show explicitly at least two iterations of the relevant algorithm.

5. $S \to ABC,\ A \to aA \mid b \mid \lambda,\ B \to bC \mid Ab \mid \lambda,\ C \to a \mid b \mid c$
6. $S \to aABc,\ A \to a \mid \lambda,\ B \to b \mid \lambda$

7. $S \to aAde, \quad A \to BCD, \quad B \to bB \mid \lambda, \quad C \to cC \mid \lambda, \quad D \to bD \mid \lambda$
8. $S \to ABC \mid Ba \mid bA, \quad A \to a \mid BC \mid Ca, \quad B \to b \mid bbCb \mid \lambda,$
   $C \to AS \mid Ba \mid \lambda$
9. Suppose in some grammar G one has the following relations:

$$FIRST(A) = \{a,\ b,\ \lambda\} \qquad FIRST(B) = \{b,\ \lambda\}$$
$$FIRST(C) = \{a,\ \lambda\} \qquad FIRST(D) = \{b\}$$

   Calculate $FIRST(ABCD)$, $FIRST(BC)$ and $FIRST(AbB)$.
10. Show that the grammar in problem 8 is not $LL(1)$ and find all the conflicts in the parsing table.
11. Consider the grammar from Example 6.5 whose parsing table is given in Figure 6.5. Show the movements of this parser on strings $\sigma_1 = dbd$, $\sigma_2 = cdbdad$, and $\sigma_3 = cdaabdc$.

CHAPTER 7

GRAMMAR TRANSFORMATIONS

7.1. PROPER GRAMMARS

Given a language L and its grammar G, it may or may not be possible to construct a deterministic $LL(1)$ parser along the lines indicated in Chapter 6. Everything hinges on the parsing table containing no conflicts. If a conflict does exist, all need not be lost. It may be possible to rewrite the grammar G into a new, equivalent grammar G' that does have an $LL(1)$ parser. (Any language L has more than one grammar.) Since we are primarily interested in parsing a language rather than any of its particular grammars, rewriting grammars to fit a particular form is quite often beneficial. We devote this chapter to various techniques of grammar transformations. In the present section we will show how to eliminate various "trivialities" from a grammar. We illustrate this first by some examples.

Example 7.1. Consider a grammar G given by

$$
\begin{array}{lcl}
S & \rightarrow & aBC \mid Db \\
B & \rightarrow & a \mid B \\
C & \rightarrow & a \mid b \mid c \\
D & \rightarrow & E \\
E & \rightarrow & D \\
F & \rightarrow & B \mid d
\end{array}
$$

Some of the productions of this grammar are what one may call *useless* and/or *inaccessible*. Consider, for example, the production $B \rightarrow B$; it is entirely obvious that it can be deleted from the list of productions without changing the language $L(G)$. Next, consider the grammatical symbols F and d. It is clear by inspection that they cannot appear in any sentential form derivable from the start symbol S. They are thus inaccessible and any production containing them may be removed without changing the resulting language. The symbols D and E are also useless, since it is impossible to derive from them any sentential form containing only terminals. Thus, if any of these symbols appears during a derivation, no amount of substitution will result in a sentence of the language. Hence, again, any production containing these symbols may be removed. Finally, we are left with a simplified grammar G':

$$S \rightarrow aBC \qquad B \rightarrow a \qquad C \rightarrow a \mid b \mid c$$

It is clear that $L(G) = L(G') =$ the language of all strings of length three that begin with aa.

We now give a formal definition of these unnecessary productions and symbols, and procedures to eliminate them.

Definition 7.1. Let $G = \{\Sigma, N, S, P\}$ be a context-free grammar. A grammatical symbol X from $\Sigma \cup N$ is called ***inaccessible*** if it does not appear in any sentential form derivable from the start symbol S. In other words, if $S \Rightarrow^* Y_1 Y_2 \ldots Y_n$, then $X \neq Y_i$ for all $i = 1, 2, \ldots, n$.

A nonterminal $Y \in N$ is said to be ***useless*** if, starting from Y, it is impossible to derive either the empty string λ or any sentential form consisting of terminals only. Thus, if $Y \Rightarrow^* Y_1 Y_2 \ldots Y_n$ then $n \geq 1$ and at least one of the Y's is a nonterminal.

Theorem 7.1. Given a context-free grammar G, there exists an equivalent grammar G' (i.e., $L(G) = L(G')$) that contains no useless or inaccessible symbols. Moreover, there exists a deterministic algorithm to construct this grammar G'.

We will prove this theorem in two stages. We will construct first an equivalent grammar with no useless symbols, and then an equivalent grammar with no inaccessible symbols. We will also show that the order of these operations is important; that is, if we first remove inaccessible symbols and then useless ones, the resulting grammar may not be of the right form.

Algorithm 7.1. Removal of useless symbols.
Input: A context-free grammar $G = \{\Sigma, N, S, P\}$.
Output: An equivalent grammar G' with no useless symbols.

The algorithm basically consists of finding all symbols that are ***not*** useless. The grammar G' is then obtained from G by deleting all the productions containing useless symbols. It is quite clear that G' is going to be equivalent to G. Formally, let

$$N_e = \{X \in N \mid X \Rightarrow^* \lambda \text{ or } X \Rightarrow^* a_1 a_2 a_3 \ldots a_n, \text{ where all } a\text{'s are in } \Sigma\}$$

be the set of all nonterminals that are not useless. The construction of the set N_e is as follows: First, we include in N_e all the nonterminals X such that there is a production of the form $X \rightarrow \lambda$ or $X \rightarrow \sigma$, where σ consists of terminals only. In the second stage, we add to N_e all the nonterminals X for which there exists a production of the form $X \rightarrow \alpha$, where α consists only of either terminals, or nonterminals that have already been included in N_e. It is clear that any nonterminal X included at this stage in not useless: One can derive from X a string in Σ^*. We continue this process until no new nonterminals are added. The procedure will surely halt since the grammar G contains only a finite number of nonterminals. Formally, the algorithm may be written as follows:

Construct a sequence of sets $N_0, N_1, N_2, \ldots$ as follows:

1. $N_0 = \emptyset$
2. Suppose $N_0, N_1, N_2, \ldots, N_i$ have been already defined. Put

$$N_{i+1} = N_i \cup \{X \in N \mid \text{There is a production of the form } X \rightarrow \alpha, \text{ where } \alpha \text{ is either } \lambda \text{ or consists entirely of symbols from } N_i \cup \Sigma\}$$

3. Repeat step 2 until $N_i = N_{i+1}$, i.e., until no new nonterminals are added. Then set $N_e = N_i$.

Since $N_0 \subseteq N_1 \subseteq N_2 \cdots \subseteq N$, it is clear that the process will end in a finit number of steps (N is a finite set).

Example 7.2. Let G be the grammar

$$S \rightarrow A \mid B \qquad A \rightarrow aB \mid bS \mid b$$
$$B \rightarrow AB \mid Ba \qquad C \rightarrow AS \mid b$$

The construction of the set N_e proceeds as follows:

Step 1: $N_0 = \emptyset$ (by definition)
Step 2: $N_1 = \{A, C\}$. The symbol A is included because of production $A \to b$ and nonterminal C because of production $C \to b$. Since $N_0 \neq N_1$, step 2 must be repeated. We get $N_2 = \{A, C, S\}$. The symbol S was added because of the production $S \to A$.
Step 3: By inspection $N_3 = N_2$, thus the algorithm terminates for $i = 2$ and $N_e = N_2 = \{S, A, C\}$.

The resulting grammar G' is then

$$\begin{aligned} S &\to A \\ A &\to bS \mid b \\ C &\to AS \mid b \end{aligned}$$

It clearly does not contain any useless nonterminals. It does, however, contain the inaccessible symbol C.

We now proceed with an algorithm for removing inaccessible symbols. The basic idea is quite similar. The starting symbol S is clearly accessible, so in the first stage we include S in the set M of accessible symbols. In the second stage we include all symbols that can be immediately derived from S, i.e., all the symbols appearing on the right-hand side of productions of the form $S \to \alpha$. In the third stage we include all the symbols that can be immediately derived from the ones included so far, etc. The formal algorithm is as follows:

Algorithm 7.2. Removal of inaccessible symbols.
Input: A context-free grammar $G = \{\Sigma, N, S, P\}$.
Output: An equivalent grammar G' with no inaccessible symbols.

Define inductively the sequence of sets $M_0, M_1, M_2, \ldots$ as follows:

1. $M_0 = \{S\}$
2. Suppose $M_0, M_1, \ldots, M_i$ have been defined. Put

$$M_{i+1} = M_i \cup \{X \in \Sigma \cup N \mid \text{There is a production of the form } Y \to \alpha X \beta, \text{ where } Y \in M_i\}.$$

3. Repeat step 2 until $M_i = M_{i+1}$, i.e., until no new nonterminal are added. Then set $M = M_i$.

To construct now the grammar G', remove from G all productions containing symbols not included in the set M.

Example 7.3. We continue with the grammar from Example 7.2. After the useless symbols were removed, the grammar was given by

$$\begin{aligned} S &\to A \\ A &\to bS \mid b \\ C &\to AS \mid b \end{aligned}$$

We now remove the inaccessible symbols using Algorithm 7.2. We set $M_0 = \{S\}$ as in step 1. Applying step 2, we get $M_1 = \{S, A\}$. The symbol A is added because of the production $S \to A$. Repeating step 2, we obtain $M_2 = \{S, A, b\}$—the symbol b was added because of the production $A \to bS$. At the third iteration of step 2 we get $M_3 = M_2$ so $M = M_2 = \{S, A, b\}$ is the set of accessible symbols, and C is inaccessible. To obtain grammar G' we delete all the productions involving C; the resulting grammar is then

$$S \to A \qquad A \to bS \mid b$$

We should emphasize that the order in which these two algorithms are applied is important. Consider, for example, the grammar

$$S \to a \mid A \qquad A \to AB \qquad B \to b \tag{7.1}$$

By inspection, A is a useless symbol. After its removal, the grammar becomes

$$S \to a \qquad B \to b$$

Now B becomes inaccessible, so its removal results in the grammar $S \to a$. In the original grammar (7.1), however, all the symbols are accessible. Thus, removing the inaccessible symbols first and the useless symbols second leads to the grammar $S \to a$, $B \to b$, which still contains an inaccessible symbol, namely B. If the above algorithms are applied in the proper order, however, the resulting grammar does not contain inaccessible or useless symbols. Indeed, it does not contain inaccessible symbols, since Algorithm 7.2 is applied last. If X is a nonterminal in the final grammar, X is not useless, since it survived application of Algorithm 7.1. This means that there is a legal derivation of the form $X \Rightarrow^* \sigma$, where σ either is λ or consists of terminals only. Since X is accessible, all the intervening nonterminals in this derivation are also accessible, thus X is not a useless nonterminal in the final grammar.

Given a nonterminal X, the phrase "production(s) whose left-hand side is X" occurs often in what follows. We introduce a piece of terminology to abbreviate this expression.

Definition 7.2. Let $G = \{\Sigma, N, S, P\}$ be a context-free grammar. If X is a nonterminal, any production whose left hand-side is X is called an X-***production.***

Thus, for example, given a grammar $S \to Aa \mid B$, $A \to aaB \mid Sa$, $B \to b \mid SA$, the production $A \to Sa$ is an A-production, and $B \to b$, and $B \to SA$ are all the B-productions of the grammar G.

It is sometime convenient to remove empty productions (of the form $X \to \lambda$) from a given grammar. We already saw that such productions call for special handling in constructing a top-down parser; they are also inconvenient when testing a grammar for being $LL(1)$. The empty productions, of course, cannot always be totally eliminated. If the empty string λ belongs to the language $L(G)$ generated by a grammar G, then G must clearly contain at least one empty production—otherwise we cannot derive λ from the start symbol S. Thus, at the very least, G must contain at least one empty production, if only $S \to \lambda$. We will show that we can make that to be the only empty production.

Definition 7.3. Let $G = \{\Sigma, N, S, P\}$ be a context-free grammar. We say that G is ***λ-free*** if one of the following conditions holds:

1. G has no productions of the form $X \to \lambda$.
2. G has exactly one empty production, namely $S \to \lambda$, and the start symbol S does not appear on the right-hand side of any of the productions.

It turns out that given any context-free grammar G one can always construct an equivalent λ-free grammar G'. Heuristically, the key to this construction is as follows: Suppose G contains a production $A \to \lambda$, and suppose all the productions of G that contain A on the right hand side are

$$\begin{aligned} B &\to aAcA \\ D &\to bA \end{aligned}$$

We could delete the production $A \to \lambda$ at the cost of adding the following additional productions:

1. Instead of production $B \rightarrow aAcA$ we include productions

$$B \rightarrow aAcA$$
$$B \rightarrow acA$$
$$B \rightarrow aAc$$
$$B \rightarrow ac$$

   The last three productions result from $B \rightarrow aAcA$ by replacing either or both occurrences of A by λ.
2. Instead of production $D \rightarrow bA$ we include productions

$$D \rightarrow bA$$
$$D \rightarrow b$$

   The last production results from $D \rightarrow bA$ by replacing A with λ.

It is clear that the resulting language $L(G)$ remains the same. For instance, if in the original grammar G the derivation tree of a string σ contains a fragment

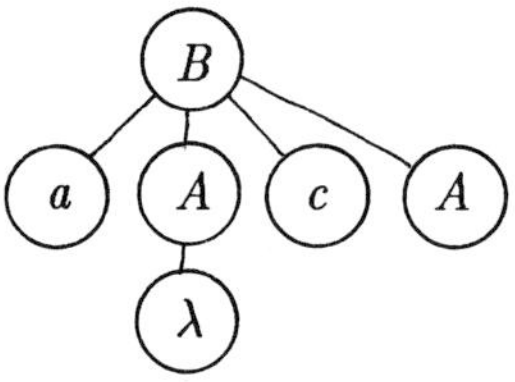

then this will be replaced by a derivation tree whose corresponding fragment is

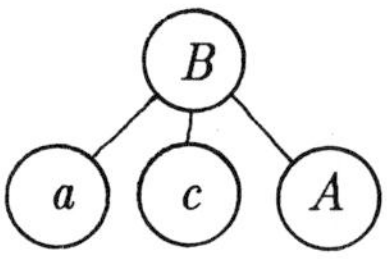

($B \rightarrow acA$ is one of the new productions). We now give a formal discussion of this algorithm. First, a preliminary result is needed about nonterminals X for which $X \Rightarrow^* \lambda$.

Definition 7.4. Let $G = \{\Sigma, N, S, P\}$ be a context-free grammar. A nonterminal $X \in N$ is said to be ***nilpotent*** if $X \Rightarrow^* \lambda$. (It is possible to derive the empty string λ from X.) The set of all nilpotent elements is denoted by $\Lambda(G)$.

Algorithm 7.3. Nilpotent nonterminals.
Input: A context-free grammar $G = \{\Sigma, N, S, P\}$.
Output: The set $\Lambda(G)$ of nilpotent nonterminals.

Define inductively the sequence of sets $\Lambda_1, \Lambda_2, \ldots$, by

1. $\Lambda_1 = \{X \in N \mid X \to \lambda$ is a production of $G\}$.
2. Suppose $\Lambda_1, \Lambda_2, \ldots, \Lambda_i$ have been defined. Put

$$\Lambda_{i+1} = \Lambda_i \cup \{X \in N \mid \text{There is production of the form } X \to Y_1 Y_2 \ldots Y_n, \text{ where each } Y_j \text{ in } \Lambda_i\}$$

3. If $\Lambda_{i+1} = \Lambda_i$, set $\Lambda(G) = \Lambda_i$, otherwise repeat step 2.

The idea behind Algorithm 7.3 should be clear. We first include in $\Lambda(G)$ all the nonterminals X such that $X \Rightarrow^* \lambda$ in one step, i.e., those X's for which $X \to \lambda$ is a production in G. In the second step we include all X's such that there is a production of the form $X \to Y_1 Y_2 \ldots Y_n$, and each Y_i can be transformed into λ. Thus Λ_2 contains all nonterminals that can be transformed into λ in two steps. We repeat the procedure (which must end, since G has only a finite number of nonterminals) until we find all the nilpotent nonterminals of G.

Example 7.4. Let G be the grammar

$$\begin{aligned} S &\to AB \\ A &\to BSB \mid BB \mid 1 \\ B &\to 0A1 \mid \lambda \end{aligned}$$

We have $\Lambda_1 = \{B\}$ since $B \to \lambda$ is a production of G. The nonterminals A and S are not in Λ_1 because neither of the productions $S \to \lambda$ and $A \to \lambda$ are productions of G. $\Lambda_2 = \{B, A\}$ because of the production $A \to BB$. The start symbol S is not in Λ_2 since $S \to AB$ is not of the right form. Finally, $\Lambda_3 = \{B, A, S\}$; here S is included because of the production $S \to AB$ (both A and B are in Λ_2). Obviously $\Lambda_4 = \Lambda_3$, so $\Lambda(G) = \Lambda_3 = \{S, A, B\}$.

The algorithm for removing empty productions is now as follows:

Algorithm 7.4. Removal of empty productions.
Input: Context-free grammar $G = \{\Sigma, N, S, P\}$.
Output: An equivalent λ-free grammar G'.

1. Construct the set $\Lambda(G)$ of nilpotent elements of G using Algorithm 7.3.
2. Write each production of G in the form

$$X \rightarrow \alpha_0 X_1 \alpha_1 X_2 \alpha_2 X_3 \ldots \alpha_{k-1} X_k \alpha_k$$

where each X_j is in $\Lambda(G)$ and each α_j contains no symbols from $\Lambda(G)$. Add to G all productions of the form

$$Z \rightarrow \alpha_0 Z_1 \alpha_1 Z_2 \alpha_2 Z_3 \ldots \alpha_{k-1} Z_k \alpha_k$$

where each Z_j is either X_j or λ, but without adding the production $X \rightarrow \lambda$. (This would happen if all α's were equal to λ.)
3. Remove all empty productions from G.
4. If S is not a nilpotent nonterminal, the algorithm stops here. If $S \in \Lambda(G)$, introduce a new start symbol S' and add two productions: $S' \rightarrow \lambda$ and $S' \rightarrow S$.

It should be fairly clear that the resulting grammar G' is λ-free and is equivalent to G.

Example 7.5. We continue with the grammar from the previous example:

$$\begin{aligned} S &\rightarrow AB \\ A &\rightarrow BSB \mid BB \mid 1 \\ B &\rightarrow 0A1 \mid \lambda \end{aligned}$$

It was calculated that $\Lambda(G) = \{S, A, B\}$. Algorithm 7.4 proceeds as follows:

From $S \rightarrow AB$ we obtain productions $S \rightarrow AB$, $S \rightarrow A$, and $S \rightarrow B$. Here $\alpha_0 = \alpha_1 = \alpha_2 = \alpha_3 = \lambda$, $X_1 = A$, and $X_2 = B$. We must, therefore, include all the productions of the form $S \rightarrow Z_1 Z_2$, where $Z_1 = A$ or λ, and $Z_2 = B$ or λ, except that the case $Z_1 = Z_2 = \lambda$ is not allowed, since it would result in the empty production $S \rightarrow \lambda$.

From $A \rightarrow BSB$ we obtain productions

$$A \rightarrow BSB \mid BS \mid BB \mid B \mid SB \mid S \mid B$$

The reasons here are pretty much as before. Notice that this procedure may lead to duplicate productions—in this case $A \rightarrow B$ occurs twice. This happens because we consider all productions of the form $A \to Z_1Z_2Z_3$, where $Z_1 = B$ or λ, $Z_2 = S$ or λ, and $Z_3 = B$ or λ. The cases $Z_1 = B$, $Z_2 = Z_3 = \lambda$, and $Z_1 = Z_2 = \lambda$, $Z_3 = B$ both lead to $A \to B$. Clearly, it is permissible to delete the duplications.

From $A \to BB$ we obtain $A \to BB \mid B$ (already included above).

From $A \to 1$ we get nothing new since this production does not contain elements from $\Lambda(G)$ on the right hand side.

From $B \to 0A1$ we obtain $B \to 0A1 \mid 01$.

Finally, the production $B \to \lambda$ is deleted altogether.

Since $S \in \Lambda(G)$ we must introduce a new start symbol S' and add two new productions $S' \to \lambda$ and $S' \to S$. The resulting grammar is given by

$$\begin{aligned} S' &\to S \mid \lambda \\ S &\to AB \mid A \mid B \\ A &\to BSB \mid BS \mid BB \mid SB \mid S \mid B \mid 1 \\ B &\to 0A1 \mid 01 \end{aligned}$$

It is also sometimes convenient to remove from a given grammar all productions of the form $X \to Y$, where both X and Y are single nonterminals. Productions such as this one are called ***single productions.*** Their removal is especially useful when one wishes to eliminate so called ***cycles.*** A cycle in a grammar G is a sequence of derivations of the form

$$X \Rightarrow \alpha_1 \Rightarrow \alpha_2 \Rightarrow \cdots \Rightarrow \alpha_n \Rightarrow X \tag{7.2}$$

where X is some nonterminal. Intuitively, if a cycle exists in a grammar G, then G must be ambiguous, that is there is a string σ in $L(G)$ having several (in this case infinitely many) distinct derivations. Indeed, let σ be a string in $L(G)$ whose derivation requires the use of nonterminal X. Let the derivation of σ be given by $S \Rightarrow^* \beta_1 X \beta_2 \Rightarrow^* \sigma$. If the cycle (7.2) is possible in G then another derivation of σ would be

$$\begin{aligned} S &\Rightarrow^* \beta_1 X \beta_2 \Rightarrow \beta_1 \alpha_1 \beta_2 \Rightarrow \beta_1 \alpha_2 \beta_2 \\ &\Rightarrow \cdots \Rightarrow \beta_1 \alpha_n \beta_2 \Rightarrow \beta_1 X \beta_2 \Rightarrow^* \sigma \end{aligned}$$

In fact, we could insert arbitrarily long loops $X \Rightarrow^* X$ into the derivation of σ. It is obvious, however, that if a λ-free grammar G contains no single productions, then cycles like (7.2) are impossible. This does not mean that such a grammar is unambiguous, only that it is more likely to be so. The basic idea behind eliminating single productions is somewhat similar to the method of eliminating empty productions. Suppose, for example, a grammar G contains a production $A \to B$, and let $B \to \beta_1$, $B \to \beta_2, \ldots, B \to \beta_n$ be all the B-productions of G (all productions having B on the left-hand side). It is clear that if we delete the production $A \to B$ and add all the productions $A \to \beta_1$, $A \to \beta_2, \ldots,$ $A \to \beta_n$, the resulting grammar is equivalent to the original one; that is, they generate the same language.

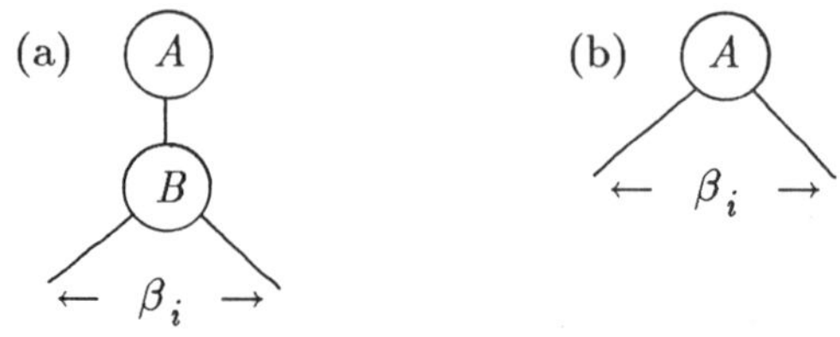

Figure 7.1. Elimination of a single production $A \to B$.

Indeed, let σ be in $L(G)$ and suppose that a fragment of the parse tree of σ that uses both $A \to B$ and $B \to \beta_i$ is given in Figure 7.1(a). The corresponding fragment of the derivation tree of σ in the modified grammar is given in Figure 7.1(b). (It uses the new production $A \to \beta_i$.) In other words, we replace instances of the application of two productions $A \to B$ and $B \to \beta_i$ by a single new production $A \to \beta_i$. The formal algorithm for removal of single productions is then as follows:

Algorithm 7.5. Removal of single productions.
Input: A λ-free context-free grammar $G = \{\Sigma, N, S, P\}$.
Output: A λ-free grammar G' with no single productions, that is equivalent to G.

1. For each nonterminal $X \in N$ construct the set

$$N(X) = \{Y \in N \mid X \Rightarrow^* Y\}$$

as follows. We define the sequence of sets $N_0(X)$, $N_1(X)$, $N_2(X)$, $\ldots$, by the following rules:

a. $N_0(X) = \{X\}$
b. Suppose $N_0(X), N_1(X), \ldots, N_i(X)$ have been defined. Put

$$N_{i+1}(X) = N_i(X) \cup \{Z \in N \mid \text{There is a production of the form } Y \to Z, \text{ where } Y \in N_i(X)\}$$

c. If $N_{i+1}(X) = N_i(X)$ the procedure stops and $N(X) = N_i(X)$. Otherwise repeat step 1b.

The set $N(X)$ consists of all nonterminals Y for which there is a legal derivation

$$X \Rightarrow \alpha_1 \Rightarrow \alpha_2 \Rightarrow \cdots \Rightarrow \alpha_n \Rightarrow Y$$

The sets $N_i(X)$ consist of those Y's that can be derived from X in i steps or less. Notice that the above procedure will always terminate in a finite number of steps since the total number of nonterminals is finite.

2. For each non-single production $Y \to \alpha$ do the following:

   a. Find all nonterminals Y such that $Y \in N(X)$ (i.e., $X \Rightarrow^* Y$)
   b. For each such X found in step 2a, add the production $X \to \alpha$ to the grammar G.

3. Remove all single productions from the grammar G.

Example 7.6. Consider the grammar G_0 of arithmetic expressions:

$$\begin{array}{lcl} E & \to & E + T \mid T \\ T & \to & T * F \mid F \\ F & \to & (E) \mid a \end{array}$$

This grammar has two single productions: $E \to T$ and $T \to F$. Notice that $F \to a$ is not a single production since a is a terminal. To find an equivalent grammar with no single productions we must first find the sets $N(E)$, $N(T)$, and $N(F)$. We proceed with step 1 for each nonterminal E, T and F.

$N_0(E) = \{E\}$ by definition.
$N_1(E) = \{E, T\}$; T is included because of the production $E \to T$.
$N_2(E) = \{E, T, F\}$; F is included because of $T \to F$.
$N_3(E) = N_2(E)$ so $N(E) = \{E, T, F\}$.
$N_0(T) = \{T\}$ by definition.
$N_1(T) = \{T, F\}$ on account of the production $T \to F$.
$N_2(T) = N_1(T)$, so $N(T) = \{T, F\}$.
$N_0(F) = \{F\}$ and $N_1(F) = N_0(F)$ since there is no single F-production. Hence $N(F) = \{F\}$.

At this point step 1 is completed and we proceed with step 2.

$E \rightarrow E + T$: We must find all X's such that $E \in N(X)$. By inspection, the only such X is E, so this non-single production generates only its own duplicate $E \rightarrow E + T$.

$T \rightarrow T * F$: Now $T \in N(T)$ and $T \in N(E)$. Therefore, we have two productions here: $T \rightarrow T * F$ and $E \rightarrow T * F$.

$F \rightarrow (E)$: Here $F \in N(F)$, $F \in N(T)$ and $F \in N(F)$, so the productions $F \rightarrow (E)$, $T \rightarrow (E)$, and $E \rightarrow (E)$ are added to G.

$F \rightarrow a$: For the same reasons, we add productions $E \rightarrow a$, $T \rightarrow a$ and $F \rightarrow a$.

Thus step 2 is completed. After applying step 3 we obtain the following grammar G':

$$\begin{aligned} E &\rightarrow E + T \mid T * F \mid (E) \mid a \\ T &\rightarrow T * F \mid (E) \mid a \\ F &\rightarrow (E) \mid a \end{aligned}$$

It should be clear that G' is equivalent to the original grammar G. By inspection, G' does not contain any single productions.

There is a name associated with grammars that have been modified to eliminate the properties we have considered.

Definition 7.5. Let G be a context-free grammar. We say that G is ***proper*** if it contains no useless or inaccessible symbols, it is λ-free, and contains no single productions.

Theorem 7.2. Given a context-free grammar G, there is an equivalent to it proper grammar G'.

Proof. Apply Algorithms 7.1–7.5 to G (in that order). Q.E.D.

Strictly speaking, we have not given formal proofs that the algorithms presented in this section do indeed work correctly. These proofs are very similar to the proof of Theorem 6.3, are tedious and do not shed any new light on the subject matter. We will give an example of one of them, the others can be constructed along the same lines.

Theorem 7.3. Algorithm 7.3 correctly determines the nilpotent nonterminals.

Proof. We must show two things:

I. Each one of the sets Λ_i defined by steps 1 and 2 of Algorithm 7.3 contains only the nilpotent elements.

II. Every nilpotent nonterminal X is included in one of the sets Λ_i.

The proof of I is by induction. Set Λ_1 consists of those X's for which there is a production of the form $X \rightarrow \lambda$; clearly all such X's are nilpotent. Assume now that Λ_i contains only nilpotent elements. The set Λ_{i+1} consists of those nonterminals X that either are already in Λ_i, or for which there is a production of the form $X \rightarrow Y_1 Y_2 \ldots Y_n$, where each $Y_i \in \Lambda_i$. By hypothesis, each one of these Y's is nilpotent, and it easily follows that the X is also nilpotent. This proves I.

Let now X_0 be a nilpotent nonterminal and let

$$X_0 \Rightarrow \alpha_1 \Rightarrow \alpha_2 \Rightarrow \cdots \Rightarrow \alpha_q = \lambda \tag{7.3}$$

be the shortest derivation of λ from X_0. For each nilpotent nonterminal X_0 define a function $\psi(X_0)$ to be the length of this shortest derivation, i.e., $\psi(X_0) = q$. We claim that every nilpotent nonterminal is included in $\Lambda_{\psi(X_0)}$. This is clearly true when $\psi(X_0) = 1$. Suppose the assertion holds for all nonterminals X for which $\psi(X) < q$ and let X_0 be a nonterminal for which $\psi(X_0) = q$, with the corresponding shortest derivation being given by (7.3). It follows that α_1 consists only of nonterminals Y for which $\psi(Y) < q$, so by hypothesis each one of these Y's is in Λ_{q-1}. Obviously, $X \rightarrow \alpha_1$ must be a production in the grammar, so by step 2 of Algorithm 7.3 $X_0 \in \Lambda_q$. This proves part II and the theorem. Q.E.D.

7.2. CONDITIONS FOR A GRAMMAR TO BE *LL*(1)

We now discuss some conditions on a grammar G that will imply that G either is or is not an $LL(1)$ grammar. Such results are obviously of interest since, as we saw in Chapter 6, the construction of parsing tables is a rather long and involved process. Any theorem, therefore, that will predict whether or not these tables contain a conflict is very useful. The basis for all the results of this kind is the following theorem.

Theorem 7.4. Let $G = \{\Sigma, N, S, P\}$ be a context-free grammar that contains nos useless or inaccessible symbols. Then G is an $LL(1)$ grammar if and only if, for any two distinct productions of the form $X \rightarrow \alpha$ and $X \rightarrow \beta$, the following condition holds:

If x and y are in $FOLLOW(X)$ then $FIRST(\alpha x) \cap FIRST(\beta y) = \emptyset$ (7.4)

Here αx and βy denote the strings α, β concatenated with symbols x and y, respectively.

Proof. Assume first that the grammar G is $LL(1)$. By definition, the parsing table of G contains no conflict, that is, the function $M[\gamma, z]$ is single valued for any stack symbol γ and any input symbol z. Suppose it is possible for the relation (7.4) not to be true. This means that there are two distinct productions: $X \to \alpha$ and $X \to \beta$ and two symbols x, y in $FOLLOW(X)$ such that there is a symbol w in both $FIRST(\alpha x)$ and $FIRST(\beta y)$. We claim this implies that the parsing table of G contains a conflict; in fact we must have $M[X, w] = APPLY(X \to \alpha)$ and $M[X, w] = APPLY(X \to \beta)$. Indeed, since $w \in FIRST(\alpha x)$ there are two possibilities:

I. $w \in FIRST(\alpha)$ in which case $M[X, w] = APPLY(X \to \alpha)$ by step 3i of Algorithm 6.1.
II. $w \notin FIRST(\alpha)$ in which case $\lambda \in FIRST(\alpha)$ and $w = x$. In this situation, by step 3ii of Algorithm 6.1, $M[X, w] = APPLY(X \to \alpha)$ also.

Exactly the same reasoning shows that since $w \in FIRST(\beta y)$, $M[X, w] = APPLY(X \to \beta)$. This proves the first half of the theorem.

Conversely, assume that the relation (7.4) holds and suppose that G is not $LL(1)$. This means that there are two distinct productions, $X \to \alpha$ and $X \to \beta$, and an input symbol w such that Algorithm 6.1 will give $M[X, w] = APPLY(X \to \alpha)$ and $M[X, w] = APPLY(X \to \beta)$. We show that this implies w is in $FIRST(\alpha x) \cap FIRST(\beta y)$ for appropriately chosen x and y in $FOLLOW(X)$. That, however, contradicts the assumption that (7.4) holds. Indeed, $M[X, w] = APPLY(X \to \alpha)$ if one of the following is true:

III. $w \in FIRST(\alpha)$
IV. $\lambda \in FIRST(\alpha)$ and $w \in FOLLOW(X)$

In case III, $w \in FIRST(\alpha x)$ for any $x \in FOLLOW(X)$. In case IV, $w \in FIRST(\alpha w)$. Thus, in both cases, $w \in FIRST(\alpha x)$ for a suitably chosen $x \in FOLLOW(X)$. By exactly the same reasoning, $M[X, w] = APPLY(X \to \beta)$ implies $w \in FIRST(\beta y)$ for a suitably chosen y in $FOLLOW(X)$. Q.E.D.

As an example of the application of this theorem we show the following negative result, giving a condition for a grammar not to be $LL(1)$.

Theorem 7.5. Suppose a context-free grammar has two distinct productions of the form $X \rightarrow \alpha\beta_1$ and $X \rightarrow \alpha\beta_2$ such that $FIRST(\alpha) \neq \{\lambda\}$. Then G is not $LL(1)$.

Proof. Since $FIRST(\alpha)$ contains an input symbol, say w, then for any x and y in $FOLLOW(X)$ we have $FIRST(\alpha\beta_1) \cap FIRST(\alpha\beta_2) \neq \emptyset$ and the result follows from Theorem 7.3. Q.E.D.

If a grammar G contains two or more productions with properties as in hypothesis of Theorem 7.5, it may be possible to rewrite the grammar to eliminate that phenomenon. The basic idea is as follows: Suppose, for example, that G contains two productions $X \rightarrow aBC$ and $X \rightarrow aBa$ (we take $\alpha = aB$, $\beta_1 = C$, and $\beta_2 = a$). We may introduce a new nonterminal, say Y, and replace these two productions by

$$\begin{aligned} X &\rightarrow aBY \\ Y &\rightarrow C \\ Y &\rightarrow a \end{aligned}$$

If $FIRST(C)$ does not contain the terminal a, this may remove the reason for G not to be $LL(1)$. Such a procedure is called ***factoring.*** We formalize this in the following result.

Theorem 7.6. Suppose a context-free grammar G has productions

$$X \rightarrow \alpha\beta_1 \mid \alpha\beta_2 \mid \ldots \mid \alpha\beta_n \tag{7.5}$$

Let G' be obtained from G by introducing a new nonterminal Y and replacing all the productions (7.5) by

$$\begin{aligned} X &\rightarrow \alpha Y \\ Y &\rightarrow \beta_1 \mid \beta_2 \mid \ldots \mid \beta_n \end{aligned}$$

Then G' is equivalent to G.

Proof: If σ is a string in the language $L(G)$ whose derivation tree contains a fragment given in Figure 7.2(a), then the derivation of σ in G' has a tree whose corresponding fragment is given in Figure 7.2(b). Q.E.D.

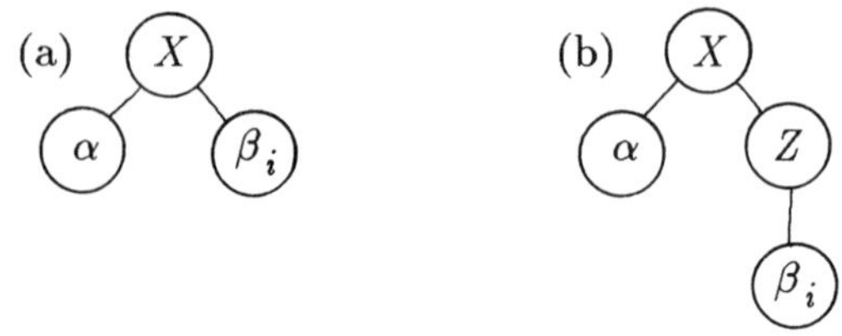

Figure 7.2. Factoring.

Definition 7.6. The transformation of a grammar described in Theorem 7.5 is called ***factoring.***

Example 7.7. Let G be the grammar

$$\begin{aligned} S &\rightarrow aBa \mid aBC \\ B &\rightarrow ba \mid bC \\ C &\rightarrow b \mid c \end{aligned}$$

It follows from Theorem 7.4 that this grammar is not $LL(1)$. (This can also be deduced directly, since the productions $S \rightarrow aBa$ and $S \rightarrow aBC$ give values $M[S, a] = APPLY(S \rightarrow aBa)$ and $M[S, a] = APPLY(S \rightarrow aBC)$, respectively.) Applying the factoring to the offending productions $S \rightarrow aBa \mid aBC$ (with $\alpha = aB$, $\beta_1 = a$, and $\beta_2 = C$) and $B \rightarrow ba \mid bC$ (with $\alpha = b$, $\beta_1 = a$, and $\beta_2 = C$) we obtain a grammar G' as follows:

$$\begin{aligned} S &\rightarrow aBZ_1 \\ Z_1 &\rightarrow a \mid C \\ B &\rightarrow bZ_2 \\ Z_2 &\rightarrow a \mid C \\ C &\rightarrow b \mid c \end{aligned}$$

This grammar is actually $LL(1)$. Indeed, let us calculate the parsing table according to Algorithm 6.1. We have $FIRST(aBZ_1) = \{a\}$, $FIRST(a) = \{a\}$, $FIRST(C) = \{b, c\}$, $FIRST(bZ_2) = \{b\}$, $FIRST(b) = \{b\}$, $FIRST(c) = \{c\}$. These values can be verified directly by inspection. There is actually no need to calculate the values of $FOLLOW(X)$ for any of the nonterminals, since $FIRST(\alpha)$ does not contain λ for any production $X \rightarrow \alpha$. The parsing table for the grammar G' is then given in Figure 7.3. Evidently there are no conflicts, thus G' is an $LL(1)$ grammar.

		Input symbol x			
		a	b	c	$
Stack	a	*POP*			
	b		*POP*		
	c			*POP*	
	S	$S \to aBZ_1$			
	B		$B \to bZ_2$		
	C		$C \to b$	$C \to c$	
	Z_1	$Z_1 \to a$	$Z_1 \to C$	$Z_1 \to C$	
	Z_2	$Z_2 \to a$	$Z_2 \to C$	$Z_2 \to C$	
	#				*ACCEPT*

Figure 7.3. Parsing table for grammar G'.

7.3. LEFT RECURSIVE GRAMMARS

We can deduce from Theorem 7.3 another criterion for a grammar not to be $LL(1)$. First we need a definition.

Definition 7.7. Let G be a context-free grammar. We say that G is ***immediately left recursive*** if there exists a production of the form $X \to X\alpha$. We say that G is ***left recursive*** if there exists a nonterminal X such that $X \Rightarrow^* X\alpha$. (It is possible to derive a sentential form $X\alpha$ from X.)

If a grammar G is immediately left recursive, it is obviously also left recursive, but not conversely. For example, if G contains productions $A \to Ba$ and $B \to Ab$ then G is left recursive since we have a legal derivation $A \Rightarrow Ba \Rightarrow Aba$, but it is clear that G need not be immediately left recursive.

Theorem 7.7. Let G be a context-free grammar without useless or inaccessible symbols. If G is left recursive then G is not $LL(1)$.

Proof. For the sake of clarity, we will prove this theorem under a stronger hypothesis, namely that G is immediately left recursive. The idea of the proof in the general case is the same; the additional complications arise from the fact that if G is assumed to be only left recursive and $X \Rightarrow^* X\alpha$ for some nonterminal X, then G may have only one production with X on the left-hand side. For full details we refer the reader to [13].

Suppose then that G is immediately left recursive and let $X \to X\alpha$ be the "guilty" production. Since X is not a useless nonterminal, $FIRST(X) \neq \emptyset$. If there is a terminal w in $FIRST(X)$ then $w \in$

$FIRST(\beta)$ for some production $X \to \beta$ that is different from $X \to X\alpha$. (Clearly the terminal w cannot be derived by applying only the production $X \to X\alpha$.) But this means that

$$w \in FIRST(X\alpha x) \cap FIRST(\beta y) \quad \text{for all } x \text{ and } y$$

Thus, G is not $LL(1)$ in this case, by Theorem 7.3. If $FIRST(X) = \{\lambda\}$ then $FIRST(X) = FIRST(X\alpha) = FIRST(\beta)$ for any production $X \to \beta$, so for any w in $FOLLOW(X)$ we must have

$$w \in FIRST(X\alpha w) \cap FIRST(\beta w)$$

Again, Theorem 7.3 shows that G is not $LL(1)$. Q.E.D.

Given a grammar G with an immediate left recursion, it is possible to transform it into an equivalent grammar with no immediate left recursion. It is even possible to get rid of ordinary left recursion, but the method tends to increase considerably the number of productions. We will present the general procedure in the next section; now we will only show a simple technique that often works quite well. We begin with an example.

Example 7.8. Consider the grammar

$$\begin{array}{lcl} S & \to & Ab \mid B \\ A & \to & Aa \mid Ab \mid c \mid d \\ B & \to & a \mid aB \end{array}$$

The nonterminal A is immediately left recursive and we wish to modify the grammar to get rid of this phenomenon. This can be done by introducing a new nonterminal, say A', and replacing all A-productions by

$$\begin{array}{lcl} A & \to & cA' \mid dA' \\ A' & \to & aA' \mid bA' \\ A' & \to & \lambda \end{array}$$

Let G' be the resulting grammar. If σ is in $L(G)$ and the production $A \to c$ was used to derive σ, in G' the sequence of productions $A \to cA'$, $A' \to \lambda$ is used instead. Pictorially, the fragment of the derivation tree of σ will change from the one given in Figure 7.4(a) to that in Figure 7.4(b).

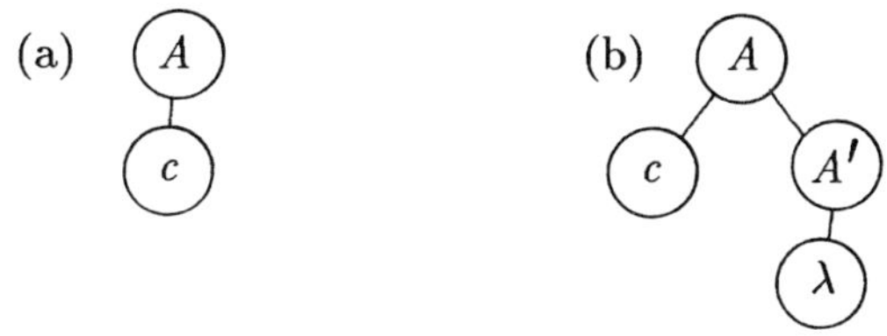

Figure 7.4. Replacement of the production $A \rightarrow c$.

Similarly, consider a portion of the derivation of σ that involves a left recursive production. It may typically look like

$$\Rightarrow \ldots A \ldots \Rightarrow \ldots Aa \ldots \Rightarrow \ldots Aba \ldots \Rightarrow \ldots cba \ldots$$

Thus, the sequence of A-productions applied here is $A \rightarrow Aa$, $A \rightarrow Ab$, and $A \rightarrow c$ (in that order). The corresponding portion in the grammar G' looks like

$$\Rightarrow \ldots A \ldots \Rightarrow \ldots cA' \ldots \Rightarrow \ldots cbA' \ldots$$
$$\Rightarrow \ldots cbaA' \ldots \Rightarrow \ldots cba \ldots$$

Thus, the sequence of productions is $A \rightarrow cA'$, $A' \rightarrow bA'$, $A' \rightarrow aA'$, and $A' \rightarrow \lambda$. In terms of parse trees, the relevant fragments change from the one given in Figure 7.5(a) to the one in Figure 7.5(b).

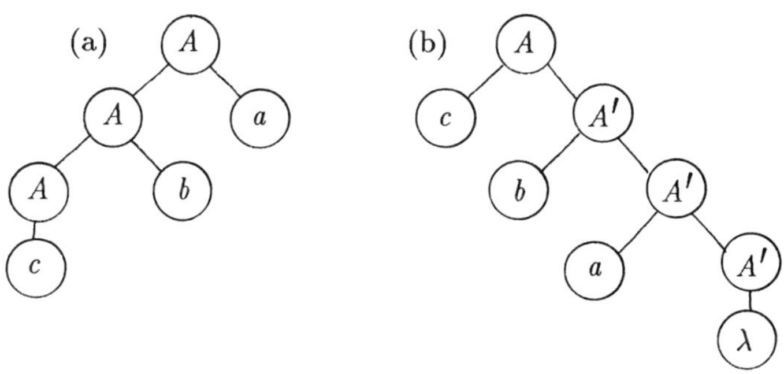

Figure 7.5. Transformation of a parse tree.

We note that the grammar transformation given here involves the introduction of an empty production ($A' \rightarrow \lambda$). This can be avoided; the details will be given in the next section. Formally, we have the following.

Theorem 7.8. Let $G = \{\Sigma, N, S, P\}$ be a context-free grammar with no useless or inaccessible symbols and no production of the form $A \rightarrow A$. Suppose X is an immediately left recursive nonterminal and let all the X-productions be

$$\begin{array}{lll} X & \rightarrow & X\alpha_1 \mid X\alpha_2 \mid \ldots \mid X\alpha_n \\ X & \rightarrow & \beta_1 \mid \beta_2 \mid \ldots \mid \beta_m \end{array}$$

where none of the β's begins with X. Let G' be the grammar obtained from G by introducing a new nonterminal, say Z, and replacing all of the above productions by

$$\begin{array}{lll} X & \rightarrow & \beta_1 Z \mid \beta_2 Z \mid \ldots \mid \beta_m Z \\ Z & \rightarrow & \alpha_1 Z \mid \alpha_2 Z \mid \ldots \mid \alpha_n Z \\ Z & \rightarrow & \lambda \end{array}$$

Then G' is equivalent to G.

Proof. Let σ be a string in $L(G)$. The derivation of σ in G' is the same as the derivation in G, except in the following situations:

I. Each time a production of the form $X \rightarrow \beta_i$ is used, it is replaced by productions $X \rightarrow \beta_i Z$ and $Z \rightarrow \lambda$. Schematically, the parse tree of σ is changed from Figure 7.6(a) to 7.6(b).

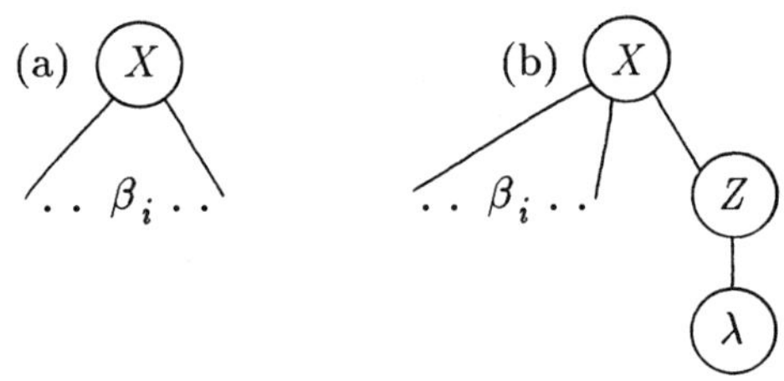

Figure 7.6. Case I of Theorem 7.5.

II. Each time the leftmost derivation of σ has the form

$$\begin{aligned} \ldots X \ldots &\Rightarrow \ldots X\alpha^{(1)} \ldots \Rightarrow \ldots X\alpha^{(2)}\alpha^{(1)} \ldots \\ &\Rightarrow \ldots X\alpha^{(p)}\alpha^{(p-1)} \ldots \alpha^{(2)}\alpha^{(1)} \ldots \\ &\Rightarrow \ldots \beta\alpha^{(p)}\alpha^{(p-1)} \ldots \alpha^{(2)}\alpha^{(1)} \ldots \Rightarrow^* \sigma \end{aligned}$$

that is, the sequence of X productions is

$$X \to X\alpha^{(1)},\ X \to X\alpha^{(2)},\ \ldots,\ X \to X\alpha^{(p)},\ X \to \beta$$

the corresponding derivation of σ in G' has the form

$$\begin{aligned} \ldots X \ldots &\Rightarrow \ldots \beta Z \ldots \Rightarrow \ldots \beta\alpha^{(p)} Z \ldots \Rightarrow \ldots \beta\alpha^{(p)}\alpha^{(p-1)} Z \ldots \\ &\Rightarrow \ldots \beta\alpha^{(p)}\alpha^{(p-1)} \ldots \alpha^{(2)}\alpha^{(1)} Z \ldots \\ &\Rightarrow \ldots \beta\alpha^{(p)}\alpha^{(p-1)} \ldots \alpha^{(2)}\alpha^{(1)} \ldots \Rightarrow^* \sigma \end{aligned}$$

The corresponding sequence of productions in G' is

$$\begin{gathered} X \to \beta Z,\quad Z \to \alpha^{(p)} Z,\quad Z \to \alpha^{(p-1)} Z,\ \ldots, \\ Z \to \alpha^{(2)} Z,\quad Z \to \alpha^{(1)} Z,\quad Z \to \lambda \end{gathered}$$

Hence the "portions" $\alpha^{(1)}, \alpha^{(2)}, \ldots, \alpha^{(p)}, \beta$ appear in reverse order. The corresponding changes in the parse tree are indicated in Figure 7.7. Q.E.D.

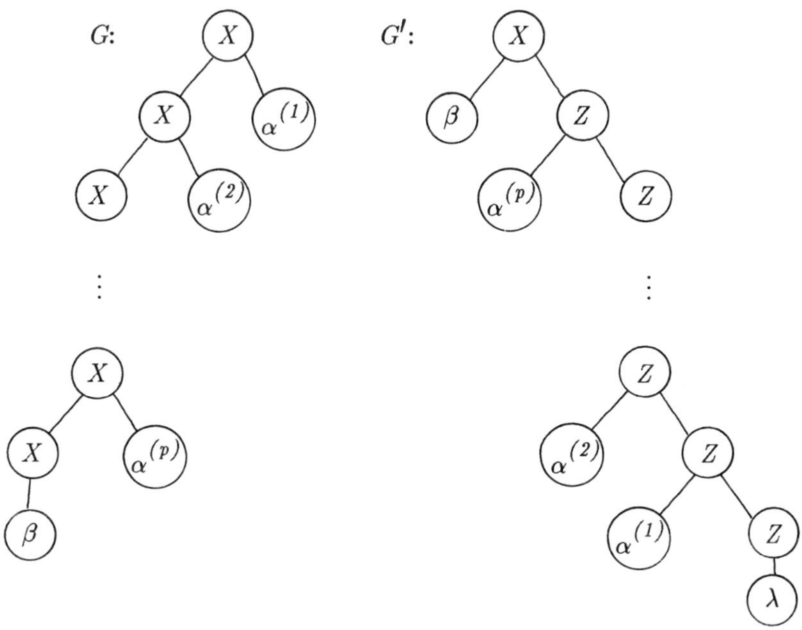

Figure 7.7. Case II of Theorem 7.7.

Definition 7.8. Let $G = \{\Sigma, N, S, P\}$ be a context-free grammar. The transformation described in Theorem 7.7. is called ***splitting*** applied to an immediately left recursive nonterminal X.

Notice that splitting is relatively efficient: it only increases the number of productions by one, at the cost of introducing a new nonterminal and an empty production. We now apply these ideas to the grammar of arithmetic expressions.

Example 7.9. Consider the grammar G_0 of arithmetic expressions:

$$E \rightarrow E + T \mid T \qquad T \rightarrow T * F \mid F \qquad F \rightarrow (E) \mid a$$

This grammar has two immediately left recursive nonterminals: E in the production $E \rightarrow E + T$, and T in the production $T \rightarrow T * F$. It is therefore not an $LL(1)$ grammar. We apply now the splitting transformation. When applied to the nonterminal E, this results in productions

$$E \rightarrow TE' \qquad E' \rightarrow +TE' \mid \lambda$$

where E' is the new nonterminal. When applied to the nonterminal T, this gives productions

$$T \rightarrow FT' \qquad T' \rightarrow * FT' \mid \lambda$$

where T' is the corresponding new nonterminal. The resulting grammar G_0' is given in full by:

$$\begin{array}{llll} 1.\ E \rightarrow TE' & & 5.\ E' & \rightarrow\ + TE' \\ 2.\ T \rightarrow FT' & & 6.\ T' & \rightarrow\ * FT' \\ 3.\ F \rightarrow (E) & & 7.\ E' & \rightarrow\ \lambda \\ 4.\ F \rightarrow a & & 8.\ T' & \rightarrow\ \lambda \end{array}$$

We now proceed with the construction of the top-down parser for G_0'. From Algorithms 6.2 and 6.3 we obtain

$$\begin{array}{lll} FIRST(TE') = \{(, a\} & FIRST(+TE') = \{+\} & FIRST(\lambda) = \{\lambda\} \\ FIRST(FT') = \{(, a\} & FIRST(*FT') = \{*\} & FIRST(a) = \{a\} \\ FIRST((E)) = \{(\} & & \\ FOLLOW(T') = \{+,), \$\} & & FOLLOW(E') = \{), \$\} \end{array}$$

We leave the justification to the reader (it is an excellent exercise). Notice that in order to obtain the parsing table, only the indicated values of $FOLLOW$ are needed. The parsing table for the grammar G_0' is then given, in accordance with Algorithm 6.1, in Figure 7.8. It is seen that G_0' is an $LL(1)$ grammar since the parsing table contains no conflicts. Thus, we have constructed a deterministic parser for the language of arithmetic expressions. We give few randomly chosen justifications of the entries in this parsing table. Consider the production $T \rightarrow FT'$. Since $FIRST(FT') = \{(, a\}$, this gives $M[T, (] = APPLY(T \rightarrow FT')$ and $M[T, a] = APPLY(T \rightarrow FT')$. Similarly, from the production $T' \rightarrow * FT'$ we get $M[T', *] = APPLY(T' \rightarrow *FT')$ because $FIRST(*FT') = \{*\}$. Next, consider the production $T' \rightarrow \lambda$. Since $FIRST(\lambda) = \{\lambda\}$ we must have $M[T', x] = APPLY(T' \rightarrow \lambda)$ for every x in $FOLLOW(T')$. This gives $M[T', +] = M[T',)] = M[T', \$] = APPLY(T' \rightarrow \lambda)$. The resulting entries are explained in a similar fashion.

		Input symbol					
		a	+	*	(	)	\$
	a	POP					
	+		POP				
	*			POP			
S	(				POP		
t	)					POP	
a	E	$E \rightarrow TE'$			$E \rightarrow TE'$		
c	T	$T \rightarrow FT'$			$T \rightarrow FT'$		
k	F	$F \rightarrow a$			$F \rightarrow (E)$		
	E'		$E' \rightarrow +TE'$			$E' \rightarrow \lambda$	$E' \rightarrow \lambda$
	T'		$T' \rightarrow \lambda$	$T' \rightarrow *FT'$		$T' \rightarrow \lambda$	$T' \rightarrow \lambda$
	#						$ACCEPT$

Figure 7.8. Top-down parser for G_0'

We now give an example of the action of the parser on the input $\sigma = a * (a + a)$. We have, in accordance with notation on p.181:

$$
\begin{aligned}
&[\![a * (a + a)\$,\ E\#]\!] \xrightarrow{1} [\![a * (a + a)\$,\ TE'\#]\!] \\
&\xrightarrow{2} [\![a * (a + a)\$,\ FT'E'\#]\!] \xrightarrow{4} [\![a * (a + a)\$,\ aT'E'\#]\!] \\
&\longrightarrow [\![* (a + a)\$,\ T'E'\#]\!] \xrightarrow{6} [\![* (a + a)\$,\ * FT'E'\#]\!] \\
&\longrightarrow [\![(a + a)\$,\ FT'E'\#]\!] \xrightarrow{3} [\![(a + a)\$,\ (E)T'E'\#]\!] \\
&\longrightarrow [\![a + a)\$,\ E)T'E'\#]\!] \xrightarrow{1} [\![a + a)\$,\ TE')T'E'\#]\!] \\
&\xrightarrow{2} [\![a + a)\$,\ FT'E')T'E'\#]\!] \xrightarrow{4} [\![a + a)\$,\ aT'E')T'E'\#]\!]
\end{aligned}
$$

$$\longrightarrow [\![+\ a)\$,\ \ T'E')T'E'\#]\!] \xrightarrow{8} [\![+\ a)\$,\ \ E')T'E'\#]\!]$$
$$\xrightarrow{5} [\![+\ a)\$,\ \ +TE')T'E'\#]\!] \longrightarrow [\![a)\$,\ \ TE')T'E'\#]\!]$$
$$\xrightarrow{2} [\![a)\$,\ \ FT'E')T'E'\#]\!] \xrightarrow{4} [\![a)\$,\ \ aT'E')T'E'\#]\!]$$
$$\longrightarrow [\![)\$,\ \ T'E')T'E'\#]\!] \xrightarrow{8} [\![)\$,\ \ E')T'E'\#]\!] \xrightarrow{7} [\![)\$,\ \ )T'E'\#]\!]$$
$$\longrightarrow [\![\$,\ \ T'E'\#]\!] \xrightarrow{8} [\![\$,\ \ E'\#]\!] \xrightarrow{7} [\![\$,\ \#]\!] \longrightarrow ACCEPT$$

Thus, the left parse of $\sigma = a * (a + a)$ is 1, 2, 4, 6, 3, 1, 2, 4, 8, 5, 2, 4, 8, 7, 8, 7, and its derivation tree is given in Figure 7.9.

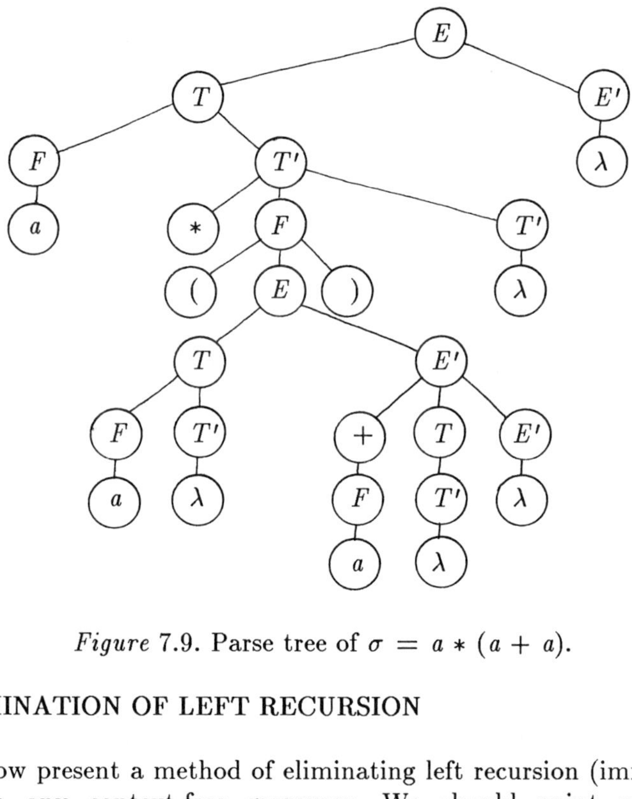

Figure 7.9. Parse tree of $\sigma = a * (a + a)$.

7.4. ELIMINATION OF LEFT RECURSION

We now present a method of eliminating left recursion (immediate or not) from any context-free grammar. We should point out at the beginning that the procedure is somewhat cumbersome and leads to grammars with large number of productions.

We first give an algorithm for eliminating immediate left recursion. This algorithm differes from the one given in Theorem 7.8; it is introduced because it does not give rise to empty productions. Roughly speaking, it is a combination of procedures from Theorem 7.8 (elimination of immediate left recursion) and Algorithm 7.4 (elimination of empty productions). The details are as follows.

Lemma 7.1. Let $G = \{\Sigma, N, S, P\}$ be a context-free grammar with no empty productions, no useless nonterminals and no productions of the form $A \rightarrow A$. Let X be an immediately left recursive nonterminal and let

$$\begin{array}{lll} X & \rightarrow & X\alpha_1 \mid X\alpha_2 \mid \ldots \mid X\alpha_n \\ X & \rightarrow & \beta_1 \mid \beta_2 \mid \ldots \mid \beta_m \end{array}$$

be all the X-productions, where none of the β's begin with X and, by hypothesis, none of the α's or β's are equal to λ. Let G' be the grammar obtained from G by introducing a new nonterminal Y and replacing all of the above productions with

$$\begin{array}{lll} X & \rightarrow & \beta_1 \mid \beta_2 \mid \ldots \mid \beta_m \\ X & \rightarrow & \beta_1 Y \mid \beta_2 Y \mid \ldots \mid \beta_m Y \\ Y & \rightarrow & \alpha_1 Y \mid \alpha_2 Y \mid \ldots \mid \alpha_n Y \\ Y & \rightarrow & \alpha_1 \mid \alpha_2 \mid \ldots \mid \alpha_n \end{array}$$

Then G' is equivalent to G. Moreover, if this transformation is applied to every immediately left recursive nonterminal X, then the resulting grammar will have no immediately left recursive nonterminals.

Proof.(Outline) The arguments are similar to those in the proof of Theorem 7.8. Suppose σ is in the language $L(G)$ and a portion of the leftmost derivation of consists of applying several productions of the form $X \rightarrow X\alpha$ followed by a production of the form $X \rightarrow \beta$. Thus, the derivation of σ has form

$$\begin{array}{l} S \Rightarrow^* \ldots X \ldots \Rightarrow \ldots X\alpha^{(1)} \ldots \Rightarrow \ldots X\alpha^{(2)}\alpha^{(1)} \ldots \\ \quad \Rightarrow^* \ldots X\alpha^{(p)} \ldots \alpha^{(1)} \ldots \Rightarrow \ldots \beta\alpha^{(p)} \ldots \alpha^{(1)} \ldots \Rightarrow^* \sigma \end{array} \tag{7.6}$$

This portion of the derivation is then replaced in G' by the sequence

$$\begin{array}{l} S \Rightarrow^* \ldots X \ldots \Rightarrow \ldots \beta Y \ldots \Rightarrow \ldots \beta\alpha^{(p)} Y \ldots \\ \quad \Rightarrow \ldots \beta\alpha^{(p)}\alpha^{(p-1)} Y \ldots \Rightarrow^* \ldots \beta\alpha^{(p)}\alpha^{(p\ 1)} \ldots \alpha^{(2)} Y \ldots \\ \quad \Rightarrow \ldots \beta\alpha^{(p)} \ldots \alpha^{(2)}\alpha^{(1)} \ldots \Rightarrow^* \sigma \end{array}$$

In other words, the sequence of productions

$$X \rightarrow X\alpha^{(1)},\ X \rightarrow X\alpha^{(2)}, \ldots,\ X \rightarrow X\alpha^{(p)},\ X \rightarrow \beta$$

is replaced by

$$X \rightarrow \beta Y,\ Y \rightarrow \alpha^{(p)} Y, \ldots,\ X \rightarrow \alpha^{(p-1)} Y,\ Y \rightarrow \alpha^{(p)}$$

The change in the parse tree is depicted in Figure 7.10.

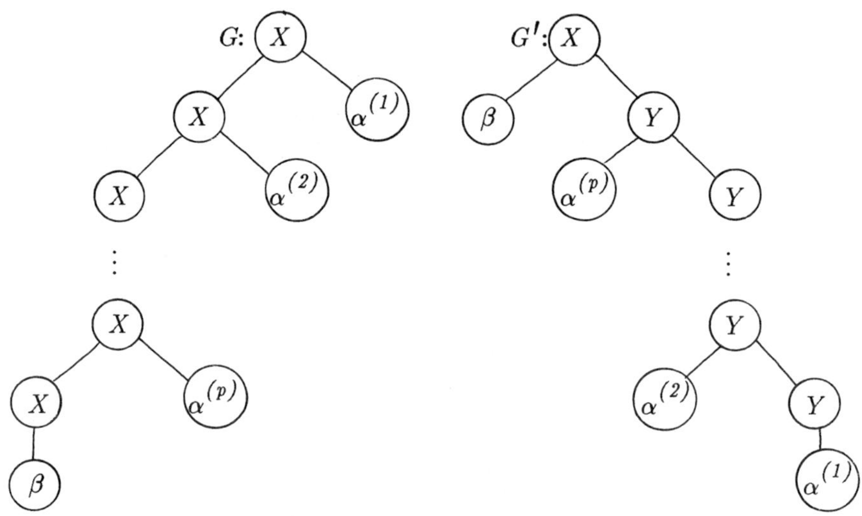

Figure 7.10. Proof of Lemma 7.1.

It should be clear that if the leftmost derivation of σ involves any X-productions then these productions must occur in a sequence such as in (7.6). Q.E.D.

Definition 7.9. We call the grammar transformation described in Lemma 7.1 a ***T1-transformation*** applied to the immediately left recursive nonterminal X.

Example 7.10. Consider a grammar G given by

$$\begin{aligned} S &\rightarrow Ab \\ A &\rightarrow Ac \mid b \mid c \end{aligned}$$

Applying transformation T1 to A we obtain grammar G'

$$\begin{array}{lcl} S & \rightarrow & Ab \\ A & \rightarrow & b \mid c \\ A & \rightarrow & bY \mid cY \\ Y & \rightarrow & cY \mid c \end{array}$$

Here Y is the new nonterminal. The derivation trees of $bccb$ in both grammars are given in Figure 7.11.

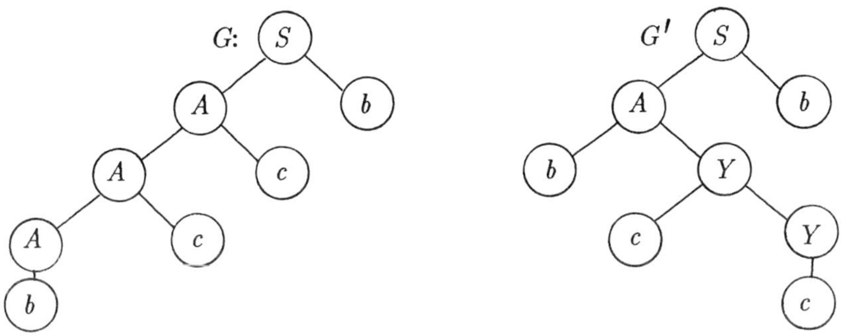

Figure 7.11. Parse tree of $\sigma = bccb$.

Notice the need for both productions $Y \rightarrow cY$ and $Y \rightarrow c$. This could be avoided, if we allowed the empty production $Y \rightarrow \lambda$.

Lemma 7.2. Let $G = \{\Sigma, N, S, P\}$ be a context-free grammar and suppose $X \rightarrow \alpha Y \beta$ is a production of G, where X and Y are nonterminals. Suppose all the Y–productions of G are $Y \rightarrow \gamma_1 \mid \ldots \mid \gamma_n$. Let G' be the grammar obtained from G by removing the production $X \rightarrow \alpha Y \beta$ and replacing it with productions $X \rightarrow \alpha\gamma_1\beta \mid \alpha\gamma_2\beta \mid \ldots \mid \alpha\gamma_n\beta$. Then G' is equivalent to G.

Proof. If σ is a string in $L(G)$ whose derivation requires productions $X \rightarrow \alpha Y \beta$ and $Y \rightarrow \gamma$, then σ can be derived in G' by using the single production $X \rightarrow \alpha\gamma\beta$. The changes in the parse tree are depicted in Figure 7.12. Q.E.D.

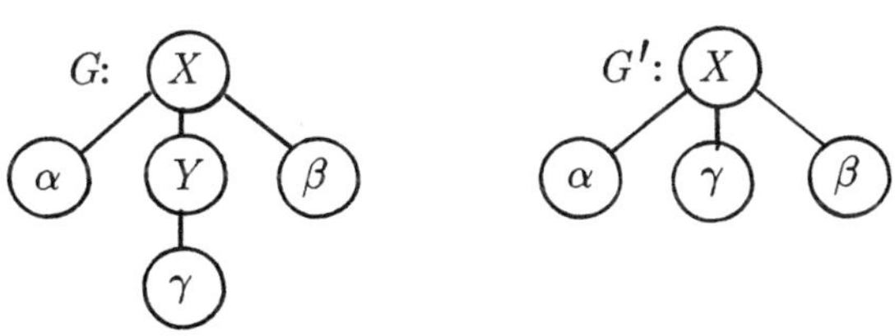

Figure 7.12. Proof of Lemma 7.2.

Definition 7.10. Let G be a context-free grammar and let $X \to \alpha Y \beta$ be a production of G. We call the transformation described in Lemma 7.2 a ***T2 -transformation*** applied to the production $X \to \alpha Y \beta$.

Example 7.11. Let G be the grammar given by

$$\begin{aligned} S &\to Ab \mid AS \\ A &\to aBa \mid c \\ B &\to AB \mid aS \mid c \end{aligned}$$

Applying transformation T2 to the production $A \to aBa$ we obtain a grammar G':

$$\begin{aligned} S &\to Ab \mid AS \\ A &\to aABa \mid aaSa \mid aca \mid c \\ B &\to AB \mid aS \mid c \end{aligned}$$

Notice that the production $A \to c$ is retained, as well as all the B-productions: $B \to AB| aS| c$. The only production that was replaced is $A \to aBa$. Consider now $\sigma = acab$, whose derivation in G is $S \Rightarrow Ab \Rightarrow aBab \Rightarrow acab$. In the grammar G' the derivation of σ is $S \Rightarrow Ab \Rightarrow acab$.

We are now ready to give an algorithm to eliminate left recursion from a given grammar. Let G be a context-free grammar and let the nonterminals of G be ordered in some arbitrary but fixed way, say X_1, $X_2, \ldots, X_n$, subject only to the condition that $X_1 = S$ is the starting symbol. We are to transform G into G' by introducing new nonterminals $Y_1, Y_2, \ldots, Y_k$ $(k \leq n)$ such that the following properties hold in G':

1. Each production in G' of the form $X_i \to \alpha$ is such that α either begins with a terminal, or a nonterminal X_j such that $j > i$.
2. Each production of the form $Y_i \to \beta$ is such that β begins either with a terminal or one of the X's.

It is clear that G' will have no recursion. Indeed, the leftmost derivation

$$X_i \Rightarrow \alpha_1 \Rightarrow \cdots \Rightarrow \alpha_m \Rightarrow X_i \gamma$$

is impossible because property 1 ensures that each α begins with either a terminal or X_j with $j > i$. Similarly, the leftmost derivation

$$Y_i \Rightarrow \beta_1 \Rightarrow \cdots \Rightarrow \beta_m \Rightarrow Y_i \delta$$

is impossible, since the properties 1 and 2 ensure that each β begins either with a terminal or one of the X's. The grammar G' will be obtained through successive applications of transformations T1 and T2 of Lemmas 7.1 and 7.2, thus it will be equivalent to G.

Algorithm 7.6. Elimination of left recursion.
Input: A context-free grammar $G = \{\Sigma, N, S, P\}$ with no empty productions and no production of the form $X \rightarrow X$.
Output: An equivalent grammar G' with no left recursion.

Step 0. Order the nonterminals of G in some fixed, but arbitrary order, say $X_1, X_2, \ldots, X_n$, such that $S = X_1$ is the start symbol.

Step 1. If X_1 is immediately left recursive, eliminate this left recursion by applying transformation T1. Otherwise, go to step 2. At the end of step 1, each X_1 production is of the form $X_1 \rightarrow \gamma$, where γ begins with either a terminal or X_j with $j > 1$. If a new terminal Y_1 was introduced as a result of applying T1, then each Y_1 production is of the form $Y_1 \rightarrow \gamma$ where γ begins with either a terminal or one of the X's.

Step 2.
(A) Apply transformation T2 to all the productions of the form $X_2 \rightarrow X_1\alpha$. At this point all the X_2-productions are of the form $X_2 \rightarrow \gamma$, where γ begins with either a terminal or X_j with $j \geq 2$ (because all X_1-productions have this property).
(B) Eliminate immediate left recursion in X_2 (if needed) by applying transformation T1. At this point all X_2-productions are of the form $X_2 \rightarrow \gamma$ with γ beginning with either a terminal or X_j with $j > 2$. The new nonterminal Y_2 (if it was introduced when T1 was applied) has the property that all productions $Y_2 \rightarrow \gamma$ have γ beginning with either a terminal or one of the X's.

Step 3.
(A) Apply transformation T2, first to all productions of the form $X_3 \rightarrow X_1\alpha$, then to all productions of the form $X_3 \rightarrow X_2\alpha$.
(B) Eliminate, if necessary, immediate left recursion in X_3 by applying transformation T1.

General i^{th} step. $(i = 4, 5, \ldots, n)$
(A) Apply transformation T2, first to all productions of the form $X_i \rightarrow X_1\alpha$, then to all productions of the form $X_i \rightarrow X_2\alpha, \ldots,$ all the way to all productions of the form $X_i \rightarrow X_{i-1}\alpha$.
(B) Eliminate the immediate left recursion in X_i, if one is present, by applying T1.

At the end of step i, all X_k-productions $(k \leq i)$ are of the form

$X_k \to \gamma$, where γ begins with either a terminal or X_j with $j > k$. All the new nonterminals Y have productions of the form $Y \to \gamma$, where γ begins either with a terminal or one of the X's.

The algorithm halts after step n (= the number of nonterminals). It is easily seen that at this point the resulting grammar has the desirable properties; the only questionable nonterminal is the last one, i.e., X_n. All of its productions will have the form $X_n \to \alpha$, where α begins with either a terminal or X_j with $j > n$. The second possibility does not arise, however, because there are only n nonterminals.

Example 7.12. Let G be a grammar given by

$$\begin{array}{lll} X_1 \to X_2X_3 & X_1 \to a & \\ X_2 \to X_3X_1 & X_2 \to X_1b & \\ X_3 \to X_3X_3 & X_3 \to X_1X_2 & X_3 \to a \end{array}$$

This grammar is left recursive: $X_1 \Rightarrow X_2X_3 \Rightarrow X_3X_1X_3 \Rightarrow X_1X_2X_1X_3$. Notice, however that the nonterminal X_1 is not immediately left recursive. Algorithm 7.6 proceeds as follows:

Step 1. Since X_1 is not immediately left recursive, we go to step 2.

Step 2.

(A) We apply transformation T2 to the production $X_2 \to X_1b$. The resulting grammar is

$$\begin{array}{l} X_1 \to X_2X_3 \mid a \\ X_2 \to X_3X_1 \mid X_2X_3b \mid ab \\ X_3 \to X_3X_3 \mid X_1X_2 \mid a \end{array}$$

(B) We apply transformation T1 to the immediately left recursive nonterminal X_2. The grammar becomes

$$\begin{array}{ll} X_1 \to X_2X_3 \mid a & X_3 \to X_3X_3 \mid X_1X_2 \mid a \\ X_2 \to X_3X_1 \mid ab \mid X_3X_1Y_2 \mid abY_2 & Y_2 \to X_3b \mid X_3bY_2 \end{array}$$

Step 3. We apply T2 to the production $X_3 \to X_1X_2$. This results in the grammar:

$$\begin{array}{l} X_1 \to X_2X_3 \mid a \\ X_2 \to X_3X_1 \mid ab \mid X_3X_1Y_2 \mid abY_2 \\ X_3 \to X_3X_3 \mid a \mid X_2X_3X_2 \mid aX_2 \\ Y_2 \to X_3b \mid X_3bY_2 \end{array}$$

We now need to apply transformation T2 to the production $X_3 \rightarrow X_2X_3X_2$. As a result, X_3-productions become

$$X_3 \rightarrow X_3X_3 \mid a \mid aX_2 \mid X_3X_1X_3X_2 \mid abX_3X_2 \mid X_3X_1Y_2X_3X_2 \mid abY_2X_3X_2$$

The productions for other nonterminals remain unchanged.
(B) We eliminate the immediate left recursion in the nonterminal X_3. This leads to the following, final version of the grammar G':

$$\begin{aligned}
X_1 &\rightarrow X_2X_3 \mid a \\
X_2 &\rightarrow X_3X_1 \mid ab \mid X_3X_1Y_2 \mid abY_2 \\
X_3 &\rightarrow a \mid aX_2 \mid abX_3X_2 \mid abY_2X_3X_2 \mid aY_3 \mid abX_3X_2Y_3 \mid \\
&\quad\ abY_2X_3X_2Y_3 \mid aX_2Y_3 \\
Y_2 &\rightarrow X_3b \mid X_3bY_2 \\
Y_3 &\rightarrow X_3 \mid X_1X_3X_2 \mid X_1Y_2X_3X_2 \mid X_3Y_3 \mid X_1X_3X_2Y_3 \mid \\
&\quad\ X_1Y_2X_3X_2Y_3
\end{aligned}$$

It is seen from this example that one obvious disadvantage of Algorithm 7.6 is that the number of productions and nonterminals increases drastically.

7.5. NORMAL FORMS

When proving that a grammar has or does not have a certain property, it is often convenient to know that all of its productions have a certain form. It may also be easier to devise a parsing strategy, given that all the productions of a grammar have special form. We describe here two such special forms that have been found to be particularly useful.

Definition 7.11. A context-free grammar G is said to be in *Chomsky normal form* if all of its productions are of the form $X \rightarrow a$ (terminal) or $X \rightarrow AB$ (A and B are nonterminals).

Definition 7.12. A context-free grammar G is said to be in *Greibach normal form* if all of its productions are of the form $X \rightarrow a\beta$, where a is a terminal and β is a string of nonterminals (possibly empty).

It turns out that any context-free grammar with no empty productions can be transformed into one of the above forms. We begin with the Chomsky normal form.

Theorem 7.9. Let G be a context-free grammar with no empty productions. Then there exists an equivalent grammar G' that is in Chomsky normal form.

Proof. By Theorem 7.2 (or Algorithm 7.5) we may assume that G does not have any single productions. We show first that G can be transformed into an equivalent grammar, each one of whose productions is either of the form $X \to a$ (terminal) or $X \to \beta$, where β is a string of nonterminals of length at least two. To this end, for each terminal a of G introduce a nonterminal X_a and a production $X_a \to a$. Further, consider a production in G of the form $X \to \beta$, where β is not a single terminal. Now replace each such production by $X \to \hat{\beta}$, where the string $\hat{\beta}$ is obtained from β as follows: 1) All the nonterminals occurring in β are left unchanged; and 2) all the terminals a in β are replaced by the nonterminals X_a just introduced.

For example, if G_1 is the grammar of arithmetic expressions from which single productions were eliminated (see Example 7.6):

$$\begin{aligned} E &\to E + T \mid T * F \mid (E) \mid a \\ T &\to T * F \mid (E) \mid a \\ F &\to (E) \mid a \end{aligned} \tag{7.7}$$

then the new nonterminals are X_+, X_* , $X_($, $X_)$ and X_a. The new productions are

$$X_+ \to + \qquad X_* \to * \qquad X_(\to (\qquad X_) \to) \qquad X_a \to a$$

and the productions in (7.7) are replaced by

$$\begin{aligned} E &\to E\,X_+T \mid T\,X_*\,F \mid X_(\,E\,X_) \mid a \\ T &\to T\,X_*\,F \mid X_(\,E\,X_) \mid a \\ F &\to X_(\,E\,X_) \mid a \end{aligned} \tag{7.8}$$

Continuing now with the proof, we may assume that the grammar G has been transformed, so all of its productions are of the form $X \to \beta$, where β is either a single terminal or a sequence of nonterminals. Since G was assumed not to have empty productions or single productions, if β consists of a string of nonterminals, then it follows from construction that this string is of length at least two. Consider now one such production, say $X \to A_1A_2A_3 \ldots A_n$, $n \geq 3$. Introduce $n - 2$ new nonterminals, say $B_1, B_2, \ldots, B_{n-2}$, and replace this production by

$$X \to A_1B_1,\ B_1 \to A_2B_2,\ B_2 \to A_3B_3, \ldots,$$
$$B_{n-3} \to A_{n-2}B_{n-2},\ \text{and}\ B_{n-2} \to A_{n-1}A_n$$

It is clear that the resulting grammar is equivalent to G and that it is in Chomsky normal form. Q.E.D.

Returning to the example above, the production $E \to EX_+T$ in (7.8) gets replaced by $E \to EB_1$ and $B_1 \to X_+T$. Similarly, $E \to TX_*F$ is replaced by $E \to TC_1$ and $C_1 \to X_*F$. Continuing in this way, we may rewrite the grammar of arithmetic expressions in Chomsky normal form as:

$$
\begin{array}{lll@{\qquad}lll}
E & \to & E\,B_1 \mid T\,C_1 \mid X_(\,D_1 \mid a & T & \to & T\,G_1 \mid X_(\,H_1 \mid a \\
F & \to & X_(\,K_1 \mid a & B_1 & \to & X_+\,T \\
C_1 & \to & X_*\,F & D_1 & \to & E\,X_) \\
G_1 & \to & X_*\,F & H_1 & \to & E\,X_) \\
K_1 & \to & E\,X_) & X_+ & \to & + \\
X_* & \to & * & X_(& \to & (\\
X_) & \to &) & & &
\end{array}
$$

Strictly speaking, the production $X_a \to a$ also should have been included, but the nonterminal X_a is inaccessible, so it can be omitted.

Theorem 7.10. Let G be a context-free grammar with no empty productions. Then there exists an equivalent grammar G' that is in Greibach normal form.

Proof. First of all, it is enough to show that G can be transformed into a grammar $\hat{G}$, all of whose productions are of the form $X \to a\beta$, where a is a terminal and β is a string of terminals or nonterminals (β can be the empty string λ). Indeed, suppose $\hat{G}$ has the stated property. For each production of the form $X \to a\beta$ let $b_1, b_2, \ldots, b_m$ all the terminals occurring in β, so this production has actually form

$$X \to a\gamma_1 b_1 \gamma_2 b_2 \ldots \gamma_m b_m \gamma_{m+1} \tag{7.9}$$

where the strings γ contain only nonterminals. Now introduce m new nonterminals $X_{b_1}, X_{b_2}, \ldots, X_{b_m}$ and replace production (7.9) by

$$X \to a\gamma_1 X_{b_1} \gamma_2 X_{b_2} \gamma_3 \ldots \gamma_m X_{b_m} \gamma_{m+1}$$
$$X_{b_1} \to b_1,\ X_{b_2} \to b_2, \ldots, X_{b_m} \to b_m$$

It is clear that the resulting grammar is equivalent to $\hat{G}$ and that it is in Greibach normal form. If all of the productions of a grammar have property (7.9), we say that this grammar is in a pre-Greibach form.

Thus, it is enough to show that any context-free grammar G has an equivalent grammar in a pre-Greibach form. The proof of this is based on Algorithm 7.6, which eliminates left recursion from a given context-free grammar G. We may assume that G has no single productions, so Algorithm 7.6 can be applied. (Apply Algorithm 7.5, if necessary.) We recall how Algorithm 7.6 works. Given a grammar G, we order its nonterminals in an arbitrary, but fixed sequence $X_1, X_2, \ldots, X_n$, subject only to the condition that X_1 is the starting symbol. When Algorithm 7.6 is finished, there are k new nonterminals $Y_1, Y_2, \ldots, Y_k$ such that all of the productions of the new grammar have the following properties.

A. Each production of the form $X_i \rightarrow \gamma$ has γ beginning either with a terminal or with X_j, $j > i$.
B. Each production of the form $Y \rightarrow \gamma$ has γ beginning with a terminal or with one of the X's.

Since there are no X's with subscript larger than n, all the X_n-productions are in pre-Greibach form. Consider now the X_{n-1}-productions. Each one of them is of the form $X_{n-1} \rightarrow a\beta$ or $X_{n-1} \rightarrow X_n\beta$. If the former is the case, the production is already in pre-Greibach form. If the latter holds, apply transformation T2 to it: replace $X_{n-1} \rightarrow X_n\beta$ by

$$X_{n-1} \rightarrow \gamma_1\beta \mid \gamma_2\beta \mid \ldots \mid \gamma_p\beta$$

where $X_n \rightarrow \gamma_1 \mid \gamma_2 \mid \ldots \mid \gamma_p$ are all the X_n-productions. It is clear that at the end of this procedure, all the X_{n-1}-productions will be in pre-Greibach form. We repeat this procedure with productions of the form $X_{n-2} \rightarrow X_{n-1}\beta$, then with productions of the form $X_{n-3} \rightarrow X_{n-2}\beta$, etc., all the way to productions of the form $X_1 \rightarrow X_2\beta$. It is clear that as a result of this, all the X-productions will be in pre-Greibach form. We then apply the transformation T2 to all the Y-productions, each one of which is of the form $Y \rightarrow \gamma$, where γ begins with a terminal or one of the X's. It is clear that the resulting grammar G' is in pre-Greibach form. Q.E.D.

Example 7.13. We will transform the grammar G_0 of arithmetic expressions into Greibach normal form. This grammar, after eliminating single productions, has form (7.6):

$$
\begin{aligned}
E &\to E + T \mid T * F \mid (E) \mid a \\
T &\to T * F \mid (E) \mid a \\
F &\to (E) \mid a
\end{aligned}
$$

We order the nonterminals by setting $E = X_1$, $T = X_2$ and $F = X_3$. A straightforward application of Algorithm 7.6 produces the grammar

$$
\begin{aligned}
E &\to T * F \mid (E) \mid a & E_1 &\to + T \mid +T E_1 \\
E &\to T * F E_1 \mid (E) E_1 \mid a E_1 \\
T &\to (E) \mid a & T_1 &\to * F \mid * F T_1 \\
T &\to (E) T_1 \mid a T_1 \\
F &\to (E) \mid a
\end{aligned}
$$

where the nonterminals E_1 and T_1 are introduced as a result of application of transformation T1 in Algorithm 7.6. All the F-productions are in pre-Greibach form, as they should be, and there are no productions of the form $X_2 \to X_3\beta$. There are, however, productions of the form $X_1 \to X_2\beta$: $E \to T * F$ and $E \to T * F E_1$. We replace the first of these by

$$E \to (E) * F \mid a * F \mid (E) T_1 * F \mid a T_1 * F$$

and the second one by

$$E \to (E) * F E_1 \mid a * F E_1 \mid (E) T_1 * F E_1 \mid a T_1 * F E_1$$

Since neither E_1-productions nor T_1-productions need to be modified, the pre-Greibach form of the grammar G_0 is

$$
\begin{aligned}
E &\to (E) \mid a \mid (E) E_1 \mid a E_1 \\
E &\to (E) * F \mid a * F \mid (E) T_1 * F \mid a T_1 * F \\
E &\to (E) * F E_1 \mid a * F E_1 \mid (E) T_1 * F E_1 \mid a T_1 * F E_1 \\
T &\to (E) \mid a \mid (E) T_1 \mid a T_1 \\
F &\to (E) \mid a \\
E_1 &\to + T \mid +T E_1 \\
T_1 &\to * F \mid * F T_1
\end{aligned}
$$

We now introduce new nonterminals X_a, $X_($, $X_)$, X_+ and X_* and replace the inside occurrences of a, (,), + and $*$ by these new nonterminals. We then add the productions $X_a \to a$, $X_(\to ($, $X_) \to)$, $X_+ \to +$ and $X_* \to *$. This, finally, results in a Greibach form of the grammar G_0. (It turns out that the nonterminals X_a , $X_($ and X_+ are inaccessible, since the terminals a, (, and + never occur in a middle of any of the right-hand side of the productions. We omitted these nonterminals from the final version.)

$$E \rightarrow (\ E\ X_)\ |\ a\ |\ (\ E\ X_)\ E_1\ |\ a\ E_1$$
$$E \rightarrow (\ E\ X_)\ X_*\ F\ |\ a\ X_*\ F\ |\ (\ E\ X_)\ T_1\ X_*\ F\ |\ a\ T_1\ X_*\ F$$
$$E \rightarrow (\ E\ X_)\ X_*\ F\ E_1\ |\ a\ X_*\ F\ E_1\ |\ (\ E\ X_)\ T_1\ X_*\ F\ E_1\ |\ a\ T_1\ X_*\ F\ E_1$$
$$T \rightarrow (\ E\ X_)\ |\ a\ |\ (\ E\ X_)\ T_1\ |\ a\ T_1$$
$$F \rightarrow (\ E\ X_)\ |\ a$$
$$E_1 \rightarrow +\ T\ |\ +T\ E_1$$
$$T_1 \rightarrow *\ F\ |\ *\ F\ T_1$$
$$X_) \rightarrow)$$
$$X_* \rightarrow *$$

This grammar has 24 productions, as opposed to six in the original G_0.

The possibility of expressing every context-free grammar in a Greibach normal form allows us to construct a simple, albeit extremely inefficient, parser for any context-free language. For simplicity, assume that a language L is generated by a grammar $G = \{\Sigma, N, S, P\}$ with no empty productions. We first transform this grammar into a Greibach normal form, say G'. Now, every production in G' adds exactly one terminal to the string being derived. Thus, if $\sigma \in \Sigma^*$ is of length n, it must be derived in exactly n steps. We then simply try out, in some systematic fashion, all possible derivations of length n and see if σ is the result of any one of them. If each nonterminal has at most N productions, this calls for at examining at most N^n sequences. There is actually a more efficient algorithm due to J. Cocke, D. H. Younger, and T. Kasami, known as the CYK algorithm, which will determine whether or not a string σ is in $L(G)$ in about n^3 steps. We refer the reader to [13].

PROBLEMS

In problems 1–3 eliminate all the useless and inaccessible symbols from the given grammar.

1.
$$\begin{array}{lll} S & \rightarrow & ABC \mid Ba \mid CA \mid bS \\ A & \rightarrow & CD \mid E \\ B & \rightarrow & bB \mid c \mid a \end{array} \qquad \begin{array}{lll} C & \rightarrow & Sa \mid Ca \mid aB \\ D & \rightarrow & DA \mid AS \mid Ea \\ E & \rightarrow & Dc \mid ED \end{array}$$

2. $S \rightarrow aB \mid AA \mid cS$
$A \rightarrow a \mid cAa \mid Bb$
$B \rightarrow aC \mid CB \mid Dab$
$C \rightarrow CBaD \mid Da \mid BB$
$D \rightarrow BC \mid BbC \mid DB$

3. $S \rightarrow cSa \mid Ba \mid bb$
$A \rightarrow Ca \mid Ba \mid bb$
$B \rightarrow cS \mid cc$
$C \rightarrow aA \mid bCAc$

In problems 4–7 eliminate empty productions from the given grammar. Give a derivation in both grammars of the indicated string.

4. $S \rightarrow aBcaCA \mid aCA$
$A \rightarrow bCa \mid Sa \mid Ba$
$B \rightarrow aC \mid bcA \mid Sa \mid CC$
$C \rightarrow Ca \mid CS \mid \lambda$
$\sigma = aacaaaaa$

5. $S \rightarrow aSa \mid b \mid AB$
$A \rightarrow BaAS \mid AaB \mid BB$
$B \rightarrow SaS \mid BA \mid \lambda$
$\sigma = aababa$

6. $S \rightarrow aSa \mid AB$
$A \rightarrow bAc \mid \lambda$
$B \rightarrow CBd \mid \lambda$
$C \rightarrow bC \mid \lambda$
$\sigma = bcbd$

7. $S \rightarrow aAd$
$A \rightarrow bAa \mid BBc$
$B \rightarrow a \mid CD$
$C \rightarrow aAb \mid \lambda$
$D \rightarrow aDb \mid \lambda$
$\sigma = abacad$

In problems 8–10 eliminate single productions from the given grammar. Give a derivation of the indicated string in both grammars.

8. $S \rightarrow Ab \mid B$
$A \rightarrow AA \mid bc$
$B \rightarrow C \mid aA$
$C \rightarrow bS \mid A \mid a$
$\sigma = abcbc$

9. $E \rightarrow E + T \mid T$
$F \rightarrow F^* \mid (E) \mid a \mid b \mid c$
$T \rightarrow TF \mid F,$
$\sigma = (a + (b + c)^*)^*$

10. $S \rightarrow Ab \mid B,$
$A \rightarrow AA \mid bc$
$B \rightarrow C \mid aA,$
$C \rightarrow bS \mid A \mid a$
$\sigma = bbcbcb$

11. Find a proper grammar equivalent to the following
$S \rightarrow A \mid B$
$A \rightarrow C \mid D,$
$B \rightarrow D \mid E$
$C \rightarrow S \mid a \mid \lambda,$
$D \rightarrow S \mid b$
$E \rightarrow S \mid c \mid \lambda$

12. Eliminate empty productions from grammar G_0' of Example 7.9.

In problems 13–15 eliminate immediate left recursion from the given grammar and give the leftmost derivation of the indicated string in both grammars.

13. $S \rightarrow aA \mid Sa \mid b$ $\quad A \rightarrow a \mid b \mid BA \mid ASb,$
$B \rightarrow aS \mid b$ $\quad \sigma = aabbbab.$

14. $S \rightarrow A \mid C$ $\quad A \rightarrow AaB \mid AaC \mid B \mid a$
$B \rightarrow Bb \mid Cb$ $\quad C \rightarrow cC \mid c$
$\sigma = aaccacb$

15. $S \rightarrow Sa \mid bA$ $\quad A \rightarrow AA \mid bc \mid Bc,$
$B \rightarrow Bcd \mid BS \mid a$ $\quad \sigma = bbcacdca$

16. Eliminate left recursion from the following grammar:
$S \rightarrow Sa \mid aA \mid B$ $\quad A \rightarrow Sa \mid b \mid BS$
$B \rightarrow Aab \mid C$ $\quad C \rightarrow BA \mid b \mid CS$

17. Find the Chomsky normal forms of the grammars in problems 13–15.

18. Find the Greibach normal forms of the grammars in problems 8–10.

CHAPTER 8

BOTTOM-UP PARSING

8.1. INTRODUCTION

A bottom-up parser operates in a way opposite to the top-down one. Given a grammar G and a string $\sigma \in L(G)$, a bottom-up parser tries to reconstruct the parse tree from the bottom up. It turns out that in such a strategy it is more convenient to reconstruct the rightmost derivation of a given string. Hence, if σ is in $L(G)$, the first question a bottom-up parser tries to answer is: What is the ***last*** production used in the rightmost derivation of σ and what was the sentential form γ immediately preceding σ? In other words, given that $S \Rightarrow^* \sigma$, the parser must find a string γ such that, in the right-most derivation, $S \Rightarrow^* \gamma \Rightarrow \sigma$, and it must also find the production that transforms γ into σ. Once this is determined, the parser tries to determine the sentential form δ that precedes γ; that is, it tries to find γ such that $S \Rightarrow^* \delta \Rightarrow \gamma \Rightarrow \sigma$ as well as the production that transforms δ into γ. The procedure is then repeated until the entire chain of derivations has been filled up, or until it has been determined that σ is not in $L(G)$. We should also keep in mind that in all these procedures we try to reconstruct the rightmost derivation, i.e., the one in which we always replace the rightmost nonterminal. To be of a practical use, such a reconstruction procedure should be deterministic. To get an idea of the complexity of the problem, we consider an example.

Example 8.1. Let G be the grammar

$$S \to aBA \qquad A \to b \qquad A \to aB$$
$$B \to a \qquad B \to bB$$

and let $\sigma = abaaa$. There are several possibilities for the predecessor of σ in the rightmost derivation. They are:

1. $Bbaaa \Rightarrow \underline{a}baaa \quad (B \to a)$
2. $aAaaa \Rightarrow a\underline{b}aaa \quad (A \to b)$
3. $abBaa \Rightarrow ab\underline{a}aa \quad (B \to a)$
4. $abaBa \Rightarrow aba\underline{a}a \quad (B \to a)$
5. $ababB \Rightarrow abaa\underline{a} \quad (B \to a)$

We have underlined the part of σ that is being "pulled back," or replaced by the corresponding left-hand side of an appropriate production (which is indicated in parentheses). From the above five possibilities we must choose the correct one. Consider, for example, the alternative 1, that is suppose the rightmost derivation of σ has the form

$$S \Rightarrow^* Bbaaa \Rightarrow \underline{a}baaa \tag{8.1}$$

By inspection, any sentential form derivable from S will begin with the terminal a, hence (8.1) is impossible. Next, consider alternative 2, i.e., assume the derivation of σ has the form

$$S \Rightarrow^* aAaaa \Rightarrow a\underline{b}aaa. \tag{8.2}$$

We know that the first sentential form derived from S is aBA, thus if (8.2) is true, it is possible to derive $aAaaa$ from aBA, or, which is the same thing, possible to derive $Aaaa$ from BA. By inspection, however, any sentential form derivable from BA will begin with either a or b. This shows that (8.2) is impossible. In a similar way, by completely ad hoc techniques, we can eliminate alternatives 4 and 5 and arrive at a conclusion that if $abaaa$ is in $L(G)$, then its rightmost derivation must have the form

$$S \Rightarrow^* abBaa \Rightarrow ab\underline{a}aa$$

and the last production used in this derivation is $B \to a$. We now repeat the procedure with the sentential form $\gamma = abBaa$ in place of $abaaa$ and consider possible predecessors of γ. Again, the possibilities are:

1. $BbBaa \Rightarrow \underline{a}bBaa \quad (B \to a)$
2. $aABaa \Rightarrow a\underline{b}Baa \quad (A \to b)$
3. $aBaa \Rightarrow a\underline{bB}aa \quad (B \to bB)$
4. $abBBa \Rightarrow abB\underline{a}a \quad (B \to a)$
5. $abBaB \Rightarrow abBa\underline{a} \quad (B \to a)$

The possibilities 1 and 2 are eliminated since they lead to derivations of σ that are not rightmost. By inspection (that wonderful technique), we see that no sentential form derivable from S contains two B's right next to each other, thus alternative 4 is out. Alternative 5 can also be eliminated by similar ad hoc techniques, which leaves 3 as the only candidate. Thus, the rightmost derivation of σ, if at all possible, must have form

$$S \Rightarrow^* aBaa \Rightarrow a\underline{bB}aa \Rightarrow ab\underline{a}aa$$

Continuing in this manner, we arrive at the complete parse of σ

$$S \Rightarrow \underline{aBA} \Rightarrow aB\underline{aB} \Rightarrow aBa\underline{a} \Rightarrow a\underline{bB}aa \Rightarrow ab\underline{a}aa \qquad (8.3)$$

In each sentential form above, we underlined the portion of the string that is being "pulled back." Which nonterminal is being replaced is, of course, determined at each stage, since we seek the rightmost derivation. The problem now is to devise a procedure that, when presented with a string σ, will automatically reconstruct such a derivation of σ.

Motivated by the above example, we can now formulate the basic problem of the bottom-up parser: Given a sentential form γ, find a substring ω of γ such that:

1. ω is the right hand side of some production $X \rightarrow \omega$.
2. If $\gamma = \alpha\omega\beta$ then the rightmost derivation of γ has form $S \Rightarrow^* \alpha X\beta \Rightarrow \alpha\omega\beta$. The last transition ($\alpha X\beta \Rightarrow \alpha\omega\beta$) is made upon application of the production $X \rightarrow \omega$.

Such a substring ω of γ, together with its location within γ, is called the ***handle*** of the sentential form γ. Consider, for example, the string $\sigma = abaaa$ from Example 8.1. The handles of σ and of all the intermediate forms are underlined in derivation (8.3). Notice, incidentally, that the handle of a sentential form is ***not*** just a substring of σ that matches the right hand side of some production—the location of such a substring is just as important. Consider, for example, the sentential form $aBaa$ in (8.3). The handle there is the last a, not any of the previous ones.

Definition 8.1. Let $G = \{\Sigma, N, S, P\}$ be a context-free grammar and let σ be a sentential form derivable from the start symbol S. The ***handle*** of σ is a triple (α, ω, β) such that

1. $\sigma = \alpha\omega\beta$.
2. There is a production in G of the form $X \rightarrow \omega$.
3. The rightmost derivation of σ is $S \Rightarrow^* \alpha X\beta \Rightarrow \alpha\omega\beta = \sigma$.

When there is no danger of confusion, we shall simply speak of the handle of a sentential form σ, but we should keep in mind that the location of this handle is an integral part of the definition. For instance, we will say that the handle of the sentential form $abBaa$ in (8.3) is bB, since the location of bB within $abBaa$ is completely determined. The basis of understanding the operation of a bottom-up parser is the following simple theorem.

Theorem 8.1. Let $G = \{\Sigma, N, S, P\}$ be a context-free grammar and let σ be a sentential form derivable from S. Let (α, ω, β) be the handle of σ with $X \rightarrow \omega$ being the relevant production, so that the rightmost derivation of σ is of the form $S \Rightarrow^* \alpha X\beta \Rightarrow \alpha\omega\beta = \sigma$, and let (δ, ψ, ϵ) be the handle of the sentential form $\alpha X\beta$. Then ψ is ***not*** entirely contained in α.

Proof. Suppose to the contrary that ψ is entirely contained in α and let $Y \rightarrow \psi$ be the relevant production, so that $\alpha = \delta\psi\zeta$ for some ζ. By definition, this means that the rightmost derivation of σ has the form

$$S \Rightarrow^* \delta\, Y \zeta\, X\, \beta \;\Rightarrow\; \underbrace{\delta\, \psi\, \zeta}_{\alpha}\, \overbrace{X\, \beta}^{\epsilon} \;\Rightarrow\; \alpha\omega\beta = \sigma$$

This, however, is ***not*** a right most derivation of σ: The nonterminal Y is replaced before the nonterminal X. Q.E.D.

We are now ready to give a rather loose description of a bottom-up parser. Such a parser will be essentially the push-down automaton depicted in Figure 8.1. The input tape of this PDA will contain the string $\sigma = a_1a_2 \ldots a_n$ to be parsed. As in the case of the top-down parser, we assume that a symbol \$, different from any of the grammatical symbols, is attached to the end of σ, so the parser can detect the end of the input. The input head initially points to the leftmost symbol a_1 of the input σ. The stack of this push-down automaton has the symbol # on the bottom (as in all other PDA's) and the stack pointer originally points to that symbol. The stack alphabet consists of all the terminals and all the nonterminals, as well as the symbol #.

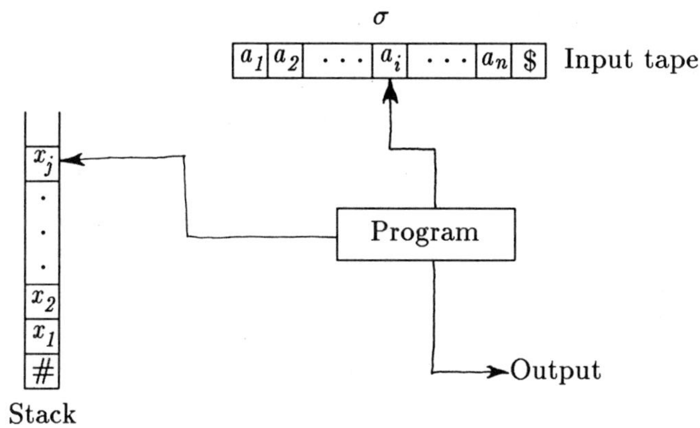

Figure 8.1. Schematic view of a bottom-up parser.

The parser begins operating by shifting the input symbols one by one onto the stack, moving the input pointer one cell to the right at each such shift. This is repeated until the handle ω of σ appears on top of the stack. Thus, if the handle of σ is $(\alpha,\ \omega,\ \beta)$, the procedure is repeated until the configuration of the machine is given in Figure 8.2(a).

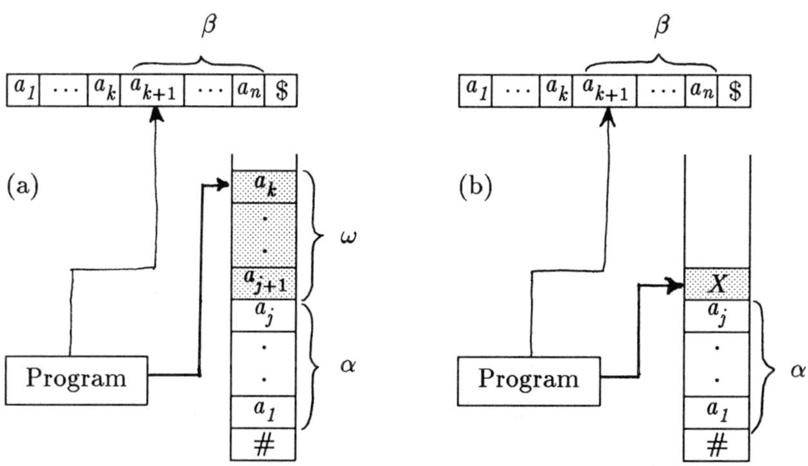

Figure 8.2. Basic move of a bottom-up parser.

At this point the handle ω is replaced by X, where $X \to \omega$ is the relevant production, and the PDA assumes the configuration given in Figure 8.2(b). This operation is called ***reduction*** by the production $X \to \omega$. Since $(\alpha,\ \omega,\ \beta)$ is the handle of σ and $X \to \omega$ is the appropriate production, the derivation of σ has the form

$$S \Rightarrow^* \alpha X \beta \Rightarrow \alpha\omega\beta = \sigma$$

After the reduction is made, the stack contains the leftmost portion of $\alpha X\beta$, namely everything up to and including symbol X. The meaning of Theorem 8.1 is that the handle of $\alpha X\beta$ is ***not*** buried in the stack, that is, it is not entirely contained in α. As a matter of fact, the handle of $\alpha X\beta$ can be placed on top of the stack by shifting more elements of the input. The handle of $\alpha X\beta$ may already be on top of the stack (in which case X is its rightmost symbol), but in any case this handle is not located below the top of the stack.

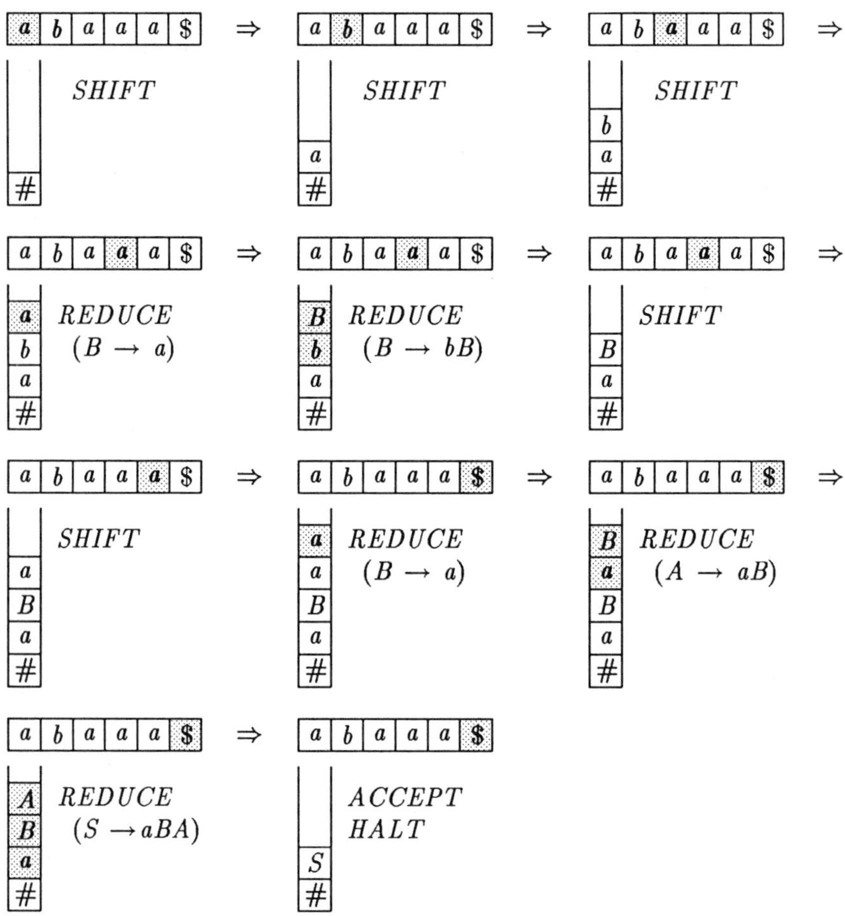

Figure 8.3. Movements of a bottom-up parser.

The parser then shifts the appropriate number of input symbols to the stack until the given handle appears on top of the stack. The appropriate reduction is then made and the procedure is repeated until the stack contains only the start symbol S, and all the input symbols have been read. If at each reduction we take note of the production number of that reduction, then after the parser goes through its movements, we obtain the right parse of σ—the sequence in reverse of the productions used in the rightmost derivation of σ.

Example 8.2. Consider again the grammar from Example 8.1 and the input string $\sigma = abaaa$. Figure 8.3 gives the sequence of configurations of a bottom-up parse of σ. The input symbol being pointed to by the input pointer is indicated by the shaded rectangle. The location of the handle on the stack is also marked at each reduction. This sequence of moves by the parser essentially duplicates the rightmost derivation of σ. The symbol of the input string being pointed to by the input pointer and the handle on top of the stack are shaded.

8.2. DESCRIPTION OF A BOTTOM-UP PARSER

The imprecise description of a bottom-up parse given in the preceding section lacks, of course, one very crucial ingredient: How does the parser know when to shift and when to reduce? In the movements of the parser in Example 8.2 it happens several times that the top of the stack contains a string exactly matching the right-hand side of a production of the grammar. The parser chooses, however, to ignore the opportunity to reduce and proceeds to shift until the correct handle of the sequential form appears on top. This knowledge of what to do can be accomplished by introducing the states in the underlying push-down automaton. The exact way of doing it is somewhat complicated and we devote this section to a precise description of these ideas.

Definition 8.2. Let $G = \{\Sigma, N, S, P\}$ be a context-free grammar. An LR *parser* of the language $L(G)$ consists of the following:

1. A finite number of states $Q_0, Q_1, \ldots, Q_m$. One of these states, say Q_0 is designated as the initial state.
2. An input tape and an input pointer IP. The input tape contains a string $\sigma = a_1a_2 \ldots a_n$ to be parsed, followed by the symbol \$, which is assumed not to be one of the terminals: $\$ \notin \Sigma$. The a's, of course, are terminals of Σ.
3. A stack and a stack pointer SP. Each entry of the stack consists of a pair (X, Q), where X is a grammatical symbol (a nonterminal or a

terminal or the symbol #) and Q is a state. We assume that # is not in $\Sigma \cup N$. The first component (i.e., X) is called the left portion of the stack entry and the second component (i.e., Q) is called the right portion.

4. A function $GOTO(Q, X)$ defined for all states Q and all grammatical symbols $X \in \Sigma \cup N$. The value of $GOTO(Q, X)$ is either a state Q' or symbol *REJECT*.
5. A function $ACTION(Q, x)$ defined for all states Q and all x's in $\Sigma \cup \{\$\}$ (i.e., x can be any symbol appearing on the tape). For each Q and each x the function $ACTION(Q, x)$ can take one of the following values:

   i. *SHIFT*
   ii. $REDUCE(X \to \alpha)$, where $X \to \alpha$ is a production of G
   iii. *ACCEPT*
   iv. *REJECT*

The parser operates according to the following rules:

I. Initially the input pointer *IP* points to the leftmost symbol a_1 of the input $\sigma = a_1 \ldots a_n\$$. The stack contains only one entry: $(\#, Q_0)$ and the stack pointer points to it. Thus, the initial configuration of the parser is given in Figure 8.4.

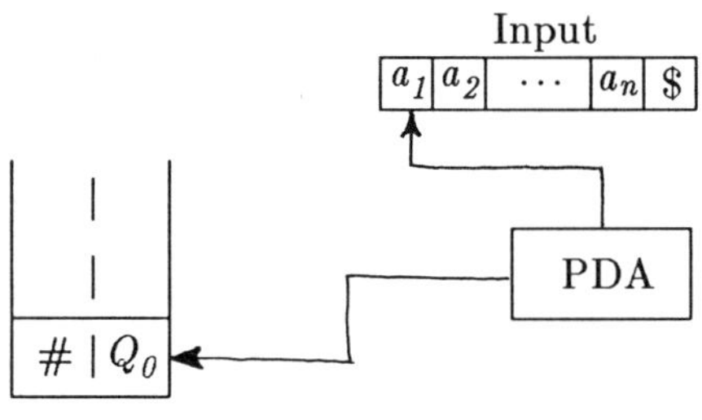

Figure 8.4. Initial configuration of an *LR* parser.

II. Suppose at some time the input pointer points at the symbol a_i and the stack pointer points at the pair (Z, Q), as in Figure 8.5(a). The action of the parser is determined then by the value of $ACTION(Q, a_i)$:

   i. If $ACTION(Q, a_i) = SHIFT$, the parser computes $GOTO(Q, a_i)$. If $GOTO(Q, a_i) = REJECT$, the parser halts and prints *REJECT* on the output tape. If, on the other hand, $GOTO\ (Q,\ a_i) = Q'$, the parser places the pair $(a_i,\ Q')$ on top of the stack and adjusts the input pointers. (The stack pointer will point to $(a_i,\ Q')$ and the input pointer to the symbol a_{i+1}.) Thus, the parser moves to the configuration in Figure 8.5(b).

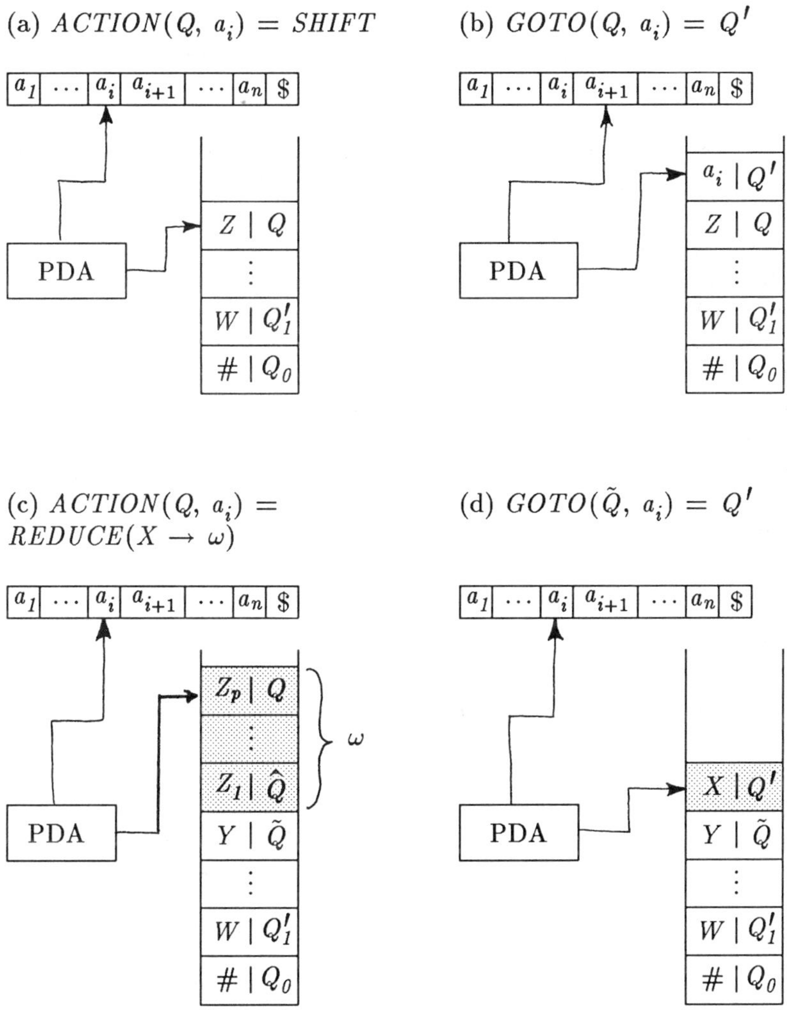

Figure 8.5. Movements of a bottom-up parser.

ii. If $ACTION(Q,\ a_i) = REDUCE(X \rightarrow \omega)$, the parser proceeds to apply the production $X \rightarrow \omega$. In this case the top of the stack matches the string ω, and ω is the handle of the sentential form $W \cdots YZ_1 \cdots Z_p a_i \cdots a_n$, $(\omega = Z_1 \cdots Z_p)$ as in Figure 8.5(c). The parser removes all the entries that constitute ω, exposing some entry $(Y,\ \tilde{Q})$. It then evaluates $GOTO(\tilde{Q},\ X) = Q'$ and places the entry $(X,\ Q')$ on top of the stack, adjusting the stack pointer only (the symbol a_i is read again). This movement is depicted in Figure 8.5(d). At the same time, the number of production $X \rightarrow \omega$ is recorded on the output tape.

iii. If $ACTION(Q,\ a_i) = REJECT$, the parser writes an appropriate phrase on the input tape and halts.

It is seen that the behavior of the parser is completely determined by two functions: *ACTION* and *GOTO*. In the next section we will give an algorithm for calculating these functions from a given grammar; at this point we are only concerned with the behavior of a parser, assuming these functions are known. A parser such as this is called an *LR* parser. The letter *L* indicates that the input is read from left to right, and *R* indicates that the rightmost derivation is reconstructed. Before giving an example, we introduce a notation for an instantaneous configuration of a parser. The diagrammatic description as in Figure 8.3 is very easily understood, but is quite cumbersome.

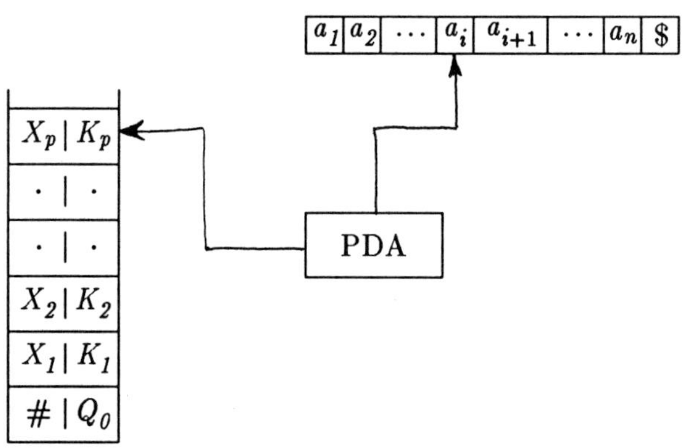

Figure 8.6. A parser in configuration $[\![\#Q_0X_1K_1 \ldots X_pK_p,\ a_i\ a_{i+1} \ldots a_n\$]\!]$.

Definition 8.3. Suppose Π is an *LR* parser whose input pointer points to symbol a_i of the input, and whose stack contains entries $(\#, Q_0)$, (X_1, K_1), . . . , (X_p, K_p) as in Figure 8.6. (X' s are grammatical symbols and K's are states. Q_0 is the initial state). This configuration of Π will be denoted by $[\![\#Q_0X_1K_1 \ldots X_pK_p,\ a_ia_{i+1} \ldots a_n\$]\!]$.

Example 8.3. We continue with the grammar G from Example 8.1:

1. $S \rightarrow aBA$
2. $A \rightarrow b$
3. $A \rightarrow aB$
4. $B \rightarrow a$
5. $B \rightarrow bB$

		States Q										
		Q_0	Q_1	Q_2	Q_3	Q_4	Q_5	Q_6	Q_7	Q_8	Q_9	Q_{10}
I	a	Q_1	Q_3			Q_3	Q_7		Q_3			
n	b		Q_4			Q_4	Q_8		Q_4			
p	S	Q_2										
u	A						Q_9					
t	B		Q_5			Q_6			Q_{10}			

GOTO function of a parser. Blank spaces indicate *REJECT*.

		Input symbol x		
		a	b	$\$$
	Q_0	*SHIFT*		
	Q_1	*SHIFT*	*SHIFT*	
	Q_2			*ACCEPT*
S	Q_3	$B \rightarrow a$	$B \rightarrow a$	$B \rightarrow a$
t	Q_4	*SHIFT*	*SHIFT*	
a	Q_5	*SHIFT*	*SHIFT*	
t	Q_6	$B \rightarrow bB$	$B \rightarrow bB$	$B \rightarrow bB$
e	Q_7	*SHIFT*	*SHIFT*	
	Q_8			$A \rightarrow b$
	Q_9			$S \rightarrow aBA$
	Q_{10}			$A \rightarrow aB$

ACTION function of a parser. Blank spaces indicate *REJECT*.

Figure 8.7. *GOTO* and *ACTION* functions of a parser.

It turns out that the *LR* parser for this grammar consists of 11 states Q_0, Q_1, . . . , Q_{10} and has the *ACTION* and *GOTO* functions given by the tables in Figure 8.7. In the next section we will show how these tables were derived; here we primarily try to explain how the parser works. The entries in the tables in Figure 8.7 are self-explanatory. An entry $X \to \alpha$ means $REDUCE(X \to \alpha)$ and the empty blank indicates the value $REJECT$. Consider now the movements of this parser on the input $\sigma = abaaa\$$. In what follows, each configuration is followed by the relevant values of the functions $ACTION$ and $GOTO$. Also, if the value of $ACTION$ is $REDUCE(X \to \alpha)$, we underline the location of the handle α on the stack. The actual movements are as follows:

$$[\![\#Q_0,\ abaaa\$]\!] \begin{bmatrix} ACTION(Q_0,\ a) = SHIFT \\ GOTO(Q_0,\ a) = Q_1 \end{bmatrix}$$

$$\to [\![\#Q_0aQ_1,\ baaa\$]\!] \begin{bmatrix} ACTION(Q_1,\ b) = SHIFT \\ GOTO(Q_1,\ b) = Q_4 \end{bmatrix}$$

$$\to [\![\#Q_0aQ_1bQ_4,\ aaa\$]\!] \begin{bmatrix} ACTION(Q_4,\ a) = SHIFT \\ GOTO(Q_4,\ a) = Q_3 \end{bmatrix}$$

$$\to [\![\#Q_0aQ_1bQ_4\underline{aQ_3},\ aa\$]\!] \begin{bmatrix} ACTION(Q_3,\ a) = \\ REDUCE(B \to a) \\ GOTO(Q_4,\ B) = Q_6 \end{bmatrix}$$

$$\to [\![\#Q_0aQ_1\underline{bQ_4BQ_6},\ aa\$]\!] \begin{bmatrix} ACTION(Q_6,\ a) = \\ REDUCE(B \to bB) \\ GOTO(Q_1,\ B) = Q_5 \end{bmatrix}$$

$$\to [\![\#Q_0aQ_1BQ_5,\ aa\$]\!] \begin{bmatrix} ACTION(Q_5,\ a) = SHIFT \\ GOTO(Q_5,\ a) = Q_7 \end{bmatrix}$$

$$\to [\![\#Q_0aQ_1BQ_5aQ_7,\ a\$]\!] \begin{bmatrix} ACTION(Q_7,\ a) = SHIFT \\ GOTO(Q_7,\ a) = Q_3 \end{bmatrix}$$

$$\to [\![\#Q_0aQ_1BQ_5aQ_7\underline{aQ_3},\ \$]\!] \begin{bmatrix} ACTION(Q_3,\ \$) = \\ REDUCE(B \to a) \\ GOTO(Q_7,\ B) = Q_{10} \end{bmatrix}$$

$$\to [\![\#Q_0aQ_1BQ_5\underline{aQ_7BQ_{10}},\ \$]\!] \begin{bmatrix} ACTION(Q_{10},\ \$) = \\ REDUCE(A \to aB) \\ GOTO(Q_5,\ A) = Q_9 \end{bmatrix}$$

$$\rightarrow [\![\#Q_0\underline{aQ_1BQ_5AQ_9}, \$]\!] \begin{bmatrix} ACTION(Q_9, \$) = \\ REDUCE(S \rightarrow aBA) \\ GOTO(Q_0, S) = Q_2 \end{bmatrix}$$

$$\rightarrow [\![\#Q_0SQ_2, \$]\!] \left[ACTION(Q_2, \$) = ACCEPT\right] \rightarrow ACCEPT.$$

The sequence of numbers of the productions used in successive *REDUCE* steps is 4, 5, 4, 3, 1 which is precisely the right parse of the string $\sigma = abaaa$.

8.3. CONSTRUCTION OF AN *LR* PARSER

We now present an algorithm for construction of an *LR* parser from a given context-free grammar *G*. Parsers constructed using algorithms from this section are called simple *LR* parsers or *SLR* parsers; the name *LR*(0) parser is also used. We will explain this a little later. The proofs that the parsers resulting from these algorithms work is beyond the scope of this book; an interested reader is referred to [2] or [3].

It turns out that in the constructions that follow it is convenient to have the underlying grammar in a certain form.

Definition 8.4. Let $G = \{\Sigma, N, S, P\}$ be a context-free grammar. An ***augmented grammar*** G' is obtained from *G* by introducing a new starting symbol S' and adding to *G* one new production $S' \rightarrow S$.

Example 8.4. Let *G* be the grammar from Example 8.1:

$$S \rightarrow aBA \quad A \rightarrow b \mid aB \quad B \rightarrow a \mid bB$$

The augmented grammar G' obtained from *G* is

$$S' \rightarrow S \quad S \rightarrow aBA \quad A \rightarrow b \mid aB \quad B \rightarrow a \mid bB$$

It is entirely obvious that if G' is an augmented grammar obtained from *G*, then $L(G) = L(G')$.

Definition 8.5. Let $G = \{\Sigma, N, S, P\}$ be a context-free grammar and let

$$X \rightarrow Y_1Y_2 \ldots Y_n \tag{8.4}$$

be a production of *G*. An ***item*** associated with the production (8.4) is an expression of the form

$$[X \rightarrow Y_1 Y_2 \ldots Y_k \bullet Y_{k+1} \ldots Y_n]$$

In other words, an item consists of a production enclosed in square brackets and a dot • placed among the symbols on the right-hand side.

Let G be the augmented grammar from Example 8.4. The production $A \rightarrow aB$ generates three items: $[A \rightarrow \bullet aB]$, $[A \rightarrow a \bullet B]$, and $[A \rightarrow aB\bullet]$. The location of the dot is part of the definition of an item, so all these three items are considered to be distinct. The production $B \rightarrow a$ generates two items: $[B \rightarrow \bullet a]$ and $[B \rightarrow a\bullet]$. An empty production $X \rightarrow \lambda$ generates only one item $[X \rightarrow \bullet]$. It is clear that given a context-free grammar G, there exists only a finite number of items generated by the productions of G. The states of the LR parser turn out to be certain sets of items. We now define some operations on sets of items.

Definition 8.6. Let $G = \{\Sigma, N, S, P\}$ be a context-free grammar and let I be a collection of items from G. A set J of items is called the ***closure*** of I if it satisfies the following conditions:

1. $I \subseteq J$.
2. If $[X \rightarrow \alpha \bullet Y\beta]$ is an item of J, where Y is a nonterminal, then for any production of the form $Y \rightarrow \gamma$, the item $[Y \rightarrow \bullet\gamma]$ is also in J.
3. J is the smallest set of items satisfying conditions 1 and 2. This means that if J' is any set of items for which 1 and 2 hold, then $J \subseteq J'$.

The closure of a set I of items will be denoted by $CLOSURE(I)$.

Example 8.5. Consider the grammar G from Example 8.1. Let I be the set of items given by

$$I = \{[S \rightarrow a\bullet BA], [A \rightarrow \bullet aB]\}$$

We heuristically construct the set $J = CLOSURE(I)$. First of all, because of condition 1, all the items of I must also belong to J. Consider now the item $[S \rightarrow a\bullet BA]$. Since B is a nonterminal, condition 2 implies that the items $[B \rightarrow \bullet a]$ and $[B \rightarrow \bullet bB]$ also belong to J. Since a is not a nonterminal, the item $[A \rightarrow \bullet aB]$ imposes no conditions on J —condition 2 does not apply here. Similarly, the two new items $[B \rightarrow \bullet a]$ and $[B \rightarrow \bullet bB]$ produce no new items in J. Thus,

$$CLOSURE(I) = \{[S \to a\bullet BA], [A \to \bullet aB], [B \to \bullet a], [B \to \bullet bB]\}$$

Algorithm 8.1. Closure of a set of items.
Input: A set I of items of a context-free grammar.
Output: The set $J = CLOSURE(I)$.

Define inductively a sequence of sets $J_0, J_1, \ldots$ as follows:

1. $J_0 = I$
2. Suppose J_n is already defined. To construct J_{n+1}, add to J_n all items of the form $[Y \to \bullet\gamma]$ where $Y \to \gamma$ is a production of G and $[X \to \alpha\bullet Y\beta]$ is an item of J_n. Formally,

$$J_{n+1} = J_n \cup \{[Y \to \bullet\gamma] \mid Y \to \gamma \text{ is a production and there is an item of the form } [X \to \alpha\bullet Y\beta] \in J_n\}$$

3. If $J_{n+1} = J_n$, i.e., no new items are added to J_n, the algorithm stops and we set $CLOSURE(I) = J_n$. If, however, J_{n+1} is properly contained in J_n, we repeat step 2.

Example 8.6. Consider the grammar G_0 of arithmetic expressions and let G_0' be the augmented grammar. The productions of G_0' are

$$\begin{array}{lcl} E & \to & E' \\ E & \to & E + T \mid T \\ T & \to & T * F \mid F \\ F & \to & (E) \mid a \end{array}$$

The starting symbol is, of course, E'. Let I be the set consisting of one item: $I = \{[E' \to \bullet E]\}$. The application of Algorithm 8.1 proceeds as follows:

$J_0 = \{[E' \to \bullet E]\}$ by step 1.
$J_1 = \{[E' \to \bullet E], [E \to \bullet E + T], [E \to \bullet T]\}$. The item $[E \to \bullet E]$ is included because it is in J_0. Since E is a nonterminal, step 2 forces the items $[E \to \bullet E + T]$ and $[E \to \bullet T]$ to be in J_1.
$J_2 = \{[E' \to \bullet E], [E \to \bullet E + T], [E \to \bullet T], [T \to \bullet T * F], [T \to \bullet F]\}$. The first three items are in J_2 because they are in J_1. The application of step 2 to the item $[E \to \bullet E + T]$ produces nothing new, but the item $[E \to \bullet T]$ gives two new items of J_2: $[T \to \bullet T * F]$ and $[T \to \bullet F]$.

$J_3 = J_2 \cup \{[F \to \bullet a], [F \to \bullet(E)]\}$. The items $[F \to \bullet a]$ and $[F \to \bullet(E)]$ are included in J_3 because of the item $[T \to \bullet F]$ in J_2.

$J_4 = J_3$ by inspection. The items $[F \to \bullet a]$ and $[F \to \bullet(E)]$ do not produce new items for J_4 since neither a nor (is a nonterminal.

Thus,

$$CLOSURE(I) = J_3 = \{[E' \to \bullet E], [E \to \bullet E + T], [E \to \bullet T], [T \to \bullet T * F], [T \to \bullet F], [F \to \bullet(E)], [F \to \bullet a]\}$$

It should be quite clear that Algorithm 8.1 stops after a finite number of steps—there exists only a finite number of items associated with a given grammar—and that it produces correct results. We should also point out that if $\emptyset$ is the empty set of items, $CLOSURE(\emptyset) = \emptyset$.

We now return to the construction of the *LR* parser. The states of this parser will be certain collections of items, and we proceed to define the *GOTO* function needed in such a parser.

Definition 8.7. Let G be a context-free grammar, let I be a collection of items of G and let Z be a grammatical symbol (a terminal or a nonterminal). Define

$$GOTO(I, Z) = CLOSURE(\{[X \to \alpha Z \bullet \beta] \mid [X \to \alpha \bullet Z\beta] \text{ is an item of } I\})$$

Heuristically, the set $GOTO(I, Z)$ is obtained as follows. We first form the set I' of items by considering all items of the form $[X \to \alpha \bullet Z\beta]$ and moving the dot $\bullet$ past Z. The set $GOTO(I, Z)$ is then the closure of I'.

Example 8.7. Let G_0' be the augmented grammar of arithmetic expressions from Example 8.6, and let

$$I = \{[E' \to \bullet E], [E \to \bullet E + T], [E \to \bullet T], [T \to \bullet T * F], [T \to \bullet F], [F \to \bullet(E)], [F \to \bullet a]\}$$

We have

$$\begin{aligned} GOTO(I, E) &= CLOSURE(\{[E' \to E\bullet], [E \to E \bullet + T]\}) \\ &= \{[E' \to E\bullet], [E \to E \bullet + T]\} \end{aligned} \tag{8.5}$$

Here $Z = E$ and there are only two items in I in which $\bullet$ appears immediately in front of E: they are $[E' \to \bullet E]$ and $[E \to \bullet E + T]$. We move the dot $\bullet$ across E and construct the closure of the resulting set. It is seen from Algorithm 8.1 that his produces no new items, thus (8.5) follows. In a similar way we get

$$\begin{aligned} GOTO(I, T) &= CLOSURE(\{[E \to T\bullet], [T \to T\bullet * F]\}) \\ &= \{[E \to T\bullet], [T \to T\bullet * F]\} \\ GOTO(I, F) &= CLOSURE(\{[T \to F\bullet]\}) = \{[T \to F\bullet]\} \\ GOTO(I, () &= CLOSURE(\{[F \to (\bullet E)]\} \\ &= \{[F \to (\bullet E)], [E \to \bullet E + T], [E \to \bullet T], [T \to \bullet F], \\ &\qquad [T \to \bullet T * F], [F \to \bullet(E)], [F \to \bullet a]\} \\ GOTO(I, a) &= CLOSURE(\{[F \to a\bullet]\}) = \{[F \to a\bullet]\} \\ GOTO(I, *) &= GOTO(I, +) = GOTO(I,)) = \emptyset \end{aligned} \tag{8.6}$$

Regarding the last line of (8.6), consider, for example $GOTO(I, *)$. There are no items in I of the form $[X \to \alpha\bullet * \beta]$, thus $GOTO(I, *) = CLOSURE(\emptyset) = \emptyset$.

We are now ready to construct the states of the parser. These states will be collections of items. If I is one such collection-state then $GOTO(I, Z)$ is the collection-state of items given by Definition 8.7. If G' is the augmented form of grammar G (see Definition 8.4), then the initial state of the parser of G' is taken to be

$$Q_0 = CLOSURE(\{[S' \to \bullet S]\})$$

We then calculate $CLOSURE(I_0, Z)$ for all possible grammatical symbols Z. This results in a set of new states $I_1, I_2, \ldots, I_n$. We calculate all the values of $GOTO(I_j, Z)$ for all these I_j's and all Z's. This, presumably, results in some new states. We repeat the procedure over and over; since there is only a finite number of possible sets of items, at some point there will be no new states appearing. This procedure determines the states of the parser and, at the same time, the function $GOTO$. Formally we have the following.

Algorithm 8.2. States of an LR parser and $GOTO$ function.
Input: A context-free grammar.
Output: States of the LR parser together with the $GOTO$ function.

1. Rewrite grammar G into the augmented form.
2. Set the initial state to be

$$Q_0 = CLOSURE(\{[S' \to \bullet S]\})$$

3. Suppose the states $Q_0, Q_1, \ldots, Q_n$ have already been defined. For each one of these states Q_j and each grammatical symbol Z calculate $GOTO(Q_j, Z)$ using Algorithm 8.1. If this results in some additional states Q, repeat step 3. Otherwise, the states of the parser are the nonempty collections among $Q_0, Q_1, \ldots, Q_n$.
4. Redefine the function $GOTO$ constructed so far by setting $GOTO(Q, Z) = REJECT$ for all those Q's and Z's for which $GOTO(Q, Z) = \emptyset$, as calculated so far.

Example 8.8. Let G be the grammar from Example 8.1. In its augmented form G' is given by

$$\begin{array}{lllllll} S' & \to & S & \qquad & A & \to & aB \\ S & \to & aBA & & B & \to & a \\ A & \to & b & & B & \to & bB \end{array}$$

The initial state is

$$Q_0 = CLOSURE(\{[S' \to \bullet S]\}) = \{[S' \to \bullet S], [S \to \bullet aBA]\}$$

We now proceed with step 3 of Algorithm 8.2.

$GOTO(Q_0, a) = CLOSURE(\{[S \to a\bullet BA]\})$
$\quad = \{[S \to a \bullet BA], [B \to \bullet a], [B \to \bullet bB]\} = Q_1$—new state.
$GOTO(Q_0, S) = CLOSURE(\{[S' \to S\bullet]\}) = \{[S' \to S\bullet]\}$
$\quad = Q_2$—new state.
$GOTO(Q_0, Z) = \emptyset$ for all other Z's.

Thus, at this stage, the states of the parser are Q_0, Q_1, and Q_2, as defined above. We execute step 3 again.

$GOTO(Q_1, a) = CLOSURE(\{[B \to a\bullet]\}) = \{[B \to a\bullet]\}$
$\quad = Q_3$—new state.

$GOTO(Q_1, b) = CLOSURE(\{[B \rightarrow b\bullet B]\})$
$= \{[B \rightarrow b\bullet B], [B \rightarrow \bullet\ a], [B \rightarrow \bullet bB]\} = Q_4$—new state.
$GOTO(Q_1, B) = CLOSURE(\{[S \rightarrow aB\bullet A]\})$
$= \{[S \rightarrow aB\bullet A], [A \rightarrow \bullet b], [A \rightarrow \bullet aB]\} = Q_5$—new state.
$GOTO(Q_1, Z) = \emptyset$ for all other Z's.

At this point, the states are Q_0, Q_1, Q_2, Q_3, Q_4, and Q_5. Since new states were introduced, we repeat step 3.

$GOTO(Q_2, Z) = GOTO(Q_3, Z) = \emptyset$ for all Z's.
$GOTO(Q_4, a) = CLOSURE(\{[B \rightarrow a\bullet]\}) = \{[B \rightarrow a\bullet]\}$
$= Q_3$—an old state.
$GOTO(Q_4, b) = CLOSURE(\{[B \rightarrow b\bullet B]\})$
$=\{[B \rightarrow b\bullet B], [B \rightarrow\bullet a], [B \rightarrow\bullet\ bB]\} = Q_4$—an old state .
$GOTO(Q_4, B) = CLOSURE(\{[B \rightarrow b\ B\bullet]\}) = \{[B \rightarrow b\ B\bullet]\}$
$= Q_6$—new state.
$GOTO(Q_4, Z) = \emptyset$ for all other Z's.
$GOTO(Q_5, a) = CLOSURE(\{[A \rightarrow a\bullet B]\})$
$= \{[A \rightarrow a\bullet\ B], [B \rightarrow\bullet a], [B \rightarrow\bullet bB]\} = Q_7$—new state.
$GOTO(Q_5, b) = CLOSURE(\{[A \rightarrow b\bullet]\}) = \{[A \rightarrow b\bullet]\}$
$= Q_8$—new state.
$GOTO(Q_5, A) = CLOSURE(\{[S \rightarrow aBA\bullet]\}) = \{[S \rightarrow aBA\bullet]\}$
$= Q_9$—new state.
$GOTO(Q_5, Z) = \emptyset$ for all other Z's.

The new states introduced during this pass through step 3 are Q_6, Q_7, Q_8, and Q_9. We thus repeat the procedure again.

$GOTO(Q_7, b) = CLOSURE\{[B \rightarrow b\bullet B]\}$
$= Q_4$—old state.
$GOTO(Q_7, B) = CLOSURE(\{[A \rightarrow aB\bullet]\}) = \{[A \rightarrow aB\bullet]\}$
$= Q_{10}$—new state.
$GOTO(Q_7, Z) = \emptyset = GOTO(Q_8, Z) = GOTO(Q_9, Z)$ for all other Z's.

The only new state introduced here is Q_{10}. Repeating step 3, we get $GOTO(Q_{10}, Z) = \emptyset$ for all Z's, thus the algorithm halts. The procedure produced states $Q_0 - Q_{10}$ and the table of $GOTO$ function in Figure 8.8. This is identical to the table in Figure 8.7.

		States Q										
		Q_0	Q_1	Q_2	Q_3	Q_4	Q_5	Q_6	Q_7	Q_8	Q_9	Q_{10}
I	a	Q_1	Q_3			Q_3	Q_7		Q_3			
n	b		Q_4			Q_4	Q_8		Q_4			
p	S	Q_2										
u	A						Q_9					
t	B		Q_5			Q_6			Q_{10}			

GOTO function of a parser. Blank spaces indicate *REJECT*.

Figure 8.8. *GOTO* function.

What remains now is to construct the function $ACTION(Q, x)$. It is at this point that one can determine whether or not the given grammar has a deterministic LR parser. The situation is analogous to the LL case. It may happen that the algorithm for constructing $ACTION(Q, x)$, which we are about to present, will give conflicting values for a given pair (Q, x). When this happens, we say that the parsing table contains a conflict. If such a conflict does not arise, a deterministic bottom-up parser for the given grammar G exists, and we say that G is an SLR grammar. We will make some additional comments on this later; first we will give the algorithm for constructing the $ACTION$ function. Strictly speaking, since functions are single valued by definition, the values of $ACTION(Q, x)$ will be sets containing the expressions $SHIFT$, $ACCEPT$, $REJECT$, and $REDUCE(p)$, where p is a production of the grammar. Thus, if $\mathfrak{Q}$ is the collection of the states of the bottom-up parser then

$$ACTION\colon \mathfrak{Q} \times \{\Sigma \cup \{\$\}\} \mapsto \mathfrak{P}(\{SHIFT,\ ACCEPT,\ REJECT, \bigcup_{p \in P} REDUCE(p)\})$$

We will, however, make an abuse of notation and regard $ACTION$ as a function assuming values $SHIFT$, $ACCEPT$, etc. Thus, strictly speaking, the expression $ACTION(Q, x) = REDUCE(p)$ should be interpreted as $REDUCE(p) \in ACTION(Q, x)$. The reader who is not very familiar with these fine points of the etiquette of set theory may safely ignore these remarks. He/she will be the better for it.

Algorithm 8.3. Action function of an LR parser.
Input: A context-free grammar $G = \{\Sigma, N, S', P\}$ in augmented form.
Output: Values of $ACTION(Q, x)$.

1. Calculate the states $Q_0, Q_1, \ldots, Q_n$ of the parser using Algorithm 8.2.
2. For every state Q (recall that Q is a collection of items) and every item of the form $[Y \rightarrow \alpha \bullet x \beta]$ in Q, such that $x \in \Sigma$, set $ACTION(Q, x) = SHIFT$.
3. For every state Q and every item of the form $[Y \rightarrow \alpha \bullet]$ in Q, where $Y \neq S'$, set $ACTION(Q, x) = REDUCE(Y \rightarrow \alpha)$ for each $x \in FOLLOW(Y)$.
4. For every state Q containing item $[S' \rightarrow S\bullet]$ set $ACTION(Q, \$) = ACCEPT$.
5. In all other situations, not defined in 1–4, put $ACTION(Q, x) = REJECT$.

Example 8.9. Consider the grammar G' from Example 8.8 (already in augmented form). The states for the LR parser for this grammar were found to be

$$
\begin{aligned}
Q_0 &= \{[S' \rightarrow \bullet S], [S \rightarrow \bullet aBA]\} \\
Q_1 &= \{[S \rightarrow a\bullet BA], [B \rightarrow \bullet a], [B \rightarrow \bullet bB]\} \\
Q_2 &= \{[S' \rightarrow S\bullet]\} \\
Q_3 &= \{[B \rightarrow a\bullet]\} \\
Q_4 &= \{[B \rightarrow b\bullet B], [B \rightarrow \bullet a], [B \rightarrow \bullet bB]\} \\
Q_5 &= \{[S \rightarrow aB\bullet A], [A \rightarrow \bullet b], [A \rightarrow \bullet aB]\} \\
Q_6 &= \{[B \rightarrow bB\bullet]\} \\
Q_7 &= \{[A \rightarrow a\bullet B], [B \rightarrow \bullet a], [B \rightarrow \bullet bB]\} \\
Q_8 &= \{[A \rightarrow b\bullet]\} \\
Q_9 &= \{[S \rightarrow aBA\bullet]\} \\
Q_{10} &= \{[A \rightarrow aB\bullet]\}
\end{aligned}
$$

An easy calculation gives $FOLLOW(S) = FOLLOW(A) = \{\$\}$ and $FOLLOW(B) = \{a, b, \$\}$. Algorithm 8.8 produces the table for the $ACTION$ function given in Figure 8.9. It is seen that this table is identical to the one in Figure 8.7. We give explanations for a few randomly selected entries. Consider the state Q_0. Since the item $[S \rightarrow \bullet aBA]$ is in Q_0, step 2 of Algorithm 8.3 calls for $ACTION(Q_0, a) = SHIFT$. There are no other items in Q_0 of the form $[Y \rightarrow \alpha \bullet x\beta]$—$[S' \rightarrow \bullet S]$ does not qualify because S is not terminal—nor any items of the form $[Y \rightarrow \alpha\bullet]$. Thus, $ACTION(Q_0, x) = REJECT$ for all $x \neq a$. The item $[B \rightarrow \bullet a]$ is responsible for the value $ACTION(Q_1, a) = SHIFT$ and the item $[B \rightarrow \bullet bB]$ causes $ACTION(Q_1, b) = SHIFT$—both result from step 2 of the algorithm. The value $ACTION(Q_2, \$) = ACCEPT$ is obtained from step 4 of the algorithm. Consider now the state $Q_3 = \{[B \rightarrow a\bullet]\}$—step 3 applies here. Since $FOLLOW(B) = \{a, b, \$\}$, we get

$ACTION(Q_3, a) = ACTION(Q_3, b) = ACTION(Q_3, \$) = REDUCE(B \rightarrow a)$. The row containing the state Q_6 is explained in the same way. Consider next the state $Q_8 = \{[A \rightarrow b\bullet]\}$. Since $FOLLOW(A) = \{\$\}$, we get $ACTION(Q_8, \$) = REDUCE(A \rightarrow b)$ and $ACTION(Q_8, x) = REJECT$ for all $x \neq \$$.

State	Input symbol x: a	b	$\$$
Q_0	*SHIFT*		
Q_1	*SHIFT*	*SHIFT*	
Q_2			*ACCEPT*
Q_3	$B \rightarrow a$	$B \rightarrow a$	$B \rightarrow a$
Q_4	*SHIFT*	*SHIFT*	
Q_5	*SHIFT*	*SHIFT*	
Q_6	$B \rightarrow bB$	$B \rightarrow bB$	$B \rightarrow bB$
Q_7	*SHIFT*	*SHIFT*	
Q_8			$A \rightarrow b$
Q_9			$S \rightarrow aBA$
Q_{10}			$A \rightarrow aB$

Figure 8.9 *ACTION* function of a parser. Blank spaces indicate *REJECT*.

By inspection, the table for the *ACTION* function contains no conflict. This does not always happen as the next example shows.

Example 8.10. Let G be the grammar given (already in augmented form) by

$$S' \rightarrow S \qquad A \rightarrow AaA$$
$$S \rightarrow A \qquad A \rightarrow b$$

Algorithm 8.2. gives the following states for the parser:

$$Q_0 = \{[S' \rightarrow \bullet S], [S \rightarrow \bullet A], [A \rightarrow \bullet AaA], [A \rightarrow \bullet b]\}$$
$$Q_1 = \{[S' \rightarrow S\bullet]\}$$
$$Q_2 = \{[S \rightarrow A\bullet], [A \rightarrow A\bullet\ aA]\}$$
$$Q_3 = \{[A \rightarrow b\bullet]\}$$
$$Q_4 = \{[A \rightarrow Aa\bullet A], [A \rightarrow \bullet AaA], [A \rightarrow \bullet b]\}$$
$$Q_5 = \{[A \rightarrow AaA\bullet], [A \rightarrow A\bullet aA]\}$$

An easy calculation gives $FOLLOW(S) = \{\$\}$, $FOLLOW(A) = \{a, \$\}$. Consider now $ACTION(Q_5, a)$. Since $[A \rightarrow A\bullet aA]$ is in Q_5, step 2 of Algorithm 8.3 gives $ACTION(Q_5, a) = SHIFT$. On the other hand

$[A \to AaA\bullet]$ is in Q_5 and a is in $FOLLOW(A)$, so we get from step 3 of the algorithm, $ACTION(Q_5, a) = REDUCE(A \to AaA)$. Thus, the table of the function $ACTION$ contains a conflict.

Definition 8.8. Let G be a context-free grammar. If the function $ACTION$ given by Algorithm 8.3 is well defined, i.e., the parsing table contains no conflicts, we say that G is an **LR(0) *grammar*** or an SLR ***grammar***. The resulting parser is called an $LR(0)$, or an SLR parser.

Thus, the grammar from Example 8.1 is an $LR(0)$ grammar, whose parser is given by the tables in Figure 8.7. On the other hand, the grammar of Example 8.10 is not an $LR(0)$ grammar. The question arises what to do if a grammar G for some language L is not $LR(0)$ and a deterministic parser is needed for L. One solution is to try to transform G into an equivalent $LR(0)$ grammar G'. Another possibility, in analogy with the LL situation, is to use "lookahead" symbols. An LR parser is constructed for the grammar G along the lines indicated above and we assume that a conflict arises in the resulting table. Thus, given a state Q and an input a_i there is more than one possibility for $ACTION(Q, a_i)$. It may very well happen, however, that if we examine the next symbol a_{i+1}, we can eliminate all but one of these possibilities. Thus, by "looking ahead" one symbol we can resolve the conflicts in the parsing table. Parsers of this kind are called $LR(1)$ parsers, where the number 1 indicates that only one symbol is needed to resolve the conflicts. The idea can be extended to looking ahead k symbols, leading to the concept of $LR(k)$ parsers and grammars. We will not pursue these concepts here, but refer the interested reader to [3] or [13].

8.4. A PARSER FOR ARITHMETIC EXPRESSIONS

We now apply the methods presented in the previous sections to the grammar G_0 of arithmetic expressions. In the augmented form, this grammar is given by

$$E' \to E \qquad\qquad T \to T * F \mid F$$
$$E \to E + T \mid T \qquad\qquad F \to (E) \mid a$$

Straightforward application of Algorithm 8.2 gives the following states for the LR parser:

$$Q_0 = \{[E' \to \bullet E], [E \to \bullet E + T], [E \to \bullet T], [T \to \bullet F], [T \to \bullet T * F], [F \to \bullet(E)], [F \to \bullet a]\}$$
$$Q_1 = \{[E' \to E\bullet], [E \to E\bullet + T]\}$$

$$
\begin{aligned}
Q_2 &= \{[E \to T\bullet],\ [T \to T\bullet *F]\}\\
Q_3 &= \{[T \to F\bullet]\}\\
Q_4 &= \{[F \to (\bullet\ E)],\ [E \to \bullet E + T],\ [E \to \bullet T],\ [T \to \bullet T * F],\\
&\qquad [T \to \bullet F],\ [F \to \bullet(\ E\ )],\ [F \to \bullet a]\}\\
Q_5 &= \{[F \to a\bullet]\}\\
Q_6 &= \{[E \to E +\bullet T],\ [\ T \to \bullet T * F],\ [T \to \bullet F],\ [F \to \bullet(E)],\\
&\qquad [F \to \bullet a]\}\\
Q_7 &= \{[F \to T *\bullet F],\ [F \to \bullet(E)],\ [F \to \bullet a]\}\\
Q_8 &= \{[F \to (\ E\bullet)],\ [E \to E\bullet + T]\}\\
Q_9 &= \{[E \to E + T\bullet],\ [T \to T\bullet * F]\}\\
Q_{10} &= \{[T \to T * F\bullet]\}\\
Q_{11} &= \{[T \to (E)\bullet]\}
\end{aligned}
$$

The *GOTO* function, given again by Algorithm 8.2, is summarized by the table in Figure 8.10. The blank spaces, as usual, indicate the value *REJECT*.

		States Q											
		Q_0	Q_1	Q_2	Q_3	Q_4	Q_5	Q_6	Q_7	Q_8	Q_9	Q_{10}	Q_{11}
I	a	Q_5				Q_5		Q_5	Q_5				
n	+		Q_6							Q_6			
p	*			Q_7							Q_7		
u	(	Q_4				Q_4		Q_4	Q_4				
t	)									Q_{11}			
	E	Q_1				Q_8							
x	T	Q_2				Q_2		Q_9					
	F	Q_3				Q_3		Q_3	Q_{10}				

Figure 8.10. $GOTO(Q, Z)$ function for the grammar G_0.

Applying Algorithm 8.3. we obtain the table for the values of the function *ACTION*; it is given in Figure 8.11. We see by inspection that this table does contains no conflicts. Thus, the grammar G_0 is an $LR(0)$ grammar and we have constructed a deterministic parser for it.

This parser can be modified slightly so that it not only parses arithmetic expressions, but also performs semantic actions associated with the derivation of these expressions, and produces their value. For simplicity of exposition, we will assume that we deal with arithmetic expressions involving only nonnegative integers. Thus, the symbol a in the description of G_0 can be any nonnegative integer.

State Q	Input symbol x: a	$+$	$*$	$($	$)$	$\$$
Q_0	*SHIFT*			*SHIFT*		
Q_1		*SHIFT*				*ACCEPT*
Q_2		$E \to T$	*SHIFT*		$E \to T$	$E \to T$
Q_3		$T \to F$	$T \to F$		$T \to F$	$T \to F$
Q_4	*SHIFT*			*SHIFT*		
Q_5		$F \to a$	$F \to a$		$F \to a$	$F \to a$
Q_6	*SHIFT*			*SHIFT*		
Q_7	*SHIFT*			*SHIFT*		
Q_8		*SHIFT*			*SHIFT*	
Q_9		$E \to E+T$	*SHIFT*		$E \to E+T$	$E \to E+T$
Q_{10}		$T \to T*F$	$T \to T*F$		$T \to T*F$	$T \to T*F$
Q_{11}		$F \to (E)$	$F \to (E)$		$F \to (E)$	$F \to (E)$

Figure 8.11. $ACTION(Q, x)$ function for the grammar G_0.

Given one such expression, say 2 + 7 * (3 + 5), the parser will not only determine whether the expression is properly formed, but will also determine its value (58 in this case). This can be done as follows: We attach another stack to the parser and call it a working stack. Originally, the working stack will contain only the symbol \$ and the working stack pointer points to this symbol. At each step the parser will perform different operations on this working stack, depending on the value of $ACTION(Q, x)$. Schematically, the entire apparatus is depicted in Figure 8.12.

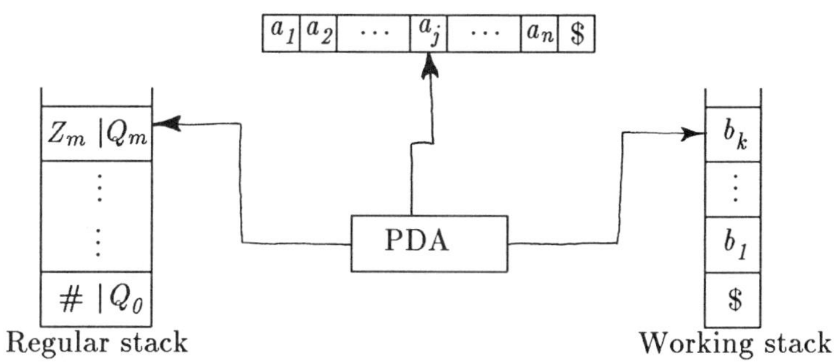

Figure 8.12. An $LR(0)$ parser for G_0.

We will denote the configuration of such a parser as in Figure 8.12 by

$$[\![\#Q_0Z_1Q_1 \ldots Z_mQ_m;\ a_ja_{j+1} \ldots a_n\$;\ b_k, b_{k-1}, b_{k-2}, \ldots, b_2, b_1, \$]\!]$$

The commas between the b's are essentially to distinguish between the sequence 1, 2, \$ (1 on top of the stack, followed by 2, followed by \$) and the sequence 12\$ (twelve on top of the stack, followed by \$). The actions of this parser on the working stack (semantic actions) are given in Figure 8.13.

Parser action	Semantic action
SHIFT	Push the current input symbol on top of the working stack.
REDUCE $(E \rightarrow E + T)$	In this case, the top three elements of the working stack are: n_1, +, n_2 (in that order). The parser removes these symbols and places the integer $n_1 + n_2$ on top of the working stack
REDUCE $(T \rightarrow T * F)$	In this case, the top three elements of the working stack are: n_1, $*$, n_2 (in that order). The parser removes these symbols and places the integer $n_1 * n_2$ on top of the working stack.
REDUCE $(F \rightarrow (E))$	In this case, the top three elements are), n, (. The parser removes these and places n on top.
All others	Do nothing.

Figure 8.13. Semantic actions of a parser.

Consider, for example, the movements of this parser on the input $\sigma = 2 + 7 * (3 + 5)$. It goes as follows (we underline the portions of handles on the stack and the top portion of the working stack being subjected to the semantic actions):

CONFIGURATION OF THE PARSER	ACTION TAKEN
$[\![\#Q_0;\ 2{+}7{*}(3{+}5)\$;\ \$]\!]$	*SHIFT*
$[\![\#Q_0\underline{2Q_5};\ {+}7{*}(3{+}5)\$;\ 2,\$]\!]$	$REDUCE(F \rightarrow a)\ a = 2$
$[\![\#Q_0\underline{FQ_3};\ {+}7{*}(3{+}5)\$;\ 2,\$]\!]$	$REDUCE(T \rightarrow F)$
$[\![\#Q_0\underline{TQ_2};\ {+}7{*}(3{+}5)\$;\ 2,\$]\!]$	$REDUCE(E \rightarrow T)$
$[\![\#Q_0EQ_1;\ {+}7{*}(3{+}5)\$;\ 2,\$]\!]$	*SHIFT*
$[\![\#Q_0EQ_1{+}Q_6;\ 7{*}(3{+}5)\$;\ {+},2,\$]\!]$	*SHIFT*
$[\![\#Q_0EQ_1{+}Q_6\underline{7Q_5};\ {*}(3{+}5)\$;\ 7,{+},2,\$]\!]$	$REDUCE(F \rightarrow a)\ a = 7$
$[\![\#Q_0EQ_1{+}Q_6\underline{FQ_3};\ {*}(3{+}5)\$;\ 7,{+},2,\$]\!]$	$REDUCE(T \rightarrow F)$

CONFIGURATION OF THE PARSER	ACTION TAKEN
$[\![\#Q_0EQ_1+Q_6TQ_9;\ \ *(3+5)\$;\ \ 7,+,2,\$]\!]$	*SHIFT*
$[\![\#Q_0EQ_1+Q_6TQ_9*Q_7;\ \ (3+5)\$;\ \ *,7,+,2,\$]\!]$	*SHIFT*
$[\![\#Q_0EQ_1+Q_6TQ_9*Q_7(Q_4;\ \ 3+5)\$;\ \ (,*,7,+,2,\$]\!]$	*SHIFT*
$[\![\#Q_0EQ_1+Q_6TQ_9*Q_7(Q_4\underline{3Q_5};\ \ +5)\$;\ \ 3,(,*,7,+,2,\$]\!]$	$REDUCE(F \to a)\ a = 3$
$[\![\#Q_0EQ_1+Q_6TQ_9*Q_7(Q_4\underline{FQ_3};\ \ +5)\$;\ \ 3,(,*,7,+,2,\$]\!]$	$REDUCE(T \to F)$
$[\![\#Q_0EQ_1+Q_6TQ_9*Q_7(Q_4\underline{TQ_2};\ \ +5)\$;\ \ 3,(,*,7,+,2,\$]\!]$	$REDUCE(E \to T)$
$[\![\#Q_0EQ_1+Q_6TQ_9*Q_7(Q_4EQ_8;\ \ +5)\$;\ \ 3,(,*,7,+,2,\$]\!]$	*SHIFT*
$[\![\#Q_0EQ_1+Q_6TQ_9*Q_7(Q_4EQ_8+Q_6;\ \ 5)\$;\ \ +,3,(,*,7,+,2,\$]\!]$	*SHIFT*
$[\![\#Q_0EQ_1+Q_6TQ_9*Q_7(Q_4EQ_8+Q_6\underline{5Q_5};\ \ )\$;\ \ 5,+,3,(,*,7,+,2,\$]\!]$	$REDUCE(F \to a)\ a = 5$
$[\![\#Q_0EQ_1+Q_6TQ_9*Q_7(Q_4EQ_8+Q_6\underline{FQ_3};\ \ )\$;\ \ 5,+,3,(,*,7,+,2,\$]\!]$	$REDUCE(T \to F)$
$[\![\#Q_0EQ_1+Q_6TQ_9*Q_7(Q_4\underline{EQ_8+Q_6TQ_3};\ \ )\$;\ \ \underline{5,+,3},(,*,7,+,2,\$]\!]$	$REDUCE(E \to E + T)$
$[\![\#Q_0EQ_1+Q_6TQ_9*Q_7(Q_4EQ_8;\ \ )\$;\ \ 8,(,*,7,+,2,\$]\!]$	*SHIFT*
$[\![\#Q_0EQ_1+Q_6TQ_9*Q_7\underline{(Q_4EQ_8)Q_{11}};\ \ \$;\ \ \underline{),8,(},*,7,+,2,\$]\!]$	$REDUCE(F \to (\ E\ ))$
$[\![\#Q_0EQ_1+Q_6\underline{TQ_9*Q_7FQ_{10}};\ \ \$;\ \ \underline{8,*,7},+,2,\$]\!]$	$REDUCE(T \to T * F)$
$[\![\#Q_0\underline{EQ_1+Q_6TQ_9};\ \ \$;\ \ \underline{56,+,2},\$]\!]$	$REDUCE(E \to E + T)$
$[\![\#Q_0EQ_1;\ \ \$;\ \ 58,\$]\!]$	*ACCEPT*

We see that, indeed, the top of the working stack contains the value (= 58) of the original arithmetic expression.

PROBLEMS

1. Consider the LR parser for the grammar G_0 of arithmetic expressions, as given in Figures 8.10 and 8.11. Show the movements of this parser on following strings: $\sigma_1 = a + a + a$, $\sigma_2 = (a + a * a) * a$ and $\sigma_3 = (a + a) * (a + a)$.

2. Let G be the grammar

   $$S \rightarrow A \mid C, \quad A \rightarrow AaB \mid AaC \mid B \mid a, \quad B \rightarrow Bb, \quad Cb, \quad C \rightarrow cC \mid c$$

   Find the $CLOSURE$ of the following sets of items:

   $$\{[S \rightarrow \bullet C], \ [B \rightarrow B\bullet b]\}, \ \{[A \rightarrow Aa\bullet C]\}, \ \{[A \rightarrow A\bullet aC]\}.$$

3. What is the initial state of an LR parser of the grammar in Problem 2?

4. Let G be the grammar given by

   $$S \rightarrow AB, \quad A \rightarrow aB \mid \lambda, \quad B \rightarrow bS \mid CA, \quad C \rightarrow aaB \mid b \mid \lambda$$

   a. What is the initial state Q_0 of an LR parser for G ?
   b. Calculate $GOTO(Q_0, A) = Q_1$ and $GOTO(Q_0, a) = Q_2$.
   c. What are the values of $ACTION(Q, X)$ for $Q = Q_0, Q_1, Q_2$ and $x \in \Sigma$?

Construct an LR parser for each grammar in Problems 5–8. Which of these grammars are $LR(0)$?

5. $E \rightarrow E + E \mid E * E \mid (E) \mid a$
6. $S \rightarrow xSyS \mid xS \mid z$
7. $E \rightarrow E+T \mid T, \quad T \rightarrow TF \mid F, \quad F \rightarrow F^* \mid (E) \mid a \mid b \mid c$
8. $S \rightarrow A \mid aB, \quad A \rightarrow BC \mid \lambda, \quad B \rightarrow Bb \mid C, \quad C \rightarrow Cc \mid cS$

CHAPTER 9

THEORY OF COMPUTATION

In this chapter we will give a brief introduction to certain theoretical aspects of computation. Some of this has already been done done in Chapter 5, when we discussed Turing machines. We will now examine more closely the intuitive notions of *algorithm*, *effective computability*, *computable functions*, etc. In Chapter 5 we equated effective computability with Turing machines (Church-Turing thesis). This was perfectly satisfactory from a formal point of view, but it needs some elaborating. When we speak loosely that a function is effectively computable, the Turing machine is not the only thing that comes to mind. What we usually think of is that there is some well-defined procedure that, when followed, will calculate the given function. We will formalize this intuitive notion and make it precise, and then show that it is indeed equivalent to computability by means of Turing machines. We will also show that the concept of effective computability can be made precise by means of grammars. Finally, we will consider again some of the undecidable problems.

9.1. RECURSIVE FUNCTIONS

We consider only the functions f defined for nonnegative integers, whose values are also nonnegative integers ($f\colon \mathbb{N} \times \mathbb{N} \times \cdots \times \mathbb{N} \mapsto \mathbb{N}$). For notational convenience we will denote a generic k-tuple $(n_1, n_2, \ldots, n_k)$ of integers by $\bar{n}$. A function f of k variables (i.e., $f\colon \mathbb{N}^k \mapsto \mathbb{N}$) will be called a **k-*place*** function. An intuitive, naive idea that a function can be effectively computed is as follows. First of all, there are some simple functions that are obviously computable, functions such as $f(n_1, n_2) = n_1$, $f(n) = 0$ for all n, etc. Secondly, given several computable functions, their simple combinations are also computable. We now proceed to formalize these concepts. To this end, it is quite convenient to extend the definition of a function and allow for the possibility that a function is not defined for all of its arguments. We say that a function $\varphi: A \rightarrow B$ is ***partial*** if $\varphi(a)$ is defined only for certain values $a \in A$. We say that φ is ***total*** if $\varphi(a)$ is defined for all values $a \in A$. For example, the function $\psi_1: \mathbb{N} \mapsto \mathbb{N}$ given by $\psi(n) = n^2$ is total. On the other hand, the function $\psi_2(n) = \sqrt{n}$ is a partial function (as a function from $\mathbb{N}$ to $\mathbb{N}$). It is defined only for $n = 0, 1, 4, 9, 16, \ldots$.

Definition 9.1. Suppose $f(n_1, n_2, \ldots, n_k)$ is a function of k variables ($f: \mathbb{N}^k \mapsto \mathbb{N}$) and $g_1, g_2, \ldots, g_k$ are k functions, each of m variables. ($g_i: \mathbb{N}^m \mapsto \mathbb{N}$, $i = 1, 2, \ldots, k$). The ***composition*** of f and $(g_1, g_2, \ldots, g_k)$ is defined to be the function

$$F(n_1, \ldots, n_m) = f(g_1(n_1, \ldots, n_m), \ldots, g_k(n_1, \ldots, n_m))$$

We denote this by $F = f \circ (g_1, g_2, \ldots, g_k)$. Clearly $F: \mathbb{N}^m \mapsto \mathbb{N}$.

For example, if $f(n_1, n_2, n_3) = n_1 + 2n_2 + (n_1 + n_3)^2$ is a function of three variables, and $g_1(n_1, n_2) = n_1 n_2$, $g_2(n_1, n_2) = n_1 + 2n_2$, and $g_3(n_1, n_2) = n_1^2 + 3n_1n_2$ are three functions of two variables each, then the function $F = f \circ (g_1, g_2, g_3)$ is a function of two variables given by

$$\begin{aligned} F(\bar{n}) &= g_1(\bar{n}) + 2g_2(\bar{n}) + (g_1(\bar{n}) + g_3(\bar{n}))^2 \\ &= n_1n_2 + 2(n_1 + 2n_2) + (n_1n_2 + n_1^2 + 3n_1n_2)^2 \end{aligned}$$

where $\bar{n} = (n_1, n_2)$. Intuitively, a composition of computable functions is computable, and our precise definition of computability should reflect this.

Definition 9.2. Let $f(n_1, n_2, \ldots, n_k)$ and $g(n_1, n_2, \ldots, n_k, n_{k+1}, n_{k+2})$ be two functions of k and $k + 2$ variables, respectively. We say that the function $F(n_1, n_2, \ldots, n_k, n_{k+1})$ is obtained from f and g by ***primitive recursion*** if

1. $F(n_1, \ldots, n_k, 0) = f(n_1, \ldots, n_k)$
2. $F(n_1, \ldots, n_k, j + 1) = g(n_1, \ldots, n_k, j, F(n_1, \ldots, n_k, j))$

The variable j is called the ***recursive variable*** and the n_i's are called ***parameters.***

The point here is that we define the function F inductively. Condition 1 defines the function $F(n_1, \ldots, n_k, j)$ for $j = 0$, and condition 2 describes a method of calculating $F(n_1, \ldots, n_k, j+1)$, provided the value $F(n_1, \ldots, n_k, j)$ is known. (And, of course, we know how to compute the functions f and g.)

Example 9.1. Let $f(n_1) = 2n_1$ and let $g(n_1, n_2, n_3) = n_1 + n_2 + n_3^2$, so that $k = 1$. The primitive recursion defines now a function F of two variables as follows:

$$
\begin{aligned}
F(n_1, 0) &= 2\,n_1 \\
F(n_1, 1) &= n_1 + 0 + (F(n_1, 0)^2 \\
&= n_1 + (2\,n_1)^2 = n_1 + 4\,n_1^2 \quad (j = 0) \\
F(n_1, 2) &= n_1 + 1 + (F(n_1, 1))^2 \\
&= n_1 + 1 + (n_1 + 4\,n_1^2)^2 \quad (j = 1) \\
F(n_1, 3) &= n_1 + 2 + (F(n_1, 2))^2 \\
&= n_1 + 2 + (n_1 + 1 + n_1^2 + 8\,n_1^3 + 16\,n_1^4)^2 \quad (j = 2)
\end{aligned}
$$

and so on. It is clear that the value of $F(n_1, j)$ can be calculated for any n_1 and j. For instance,

$$
\begin{aligned}
F(1, 0) &= 2 \\
F(1, 1) &= 1 + 0 + (F(1, 0))^2 = 5 \\
F(1, 2) &= 1 + 1 + (F(1, 1))^2 = 27 \\
F(1, 3) &= 1 + 2 + (F(1, 2))^2 = 732 \\
F(1, 4) &= 1 + 3 + (F(1, 3))^2 = 535828
\end{aligned}
$$

and so on.

It is quite clear that very complicated functions can be built up from very simple functions using a primitive recursion and each such function conforms to our intuition of being effectively computable. We have to begin, of course, with some simple functions that are computable by definition. We define the ***basic primitive functions*** to be very simple indeed:

1. The ***zero function*** $Z(n) = 0$ for all $n \in \mathbb{N}$
2. The ***successor function*** $S(n) = n + 1$
3. The ***projection functions*** $\pi_k^{(j)} : \mathbb{N}^k \mapsto \mathbb{N}$ defined by

$$\pi_k^{(j)}(n_1, \ldots, n_k) = n_j \quad 1 \leq j \leq k.$$

The function $\pi_k^{(j)}(\bar{n})$ simply assumes the value of the jth coordinate of the vector $\bar{n} = (n_1, \ldots, n_k)$. For example $\pi_4^{(3)}(3, 17, 6, 9) = 6$.

Definition 9.3. A function f is said to be ***primitive recursive*** if it can be obtained from the basic primitive functions by a finite number of applications of primitive recursion and composition (in any order).

Example 9.2. We show here that some of the familiar functions are primitive recursive. We begin with constant functions, such as $f(n_1, n_2) = 5$ for all n_1 and n_2. The function $f_0(n_1, \ldots, n_k) = 0$ is primitive recursive:

$$f_0(n_1, \ldots, n_k) = Z \circ \pi_1^{(1)}(n_1, \ldots, n_k) = Z(n_1) = 0$$

The function $f_1(\bar{n}) = 1$ is also primitive recursive: $f_1(\bar{n}) = S \circ f_0(\bar{n}) = S(f_0(\bar{n})) = S(0) = 0 + 1 = 1$. Similarly, $f_2(\bar{n}) = 2$ can be expressed as $S(f_1(\bar{n})) = S(1) = 2$. Clearly any constant function is primitive recursive.

Next, we consider the function $Add(n, m) = n + m$. The function $f(n) = n$ is primitive recursive, in fact it is a basic primitive function: $f(n) = \pi_1^{(1)}(n) = n$. The function $g(n_1, n_2, n_3) = n_3 + 1$ is also primitive recursive: $S(\pi_3^{(3)}(n_1, n_2, n_3)) = S(n_3) = n_3 + 1$. The function $Add(n, m)$ can be now obtained from f and g by primitive recursion:

$$\begin{aligned} Add(n, 0) &= f(n) = n \\ Add(n, m + 1) &= g(n, m, Add(n, m)) = Add(n, m) + 1 \end{aligned}$$

A moment of reflection should convince the reader that, indeed, $Add(n, m) = n + m$ for all n and m. For example

$$Add(3, 2) = Add(3, 1) + 1 = (Add(3, 0) + 1) + 1 = (3 + 1) + 1 = 5$$

In a similar way we show that the multiplication function $Mult(n, m) = n \cdot m$ is primitive recursive: The function $h(n_1, n_2, n_3) = n_1 + n_3$ is primitive recursive, since $h(\bar{n}) = Add(\pi_3^{(1)}(\bar{n}), \pi_3^{(2)}(\bar{n}))$. We now define $Mult(n, m)$ by primitive recursion:

$$Mult(n, 0) = Z(n) = 0$$
$$Mult(n, m+1) = h(n, m, Mult(n, m)) = n + Mult(n, m)$$

It should be clear again that this gives the correct definition of multiplication.

The notion of primitive recursive function formalizes our intuitive notion of computable functions. We have already encountered another formal definition of computable functions using the concept of a Turing machine. Recall that a function $m = f(n)$ is called Turing computable if there is a Turing machine T_f that will compute f. More precisely, such a Turing machine, when started in configuration $[\![Q_0, \#11 \ldots 1]\!]$ (i.e., in the initial state Q_0 with n 1's on the tape), will always halt in configuration $[\![H, \#11 \ldots 1]\!]$ ($f(n)$ 1's). It turns out that every primitive recursive function is Turing computable.

Theorem 9.1. Every primitive recursive function is Turing computable.

To prove this theorem one has to show the following:

1. The basic primitive recursive functions are Turing computable.
2. Compositions of Turing computable functions are Turing computable.
3. If f and g are Turing computable and F is obtained from f and g by primitive recursion, then F is also Turing computable.

Completely formal and rigorous proof of these assertions is not very difficult, but quite long and tedious. We refer the interested reader to the excellent treatise [13] for details. Here we only explain the main idea of the proof.

To construct a Turing machine for each of the basic primitive functions is quite easy, and we leave it as an exercise. Consider now the composition of two functions. As an example, suppose $f(n_1, n_2)$ is a function of two variables, whose Turing machine is T_f, and $g(n)$ and $h(n)$ are functions of one variable with corresponding Turing machines T_g and T_h. A Turing machine T_F for the composition function $F(n) = f(g_1(n), g_2(n))$ can be constructed as follows: The machine T_F, when presented with n 1's on the tape, will pass the contents of this tape to the machines T_g and T_h. When these machines are done with their calculations and return the appropriate values, T_F will pass these values to the machine T_f which will then return the value $F(n)$. Storage of these intermediate values can be accomplished by endowing the machine T_g with more than one tape. It is easy to see that this scheme will construct a Turing machine for any composition of functions.

We next take up the primitive recursion. Again, for simplicity, assume that $f(n)$ is a function of one variable with Turing machine T_f, and $g(n_1, n_2, n_3)$ is a function of three variables and $F(m, j)$ is defined by primitive recursion as

$$F(m, 0) = f(m)$$
$$F(m, j + 1) = g(m, j, F(m, j))$$

A Turing machine T_F for the function F can be constructed as follows: T_F will have four tapes. When the input (m, j) is presented to T_F, it stores m on the first tape and j on the second tape, and enters 0 on the third tape, which will be used as a counter. It then passes the value m to the machine T_f and stores the resulting value, i.e., $f(m)$. It next compares the value of the second tape, i.e., j, with the value stored in the counter. If these are equal, $m = 0$ and $F(m, 0) = f(m)$ has been calculated. If the counter and the second tape are different, the counter is incremented and the values m, 1, and $F(m, 0)$ are passed to the machine T_g, resulting in the value $F(m, 1)$, which is stored on tape #4. The counter and the second tape are compared again. If they are equal, then $j = 1$ and $F(m, j)$ has been calculated. If they are not, the counter is incremented again and the values m, 1, and $F(m, 1)$ are passed again to T_g, which returns the value $F(m, 2)$. The process is repeated until the counter and the second tape are equal and $F(m, j)$ is calculated.

An obvious question arises as to whether every function is primitive recursive. It is actually very easy to see that this is not so. We saw in Chapter 5 (Theorem 5.3) that there are only countably many Turing machines. Since there are uncountably many functions $\mathbb{N} \mapsto \mathbb{N}$ (see Appendix 1), it follows immediately that there exist total functions which are not Turing computable and hence not primitive recursive. This argument does not, of course, give any clue as to what such a function may be. We provide here one example due to Ackermann [1]. The definition given is deceptively similar to the definition by primitive recursion, but the function is actually not primitive recursive.

Example 9.3. A function $A(n, m)$ that is not primitive recursive. This function is defined as follows:

1. $A(0, m) = m + 1$
2. $A(n + 1, 0) = A(n, 1)$
3. $A(n + 1, m + 1) = A(n, A(n + 1, m))$

We must actually show that the function $A(n, m)$ is defined for all of its arguments (i.e., that it is total). equation 1 shows that $A(0, m)$ is defined for all m's. Suppose now that $A(n, m)$ is defined for all m's; we wish to show that $A(n+1, m)$ is defined for all m's. By equation 2, $A(n + 1, 0) = A(n, 1)$ so $A(n + 1, 0)$ is defined. Assuming that $A(n + 1, m)$ is defined, Equation 3 shows that $A(n + 1, m + 1)$ is also defined. This induction within induction proves that $A(n, m)$ is defined for all n's and m's. It is remarkable how fast this function grows for even small values of its arguments. We have a rather innocuous start:

$$A(1, 0) = A(0, 1) = 2$$
$$A(1, m+1) = A(0, A(1, m)) = A(1, m) + 1$$

It follows now by induction that $A(1, m) = m + 2$. Next,

$$A(2, 0) = A(1, 1) = 3$$
$$A(2, m + 1) = A(1, A(2, m)) = A(2, m) + 2$$

and so, by induction, $A(2, m) = 2m + 3$. The values of $A(3, m)$ are still manageable:

$$A(3, 0) = A(2, 1) = 5$$
$$A(3, m + 1) = A(2, A(3, m)) = 2\,A(3, m) + 2$$

which leads to $A(3, m) = 2^{m+3} - 3$. From then on, the function A grows very fast indeed.

$$A(4, 0) = A(3, 1) = 13$$
$$A(4, m + 1) = A(3, A(4, m)) = 2^{A(4,\ m) + 3} - 3$$

Induction then gives

$$A(4, m) = 2^{2^{\cdot^{\cdot^{\cdot^{2^{16}}}}}} - 3$$

where the number of 2's in the exponent is m. It is this very fast growth of the function A that makes it not primitive recursive.

We state, without proof, the following result.

Theorem 9.2. If $f(n)$ is a one-variable primitive recursive function, then there is a positive integer i (depending on f) such that $f(i) < A(i, i)$.

Hence the function $A(n, n)$, for example, is not primitive recursive.

We have been trying to formalize a vague concept of computable functions and the primitive recursive functions are the result of this effort. Is it true, however, that they indeed represent what we want? Ackermann's function is intuitively computable, but it is not primitive recursive. Let us consider another example. Every primitive recursive function can be described completely by a finite string of symbols from the alphabet

$$\Sigma = \{Z, S, \pi, 0, 1, 2, 3, 4, 5, 6, 7, 8, 9, (,), \circ , [,], R, |\} \tag{9.1}$$

The zero function will be denoted by $[Z]$, the successor function by $[S]$, and the projection functions $\pi_k^{(j)}$ by $[\pi|k|j]$. The composition of functions f and g will be denoted by $[[f]\circ[g]]$, where $[f]$ and $[g]$ are descriptions of f and g, respectively, and the primitive recursion from functions f and g will be denoted by $[[f]\,R[g]]$. Intuitively, this encoding of primitive recursive functions is effective. For example, the function $Add(m, n)$ from Example 9.2 was obtained by primitive recursion from the functions $f(n) = n$ and $g(n_1, n_2, n_3) = n_3 + 1$. The function f was a basic primitive function $\pi_1^{(1)}$ and g was obtained by composing the successor function S and $\pi_3^{(3)}$. Thus, we encode $Add(m, n)$ as a string

$$[[\pi|1|1]\ R\ [[S]\circ[\pi|3|3]]]$$

We can thus effectively produce the list of all primitive recursive functions. We can just as easily and effectively make a list of all primitive recursive functions of one variable:

$$F_1, F_2, F_3, \ldots$$

We do this in the same way as we constructed a list of all possible

Turing machines: The set Σ from (9.1) consists of 20 symbols. For any given k, there are 20^k strings of elements from Σ that are of length k. We list all the strings of length 1, then all the strings of length 2, etc. We delete from this list all the strings that do not describe a primitive recursive functions; what remains is the list of all possible primitive recursive functions. Now define a function $G(n) = F_n(n) + 1$. It is clear that G is not on this list: $G \neq F_1$, since $G(1) \neq F_1(1)$; $G \neq F_2$ since $G(2) \neq F_2(2)$, etc. Thus G is not primitive recursive, in spite of the fact that we feel it should be included among effectively computable functions. This idea is not really new, it is just a diagonalization procedure and we have used essentially the same argument in showing that the halting problem for Turing machines is unsolvable. It is also clear that any definition of effectively computable functions, that allows one to list all such functions in a sequence will lead to the same paradox. Thus, to capture the notion of effective computability we must extend the methods used to define such functions. We present one such extension. In essence, we allow the set of computable functions to include partial functions, i.e., functions that are not defined for all possible values of their arguments.

Definition 9.4. Let $k \geq 0$ and let f be a function of $k + 1$ variables. The ***unbounded minimization*** of f is a function g of k variables such that

$$g(n_1, \ldots, n_k) = \text{The smallest } m \text{ such that } f(n_1, \ldots, n_k, m) = 0$$

We say that g is obtained from f by ***unbounded minimization*** and denote it by

$$g(\overline{n}) = \mu\ m\ [f(\overline{n}, m) = 0]$$

or, simply $g(\overline{n}) = \mu m f(\overline{n}, m)$.

Definition 9.5. A function f is said to be ***μ-recursive*** if and only if it can be obtained from the basic primitive functions (zero, successor, and projection) by a finite number of applications of composition, primitive recursion and unbounded minimization, where the process of unbounded minimization is applied only to total functions.

The μ-recursive functions need not be defined everywhere: If the function f is such that $f(\overline{n}, m) \neq 0$ then $\mu m f(\overline{n}, m)$ is not defined. In this way the diagonalization paradox is resolved: We can still list all the μ-recursive functions of one variable in a sequence $F_1, F_2, \ldots$ and define $G(n) = F_n(n) + 1$, but we cannot conclude that G is different from all the F's: If $F_n(n)$ is undefined, so is $G(n)$, and we cannot conclude that $G \neq F_n$. An argument can be made that the unbounded minimization does confirm to an intuitive concept of effective computability. If $f(\bar{n})$ is defined for all $\bar{n}$'s and one is called upon to evaluate $\mu m f(\bar{n}, m)$, one can start evaluating $f(\bar{n}, 0)$, $f(\bar{n}, 1)$, $f(\bar{n}, 2)$, etc., and wait until $f(\bar{n}, m) = 0$ for some m. The problem, of course is, that there is no way of knowing beforehand whether such m will be encountered or not. It is clear, however, that any formal definition of effectively computable function, that allows us to list all such functions in a sequence and requires that all such functions be defined everywhere, will result in some functions, which we feel should be effectively computable, not being included in this list. This is one of the main reasons why we adopt the concept of μ-recursive functions as being the formalization of the concept of effectively computable functions.

We can extend the definition of Turing computable functions to partial functions. Recall that a function $f(n)$, of one variable say, is Turing computable if a Turing machine $T = T_f$ exists such that for any n, the machine T, when started in configuration $[\![Q_0, \#11 \ldots 1]\!]$ (n 1's), will halt in configuration $[\![H, \#11 \ldots 1]\!]$ ($f(n)$ 1's).

Definition 9.6. A partial function f is said to be ***Turing computable*** if there is a Turing machine T_f that will compute the values of $f(\bar{n})$ for those $\bar{n}$'s for which $f(\bar{n})$ is defined, and will not halt for those $\bar{n}$'s for which $f(\bar{n})$ is not defined.

Thus, for example, if $f(n)$ is a function of one variable, the Turing machine T_f, when started in configuration $[\![Q_0, \#11 \ldots 1]\!]$ (n 1's), will halt in configuration $[\![H, \#11 \ldots 1]\!]$ ($f(n)$ 1's) for those n's for which $f(n)$ is defined, and go into an infinite loop for other n's. It turns out that the μ-recursive functions are Turing computable. For a complete, formal proof we refer the reader to [13], here we only present the main idea. Since the primitive recursive functions were shown to be Turing computable (Theorem 9.1) it is enough to show that if $f(\bar{n}, m)$ is Turing computable, then so is $g(\bar{n}, m) = \mu m f(\bar{n}, m)$. To construct a Turing machine for T_g from the machine of T_f we proceed as follows: The machine T_g will have two tapes. When T_g is called upon to evaluate $g(\bar{n})$, it places the argument $\bar{n}$ in the first tape and the number 0 in the second tape. It then passes the values of $\bar{n}$ and 0 to T_f and waits for it to complete the calculation. If T_f returns 0, T_g also returns 0. If T_f returns anything else, T_g increments the value 0 on the second tape to 1, and passes the values $(\bar{n}, 1)$ to T_f; T_f the proceeds to evaluate $f(\bar{n}, 1)$. If the result is 0, this is passed back to T_g, which returns the value 1. If the result not 0, the second tape is incremented to 2, and the value $(\bar{n}, 2)$ is passed to T_f. The process is repeated until the value m such that $f(\bar{n}, m)$

$= 0$ is obtained, if m exists. The machine T_g may not halt, of course—it may happen that there is no m such that $f(\overline{n}, m) = 0$. However, if $g(\overline{n})$ is defined, T_g will find its value. We thus have the following theorem:

Theorem 9.3. Every μ-recursive function is Turing computable.

It turns out that the converse of this theorem is also true.

Theorem 9.4. Every Turing computable function is μ-recursive.

The proof of Theorem 9.4. is beyond the scope of this book; the reader is referred to an excellent presentation of this proof in [8]. We will now turn our attention to the concept of computation using grammars.

9.2. GRAMMATICAL COMPUTATIONS

When talking about functions, we need not restrict our attention to numerical functions. For example, let Δ be a finite set and let Δ^* denote the set of all strings of elements of Δ. A function f: $\Delta^* \mapsto \Delta^*$ is a rule that assigns to every string $\sigma \in \Delta^*$ another string $f(\sigma)$. (The seemingly more general version of f: $\Delta_1^* \mapsto \Delta_2^*$ can be viewed as a special case of this by taking $\Delta = \Delta_1 \cup \Delta_2$.) We would like to make precise the notion that functions such as these are effectively computable. One obvious way is to say that a function f: $\Delta^* \mapsto \Delta^*$ is effectively computable if there is a Turing machine that will simulate the function f. Such a Turing machine would have as its tape alphabet the set Δ and will mimic the function f—when started in configuration $[\![Q_0, \sigma]\!]$ it will halt in configuration $[\![H, f(\sigma)]\!]$. Another way to view such functions is to consider them as string transformations by means of a grammar. To say that a function f: $\Delta^* \mapsto \Delta^*$ is grammatically computable is to say that there is a grammar $G = \{\Sigma, N, S, P\}$ such that $\Delta = \Sigma \cup N$ and such that $f(\sigma) = \tau$ if and only if the string τ is derivable from σ using the rules of this grammar. It turns out that these concepts are equivalent, if we take our grammars to be of Chomsky type-0. We now formalize these concepts.

Recall from Chapter 1 that a grammar G of type-0 consists of a finite set Σ, the elements of which are called terminals; a finite set N of nonterminals, with $\Sigma \cap N = \emptyset$; the start symbol $S \in N$; and a collection of production rules of the form $u \rightarrow v$, where $u \neq \lambda$ and v are strings of terminals and nonterminals (u, $v \in (\Sigma \cup N)^*$). If $\sigma = \alpha u \beta$ is a sentential form (again, a string of terminals or nonterminals) then we may replace u by v and obtain the string $\alpha v \beta$. We denote this by $\alpha u \beta \Rightarrow \alpha v \beta$ and say that $\alpha v \beta$ is immediately derivable from $\alpha u \beta$ using the production $u \rightarrow v$. If $\sigma_1, \sigma_2, \ldots, \sigma_n$ is a sequence of sentential forms such that

$$\sigma_1 \Rightarrow \sigma_2 \Rightarrow \cdots \Rightarrow \sigma_n$$

we say that σ_n is derivable from σ_1 and denote this by $\sigma_1 \Rightarrow^* \sigma_n$.

Grammars of type-0 are considerably more powerful than the context-free grammars. Here is an example of such a grammar which, generates the language $L = \{a^n b^n c^n \mid n = 0, 1, 2, \ldots\}$ that was shown not to have a context free grammar (see Chapter 4, p. 138).

Example 9.4. Let G be the grammar

$$\begin{aligned} S &\rightarrow aAbc \mid \lambda \\ A &\rightarrow aAbC \mid \lambda \\ Cb &\rightarrow bC \\ Cc &\rightarrow cc \end{aligned}$$

The grammar G generates the language $L = \{a^n b^n c^n \mid n = 0, 1, 2, \ldots\}$. Indeed, the production $S \rightarrow \lambda$ insures that $\lambda \in L$, as it should. When the production $S \rightarrow aAbc$ is applied, followed by $n - 1$ applications of the production $A \rightarrow aAbC$, the resulting sentential form will have form $a^n A\sigma$ where σ consists of equal number of C's and b's. The production $Cb \rightarrow bC$ will then "slide" the C's to the right past all the b's, and repeated application of $Cc \rightarrow cc$ and $A \rightarrow \lambda$ will produce the desired string. It is also clear that the only strings of terminals that can be derived from the start symbol S are of the form $a^n b^n c^n$.

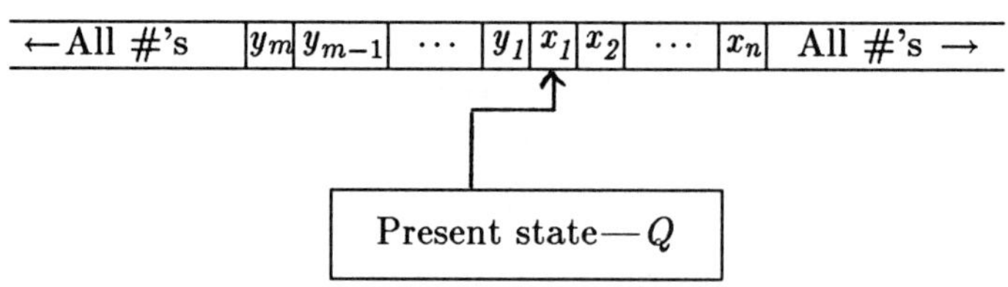

Figure 9.1. Turing machine in configuration $[\![y_m \ldots y_1 Q x_1 \ldots x_n]\!]$.

We now show that any Turing machine can be simulated by a type-0 grammar. For convenience, we assume that such a Turing machine has its tape extending indefinitely to the left and to the right. We will revise slightly the notation for instantaneous description of a Turing machine, i.e., configuration. If at some moment the machine T looks as in Figure 9.1, we denote this configuration by

$$[\![y_m y_{m-1} \dots y_1 Q x_1 x_2 \dots x_n]\!]. \tag{9.2}$$

This means that the current state of T is Q, the reading head points to x_1, and the tape is blank to the left of y_m and to the right of x_n. Such a configuration was denoted by $[\![Q,\ y_m \dots y_1 \underline{x_1} \dots x_n]\!]$ in Chapter 5. The sentential forms of our grammar G will be strings of the form (9.2). The productions of the grammar G will have to simulate the movements of the machine T. This means, for example, that if the machine is in configuration $[\![adQ_3cdd]\!]$ and $\delta(Q_3,\ c) = (Q_5,\ a,\ R)$—that is the symbol c under the head is replaced by a, the head moves one cell to the right and the new state is Q_5—the grammar G should transform the string $[\![adQ_3cdd]\!]$ into $[\![adaQ_5dd]\!]$. This can be done by having a production

$$Q_3c \rightarrow aQ_5$$

in the grammar G. Thus, each transition of the Turing machine will generate a corresponding production of the grammar. The precise description of the entire process is as follows: Let $T = \{\mathbb{Q},\ \Sigma,\ Q_0,\ \delta\}$ be a Turing machine whose set of states is $\mathbb{Q}$, with initial state Q_0, whose tape alphabet is Σ; and whose transition function is δ. We assume that the symbols R, L, S (for right, left and stay) are not in Σ. We further assume that the delimiters $[\![$ and $]\!]$ are also not in Σ. The set Δ of terminals for corresponding grammar G will be $\Sigma \cup \{[\![,\ ]\!]\}$, and the nonterminals will be the states of T. The start symbol will be the state Q_0, and the productions will be as follows:

1. For every transition rule $\delta(Q,\ a) = (Q',\ b,\ S)$, include in G the production $Qa \rightarrow Q'b$.
2. For every transition $\delta(Q,\ a) = (Q',\ b,\ R)$ include in G all the productions of the form $Qax \rightarrow bQ'x$ for all $x \in \Sigma$, and the production $Qa]\!] \rightarrow bQ'\#]\!]$. This last production is needed in case the reading head of T points to the rightmost non-blank symbol of the tape and the instructions call for moving the head to the right.
3. For every transition of the form $\delta(Q,\ a) = (Q',\ b,\ L)$, include in G all the productions of the form $xQa \rightarrow Q'xb$ for all x's in Σ and the production $[\![Qa \rightarrow [\![Q'\#b$.
4. Include in G the production $H \rightarrow \lambda$, where H is the halting state of T.

It should be clear that if the machine T transforms string σ into a string

τ (i.e., it moves from configuration $[\![Q_0, \sigma]\!]$, with the head pointing to the leftmost symbol of, say σ, to the configuration $[\![H, \tau]\!]$) then it is possible to derive, in the grammar G, the sentential form $[\![\tau]\!]$ from the sentential form $[\![Q_0\sigma]\!]$: $[\![Q_0\sigma]\!] \Rightarrow^* [\![\tau]\!]$.

Example 9.5. Consider, for example, a simple Turing machine that, when presented with a string of a's and b's (with no blanks in between), will place an additional a at the right end of the string and an additional b at the left end of the string. The transitions of such a machine are as follows:

1. $\delta(Q_0, a) = (Q_0, a, R)$, $\delta(Q_0, b) = (Q_0, b, R)$—this moves the head to the right end of the string.
2. $\delta(Q_0, \#) = (Q_1, a, S)$—the right end of the string is detected.
3. $\delta(Q_1, x) = (Q_1, x, L)$ for $x = a, b$—the head moves to the left end of the string.
4. $\delta(Q_1, \#) = (H, b)$—symbol b is placed at the left end of the string.

The corresponding productions of the grammar G are as follows:

1. $Q_0aa \rightarrow aQ_0a, \quad Q_0ab \rightarrow aQ_0b, \quad Q_0a]\!] \rightarrow aQ_0\#]\!]$
2. $Q_0\# \rightarrow Q_1a$
3. $aQ_1 \rightarrow Q_1a, \quad bQ_1 \rightarrow Q_1b, \quad [\![Q_1 \rightarrow [\![Q_1\#$
4. $Q_1\# \rightarrow Hb$
5. $H \rightarrow \lambda$

The movements of the machine T on input $\sigma = aaba$ are

$$[\![Q_0aaba]\!] \rightarrow [\![aQ_0aba]\!] \rightarrow [\![aaQ_0ba]\!] \rightarrow [\![aabQ_0a]\!] \rightarrow [\![aabaQ_0\#]\!]$$
$$\rightarrow [\![aabaQ_1a]\!] \rightarrow [\![aabQ_1aa]\!] \rightarrow [\![aabQ_1aa]\!] \rightarrow [\![aaQ_1baa]\!]$$
$$\rightarrow [\![aQ_1abaa]\!] \rightarrow [\![Q_1aabaa]\!] \rightarrow [\![Q_1\#aabaa]\!] \rightarrow [\![Hbaabaa]\!]$$

The derivation in G is almost identical, with $\rightarrow$ replaced by $\Rightarrow$,

$$[\![Q_0aaba]\!] \Rightarrow [\![aQ_0aba]\!] \Rightarrow [\![aaQ_0ba]\!] \Rightarrow [\![aabQ_0a]\!] \Rightarrow [\![aabaQ_0\#]\!]$$
$$\Rightarrow [\![aabaQ_1a]\!] \Rightarrow [\![aabQ_1aa]\!] \Rightarrow [\![aabQ_1aa]\!] \Rightarrow [\![aaQ_1baa]\!]$$
$$\Rightarrow [\![aQ_1abaa]\!] \Rightarrow [\![Q_1aabaa]\!] \Rightarrow [\![Q_1\#aabaa]\!] \Rightarrow [\![Hbaabaa]\!]$$
$$\Rightarrow [\![baabaa]\!].$$

Definition 9.7. Let Δ be a finite set. We say that a function f: $\Delta^* \mapsto \Delta^*$ is ***grammatically computable*** if there is a type-0 grammar G such that $\tau = f(\sigma)$ if and only if τ is derivable from σ in the grammar G.

The foregoing discussion shows the following:

Theorem 9.5. Any Turing computable function is grammatically computable.

Given a Turing machine T, the grammar G constructed above does not have the property that $\sigma \Rightarrow^* \tau$ if and only if T transforms σ into τ, but the exact formal proof can be constructed using arguments and constructions along the indicated lines.

We show next that given a type-0 grammar G, there is a Turing machine T that will simulate derivations in G. More precisely, if $G = \{\Sigma, N, S, P\}$, the language $L(G)$ is defined to be the set of strings $\sigma \in \Sigma^*$ that are derivable from the start symbol S. We will show how to construct a Turing machine T that, when started in the initial state Q_0 with a string $\sigma \in \Sigma^*$ on its tape, will halt whenever $\sigma \in L(G)$. It will not necessarily always halt; in particular it need not halt when σ is not in the language—issues that we will discuss later in the chapter.

First of all, suppose we are given a tape (of some Turing machine T) that contains a string of the form $\sigma = \alpha u \beta$ and we are given another string, say v. There exists a Turing machine $T(u, v)$ that will replace u in the string σ with v, resulting in a string $\tau = \alpha v \beta$. Such a machine $T(u, v)$ will have three tapes. It will copy the string $\alpha u \beta$ onto the first tape. It will then copy the substring α onto the second tape and the string β onto the third tape. It will then erase the first tape, copy α back onto the first tape, then copy v, then β. The first tape will then contain the string $\alpha v \beta$. The exact details are not that important.

Now let $G = \{\Sigma, N, S, P\}$ be a type-0 grammar. The machine $T = T_G$, which will simulate the derivations of G, will be a nondeterministic machine as follows: It will have two tapes and will have at its disposal all the Turing machines $T(u, v)$, as described above, for all possible productions $u \to v$ of the grammar G. Given now a string $\sigma \in L(G)$, it will place σ on the first tape and then simulate the derivation of σ on the second tape as follows. Suppose the derivation of σ in G has the form

$$\begin{aligned} S \Rightarrow\ & \sigma_1 = \alpha_1 u_1 \beta_1 \Rightarrow \\ & \sigma_2 = \alpha_1 v_1 \beta_1 = \alpha_2 u_2 \beta_2 \Rightarrow \\ & \sigma_3 = \alpha_2 v_2 \beta_2 = \alpha_3 u_3 \beta_3 \Rightarrow \end{aligned}$$

$$\sigma_4 = \alpha_3 v_3 \beta_3 = \alpha_4 u_4 \beta_4 \Rightarrow$$
$$\vdots$$
$$\sigma_n = \alpha_{n-1} v_{n-1} \beta_{n-1} = \alpha_n u_n \beta_n \Rightarrow$$
$$\alpha_n v_n \beta_n = \sigma$$

where the string $\sigma_{i+1} = \alpha_i v_i \beta_i$ was derived from the string $\sigma_i = \alpha_i u_i \beta_i$ by applying production $u_i \rightarrow v_i$. The machine T will place the start symbol S on the second tape and begin a sequence of transformations of the content of this second tape as follows: At each step, the content of the second tape is compared with the content of the first tape. If these two tapes are identical, T halts. If the tapes are different, then the content of the second tape, say σ, is written as $\sigma = \alpha u \beta$, where u is the left-hand side of some production $u \rightarrow v$ in the grammar G. (There may be many such ways of writing σ and several available productions; T chooses one of them in a nondeterministic way.) The content of the second tape is then passed to the machine $T(u, v)$, described above, which transforms the content of the second tape into $\alpha v \beta$. The process is then repeated. It is clear that if a string σ is in the language $L(G)$, then there is a sequence of choices for T that, when started with the string σ on tape, will cause T to halt. Conversely, it is also clear that if T will halt on some input σ and some choice of moves, then the string σ is in the language $L(G)$. The derivation of σ can be deduced from the movements of T. This gives a rough sketch of the proof of the following theorem:

Theorem 9.6. Any grammatically computable function is also Turing computable.

Combining this result with Theorem 9.5, we see that the computational power of Turing machines and grammatically computable functions is the same. We now turn our attention to the connection between grammatically computable functions and μ-recursive functions.

9.3. GÖDEL NUMBERING

Let Δ be a finite set and let f: $\Delta^* \mapsto \Delta^*$ be a function that transforms strings σ from Δ^* into strings $f(\sigma)$, again from Δ^*. It turns out that every such function can be uniquely described by a function f': $\mathbb{N} \mapsto \mathbb{N}$. Moreover, f is grammatically computable if and only if the corresponding function f' is μ-recursive. We describe some of the basic ideas behind these assertions.

To represent a string function f by a numerical function f' we only need to represent the strings themselves by numbers. The scheme for doing this was first presented by K. Gödel [11], we give here one of the variants of the method. When the set Δ (the alphabet) consists of only one symbol, say a, the representation of strings from Δ^* by a number is easy enough: Any such string is of the form $\sigma = aa \ldots a$ (n times). We then represent this string by the number n. We may therefore assume that the set Δ has more than one element, and we seek an explicit function $\gamma\colon \Delta^* \mapsto \mathbb{N}$ that is one-to-one. Let Δ consist of δ elements, which we arbitrarily enumerate as $\Delta = \{a_1, a_2, \ldots, a_\delta\}$ and put $b = \delta + 1$. For strings of length 1, define the function γ by $\gamma(a_j) = j$. Each string $\sigma = \epsilon_1\epsilon_2 \ldots \epsilon_n$ from Δ^* can be now interpreted as an integer in base b notation, we denote this integer by $\gamma(\sigma)$:

$$\gamma(\sigma) = k_1 b^{n-1} + k_2 b^{n-2} + \cdots + k_{n-2} b^2 + k_{n-1} b^1 + k_n \qquad (9.3)$$

where $k_j = \gamma(\epsilon_j)$. When $\sigma = \lambda$, we define $\gamma(\lambda) = 0$. It is entirely clear that this mapping is one-to-one, i.e., the string σ is completely determined by the value $\gamma(\sigma)$—provided the initial enumeration of the elements of Δ is agreed upon.

Example 9.5. Suppose $\Delta = \{a, b, c, d\}$. We arbitrarily assign the values of γ to a, b, c, d by

$$\gamma(a) = 1 \quad \gamma(b) = 2 \quad \gamma(c) = 3 \quad \gamma(d) = 4$$

The number $\gamma(\sigma)$ associated to each string σ from Δ^* is then completely determined. Indeed, in this case $\delta = 4$, so $b = 5$ and if $\sigma = \epsilon_1\epsilon_2 \ldots \epsilon_n$, then, in accordance with (9.3)

$$\gamma(\sigma) = \gamma(\epsilon_1)5^{n-1} + \gamma(\epsilon_2)5^{n-2} + \cdots + \gamma(\epsilon_{n-1})5^1 + \gamma(\epsilon_n)$$

For example,

$$\gamma(aab) = \gamma(a)5^2 + \gamma(a)5^1 + \gamma(c) = (113)_{\text{base } 5} = 33$$
$$\gamma(cdab) = \gamma(c)5^3 + \gamma(d)5^2 + \gamma(a)5^1 + \gamma(b) = 482\ , \text{etc.}$$

It is clear that each string σ is uniquely described by its Gödel number $\gamma(\sigma)$; for example, to find the unique string σ for which $\gamma(\sigma) = 87$, we express 87 in base 5 as $87 = 3 \cdot 5^2 + 2 \cdot 5 + 2 = (322)_{\text{base } 5}$, from which we conclude that $\sigma = cbb$.

The function $\gamma: \Delta^* \mapsto \Delta^*$ defined above is not onto, but is one-to-one. For example, there is no string σ in Example 9.5 for which $\gamma(\sigma) = 76$. This is because $76 = 3 \cdot 5^2 + 0 \cdot 5^1 + 1$, and there is no symbol x in the set Δ for which $\gamma(x) = 0$. Hence, if we define the inverse function γ^{-1}, this function is a partial function; it need not be defined for all integers n. ($\gamma^{-1}(n)$ is the string σ such that $\gamma(\sigma) = n$. Given n, such a string may not exist, if it does exist; however, it is unique. In Example 9.5, the value $\gamma^{-1}(76)$ is undefined.)

Now let Δ be a finite nonempty set and let γ be a Gödel numbering of the strings from Δ^*. For a string σ, the number $\gamma(\sigma)$ will be called the ***Gödel number*** of σ. If $f: \Delta^* \mapsto \Delta^*$ is now a function that transforms the strings from Δ^* to other strings from Δ^*, we may associate with this function a function $f': \mathbb{N} \mapsto \mathbb{N}$ by

$$f'(n) = \gamma(f(\gamma^{-1}(n)) \tag{9.4}$$

The function f is, in general, a partial function, it is defined only for those n's for which $\gamma^{-1}(n)$ is defined.

Example 9.6. Consider the set $\Delta = \{a, b, c, d\}$ as in Example 9.5, together with the Gödel numbering function γ introduced there. Let $f: \Delta^* \mapsto \Delta^*$ be given by $f(\sigma) = \sigma^R =$ the reverse of the string σ. Thus $f(abc) = cba$, $f(cdd) = ddc$, etc. We compute here several values of the associated function f'. Consider, for example $f'(222)$. In base 5, the number 222 is expressed as $(1342)_5 = 1 \cdot 5^3 + 3 \cdot 5^2 + 4 \cdot 5 + 2$, so that $\gamma^{-1}(222) = acdb$. Next, $f(acdb) = bdca$ and $\gamma(bdca) = 2 \cdot 5^3 + 4 \cdot 5^2 + 3 \cdot 5 + 1 = 366$. Hence, $f'(266) = \gamma(f(\gamma^{-1}(222) = 366$. On the other hand, $f'(528)$ is undefined, since in base 5 the number 528 is written as $(4103)_5$, and there is no σ such that $f(\sigma) = (4103)_5$.

It turns out that there is a close connection between the concept of grammatical computability of a function f and μ-recursiveness of the corresponding function f'—as a matter of fact these two concepts turn out to be identical:

Theorem 9.7. Let $f: \Delta^* \mapsto \Delta^*$ be a function transforming strings into strings (over some finite alphabet Δ). Then f is grammatically computable if and only if the corresponding function $f': \mathbb{N} \mapsto \mathbb{N}$, obtained from Gödel numbering as above, is μ-recursive.

We sketch here only the underlying idea of the proof, for complete details the reader is referred to [15]. It should be reasonably clear that the functions f and f' completely determine each other—if we know one, we can effectively compute the other. In fact, one can construct a Turing machine that, given a description of f, say, will calculate f', and conversely. The functions f and f' can, therefore, be viewed as two different descriptions of the same computational device. However, f is grammatically computable if and only if it is Turing computable (Theorems 9.5 and 9.6) and this, in turn, happens if and only if the function is μ-recursive.

We have thus established that, as far as their computational powers are concerned, the concepts of μ-recursive functions, grammatical computations, and Turing machines are all equivalent. It is this equivalence that is perhaps the strongest argument in favor of accepting the Church thesis, namely that the notions of effective computability and the Turing machine are one and the same. Whatever reasonable definition of effective computability one develops, it turns out to be equivalent to the concept of the Turing machine.

9.4. ENUMERABILITY

In this section we take up the issue of enumerating, or effectively listing elements of a set. Intuitively, there are some sets the elements of which can be effectively written out. For example, if S is a set of all positive even integers, one can start listing all the elements of S:

$$2, 4, 6, 8, \ldots$$

It is clear that if a set S can be effectively enumerated, this set must be at most countable. What we would like to do is to give a precise definition of what it means to effectively enumerate elements of a set. In keeping with the spirit of the Church-Turing thesis, we say that elements of a set can be effectively enumerated if and only if this enumeration can be done by a Turing machine. The sets to be enumerated are going to be only countable sets that are subsets of Σ^* for some finite set Σ. This means that an element of a set in question can be described by a finite string of symbols from a fixed alphabet Σ^*. Thus, we consider only sets that are languages over some finite alphabet. Intuitively, such a set (language) will be considered enumerable if there is a Turing machine that will write out, one by one, all the elements of the set. Formally we have the following:

Definition 9.8. Let Σ be a finite, nonempty set and let L be a subset of Σ^*, i.e., L is a language over Σ. We say that L is ***effectively enumerable*** or ***recursively enumerable*** if there is a Turing machine T_L with the following properties:

1. The set Σ does not contain the blank symbol # of T_L.
2. The tape alphabet of T_L contains the set Σ.
3. The machine T_L has one distinguished tape, called the output tape, for which the following holds:
   a) Once a symbol has been written on the output tape, it is never erased.
   b) Only the symbols from Σ and the blank symbol # can appear on the output tape.
   c) The read-write head on the output tape can move only to the right.
4. If we start the machine T_L in the initial state with the output tape being empty, then for any element σ of L, the output tape will eventually contain a segment $\#\sigma\#$, and, conversely, if the output tape contains a fragment of the form $\#\sigma\#$, where $\sigma \in \Sigma^*$, then σ is in L.

If the language L is recursively enumerable by a Turing machine T_L as above, we also say that L is ***generated*** by T_L and denote this by $L = G(T_L)$.

What all this means is that we call a language L recursively enumerable, if there is a Turing machine that will, one by one, write all the elements of L on one of its tapes (and will not write anything else on that tape). Notice that we do not require that each element of the set be written out by the Turing machine exactly once; the list of the elements of the set produced by the Turing machine may contain duplicates. We also do not stipulate the order in which order the elements of the set are produced.

We thus have a second way of describing a language by a Turing machine. Recall that in Chapter 5 we said that a language L is recognized by a Turing machine T, if T is able to decide the membership in L of any string σ. Such languages are also called Turing decidable. Precisely speaking, this means that a Turing machine T that recognizes the language L has the following properties:

1. T halts on every input σ.
2. If T is started in the initial state Q_0 and a string σ on its tape, then T will halt with Y on its tape whenever σ is in L, and will halt with N on its tape if σ is not in L.

In other words, the machine T is able to ***decide*** whether or not a given string σ is in the language L. There is yet another way of describing a language by means of a Turing machine.

Definition 9.9. Let L be a language over a finite alphabet Σ. We say that L is ***accepted*** by a Turing machine T if the following is true:

1. T has only one tape.
2. The tape alphabet of T includes the set Σ, and the blank symbol # is not included in Σ.
3. The language L consists precisely of those σ's in Σ^* for which T, when started in the initial state Q_0 with σ on its tape, will halt.

Hence, to say that a language L is accepted by a Turing machine T is to say that L consists precisely of those strings σ that cause T to halt. Given a language L, we say that L is Turing generated, Turing recognized, or Turing accepted, if there is a Turing machine that respectively generates, recognizes, or accepts L. It turns out that the concepts of a language being Turing generated or accepted are actually equivalent, but that the concept of a language being Turing recognized is profoundly different. As a matter of fact, this difference is the essence of the undecidability of the halting problem. We now give a brief discussion of these ideas.

Theorem 9.8. Let $L = \Sigma^*$ be the language of all strings over a finite set (alphabet) Σ. Then L is recursively enumerable, Turing acceptable, and Turing recognizable.

The proof of this theorem is quite easy and we leave it as an exercise.

Theorem 9.9. A language $L \subseteq \Sigma^*$ is recursively enumerable if and only if it is Turing acceptable.

Proof. Suppose first that L is recursively enumerable by a Turing machine T_1. We wish to construct a Turing machine T_2 that will halt only on the strings generated by T_1. The machine T_2 will operate roughly as follows: When presented with an input σ it will enter the input onto its tape and then start the machine T_1. Each time T_1 produces a string τ on its output tape, σ is compared with τ. If they are equal, T_2 halts. If not, T_1 is allowed to run again, until a new string τ' is produced. (Should T_1 halt without producing σ on its output tape, T_2 continues to run—its sits idly waiting for T_1 to do something.) It is clear that, given an input string σ, T_2 will halt if and only if σ appears on the output tape of T_1. Thus, if L is recursively enumerable, it is Turing acceptable.

Suppose, conversely, that a language $L \subseteq \Sigma^*$ is Turing acceptable by a Turing machine M_1. Intuitively, a Turing machine M_2 enumerating L

can be constructed as follows. M_2 will have at its disposal the machine M_1 accepting L, as well as the machine K enumerating the language Σ^*. M_2 will take the strings $\sigma_1, \sigma_2, \ldots$, generated by K and will feed them, as they are generated, to M_1. If M_1 halts on input σ_i, M_2 will write that σ_i on its output tape. This scheme does not quite work, and has to be adjusted slightly. The trouble is that the first time K produces a string σ_{i_0} that is not in L, M_2 will pass it to M_1, which will proceed to churn on it indefinitely. Thus, M_2 will not be able to generate strings that appear past σ_{i_0} in the enumeration by K. We can fix this problem, however, as follows: We may assume, without loss of generality, that M_1, accepting the language L, never hangs (i.e., it either halts or continues to move indefinitely). This can be accomplished by assuming that M_1 has its tape extending indefinitely in both directions. We can now make M_2, generating L, operate in stages. During the kth stage, M_2 will wait for K to generate the first k strings of Σ^*, say $\sigma_1, \sigma_2, \ldots, \sigma_k$. It will then feed each one of the σ_i's, $i = 1, 2, \ldots, k$, to M_1 and wait in each instance for M_1 to execute k moves. If during these k moves M_1 halts, M_2 writes out the relevant string σ on its output tape. Thus, it takes only a finite amount of time to execute stage k. It is also clear that the only strings σ which that appear on the output tape of M_2 are those for which M_1 will halt. Hence L is generated by M_2. Q.E.D.

We have thus proved that a language L is Turing acceptable if and only if it is recursively enumerated (Turing generated). Any Turing recognizable language is also Turing accepted.

Theorem 9.10. If a language L is Turing recognizable, it is Turing generated.

Proof. The proof is actually quite simple and straightforward. Let T be a machine recognizing the language L. This means, first of all, that T halts on every input. Moreover, given a string σ, if T is started in the initial state Q_0 with σ on its tape, T will halt in the configuration $[\![H, \underline{Y}]\!]$ whenever $\sigma \in L$ and will halt in configuration $[\![H, \underline{N}]\!]$ whenever $\sigma \notin L$. To construct a Turing machine M generating the language L we proceed as follows. We start with machine K generating the language Σ^* (cf. Theorem 9.8.) For each σ generated by K, machine M feeds σ to T. If T halts in configuration $[\![H, \underline{Y}]\!]$, machine M prints σ on its output tape, otherwise T gets the next σ from K. It is clear that the only σ's appearing on the output tape of M will be those in the language L. Q.E.D.

The converse of Theorem 9.10, however, is not true. There are languages that are generated by a Turing machine, but for which there is no Turing machine that will provide a decision procedure for whether or not any given string belongs to that language. We will discuss these and other connected issues in the next section.

9.5. DECIDABILITY

We first show that there are languages which are not recursively enumerable (generated by a Turing machine). This was essentially done in Chapter 5; we repeat and amplify some of the arguments here. Recall from Section 5.5 that any Turing machine can be uniquely and completely described by a finite string of symbols from the set $\Sigma_T = \{B, A, E, P, X, Y, R, L, S, 0, 1\}$. Given a Turing machine T, its description in terms of symbols from Σ_T is denoted by $D_1(T)$. Thus, the set of all Turing machines can be viewed as a language $\mathcal{T}$ over the alphabet Σ_T. We are not going to prove all the details, but it should be intuitively clear that $\mathcal{T}$ is recursively enumerable. Indeed, a Turing machine T_0 enumerating all the Turing machines can be constructed as follows. T_0 will have at its disposal the Turing machine K_0 enumerating all the strings from Σ_T^*. It will then take each string σ presented by K_0 and examine whether or not it is a valid description of a Turing machine, as described in Section 5.5. If the description is valid, the machine T_0 writes out that string σ on its output tape.

In exactly the same way, all the initial inputs to Turing machines can be uniquely and completely described by a string from the alphabet $\Sigma_I = \{A, F, W, Z, 0, 1\}$—again as explained in Section 5.5. Given an initial input σ to a Turing machine, we denote the description of σ in terms of symbols from Σ_I by $D_2(\sigma)$. Again, we may view the set of all possible initial inputs to all possible Turing machines as a language $\mathcal{I}$ over the alphabet Σ_I^*. Just as in the case of the language $\mathcal{T}$, the language $\mathcal{I}$ is recursively enumerable.

We may thus effectively construct listings of both $\mathcal{T}$ and $\mathcal{I}$:

$$\begin{aligned} \mathcal{T} &= \{\tau_1, \tau_2, \tau_3, \ldots\} \\ \mathcal{I} &= \{\sigma_1, \sigma_2, \sigma_3, \ldots\} \end{aligned} \tag{9.5}$$

where each τ is a string over Σ_T^* and each σ is a string over Σ_I^*. Each τ, of course, is a description of some Turing machine, and each σ is a description of an input to some such machine. Now, define a language L_0 over Σ_I by

$$L_0 = \{\, \sigma_n \mid \tau_n \text{ does not halt on the input } \sigma_n\} \tag{9.6}$$

Theorem 9.11. The language L_0 defined by (9.6) is not recursively enumerable.

Proof. Suppose there exists a Turing machine T_0 that accepts L_0; that is, T_0 will halt on each input σ in L_0. The description of this Turing machine T_0 is of course listed in the enumeration of all Turing machines given in (9.5). Suppose T_0 is described by τ_{n_0}. This, however, immediately causes a contradiction as follows: Consider the string σ_{n_0}, and the question whether or not this string belongs to the language L_0. If σ_{n_0} belongs to L_0, then T_0 accepts σ_{n_0}, i.e., T_0 halts on input σ_{n_0}. The description of T_0 is, however, τ_{n_0} and by virtue of the definition of L_0, τ_{n_0} does not halt on σ_{n_0}. Hence the hypothesis that $\sigma_{n_0} \in L_0$ leads to a contradiction. But the hypothesis $\sigma_{n_0} \notin L_0$ also results in a contradiction. Indeed, if σ_{n_0} is not in L_0, this means that τ_{n_0} halts on the input of σ_{n_0}, which in turn means that σ_{n_0} is in L_0 (since τ_{n_0} is the encoding of the machine T_0 accepting L_0). Q.E.D.

Our next goal is to exhibit a language that is recursively enumerable, but is not recognized (decidable) by any Turing machine. What this entails is an example of a language L_1, the sentences of which can successively be effectively generated, but for which there is no effective algorithm that will decide for any string σ whether or not the string σ belongs to the language L_1. Again, when speaking of an effective procedure or effective algorithm we adopt the Church-Turing thesis that such a procedure or algorithm is equivalent to a Turing machine. The example we are going to provide is actually the essence of the theorem about the undecidability of the halting problem given in Chapter 5. The language L_1 to be constructed will be a combination of languages $\mathfrak{T}$ and $\mathfrak{I}$ in (9.5). The language $\mathfrak{T}$ is a language, over the alphabet Σ_T, whose sentences completely describe all possible Turing machines. Similarly, the language $\mathfrak{I}$ over the alphabet Σ_I lists all possible inputs to a Turing Machine. We choose a symbol, say \$, that is not in $\Sigma_T \cup \Sigma_I$ and define L_1 to be the language over $\Sigma_T \cup \Sigma_I \cup \{\$\}$ given by

$$L_1 = \{\tau\$\sigma \mid \tau \in \mathfrak{T},\ \sigma \in \mathfrak{I},\ \tau \text{ halts on input } \sigma\} \tag{9.7}$$

What precisely is meant by the phrase "τ halts on input σ" is that the Turing machine described by the string τ, when started in the initial state Q_0 and with the content of its tape described by the string σ, will eventually halt.

Theorem 9.12. The language L_1 given by (9.7) is recursively enumerable.

Proof. We sketch an outline of a construction of a Turing machine U that will accept the language L_1, i.e., the machine U, when presented with the string $\alpha = \tau\$\sigma$, will halt if and only if the Turing machine τ will halt on input σ. Theorem 9.9 will imply then that L_1 is, indeed, recursively enumerable. U will simulate the behavior of τ on input σ. It will have three tapes. When a string $\alpha \in \{\Sigma_T \cup \Sigma_I \cup \{\$\}\}^*$ is presented, U will first check that α is of the form $\tau\$\sigma$, where τ is a correct encoding of a Turing machine and σ is a correct encoding of a string. What this entails is that U must check that the string α is of the proper form: that there is only one symbol \$ in α; that the string τ preceding \$ is indeed an encoding of a Turing machine, as defined in Section 5.5; and that the string σ following \$ is an encoding of an initial content of a tape of a Turing machine, again as defined in Section 5.5. It is clear that these functions are purely mechanical and can be implemented by a Turing machine. If the string α is not of the proper form, U will go into an infinite loop. If, however, α is of the form $\tau\$\sigma$, the simulation of τ on the input σ begins. The string τ is entered on the first tape; the string σ on the second tape; the current state of τ and the current position of the read-write head of τ are on the third tape. (Originally, the third tape contains the encoding of the initial state of τ and the initial position of the read-write head, i.e., the encoding of the leftmost cell of the tape of τ.) U takes note of the current state of τ and the current input symbol of τ (these can be deduced from the information on the third and second tape of U); it then goes to the first tape and obtains the information of what has to be done in this situation (the new state, the movements of the head of τ, the new symbol under the read-write head, etc.). U will then make the necessary changes on the third and second tape to reflect the new configuration of τ. The procedure repeats until the encoding of τ calls for τ to halt. If that happens, U will halt. If, however, τ on input σ will never halt, then neither will U. A moment of reflection shows that, indeed, the machine U accepts the language L_1. Q.E.D.

The machine U in the proof of Theorem 9.13 can be viewed as a ***universal Turing machine*** already discussed in Section 5.5. It is called universal because it simulates the behavior of any other Turing machine.

Theorem 9.13. The language L_1 from Theorem 9.12 is not Turing decidable.

Proof. We will show that if there is a Turing machine that is capable of deciding membership in the language L_1, then the language L_0 of Theorem 9.11 is recursively enumerable. That, however, is not the case, as was shown by Theorem 9.11. Suppose then that there exists a hypothetical Turing machine A that recognizes the language L_1. In precise terms this means the following:

1. A halts on every input σ.
2. If A is started in the initial state Q_0 and a string σ on its tape, then A will halt with Y on its tape whenever σ is in L_1, and will halt with N on its tape if σ is not in L_1.

We construct a machine B that will enumerate the language L_0 as follows: B will have at its disposal two machines $T_{\mathfrak{T}}$ and $T_{\mathfrak{I}}$ enumerating the languages $\mathfrak{T}$ and $\mathfrak{I}$ respectively. At stage n of the computation $T_{\mathfrak{T}}$ and $T_{\mathfrak{I}}$ produce strings τ_n and σ_n respectively. B feeds the string $\alpha_n = \tau_n\$\sigma_n$ to the machine A and awaits whether or not the Turing machine τ_n will halt on input σ_n. (By hypothesis, such a decision is forthcoming from A in a finite amount of time.) If the answer is No, B will write the string σ_n on its output tape; if the answer, given by A, is Yes, machine B proceeds to the next stage without writing anything on its output tape. It is quite clear that B enumerates the language L_0. Q.E.D.

Theorem 9.13 provides an example of an undecidable problem. What it expresses, in precise mathematical terms, is that there is no effective procedure or an algorithm that will, given a description of a Turing machine and its initial input, determine whether or not the machine will eventually halt. In accordance with the Church-Turing thesis, we have defined the intuitive concepts of effective procedure and algorithm to be exactly those computations and procedures which can be carried out by a Turing machine. It thus becomes possible to give a rigorous proof that some problems are undecidable.

PROBLEMS

1. Let a function $f(x, y)$ be defined by the primitive recursion as follows:
   $$f(x, 0) = 2x + 1$$
   $$f(x, y + 1) = (f(x, y))^2 + x + y$$
   Calculate the values $f(2, 1)$, $f(3, 3)$, $f(1, 3)$.
2. Show that the following functions are primitive recursive:
   a. The predecessor function $prd(x)$ defined by $prd(x) = x - 1$ for $x > 0$ and $prd(0) = 0$.
   b. The factorial function $fac(x) = x!$
   c. The exponential function $exp(x, y) = x^y$.

d. $abs(x, y) = | x - y |$
e. The zero function $zer(0) = 1$ and $zer(x) = 0$ for $x > 0$.
f. $min(x, y) =$ the smaller of the numbers x and y.
g. $max\ (x, y)$

3. Let $F(n)$ be the sequence of Fibonacci numbers defined by
$$F(1) = 0, \quad F(2) = 1, \quad F(n + 2) = F(n + 1) + F(n)$$
Show that the function $F(n)$ is primitive recursive.

4. Let $A(x, y)$ be the Ackermann function defined in Example 9.3. Use induction to show the following.
a. $A(1, m) = m + 2$
b. $A(2, m) = 2m + 3$
c. $A(3, m) = 2^{m+3} - 3$
d. $A(4, m) = 2^{2^{\cdot^{\cdot^{\cdot^{2^{16}}}}}} - 3$, where the number of 2's in the exponent is m.

5. Show that the square root function $sqrt(n) = k$ if $n = k^2$, and $sqrt(n)$ is undefined for other n's, is μ-recursive function.
6. Encode the function $Mult(x, y)$ as a sequence of symbols from the set Σ defined in (9.1).
7. a. Show that the language $L = \{a^i b^j c^i d^j \mid j \geq 0\}$ is not context free.
b. Construct a type-0 grammar generating the language L.
8. Construct type-0 grammars that simulate the following Turing machines (first, formally construct the machines):
a. A machine that calculates function $f(n) = 2n$. Precisely speaking, this machine will move, in the notation of Section 9.2, from configuration $[\![\lambda Q_0 11 \ldots 1]\!]$ (n 1's) to configuration $[\![\lambda H 11 \ldots]\!]$ ($2n$ 1's).
b. A machine that, when presented with a string $\sigma \in \{a, b\}^*$, with the head on the leftmost symbol, will transform σ into the string $\sigma\sigma^R$.
9. Let $\Delta = \{a, b, c, d, e\}$. Calculate the Gödel number $\gamma(\sigma)$ of the following strings σ from Δ^*: *aadecb*, *bbdac*, *dadacb*.
10. Let γ be the Gödel numbering function from problem 9. Find the four smallest numbers n for which $\gamma^{-1}(n)$ is undefined.
11. Let Δ and γ be as in Problems 9 and 10. Define a function $f: \Delta^* \mapsto \Delta^*$ by $f(\sigma) = ab\sigma^R cd$ and let f' be the corresponding function $\mathbb{N} \mapsto \mathbb{N}$, as described in Section 9.3. Calculate $f'(n)$ for $n = 12, 2534, 856,$ and 7345.
12. Show that if a recursively enumerable language L is such that $\overline{L}$ is also recursively enumerable, then L is Turing decidable.

APPENDIX 1

SET THEORY ETIQUETTE

A.1. SETS

We take the concept of a ***set*** to be a primitive one, requiring no further definition. Other names used to denote this concept are collection, aggregate, family, etc.—they all mean the same thing. Sets consist of ***elements***, again we take this to be a primitive notion, with no definition required. Elements of a set are also called members of this set. Thus, for example, a set A may consist of three elements: a number 1, a letter b, and a symbol \$. We denote this by

$$A = \{1,\ a,\ \$\} \tag{A.1}$$

If x is an element of a set A, we denote this by $x \in A$ and if x does not belong to a set A, this is denoted by $x \notin A$. In the example above, $\$ \in A$ and $b \notin A$. A set may be described by listing its members, as in (A.1), or by the notation

$$A = \{x \mid \text{Property } x \text{ is required to posses in order to belong to } A\} \tag{A.2}$$

For example, $A = \{x \mid x \text{ is an even positive integer}\}$ describes an infinite set $A = \{2, 4, 6, \ldots\}$.

Many of the more popular sets have their own notation associated with them. Thus, for example, the set of all integers, positive or negative (or zero), is usually denoted by $\mathbb{Z}$. The set of all positive integers is denoted by $\mathbb{N}$, the set of all real numbers by $\mathbb{R}$, the set of all rational numbers (fractions or quotients of integers) by $\mathbb{Q}$, and the set of all complex numbers by $\mathbb{C}$. Sometimes this notation is modified by sub-

and/or superscript, hence $\mathbb{R}_+$ or $\mathbb{R}^+$ often denotes the set of positive real numbers, etc.

If A and B are two sets, we define

$$A \cup B = \{x \mid x \in A \text{ or } x \in B\} \quad \text{union of } A \text{ and } B$$
$$A \cap B = \{x \mid x \in A \text{ and } x \in B\} \quad \text{intersection of } A \text{ and } B.$$

These concepts extend easily to more than two sets, even to infinite families of sets: Let $\{A_\alpha \mid \alpha \in \mathcal{A}\}$ be a family of sets. (This means that for every α in set $\mathcal{A}$ we have a set A_α.) Define

$$\bigcup_{\alpha \in \mathcal{A}} A_\alpha = \{x \mid x \in A_\alpha \text{ for some } \alpha \in \mathcal{A}\} \quad \text{union of sets } A_\alpha$$

$$\bigcap_{\alpha \in \mathcal{A}} A_\alpha = \{x \mid x \in A_\alpha \text{ for every } \alpha \subset \mathcal{A}\} \quad \text{intersection of sets } A_\alpha$$

If A and B are two sets, we say that A is contained in B if every element of A is also an element of B. We denote this by $A \subseteq B$ or $B \supseteq A$. Two sets are considered to be equal if they consist of the same elements, i.e., if $A \subseteq B$ and $B \subseteq A$. If A is a set, the complement of A is a collection of elements not in A. The complement of a set A is denoted variously by $\overline{A}$, A', A^{C}, etc. When speaking of a complement of a set, it is usually understood that the elements of this complement are restricted to be of the same kind as the elements of the set. This is hard to pin down, but is usually clear from the context. More precisely, when speaking of various sets, we always assume that they are all contained in some universal set E. Thus, for instance, if $A = \{x \mid x \text{ is an even integer}\}$, then the complement $\overline{A}$ of A is understood to be the set of all odd integers, provided E is the set of all integers. Perhaps in some other circumstances the set E consists all real numbers, in which case $\overline{A}$ is more complicated. The exact nature of such a universal set is often not explicitly stated, but should be clear from the context. In any case, unless specifically so stated, the complement of the set $\mathbb{N}$ of all positive integers does not contain a heavy locomotive.

There is a special set, called an empty set, which contains no elements at all. It will always be denoted by $\emptyset$. The empty set $\emptyset$ is a subset of every set. Two sets A and B are disjoined if their intersection $A \cap B = \emptyset$.

Here some easily established facts about the unions of sets:

$$A \cup B = B \cup A \quad \text{commutativity}$$
$$A \cup (B \cup C) = (A \cup B) \cup C \quad \text{associativity}$$
$$A \cup A = A \quad \text{idempotence}$$
$$A \cup \emptyset = A$$
$$A \subseteq B \text{ if and only if } A \cup B = B$$

The basic facts about intersection are similar:

$$A \cap B = B \cap A \quad \text{commutativity}$$
$$A \cap (B \cap C) = (A \cap B) \cap C \quad \text{associativity}$$
$$A \cap A = A \quad \text{idempotence}$$
$$A \cap \emptyset = \emptyset$$
$$A \subseteq B \text{ if and only if } A \cap B = A$$

The properties relating to both the union and the intersection of sets are the distributive laws:

$$A \cap (B \cup C) = (A \cap B) \cup (A \cap C)$$
$$A \cup (B \cap C) = (A \cup B) \cap (A \cup C)$$

Let us, as an example, prove the second property above. If x belongs in the left-hand side, then x is a member of A or $B \cap C$. In the first case, x belongs to both $A \cup B$ and $A \cup C$, so it belongs to their intersection $(A \cup B) \cap (A \cup C)$. In the second case, x is in both B and C, so $x \in A \cup B$ and $x \in A \cup C$, hence x is a member of $(A \cup B) \cap (A \cup C)$. Hence, the left-hand side is contained in the right-hand side. To prove the reverse inclusion, notice that if $x \in (A \cup B)$ and $x \in (A \cup C)$, then x must belong either to A, or to both B and C. A great many of proofs of equality of sets follow this pattern.

Let E be some universal set, and let A, B, C, . . . all be subsets of E. This means that the complement of a set A, denoted by $\overline{A}$, is the collection of all x's in E that do not belong to E:

$$\overline{A} = \{x \mid x \in E \text{ but } x \notin A\}$$

With this understanding, the basic facts about complementation are as follows:

$$\overline{(\overline{A})} = A$$
$$\overline{\emptyset} = E \text{ and } \overline{E} = \emptyset$$
$$A \cap \overline{A} = \emptyset \text{ and } A \cup \overline{A} = E$$

The concepts of union, intersection, and complementation are related to each other through the so-called De Morgan laws:

$$\overline{(A \cup B)} = \bar{A} \cap \bar{B} \text{ and } \overline{(A \cap B)} = \bar{A} \cup \bar{B}$$

These laws are not restricted to pairs of sets, but hold for any collections of sets: If $\{A_\alpha \mid \alpha \in \mathcal{A}\}$ is any family of sets then

$$\overline{\bigcap_{\alpha \in \mathcal{A}} A_\alpha} = \bigcup_{\alpha \in \mathcal{A}} \bar{A}_\alpha$$

$$\overline{\bigcup_{\alpha \in \mathcal{A}} A_\alpha} = \bigcap_{\alpha \in \mathcal{A}} \bar{A}_\alpha$$

If A and B are two sets, the difference between A and B is a set, denoted by $A - B$ or $A \setminus B$, and defined by

$$A - B = \{x \mid x \in A \text{ and } x \notin B\}$$

It is easily seen that $A - B = A \cap \bar{B}$. Some of the properties of this difference are as follows:

$$A \cap (B - C) = (A \cap B) - (A \cap C),$$
$$A - (A - B) = A \cap B,$$
$$A \subseteq B \text{ if and only if } A - B = \emptyset.$$

If A is a set, we denote by $\mathfrak{P}(A)$ the set of all subsets of A. We include the empty set $\emptyset$ and the entire set A in $\mathfrak{P}(A)$. Thus, if $A = \{a, b, c\}$, the set $\mathfrak{P}(A)$ has 8 elements:

$$\mathfrak{P}(A) = \{\emptyset, \{a\}, \{b\}, \{c\}, \{a, b\}, \{a, c\}, \{b, c\}, \{a, b, c\}\}$$

The set $\mathfrak{P}(A)$ is called the ***power set*** of A. If a set A is finite and has n elements, the power set $\mathfrak{P}(A)$ has 2^n elements. Indeed, suppose $A = \{a_1, a_2, \ldots, a_n\}$. We will describe each subset B of A by a sequence $p(B) = \epsilon_1\epsilon_2 \ldots \epsilon_n$ of 0's and 1's as follows: We put $\epsilon_i = 1$ if $a_i \in B$ and $\epsilon_i = 0$ if $a_i \notin B$. Thus, if $A = \{a_1, a_2, a_3, a_4\}$ and $B = \{a_2, a_4\}$, then $p(B) = 0101$. Also $p(\emptyset) = 0000$ and $p(A) = 1111$. It is clear that the number of subsets of A and the number of sequences $\epsilon_1\epsilon_2 \ldots \epsilon_n$ of 0's and 1's are the same. On the other hand, there are exactly 2^n such sequences: There are 2 choices for ϵ_1, 2 choices for ϵ_2, etc., and all possible combinations of 0's and 1's are allowed.

If A and B are two sets, the set $A \times B$ is defined to be the set of all expressions of the form (a, b), where $a \in A$ and $b \in B$:

$$A \times B = \{(a, b) \mid a \in A, b \in B\}$$

The entity (a, b) is called an ordered pair. It should be pointed out that (a, b) is ***not*** the set consisting of a and b, and that the order is important. Thus $(a, b) \neq (b, a)$. For example, if $A = \{a, b, c\}$ and $B = \{0, 1\}$, then $A \times B = \{(a, 0), (a, 1), (b, 0), (b, 1), (c, 0), (c, 1)\}$ and $B \times A$ is the set $\{(0, a), (0, b), (0, c), (1, a), (1, b), (1, c)\}$. These are two different sets, although they have the same number of elements. The set $A \times B$ is also called ***Cartesian product*** of A and B. In a similar way, we define the Cartesian product of n sets $A_1, A_2, \ldots, A_n$ as a collection expressions $(a_1, a_2, \ldots, a_n)$, called ordered n-tuples, where each $a_i \in A_i$:

$$A_1 \times A_2 \times \ldots \times A_n = \{(a_1, a_2, \ldots, a_n) \mid a_1 \in A_1, a_2 \in A_2, \ldots, a_n \in A_n\}.$$

There is a certain amount of abuse of notation (and of concepts) associated with this notion. Suppose we have three sets A, B, and C. Then, according to what has been said, the three sets $A \times B \times C$, $(A \times B) \times C$, and $A \times (B \times C)$ are all different. Usually, however, these three sets are taken to be the same. Here are some simple properties of Cartesian products:

$$(A \cup B) \times C = (A \times C) \cup (B \times C)$$
$$(A \cap B) \times C = (A \times C) \cap (B \times C)$$
$$\text{If } A = \emptyset \text{ or } B = \emptyset \text{ then } A \times B = \emptyset.$$

The reason for the last equality is that if, say, $A = \emptyset$, then there are no ordered pairs (a, b) such that $a \in A$ and $b \in B$, since the existence of such a pair would imply that A contained an element a.

A.2. FUNCTIONS

Given two sets A and B, a function f from A to B is a rule, that associates to every element $a \in A$ a unique element $b \in B$. This element b is usually denoted by $f(a)$, but fa and af are also used. In more precise and pedantic way, a function f from A to B is a subset f of $A \times B$ with the following properties:

1. For every $a \in A$ there is a $b \in B$ such that $(a, b) \in f$.
2. If (a, b_1) and (a, b_2) are in f then $b_1 = b_2$.

Other names used for functions are: mapping, map, transformation, correspondence, etc. If f is a function from A to B, we denote this by $f: A \mapsto B$. If $f: A \mapsto B$ is a function and $a \in A$, the element of B associated to a by f is denoted by $f(a)$ and is called the value of f at a, or the image of a under f. The set A is called the domain of the function f and the set of all possible values of f is called the range of f. A function f: $A \mapsto B$ is said to be ***one-to-one*** or $1-1$ if, whenever $a_1 \neq a_2$ then $f(a_1) \neq f(a_2)$. Such functions are also called injective. A function f: $A \mapsto B$ is said to be ***onto***, if for every $b \in B$ there is an element $a \in A$ such that $f(a) = b$ (there may be more than one such a). An onto function is also called ***surjective***. A function that is both injective and surjective is called ***bijective***. If A, B, and C are sets and f: $A \times B \rightarrow C$ is a function, then this function associates an element c to every ordered pair (a, b). Strictly speaking, this should be denoted by $f((a, b)) = c$, but it is almost never done. Instead, we write $c = f(a, b)$ and say that f is a function of two variables.

A.3. CARDINALITY

We would like to be able to compare sizes of different sets. If A and B are two finite sets there is no problem. We count the number of elements in both of them and see which one has more. The situation is less clear when we deal with infinite sets. Are there more fractions than integers? more points in the plane than in the line?, more points in the line than integers? These questions are a bit more subtle than they seem at first sight.

Definition A.1. We say that two sets A and B have the same ***cardinality*** if a ono-to-one function from A onto B exists.

Thus, two sets A and B are said to have the same cardinality if there is a one-to-one correspondence between the elements of A and the elements of B.

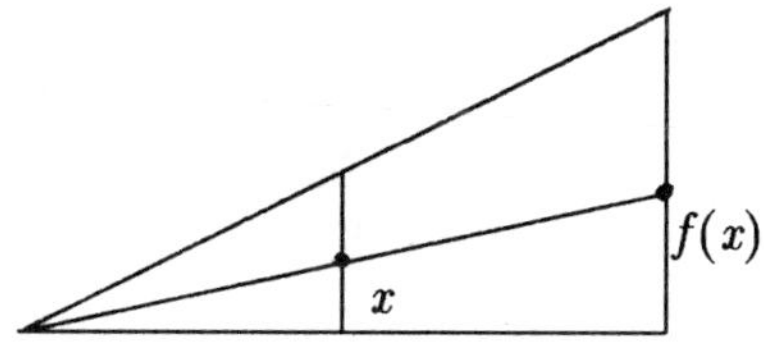

Figure A.1. Different length intervals with the same cardinality.

It is quite clear that if A and B are two finite sets, then they have the same cardinality if and only if they have the same number of elements: One cannot put 10 oranges in 9 boxes, at most one orange to a box. The subtleties arise when we start dealing with infinite sets. Thus, for example, two intervals of different length have the same cardinality, as in Figure A.1.

A proper subset of a set may also turn out to have the same cardinality as the entire set: Let $A = \mathbb{N}$ be the set of all positive integers, $\mathbb{N} = \{1, 2, 3, \ldots\}$ and let B be the set of all positive even integers, $B = \{2, 4, 6, 8, \ldots\}$. It is clear that B is properly contained in A; the cardinalities of A and B are, however, the same. The desired one-to-one onto function $f\colon A \mapsto B$ can be taken to be $f(x) = 2x$. When proving that two infinite sets have the same cardinality, the construction of a specific one-to-one correspondence is sometimes a bit cumbersome. The following intuitively obvious result is quite handy in these situations: Given two sets A and B, we say that the cardinality of A is less then or equal to the cardinality of B if there is a one-to-one mapping from A to B, or $f\colon A \mapsto B$. We denote this by $card(A) \leq card(B)$. In other words, $card(A) \leq card(B)$ if and only if A has the same cardinality as a subset of B.

Theorem A.1. (Schroeder-Bernstein). If $card(A) \leq card(B)$ and $card(B) \leq card(A)$, then $card(A) = card(B)$.

The point of the theorem is that it is often quite easy to construct one-to-one functions from one set to the other, but constructing a one-to-one function that is also onto is sometime a bit cumbersome. The theorem asserts that it can be indeed done. For the proof, see [12]. We illustrate this on some examples.

Example A.1. The set $\mathbb{N}$ of positive integers and the set $\mathbb{Q}$ of all rational numbers have the same cardinality. To construct a $1-1$ function $f\colon \mathbb{N} \mapsto \mathbb{Q}$ is quite easy, take $f(x) = x$, for example. We now construct a $1-1$ function g in the other direction—$g\colon \mathbb{Q} \mapsto \mathbb{N}$. Any rational number α can be uniquely written as $\alpha = +p/q$ or $\alpha = -p/q$, where $p > 0$, $q > 0$ and p and q have no factors in common. We also agree to represent the rational number 0 by $+0/1$. Thus, any rational number α can be thought of as a triple $\alpha = (+, p, q)$ or $(-, p, q)$, with p and q as before. It is clear that given any integer $N > 1$, there is only a finite number of rational numbers such that $p + q = N$ in this representation. We can, therefore, list all the fractions corresponding to each N:

$$N = 1: \ +\tfrac{0}{1}$$

$$N = 2: \ +\tfrac{1}{1}, -\tfrac{1}{1}$$

$$N = 3: \ +\tfrac{1}{2}, -\tfrac{1}{2}, +\tfrac{2}{1}, -\tfrac{2}{1}$$

$$N = 4: \ +\tfrac{1}{3}, -\tfrac{1}{3}, +\tfrac{3}{1}, -\tfrac{3}{1}$$

$$N = 5: \ +\tfrac{1}{4}, -\tfrac{1}{4}, +\tfrac{2}{3}, -\tfrac{2}{3}, +\tfrac{3}{2}, -\tfrac{3}{2}, +\tfrac{1}{4}, -\tfrac{1}{4}$$

and so on. We thus can make a list of all the fractions from **Q**:

$$\alpha_1, \alpha_2, \alpha_3, \ldots.$$

We first list all the fractions corresponding to $N = 1$, then all the fractions corresponding to $N = 2$, then those corresponding to $N = 3$, etc. The desired function g is then given by $g(\alpha_n) = n$—the order of listing of α_n. For instance, $f(+\frac{1}{2}) = 4$ in the above scheme.

Another way to construct the function g, perhaps a bit less intuitive but just as effective, is as follows: Express each rational α as a triple (ϵ, p, q) as before: $\epsilon = +$ or $-$, $p > 0$, $q > 0$ and p and q have no divisors in common. Define g by

$$g(\alpha) = \begin{cases} 0 \text{ if } \alpha = 0 \\ 2 \cdot 3^p \cdot 5^q \text{ if } \epsilon = + \\ 3^p \cdot 5^q \text{ if } \epsilon = -1 \end{cases}$$

A moment of reflection shows that, indeed, this function g is also $1-1$.

Example A.2. Any finite interval $I = \{x \mid a \leq x \leq b\}$ of real numbers has the same cardinality as the set $\mathbb{R}$ of all real numbers. To construct a $1-1$ function $f\colon I \mapsto \mathbb{R}$ is easy enough: just take $f(x) = x$. In the reverse direction, suppose I is the interval $[-1, +1]$. The function g given by

$$g(x) = \frac{x}{1 + |x|}$$

is clearly $1-1$ and maps $\mathbb{R}$ into $[-1, +1]$. It can easily be modified in case I is another interval.

Example A.3. The unit square $S = (0, 1) \times (0, 1)$ and the unit interval $I = (0, 1)$ have the same cardinality. Constructing a function f: $I \mapsto S$ is easy enough; put $f(x) = (x, 0)$. To construct a $1-1$ function g: $S \mapsto I$ we argue as follows: Every number α, $0 < \alpha < 1$ can be represented in its decimal expansion as

$$\alpha = 0.a_1a_2a_3 \ldots$$
$$= \sum_{n=1}^{\infty} \frac{a_n}{10^n} \text{ where each } a_n \text{ is an integer between 0 and 9} \quad (A.3)$$

This representation is not unique since, for instance, 0.1299999 . . . and 0.130000 . . . represent the same number. If we stipulate, however, that in the above representation infinitely many a_n's are different from 9, then this representation is unique. Any x in the square S is represented by a pair of such numbers $x = (\alpha, \beta)$ where

$$\alpha = 0.a_1a_2a_3 \ldots$$
$$\beta = 0.b_1b_2b_3 \ldots$$

and infinitely many a's and b's are different from 9. We define a function g: $S \mapsto I$ by interweaving the digits of α and β:

$$g(x) = g((\alpha, \beta)) = 0.a_1b_1a_2b_2a_3b_3 \ldots$$

It is clear that g is indeed $1-1$.

It may seem at this point that any two infinite sets have the same cardinality. It was discovered in 1874 by G. Cantor that this is not so.

Theorem A.2. The cardinality of the set $\mathbb{N}$ of all natural numbers is strictly less then the cardinality of the set $\mathbb{R}$ of all real numbers.

Proof. What we must show is that there is a $1-1$ function f: $\mathbb{N} \mapsto \mathbb{R}$, but there is no $1-1$ function g: $\mathbb{R} \mapsto \mathbb{N}$. To find a function f is easy, put $f(n) = n$. We will show that there is no $1-1$ function g from the open interval $I = (0, 1) = \{x \mid 0 < x < 1\}$ to $\mathbb{N}$. If such a function g existed, then by the Schroeder-Bernstein theorem the sets $\mathbb{N}$ and I would have the same cardinality and one would be able to construct a $1-1$ function F: $\mathbb{N} \mapsto I$ that is ***onto***. We will show that this is impossible. Let F be any $1-1$ function from $\mathbb{N}$ to I. We will show that there is $z_0 \in (0, 1)$ such that $F(n) \neq z_0$ for any $n \in \mathbb{N}$, i.e., F is ***not onto***. Let F be a

$1-1$ function from $\mathbb{N}$ to I. For each $n \in \mathbb{N}$ the number $F(n)$ is between 0 and 1 and can be represented in decimal expansion as in (A.3):

$$F(n) = 0.a_1^{(n)} a_2^{(n)} a_3^{(n)} \ldots$$

We now list all the values of F:

$$F(1) = 0.a_1^{(1)} a_2^{(1)} a_3^{(1)} \ldots$$

$$F(2) = 0.a_1^{(2)} a_2^{(2)} a_3^{(2)} \ldots$$

$$F(3) = 0.a_1^{(3)} a_2^{(3)} a_3^{(3)} \ldots$$

and so on. Consider now a number $x = 0.a_1^{(1)} a_2^{(2)} a_3^{(3)} \ldots$ made up of the diagonal digits and, finally, the number z_0 obtained from x by changing all of its digits, $z_0 = 0.b_1 b_2 b_3 \ldots$, where each b_n is taken to be different from $a_n^{(n)}$. (We may also choose the numbers b_n so that infinitely many of them are different from 9.) It is clear that there is no n such that $F(n) = z_0$: Indeed $F(1)$ and z_0 differ in the first digit, $F(2)$ and z_0 differ in the second digit, $F(3)$ and z_0 differ in the third digit, etc. Q.E.D.

A set A is said to be ***countable***, or ***denumerable***, if it has the same cardinality as the set $\mathbb{N}$ of all natural numbers. The cardinality of $\mathbb{N}$ is denoted by $\aleph_0$. An infinite set that is not countable is called uncountable. The cardinality of the set $\mathbb{R}$ of the real numbers is denoted by c and is called ***continuum.***

We conclude by showing that the set $\mathcal{F}$ of all functions from $\mathbb{N}$ with values 0 or 1 is a set of cardinality continuum. This was discussed briefly in Chapter 5 in connection with proving that there are unsolvable problems. Let, then, $\mathcal{F} = \{\varphi : \mathbb{N} \mapsto \{0, 1\}\}$.

Theorem A.3. The set $\mathcal{F}$ has the cardinality c.

Proof. We will show that the set $\mathcal{F}$ has the same cardinality as the half-open interval $I = [0, 1) = \{x \mid 0 \leq x < 1\}$. It was shown above that I has the same cardinality as $\mathbb{R}$.

To construct a $1-1$ function from I to $\mathcal{F}$ we proceed as follows. Each $x \in I$ can be written in binary notation as

$$x = (0.\epsilon_1 \epsilon_2 \epsilon_3 \ldots)_2 = \sum_{n=1}^{\infty} \frac{\epsilon_n}{2^n} \quad \text{where each } \epsilon_n = 0 \text{ or } 1. \qquad \text{(A.4)}$$

To each such x we correspond a function $\varphi_x \in \mathcal{F}$ defined to be $\varphi_x(n) = \epsilon_n$. It is clear that the mapping $x \mapsto \varphi_x$ is $1-1$.

To construct now a $1-1$ function $f\colon \mathcal{F} \mapsto [0, 1)$ we essentially reverse the procedure. Given a function $\varphi \in \mathcal{F}$, we may think of it as a sequence of 0's and 1's:

$$\varphi(1),\ \varphi(2),\ \varphi(3),\ \ldots$$

We correspond to this function φ a number x_φ by

$$x_\varphi = (0.\varphi(1)\varphi(2)\varphi(3)\ \ldots\ )_2 = \sum_{n=1}^{\infty} \frac{\varphi(n)}{2^n}$$

This almost works. The problem is that two distinct functions φ_1 and φ_2 from $\mathcal{F}$ may give the same point x: If

$$\begin{aligned} \varphi_1(1) = 0, \quad \varphi_1(2) = \varphi_1(3) = \varphi_1(4) = \cdots = 1 \\ \varphi_2(1) = 1, \quad \varphi_2(2) = \varphi_2(3) = \varphi_2(4) = \cdots = 0 \end{aligned}$$

then φ_1 gets mapped to the number 0.0111 . . . (in binary) and φ_2 gets mapped to the number 0.100 . . . (also in binary).These two numbers are, however, the same (both are equal to 1/2). This can be circumvented very easily. Instead of expanding numbers in base 2, we expand them in base 3: Each x can be written as

$$x = (0.\gamma_1\gamma_2\gamma_3 \cdots)_3 \quad = \sum_{n=1}^{\infty} \frac{\gamma_n}{3^n} \quad \text{where each } \gamma_n = 0,\ 1, \text{ or } 2$$

Given now $\varphi \in \mathcal{F}$ we map it into a number $x_\varphi \in [0, 1)$ by

$$x_\varphi = \sum_{n=1}^{\infty} \frac{\varphi(n)}{3^n} = (0.\varphi(1)\varphi(2)\varphi(3)\ \ldots\ )_3$$

It is clear that two distinct functions φ_1 and φ_2 give rise to two distinct numbers x_{φ_1} and x_{φ_2}.

APPENDIX 2

PASCAL GRAMMAR

We give here the grammar for the programming language Pascal. This language was developed by N. Wirth and its grammatical description is taken from his book [14]. The notation used is slightly different from the usual one. The nonterminals are written as self explanatory phrases enclosed by $< \ . \ . \ . \ >$. Thus, the start symbol is $<\mathit{program}>$. To save space and for the sake of clarity, the notation $\{\alpha\}$ means that the string α can be repeated zero or more times. Thus, the production

$$<\mathit{identifier}> \ \to \ <\mathit{letter}> \mid \{ \ <\mathit{letter\ or\ digit}> \ \}$$

should be expanded to

$$\begin{array}{l} <\mathit{identifier}> \ \to \ <\mathit{letter}><A> \\ <A> \ \to \ < A ><\mathit{letter\ or\ digit}> \ \mid \ \lambda \end{array}$$

where $<A>$ is a new nonterminal.

The words written out in boldface, such as ***program***, ***begin***, ***end***, etc., are called reserved words, and are part of the alphabet (in addition to all the letters, digits, arithmetic operators, etc.). This means, for instance, that ***begin*** is considered to be one single terminal. Thus, according to the grammar below, a variable can be named *begin*, with the understanding that the string *begin* is not equal to the single symbol ***begin***. Without exception, however, the compilers are font insensitive and all the implementations impose a restriction that an identifier cannot be named "begin", in whatever font it is written. The grammar could actually be modified in such a way that the string *begin*, say, could not be derived from the nonterminal *<identifier>*. The result, however, would be much more complicated and obscure, and the overall design would be hidden behind a plethora of artificial productions.

The grammar given here is an ambiguous one, due to the production

<if statement> → ***if*** *<expression>* ***then*** *<statement>* |
  if *<expression>* ***then*** *<statement>* ***else*** *<statement>*

(see discussion in Example 1.9). Again, the grammar could be modified along the lines indicated on page 21 to remove this ambiguity—the result, however, would be considerably longer and less elegant.

<program> → *<program heading>* *<block>*.
<program heading> →
  program *<identifier>* (*<file identifier>* { , *<file identifier>*});
<file identifier> → *<identifier>*
<identifier> → *<letter><letter or digit>*
<letter or digit> → *<letter>* | *<digit>*
<letter> → *a* | *b* | *c* | *d* | *e* | *f* | *e* | *g* | *h* | *i* | *j* | *k* | *l* | *m* | *n* | *o* | *p* |
  q | *r* | *s* | *t* | *u* | *v* | *w* | *x* | *y* | *z* |
  A | *B* | *C* | *D* | *E* | *F* | *G* | *H* | *I* | *J* | *K* | *L* | *M* |
  N | *O* | *P* | *Q* | *R* | *T* | *U* | *V* | *W* | *X* | *Y* | *Z*
<digit> → 0 | 1 | 2 | 3 | 4 | 5 | 6 | 7 | 8 | 9
<block> → *<label declaration part><constant definition part>*
  <type declaration part><variable declaration part>
  <procedure and function declaration part>
  <statement part>
<label declaration part> → λ | ***label*** *<label>* {, *<label>*};
<label> → *<unsigned integer>*
<constant definition part> → λ |
  const *<constant definition>* {; *<constant definition>*};
<constant definition> → *<identifier>* = *<constant>*
<constant> → *<unsigned integer>* | *<sign>* *<unsigned number>* |
  <constant identifier> | *<sign>* *<constant identifier>* | *<string>*
<unsigned number> → *<unsigned integer>* | *<unsigned real>*
<unsigned integer> → *<digit>*{*<digit>*}
<unsigned real> → *<unsigned integer>*.*<digit>*{*<digit>*} |
  <unsigned integer>.*<digit>*{*<digit>*}*E<scale factor>* |
  <unsigned integer>E<scale factor>
<scale factor> → *<unsigned integer>* | *<sign><unsigned integer>*
<sign> → + | −
<constant identifier> → *<identifier>*
<string> → ' *<character>*{*<character>*}'

<type definition part> → λ | **type** <type definition>{; <type definition>};

<type definition> → <identifier> = <type>

<type> → <simple type> | <structured type> | <pointer type>

<simple type> → <scalar type> | <subrange type> | <type identifier>

<scalar type> → (<identifier>{, <identifier>})

<subrange type> → <constant> . . <constant>

<type identifier> → <identifier>

<structured type> → <unpacked structured type> | **packed** <packed structured type>

<unpacked structured type> → <array type> | <record type> | <set type> | <file type>

<array type> → **array** [<index type>{, <index type>}] **of** <component type>

<index type> → <simple type>

<component type> → <type>

<record type> → **record** <field list> **end**

<field list> →
<fixed part> | <fixed part> ; <variant part> | <variant part>

<fixed part> → <record section> {; <record section>}

<record section> → λ | <field identifier> {, <field identifier>} : <type>

<variant part> → **case** <tag field> <type identifier> **of** <variant>{; <variant>}

<tag field> → λ | <field identifier> :

<variant> → λ | <case label list> : (<field list>)

<case label list> → <case label> {, <case label>}

<case label> → <constant>

<set type> → **set of** <base type>

<base type> → <simple type>

<file type> → **file of** <type>

<pointer type> → ↑ <type identifier>

<variable declaration part> → λ | **var** <variable declaration> {; <variable declaration>}

<variable declaration> → <identifier> {, <identifier>} : <type>

<procedure and function declaration part> → {<procedure or function declaration>;>}

<procedure or function declaration> → <procedure declaration> | <function declaration>

<procedure declaration> → <procedure heading><block>

<procedure heading> → **procedure** <identifier> ; | **procedure** <identifier> (<formal parameter section> {;<formal parameter section>})

```
<parameter group> → <identifier> {, <identifier>}: <type identifier>
<function declaration> → <function heading> <block>
<formal parameter section> → <parameter group> |
        var <parameter group> | function <parameter group> |
                procedure <identifier> {, <identifier>}
<function heading> → function <identifier> : <result type>; |
        function <identifier>( <formal parameter section>
            {; <formal parameter section>}) : <result type>;
<result type> → <type identifier>
<statement part> → <compound statement>
<statement> → <unlabeled statement> |
                <label> : <unlabeled statement>
<unlabeled statement> → <simple statement> | <structured statement>
<simple statement> → <assignment statement> | <go to statement>
                <procedure statement> | <empty statement>
<assignment statement> → <variable> := <expression> |
                <function identifier> := <expression>
<variable> → <entire variable> | <component variable> |
                <referenced variable>
<entire variable> → <variable identifier>
<variable identifier> → <identifier>
<component variable> → <index variable> | <field designator> |
                <file buffer>
<indexed variable> →
        <array variable> [ <expression> {, <expression>}]
<array variable> → <variable>
<field designator> → <record variable> . <field identifier>
<record variable> → <variable>
<field identifier> → <identifier>
<file buffer> → <file variable> ↑
<file variable> → <variable>
<referenced variable> → <pointer variable> ↑
<pointer variable> → <variable>
<expression> → <simple expression> |
        <simple expression><relational operator><simple expression>
<relational operator> → = | <> |< | <= | >= | > | in
<simple expression> → <term> | <sign><term> |
        <simple expression> <adding operator> <term>
<adding operator> → + | − | or
<term> → <factor> | <term> <multiplying operator> <factor>
<multiplying operator> → * | / | div | mod | and
<factor> → <variable> | <unsigned constant> | (<expression>) |
        <function designator> | <set> | not <factor>
```

<unsigned constant> → <string> | <constant identifier> | **nil**

<function designator> → <function identifier> |
<function identifier> (<actual parameter> {, <actual parameter>})

<function identifier> → <identifier>

<set> → [<element list>]

<element list> → <element> {, <element>} | λ

<element> → <expression> | <expression> . . <expression>

<procedure statement> → <procedure identifier> |
<procedure identifier> (<actual parameter> {, <actual parameter>})

<procedure identifier> → <identifier>

<actual parameter> → <expression> | <variable> |
<procedure identifier> | <function identifier>

<go to statement> → **goto** <label>

<empty statement> → λ

<structured statement> → <compound statement> |
<conditional statement> | <repetitive statement> | <with statement>

<compound statement> → **begin** <statement> {; <statement> } **end**

<conditional statement> → <if statement> | <case statement>

<if statement> → **if** <expression> **then** <statement> |
if <expression> **then** <statement> **else** <statement>

<case statement> →
case <expression> **of** <case list element> {; <case list element>} **end**

<case list element> → <case label list> : <statement> | <empty>

<case label list> → <case label> {, <case label>}

<repetitive statement> →
<while statement> | <repeat statement> | <for statement>

<while statement> → **while** | <expression> **do** <statement>

<repeat statement> →
repeat <statement> {; <statement>} **until** <expression>

<for statement> →
for <control variable> := <for list> **do** <statement>

<for list> → <initial value> **to** <final value> |
<initial value> **downto** <final value>

<control variable> → <identifier>

<initial value> → <expression>

<final value> → <expression>

<with statement> → **with** <record variable list> **do** <statement>

<record variable list> → <recrd variable> {, <record variable>}

<unsigned constant> → <string> | <constant identifier> | **nil**
<function designator> → <function identifier> |
<function identifier> (<actual parameter> {, <actual parameter>})
<function identifier> → <identifier>
<set> → [<element list>]
<element list> → <element> {, <element>} | λ
<element> → <expression> | <expression> . . <expression>
<procedure statement> → <procedure identifier> |
<procedure identifier> (<actual parameter> {, <actual parameter>})
<procedure identifier> → <identifier>
<actual parameter> → <expression> | <variable> |
<procedure identifier> | <function identifier>
<go to statement> → **goto** <label>
<empty statement> → λ
<structured statement> → <compound statement> |
<conditional statement> | <repetitive statement> | <with statement>
<compound statement> → **begin** <statement> {; <statement> } **end**
<conditional statement> → <if statement> | <case statement>
<if statement> → **if** <expression> **then** <statement> |
if <expression> **then** <statement> **else** <statement>
<case statement> →
case <expression> **of** <case list element> {; <case list element>} **end**
<case list element> → <case label list> : <statement> | <empty>
<case label list> → <case label> {, <case label>}
<repetitive statement> →
<while statement> | <repeat statement> | <for statement>
<while statement> → **while** | <expression> **do** <statement>
<repeat statement> →
repeat <statement> {; <statement>} **until** <expression>
<for statement> →
for <control variable> := <for list> **do** <statement>
<for list> → <initial value> **to** <final value> |
<initial value> **downto** <final value>
<control variable> → <identifier>
<initial value> → <expression>
<final value> → <expression>
<with statement> → **with** <record variable list> **do** <statement>
<record variable list> → <recrd variable> {, <record variable>}

REFERENCES

1. Ackermann, W., Zum Hilbertschen Aufbau der reellen Zahlen, *Mathematische Annalen*, 99(1928), 118-133.
2. Aho, A. A., and Ullman, J. D., *Principles of Compiler Design*, Addison-Wesley, Reading, Mass., 1978.
3. Aho, A. V., and Ullman, J. D., *The Theory of Parsing, Translation, and Compiling*, Prentice Hall, Englewood Cliffs, N. J., 1972.
4. Chomsky, N., Three models for a description of a language. *IRE Trans. on Information Theory*, 2 *No.* 3(1956), 113-124.
5. Chomsky, N., *Syntactic Structures*, Moughton & Co., The Hague, 1964.
6. Church, A., An unsolvable problem of elementary number theory, *Amer. J. Math.*, 58(1936), 345-363.
7. Cohen, D. I. A., *Introduction to Computer Theory*, John Wiley & Sons, New York, N.Y., 1986.
8. Denning, P. J., Dennis, J. B., and Qualitz, J. E., *Machines, Languages, and Computation*, Prentice Hall, Englewood Cliffs, N.J., 1978.
10. *FORTRAN Manual for CDC*6000. Control Data Corp., Minneapolis, Minn., 1968.
11. Gödel, K., Über formal unentscheidbare Sätze der Principia Mathematica und verwandter Systeme, I. *Monatschafte für Mathematik und Physik*, 38(1931), 173-198.
12. Halmos, P. R., *Naive Set Theory*, Springer Verlag, New York, N.Y., 1985.
13. Hopcroft, J. E., and Ullman, J. D., *Introduction to Automata Theory, Languages, and Computation*, Addison-Wesley, Reading, Mass., 1979.
14. Jensen K., and Wirth N., *Pascal, User Manual and Report*, 2nd ed., Springer Verlag, New York, N.Y., 1974.
15. Lewis, R. L., and Papadimitriou C. H., *Elements of the Theory of Computation*, Prentice Hall, Englewood Cliffs, N.J., 1981.
16. Mealy, G. D., A method for synthesizing sequential circuits, *BSTJ*, 34(1955), 1045-1079.

17. Moore, E. F., Gedanken-experiments on sequential machines. In C. E. Shannon and J. McCarthy (eds.), *Automata Studies*, Princeton University Press, Princeton N.J., 1956.
18. Shannon, C. E., A universal Turing machine with two internal states. In C. E. Shannon and J. McCarthy (eds.), *Automata Studies*, Princeton University Press, Princeton N.J., 1956.
19. Turing, A. M., On computable numbers, with an application to Entscheidungsproblem, *Proc. London Math. Soc.*, 2-42(1936), 230-265.

INDEX